M000317217

College Basketball Prospectus 2009-10

Major-Conference Preview

THE ESSENTIAL GUIDE TO THE ACC, BIG 12, BIG EAST, BIG TEN, PAC-10 & SEC

by the authors of Basketball Prospectus

Edited by John Gasaway

Foreword by Jay Bilas

Layout by Vince Verhei

Table of Contents

Foreword   v

Introduction   vi

Terms Used In This Book   viii

Thoughts For
A New Season

The Recent Experience Of Experience   3

The True Value of DeJuan Blair's
Historic Offensive Rebounding   7

Can The Right Coach Get
You To The Final Four?   10

Evaluating NBA Drafts Before They Happen   13

The Hardwood And The Damage Done   20

2010 Previews

ATLANTIC COAST CONFERENCE   **25**
Boston College   26
Clemson   28
Duke   29
Florida State   31
Georgia Tech   33
Maryland   35
Miami   36
North Carolina   38
North Carolina State   40
Virginia   42
Virginia Tech   43
Wake Forest   45

BIG 12 CONFERENCE   **47**
Baylor   49
Colorado   50
Iowa State   52
Kansas   54
Kansas State   57
Missouri   58
Nebraska   60
Oklahoma   62
Oklahoma State   64
Texas   66
Texas A&M   68
Texas Tech   70

BIG EAST CONFERENCE   **72**
Cincinnati   73
Connecticut   75
DePaul   76
Georgetown   78
Louisville   80
Marquette   82
Notre Dame   84
Pitt   86
Providence   87
Rutgers   89
St. John's   91
Seton Hall   92
South Florida   94
Syracuse   95
Villanova   97
West Virginia   98

BIG TEN CONFERENCE   **101**
Illinois   102
Indiana   104
Iowa   106
Michigan   108
Michigan State   110

TABLE OF CONTENTS

Minnesota	112
Northwestern	114
Ohio State	116
Penn State	119
Purdue	121
Wisconsin	122
PACIFIC-10 CONFERENCE	**125**
Arizona	126
Arizona State	128
California	129
Oregon	131
Oregon State	133
Stanford	134
UCLA	136
USC	138
Washington	139
Washington State	141
SOUTHEASTERN CONFERENCE	**143**
Alabama	144
Arkansas	146

Auburn	147
Florida	149
Georgia	151
Kentucky	152
LSU	155
Mississippi	156
Mississippi State	158
South Carolina	160
Tennessee	162
Vanderbilt	164
THE MID-MAJORS	**167**
Atlantic 10 Conference	167
Conference USA	169
Mid-American Conference	171
Missouri Valley Conference	172
Mountain West Conference	173
West Coast Conference	175
Western Athletic Conference	176
Best Of The Rest	178
Author Bios	181

Foreword

I love basketball. I have been a player, coach and broadcaster, but above all I am an unabashed fan. Basketball is the purest team game of all, and beautiful in its simplicity. Basketball requires its players to play both offense and defense in a continuous flow, with players converting from offense to defense without stoppages in play like you would see in football or baseball.

But basketball is not without complexity, and a true understanding of the game requires in-depth analysis of it. From playing and coaching under Duke's Mike Krzyzewski, I learned to look deeper into the game by breaking it down through the use of statistics. Using skillfully targeted and established metrics and measures helps to determine the true efficiency and productivity of players, plays, combinations, and teams, and illuminates that which can go unseen by even the most trained basketball observers. While statistical analysis does not tell you the complete story about a game, a half, a possession, a team's offense, a team's defense or a player, it takes you much deeper into your analysis and judgments of all of the above. The thoughtful use of statistics and metrics is an invaluable tool in scouting and evaluation, and it is a useful means to deepen the understanding and enjoyment of the game for any fan.

Basketball Prospectus is one of the essential tools I use in analyzing the game and those that play and coach it. In evaluating tape and live performance, the targeted numbers presented by BP supplement and often drive judgments that once were made solely by my eyes. Often the statistical analysis so expertly presented in BP will open my eyes and my mind to new thoughts and ideas about the relative strengths and weaknesses of teams and players. I know that when I read and absorb BP's easy to use and understand data, which is always presented in precise context, I will learn something. I use Basketball Prospectus as an important part of scouting college basketball teams and players, and in my player evaluations for the NBA Draft.

The true experts in the game, those teaching, coaching, scouting and making day-to-day management decisions in the NBA, all use Basketball Prospectus to gain a competitive edge. If you are a fan, like me, wishing to delve deeper into the game, you will truly benefit from and enjoy Basketball Prospectus. I know that I have. It is a vital tool for my work, and helps me figure out this ever changing and evolving game.

Jay Bilas
ESPN Basketball Analyst

Introduction

When I was eight or nine years old the Harlem Globetrotters came to my town, Springfield, Illinois, to put their winning streak on the line against the Washington Generals yet again. The game was played at the old Armory downtown, and seating arrangements and security staff were both casual enough that my friends and I quickly congregated around one of the baskets as the game got underway.

We hadn't been there long when, thanks to an errant pass from the Generals, the ball came straight at my little group and lodged itself in the structural supports that held up the basket. I immediately dove behind the padding covering the supports and got a good grip on the ball. As I did so I could feel all my friends grabbing at me from every direction as they too tried for the same prize.

Then I felt a much different pair of hands. Impossibly large, strong, and preemptively fast, the two giant mitts fastened onto my ribcage and abruptly hoisted me out from behind the padding and up into the air.

Having toggled from euphoria to paranoid terror in an instant, I assumed a security guard had grabbed me and that I was about to be thrown out. Still clutching the ball instinctively with both hands, I was trying to think of how I'd explain myself to my parents when I noticed I was in fact being carried out onto the court itself. It was then that I heard a voice, somehow familiar and very close to my ear, booming out in a practiced and clearly enunciated vaudeville punchline cadence: "I GOT THE BALL!"

I turned around and saw that Curly Neal was holding me high in the air, grinning with a showman's contentment as the crowd's laughter and applause washed over us both. When he set me back down on the sideline, my friends regarded me with awed silence. I let them.

Curly had a point. Basketball is fairly consumed with who has the ball, for the simple reason that no other sport gives its players as much discretion in deciding who gets a chance to score.

In fact "discretion" puts it too mildly. In basketball these decisions are, for the most part, made by players in real time. Conversely in your other major team sports these choices are made in advance by the nearest non-player authority figure. Managers set the batting order in baseball and offensive coordinators call each play in football, but to a striking degree these know-it-alls are banished quite literally to the sidelines in hoops. (The idea of a basketball player being tethered to his coach electronically via an earpiece should send a chill down the spine of any true fan of the game.)

Instead Dr. Naismith's game sets aside vast tracts of strategic space for creative improvisation, space in which each player is expected to contribute in multiple ways. Even in the free-flowing kindred spirits of soccer and hockey, a substantial minority of players never strays too far from the physical space that marks their primary responsibility as defensive. Basketball is different. No other team sport gives this much freedom to each player to score if they get the chance.

Alas, with that freedom came 100 years of confusion. Who are the best players in this sport? Which of these two undefeated teams is better? Why are these two teams undefeated, anyway? The ceaseless flow of action in basketball made answers hard to attain.

I'd watch a game and I'd come away with impressions—I still do, and if I'm lucky they're indelible—but the kind of evaluative declarations that baseball yields up so effortlessly were often in short supply in hoops. Why did this team have a disappointing year? We thought we had some pretty good ideas, but we didn't really know. (And by that I mean we knew that we didn't know.) Because the game itself doesn't equalize opportunity across players—be it opportunities to score, rebound, record an assist, or what have you—someone was going to have to come in after the fact and place that kind of analytic frame around basketball.

To my knowledge the first person to do so was Dean Smith. About 50 years ago when Smith was still an assistant at North Carolina, the Tar Heels began to chart their games and keep track of things that the official scorer didn't bother with, things like turnovers, shot locations, and, most crucially, possessions. Smith's innovations enabled the UNC staff to track with unprecedented accuracy and detail how well their team performed from game to game.

It would be another 30 years, however, until a basketball analyst named Dean Oliver gave us the ability to compare Team A to Teams B through infinity. When my colleague Ken Pomeroy came along 15 years after Oliver, trained his focus on 300-some Division I college teams, retrieved all the information that Smith and Oliver had showed could be gathered, and posted the results for everyone to see online, all the pieces were finally in place. Now we can answer the most basic questions about basketball's players, teams, and seasons in a way that starts with and works alongside our impressions but does not end with them.

The manner in which we reach these answers comes freighted with some fancy labels: "Advanced metrics," "tempo-free stats," etc. But the activity here is fundamentally un-fancy and indeed at its core is much more journalistic than quantitative: I just want to know what really happened. If numbers can help that along, so be it. This English major will thank the digits heartily. Either way, I just want to know what really happened.

Any given season will feature performances that are extreme and thus "historic" in the literal sense of that term: Here's something you don't see every day. Recognizing the historic as it happens is journalistic job one.

If you want to talk about Kentucky, for example, it helps to know what really happened last year. It helps to know that Jodie Meeks and Patrick Patterson were historically efficient as a duo on offense, almost as spectacular as Ty Lawson and Tyler Hansbrough, but that their efforts were negated to a large extent by the unbelievable number of turnovers recorded by Wildcat role players.

Or if you want to talk about UCLA or Ohio State, it helps to know that both teams were historically accurate from the field in conference play in 2009 and that it is therefore highly unlikely that they will miss so few shots again in 2010.

And if you want to talk about Oregon State, it helps to know that the Beavers were historically fortunate to go 7-11 in the Pac-10 in 2009 when their level of performance on a possession-by-possession basis would ordinarily have netted them a 3-15 record.

In other words this slender little *College Basketball Prospectus 2009-10: Major-Conference Preview* stands on the shoulders of giants—many of them named Dean for some reason—and attempts to share what we've learned about the 73 major-conference teams and their players. Certainly we wish could have covered all 347 D-I teams with this level of analytic TLC. With the exception of John Perrotto's excellent mid-major capsule summaries, however, in this edition we trained our focus for the most part on the six leagues whose current membership can claim 42 of the last 43 national championships.

If we're doing justice to the game, you should be able to piece together what really happened in these conferences in 2009, as well as what may take place in 2010. At a minimum I can promise you that reading the likes of Ken Pomeroy, Dan Hanner, Bradford Doolittle, Kevin Pelton, Will Carroll, and John Perrotto will make you a more observant, more informed, and above all more appreciative fan of college basketball. I know these writers have done that for this reader.

Lastly, speaking only for myself, finding out what really happened between the lines on a basketball court has been a recurring pursuit of mine ever since I was unexpectedly brought onto the floor at the Springfield Armory. That pursuit continues here, and as part of that effort let me point out that Curly Neal was wrong. *I* got the ball.

Enjoy.

John Gasaway
November 2009

Terms Used In This Book

Here it is 2009 and what we said in our *College Basketball Prospectus* a year ago is still true today: The language we use is a little different than what you'll see in any other preview. If you're a regular visitor to the site, you should be familiar with this language. If not, don't fret. Here's what you need to know.

We judge a team's offense and defense in terms of their **points scored or allowed per possession**. In this way, we remove the corrupting influence of a team's pace from our judgment of their skills. We'll call these stats **offensive and defensive efficiency** from time to time. We tend to focus on how these measures look during regular-season conference games only in order to get the best estimate of how a team stacks up to its conference brethren in a setting that equalizes home and road games. Occasionally, though, we'll refer to **adjusted efficiencies** which includes all games played and accounts for schedule strength, among other things, to provide an estimate of how a team stacks up nationally.

We're also big believers in Dean Oliver's Four Factors. For the uninitiated, nearly all of a team's offensive and defensive efficiency can be explained by its performance in four areas: Shooting, rebounding, turnovers, and free throws.

For shooting, we use **effective field goal percentage** (typically shortened to eFG) in lieu of traditional field goal percentage. The version we use gives 50 percent more credit for a made three-pointer, just like the scoreboard does. Thus, a player going 4-for-10 from the field while making all of his shots from beyond the arc would have an eFG of 60 percent. His two-point making counterpart would have an eFG of just 40 percent.

In the rebounding department, we also use a percentage. In this case, the number of rebounding opportunities is the divisor. When we talk about a **defensive rebounding percentage**, we mean the percentage of rebounds a defense grabbed among those available. The same principle applies for **offensive rebounding percentage**.

With ball security, we use **turnover percentage**. (Sensing a theme here?) This is just the percentage of possessions where a team commits or forces a turnover.

Finally, for free throws we'll refer to something called **free throw rate** which is just free throw attempts divided by field goal attempts.

We use similar measures to define a player's ability. Additional terms on the personal level you should acquaint yourself with are **offensive rating**, which is just the player version of offensive efficiency, and **usage** or **possessions used**, which described how often a player did something statistically on the offensive end. This helps us distinguish the go-to guy from the screen-setter.

Thoughts For A New Season

The Recent Experience Of Experience

This season teams like Kansas, Tennessee, and Cal will have "everyone back" from last year, while at the other extreme programs like North Carolina, Pitt, and USC will fill their starting lineups with a whole host of relatively or even completely new faces.

As fans with a few years of accumulated wisdom under our collective belts, we therefore assume that the Jayhawks, Volunteers, and Bears will all be very good this season. Yet we also understand that the Tar Heels, Panthers, and Trojans will not be uniformly "bad" this year simply because their players are relatively inexperienced. For one thing Roy Williams has a veritable truckload of McDonald's All-Americans arriving in Chapel Hill to complement veterans like Deon Thompson, Marcus Ginyard, and Ed Davis. UNC may be young but they'll be talented and most likely very good.

Such is the folk wisdom of college hoops. Experience is good to have. So is talent. Experienced talent is the best scenario of all.

Just how sound is that folk wisdom? To find out, I looked at the relationship between experience and performance as demonstrated over the past few seasons by the teams of the ACC, Big 12, Big East, Big Ten, Pac-10, SEC, C-USA, MVC, and MWC. Specifically I looked at how well the 104 teams in those conferences have performed in league play during 272 separate team-seasons since 2006.

Returning possession-minutes: RPM's

To measure "performance," I simply used a team's in-conference efficiency margin, the difference between how many points they scored and allowed on each possession. And to measure "experience," I tweaked the returning-minutes measure that we've traditionally used here at Basketball Prospectus and came up with something that I call returning possession-minutes, or RPM's. With RPM's we're measuring not only how many minutes a player recorded the previous year, but

also how many possessions he accounted for within his offense. In other words, RPM's speak to not only how experienced a player is, but also how prominent he is in his team's offense.

To be honest, four out of every five times there isn't going to be much difference between good old returning minutes and this fancy new RPM thing. All the new metric gives us, really, is one further sift that catches the occasional notably weird case.

For instance Iowa State and Arizona State are both notably weird this year. On paper the Cyclones and the Sun Devils each return virtually the exact same level of experience from last year: ISU is bringing back 65 percent of its minutes while ASU returns 66. But in fact the two teams couldn't be more different in terms of how much uncertainty their head coaches are facing right now. In Ames, Greg McDermott knows exactly what he'll see on offense in 2009-10: Craig Brackins, Craig Brackins, and more Craig Brackins, likely followed by some additional Craig Brackins and topped off by a final dash of Craig Brackins. The fact that Brackins was one of the highest possession-usage players in the nation last year means the Cyclones actually return 77 percent of their possession-minutes. In Tempe, on the other hand, Herb Sendek has said goodbye to both James Harden and Jeff Pendergraph, meaning just 54 percent of the Sun Devils' possession-minutes will be back for another go this season. So while Iowa State and Arizona State look identical in terms of returning minutes, they're actually poles apart. With RPM's we can catch these admittedly rare instances.

Naturally our interest in the relationship between experience and performance over the past four seasons is driven to a large extent by a desire to forecast what's going to happen in future seasons. Still, it's a little early in the game to call this a true team projection system. I prefer to think of it as a beta effort. Anyway, this RPM thing has already coughed up some observations that have at least made me take another look at some of my assumptions.

First things first. Since it's incumbent upon any presenter of a multi-year survey of results to include an ugly scatter plot, here is my ugly scatter plot.

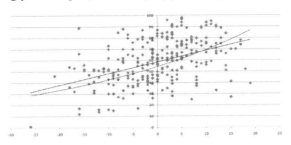

Yes, Indiana fans, that's your 2009 team all by itself there in the *extreme* lower-left. The Hoosiers last year were both historically inexperienced and historically unsuccessful compared to the team's previous season. Sometimes your immediate sensory impressions are indeed precisely correct. In such cases no further analysis is required.

Anyway, behold 272 team-seasons in conference play since 2006. Year-to-year change in efficiency margin is indicated by the numbers running along the bottom; RPMs are denoted by the numbers running up the center of the chart.

Looking at my ugly scatter plot we can see there is indeed a vague tendency here for performance to improve as RPM's increase. But when we're looking at this entire population of teams, the performance-experience relationship actually isn't all that strong. Why not?

Because this scatter plot throws very different teams together in one huge mass: North Carolina's 2009 national championship team is shown here alongside DePaul's 2009 team that went 0-18 in the Big East. Sure, experience was one factor behind the Tar Heels winning it all. Another equally weighty variable, however, was the fact that Roy Williams' experienced players were really good—and had demonstrated this quality beyond doubt with a Final Four season in 2008. Simply put, a team's experience alone is not going to determine how well they're going to perform this year. The other half of that equation is, of course, how well they performed last year with all those players that either are or are not returning.

When we hold performance the previous year constant, however, the relationship between past experience and current performance becomes much clearer. For example, let's look at teams that are good but not great. These are teams that outscored their

conference opponents by about 0.05 points per trip the previous year. What should such teams expect the following season?

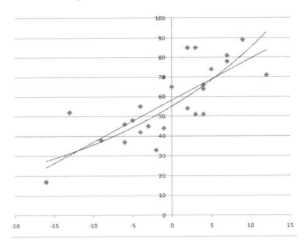

That's much cleaner. For these 25 teams, all of whom were pretty good the previous year, the relationship between experience and performance was strong. This group includes major-conference teams from last year like Pitt, USC, and Arkansas. (Meaning the Panthers, Trojans, and Razorbacks all outscored their conference opponents by about 0.05 points per trip in 2008.) You've probably guessed that the dot way out there on the far right represents Pitt: Jamie Dixon's team last year returned 71 percent of its possession-minutes and improved by leaps and bounds over 2008. In other words the Panthers in 2009 were clear outliers. If you want to know why, I suggest you read Ken Pomeroy's piece, which follows this one.

As for the teams in this group that (spoiler alert) did *not* have an incomparably monstrous Thabeet-flipping man-weapon in the paint, the results they achieved tended to stick pretty close to what we'd expect based on recent history. USC last year, for example, brought in DeMar DeRozan, a highly-anticipated one-and-done player who is now a member of the Toronto Raptors. For all we know DeRozan may go on to be a ten-time All-Star and get himself a Jordan-esque statue outside the Air Canada Centre. During his one year of college ball, however, DeRozan by himself did not appear to move the Trojans off the performance dime, as it were. A team that performed at the level that USC did in 2008—again, good but not great—and that returned 55 percent of its possession-minutes would be expected to take a small step back in 2009. That is more or less exactly what happened, even with DeRozan.

But enough of the past tense. Let's take this same definition of a good-but-not-great team and carry it forward. In 2009 there were five new members added to this club of teams that outscored conference opponents by about 0.05 points per trip. I find these new members to be a rather interesting group:

- Wake Forest
- Illinois
- Texas
- Kentucky
- Tennessee

Let's take a quick look at how RPM (beta!) sees each team doing in 2010.

Wake Forest. The Demon Deacons lost Jeff Teague and James Johnson to the NBA, but Dino Gaudio does return Al-Farouq Aminu, meaning Wake's number for RPM's is a relatively skimpy but not disastrous 57 percent. In theory that should put the Deacons on a trajectory to slip a little from where they finished in the ACC last year (11-5), only without the highs of a number one ranking nationally and the lows of losing to Georgia Tech and NC State. Still, while I projected Wake as going 8-8 in my ACC preview, RPM would not be surprised by something more in the neighborhood of 10-6.

Illinois. As I note in my Big Ten preview, losing Chester Frazier and Trent Meacham means Bruce Weber has said goodbye to many more minutes than RPM's. Frazier and Meacham both logged a lot of minutes without using a lot of possessions (though, of course, Frazier earned his keep on defense). And because offensive mainstays Demetri McCamey, Mike Davis, and Mike Tisdale are all back, the Illini this year return 64 percent of their possession-minutes. Three recent teams in our sample fit this profile pretty well: Tulsa last year, and Mississippi State and UCF in 2008. Of this threesome, the first two improved while the third stayed the same from year to year. In fact MSU won the SEC West in 2008 after not even making the NCAA tournament the previous year. (Then again that team won with defense supplied in large part by one Jarvis Varnado. If the Illini want to follow this particular example they'll have to get it done a different way.) On balance, then, RPM would expect Illinois to improve by a game to 12-6 from last year's 11-7. In my preview, however, I have the Illini at 10-8. Once again RPM thinks I'm being pessimistic.

Texas. The Longhorns are everyone's pick as the Big 12's best chance to provide any kind of competition for Kansas this season. With 75 percent of their possession-minutes coming back from a team that finished 9-7 in-conference and McDonald's All-American Avery Bradley arriving in Austin, it's easy to see why the 'Horns are getting the love. In terms of recent history, the closest parallels here would seem to be Pitt in 2007 and Duke in 2008. Those are two encouraging precedents for Texas fans looking toward 2010. (The 2007 Panthers rode big man Aaron Gray to a 12-4 record in the Big East and a trip to the Sweet 16. The 2008 Blue Devils—led by Gerald Henderson, DeMarcus Nelson, and freshman phenom Kyle Singler—stood at 22-1 and 10-0 in the ACC in mid-February before finishing at 13-3 and losing to West Virginia in the second round.) In other words, RPM likes the Horns this year and so do I: We both pick Texas to finish somewhere in the neighborhood of 12-4. Hey, we agree on one! The only question is whether both RPM and I might be underrating Rick Barnes' team just a bit. Assuming Bradley lives up to his clippings, he might be one of those rare freshmen that can help a team outperform what's been done previously by mere mortals.

Kentucky. If Kentucky this year were a normal team with normal recruits, RPM would look at this roster that returns 60 percent of its possession-minutes and expect the Wildcats to stay exactly where they are, outscoring opponents by about 0.05 points per possession. (Though note that most years this level of performance is more likely to get you a 10-6 record than the 8-8 that UK recorded in 2009.) But since Kentucky this year is in fact anything but normal and their recruits are anything but average, we need to ever so slightly tap RPM on the shoulder and point out a few simple facts. Like the fact that UK freshman John Wall is widely expected to be the first player chosen in the 2010 NBA draft. So the real question becomes whether Kentucky can outperform expectations with Wall (and Patrick Patterson, DeMarcus Cousins, Eric Bledsoe, et al.) in 2010 to the same extent that Pitt outperformed expectations with DeJuan Blair in 2009. Obviously I think the Wildcats can come close to that precedent: I have UK this year finishing at 12-4 in the SEC, tied with a certain team….

Tennessee. It's rare that the phrase "everyone's back" is as close to literally true as it is in Knoxville this season, to the tune of 99+ percent of possession-minutes returning. In our brief era of tracking these good-but-not great teams, no roster that performed at this particular level the previous year has ever brought back this much experience. The closest example would be Wisconsin in 2007, which returned "only" 89 percent of their possession-minutes and still improved from 9-7 to 13-3 in the Big Ten. So once again RPM thinks I'm being too cautious with my 12-4 prediction for the Vols. The nascent projection system thinks an outcome that's one or perhaps even two wins better than that is not unlikely for Bruce Pearl's team. We'll see.

The flexible but very nevertheless very real ceiling above the best teams

Last scatter plot, promise. Let's look at really good teams, those that outscore their conference opponents by 0.16 points per trip or more. If you dominate your league to that extent, you are clearly a threat to reach the Final Four.

Here's how hard it is for really good teams to improve from year to year.

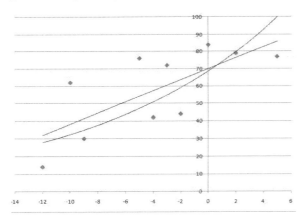

The data here is skimpy, sure, but it's interesting not for what it "proves" but rather for what it merely suggests. Since 2006, ten teams out of the 272 in my sample have outscored their conference opponents by 0.16 points or more per trip, and of those ten teams only two were able to improve the following year. The 2007 Kansas team that lost to UCLA in the Elite Eight was better than KU in 2006, and the Derrick Rose Memphis team in 2008 that never officially existed was better than the 2007 Tigers that are still on the books. A third team, the Kansas squad that won the national championship in 2008, stayed right where it had been the previous year in terms of in-conference performance. The other seven members of this elite group all declined in performance the following year.

There's a lesson here. North Carolina in the mid-to late-aughts notwithstanding, fans of great teams should definitely adhere to the principle of carpe diem. If your team is dominant this year, enjoy it while it lasts. There's a 70 percent chance that next year you won't be as dominant.

When everyone's back from a really good team, the expectation shouldn't be that they'll improve greatly, or even at all, but rather that they'll simply be really good again—and that is no small feat. There's a ceiling to how good a team can be and the best-case scenario for a team that is already outstanding and that brings everyone back is that they will stick to this ceiling.

The folk wisdom is sound -- mostly

We have seen that how well a team does in a given year is not as simple as how many seniors it has. What matters is not only how many starters are returning, but also how those returning starters performed last year.

Which is all well and good, but college basketball wouldn't command our interest if there weren't the occasional outlier. And in the field of performance not corresponding to experience, there are definitely outliers, teams that obviously make this RPM thing scratch its head and say "What the...?"

• In 2008 Drake returned just 39 percent of its possession-minutes from a team that finished 6-12 in the Missouri Valley. That year the Bulldogs went 15-3 in the MVC and earned a five-seed in the NCAA tournament.

• Last year Southern Miss brought back 89 percent of the possession-minutes from a group that went 9-7 in Conference USA. In 2009 the Golden Eagles finished 4-12 in C-USA.

Drake in 2008 and Southern Miss in 2009 remind us that if you're foolhardy enough make predictions in public, sooner or later you will look silly. Nevertheless, we can't stop making predictions.

For its part, this RPM thing should get better at making those predictions this year, as more information's added to its memory bank. I'll keep you posted.

John Gasaway

Much of my interest in quantifying things comes from the desire to be aware when something crazy happens. Without some context of what's normal, there's no way to know what's abnormal.

Unless you were paying close attention to advanced stats, you probably didn't realize that Pitt's DeJuan Blair may well have had a season for the ages in 2008-09. During his time on the floor, Blair pulled down nearly one in four of his team's missed shots. The exact figure was 23.6 percent. That's a number that by itself isn't all that significant, so let's put it in perspective.

• The next highest offensive rebounding rate last season was turned in by Santa Clara's John Bryant at 18.6 percent. Bryant would have needed to grab 35 more offensive rebounds to match Blair.

• In our five seasons of tracking this data, the next best rate was posted by Morehead State's Kenneth Faried in 2007-08 at 20.3 percent.

• Only 40 players in the country had a better *defensive* rebounding rate last season.

• In 6,700 player-minutes, the University of Colorado grabbed a total of 201 offensive rebounds last season. In 955 minutes, Blair pulled down 195.

Let it be known that Blair's season was historic. Even though offensive rebounding like this has been observed now once in five seasons of tracking, it's plausible that a season this extreme is far rarer than that. A season like this deserves a complete examination, if for no other reason than to preserve its greatness in print for future generations. But also to answer a more fundamental question: Exactly how valuable was Blair's performance? How valuable was the best offensive rebounding season that we've (possibly) ever seen?

I put my team of number-crunching robots to the task of looking at each one of Pitt's possessions in an effort to answer those questions. Short of going back in time and forcing Jamie Dixon to replay the entire season without Blair, we can never know with certainty just how large a difference he really made for his team. But I do think we can come up with some very interesting clues in that direction.

Finding 1: Blair came by his record honestly, except for one case

What I thought I would find is that Blair had incidents where he racked up multiple offensive boards through a sequence of missed layups or tip-ins. However, Blair didn't benefit from many of these situations. In fact, only once during the entire season did he record as many as three offensive rebounds in a single possession. It occurred in the January 14 game against South Florida. I specifically say "recorded" three rebounds because in this particular instance, it appears Blair was given one that he didn't deserve. Here are the details of that possession from the game's official play-by-play:

07:15 Beginning of Possession (Score: Pittsburgh 66, South Florida 53)
07:15 REBOUND (DEF) by Fields, Levance
07:01 MISSED JUMPER by Fields, Levance
07:01 REBOUND (OFF) by Blair, DeJuan
06:55 MISSED LAYUP by Blair, DeJuan
06:55 BLOCK by GILCHRIST, Augustus
06:52 REBOUND (OFF) by Blair, DeJuan
06:51 FOUL by GILCHRIST, Augustus (P3T8)
06:51 MISSED FT SHOT by Blair, DeJuan
06:51 REBOUND (OFF) by Blair, DeJuan
06:51 GOOD! FT SHOT by Blair, DeJuan
06:51 End of Possession (Score: Pittsburgh 67, South Florida 53)

If you follow the possession through, you should notice something unusual near the end of it. Blair goes to the line after getting fouled by the Bulls' Gus Gilchrist (who, by the way, had his best game of the season, scoring 22 points in 32 minutes off the bench). Blair misses the first, gets his own rebound, and is suddenly back at the line shooting again without another foul being recorded. He makes that free throw and then the Bulls get the ball for some reason.

What I expect happened here was that Blair was at

the line for two. Normally, when a player misses the first free throw in this situation, the scorekeeper will record a team deadball rebound for accounting purposes, which gets dropped on the floor when the official box score is created. However, a rebound was erroneously assigned to Blair while he was simply standing at the line waiting to get the ball for his second attempt.

This serves to illustrate that all stats are measurements and all measurements have errors. Blair's official total for the season was 195. He probably didn't have that many offensive rebounds. He may not have truly had 194, either—undoubtedly there were other cases where either a teammate was credited with a rebound Blair got, or vice versa. College basketball is a fast-paced game and stats are recorded by people not getting paid much to do it. Because of that, the precision of large numbers accumulated over the season should not be taken for granted.

Regardless, DeJuan Blair's 195 offensive rebounds were spread across 178 possessions. While he got help from the scorekeeper on one occasion, it would appear he did little padding of his own stats.

Finding 2: Blair's boards were very good for the Pitt offense

Part of the reason for this exercise was that I thought Blair's efforts were quite valuable. I mean, I've always felt like the offensive rebound is an underappreciated play. For instance, the blocked shot gets incredible publicity. It can erase points, but it also doesn't necessarily end a possession. Likewise, an offensive rebound erases a missed shot. It doesn't necessarily lead to points but it gives the offense an opportunity for points that it otherwise wouldn't get.

I suspect the reason that the block gets all the attention is that (a) it's exciting, and (b) it's more rare. There were about three times as many offensive rebounds as blocked shots last season. In addition, the frequent shot-blockers account for a lot of those blocks. For instance, Mississippi State's Jarvis Varnado by himself was responsible for 0.46% of all blocked shots in the game last season. Of the 4,630 players to see action last season, 153 of them accounted for a quarter of D-I's blocked shots. (By contrast, it took 315 players to account for a quarter of all offensive boards.)

Towards the end of the season, as Pitt was battling

UNC for top honors in offensive efficiency –a battle the Panthers would concede with a slump in March— I couldn't help but wonder about the value of Blair's amazing season on the boards. It had to be extremely liberating for Blair's teammates. They didn't need to think twice about taking a shot. Over 40 percent of the time it would end up in a teammate's hands. And when Blair was on the floor, he was getting over half his team's offensive boards, often in a good position to finish.

On those 178 possessions when Blair grabbed a Pitt miss, the Panthers scored 257 points after the offensive rebound. That's 1.44 points per possession, which is better than the typical D-I team's fast break efficiency. Strictly speaking, that's 257 points (or 7.1 points per game) that Pitt wouldn't have scored without a Blair-created second chance. (More amazingly, Blair scored 191 of those points himself—that's 36 percent of all the points he scored during the season. It was almost as effective to pass him the ball off the rim as it was to dish it to him directly.)

We can be a little more precise about this, though. If DeJuan Blair didn't exist, Pitt still would have someone playing center and would have converted some additional points after offensive rebounds. In addition, Blair may have been such a tenacious rebounder that he stole offensive boards from teammates. One way to get a grasp on Blair's overall worth is to compare the Panthers' offensive rebounding rates (and subsequent conversions) with him on and off the floor.

Finding 3: Blair's offensive rebounds didn't come at the expense of his teammates

There's some anecdotal evidence to assess the Blair effect. Pitt played one game without him, a November 25 contest against Belmont. The Bruins had a pretty good season—they went 20-12 and tied for second in the Atlantic Sun. But they weren't a good defensive rebounding team, ranking 217th nationally against a weak schedule. Even so, Pitt had its worst offensive rebounding game of the season against Belmont, grabbing just 21 percent of the available boards. I must point out that there were only 24 such boards available because Pitt missed so few shots, and that's a small enough sample for something fluky to happen, but it's at least an interesting coincidence. Fortunately, through official play-by-play data we can determine if it was more than a fluke.

In looking at Pitt's offensive rebounding rate as a team with Blair on and off the floor, it doesn't appear he was taking many rebounds from teammates.

Pittsburgh's Offensive Rebounding Percentage With Blair On/Off The Court	
	Rebound Percentage
Blair on	46.7%
Blair off	35.7%

So on the surface it appears Blair's work was mostly additive. When he was on the bench, either Tyrell Biggs or Gary McGhee was often on the floor in his place. Biggs and McGhee each had offensive rebounding percentages ten to 14 points lower than Blair's, which would explain the difference above. What's amazing is that if you take away free throws, which are much more difficult for the offense to rebound, Pitt's field goal attempts with Blair on the floor were astonishingly close to true 50/50 propositions when it came to which team got the rebound.

Finding 4: Blair's offensive rebounds were of very high quality

But Blair's impact was not merely that he gave his team more shots per possession.

Offensive Rebounding Efficiency With Blair On/Off The Court			
	OR Poss	OR Points	Points Per OR Poss
Blair on	315	435	1.38
Blair off	113	140	1.24

It was that those second looks were of a higher quality when he was in the game.

Conclusion: Blair's incredible skill improved Pitt's offensive efficiency significantly.

Now that we know how much an offensive rebound possession was worth with Blair both on and off the floor, we need just one more table to connect all of the dots here and determine how much Blair's offensive rebounding presence was worth over his replacements.

Offensive Rebounding Frequency With Blair On/Off The Court			
	Total Poss	OR Poss	%OR Poss
Blair on	1518	315	20.8
Blair off	795	113	14.2

With Blair off the court, an offensive rebound occurred on 14.2 percent of Pitt's possessions. With him on the court that number improved by 6.6 percent. We can apply that difference to the 1,518 possessions Blair was in the game and determine that his presence gave Pitt an extra 99 possessions where at least one offensive rebound occurred. Since each of those possessions was worth 1.38 points, the total value of those 99 possessions was 137 points.

In addition, of the 216 offensive rebound possessions that would have occurred anyway whether Blair was in the game or not, his presence improved their rate of return by 0.14 points per possession, or a total of 30 additional points. Thus, the conclusion is that the total value of Blair's offensive rebounding was 167 points.

This methodology is not perfect—it's trying to create a situation that didn't occur, namely Pitt's life without DeJuan Blair. But it seems like a reasonable way to estimate the effect of a supernatural offensive rebounder. In this case, Blair's talent was worth 4.6 points per game, or 0.07 points per possession over the entire season.

Without those points, Pitt's offense would have ranked on the fringe of the nation's top 20. As it was, the Panthers were only exceeded by North Carolina. Case closed.

Ken Pomeroy

Can The Right Coach Get You To The Final Four?

When it comes to Final Four coaches, doesn't it seem like we see a lot of the same faces April after April?

That was certainly the case last season in Detroit. North Carolina's Roy Williams was coaching in his seventh Final Four. Michigan State's Tom Izzo was making his fifth appearance. For UConn's Jim Calhoun, last spring completed his Final Four trifecta. The only newcomer to the party was Villanova's Jay Wright, who took the Wildcats to the Final Four for the first time in his eight years at the school.

Last season's Final Four was fairly typical in terms of the caliber of the teams that survived the Elite Eight. North Carolina and Connecticut were expected to make the trip to Detroit by virtue of their one-seeds. Michigan State was the second seed in the Midwest Region, needing only to knock off top-seeded Louisville in terms of "unexpected wins." Villanova was the Cinderella team in the bunch, comparatively, but the Wildcats were the three-seed in the East. The Wildcats edged Big East rival and top-seed Pittsburgh to punch their ticket to Ford Field.

If you add up the seeds of last season's Final Four participants, you get seven. Twenty-one of the 25 NCAA tournaments played since the field expanded to 64 teams in 1985 have been within five of that number. The outliers all stem from a true Cinderella crashing the party. Those include LSU (1986, 11-seed); Michigan and Cincinnati (six- and four-seeds, respectively), who squared off in the 1992 semifinals; Wisconsin (2000, eight-seed) and George Mason (2006, 11-seed).

So with the Final Four generally consisting of top-seeded teams (who in turn are typically top programs from power conferences), we do tend to end up with a lot of the same coaches squaring off to decide each season's national champion. The coaches are always at the forefront of media attention and fan adoration. Unlike the NBA, college basketball is a coach's game and those that walk on the biggest stage—the Final Four—are treated like the upperclassmen in an exclusive fraternity.

To a certain extent, the success of the Roy Willamses and Tom Izzos of the world ought to be expected. Because they lead programs rich in tradition and success, some of it of their own creation, proven coaches are able to create self-reinforcing success cycles. They get top talent because they win and they win because they get top talent. However, does that really tell us anything about a coach's ability to win in the tournament?

There is an industry built up around trying to profile the type of teams that win at tournament time. People take those office pools seriously and treat their brackets as if it was the Magna Carta. Until, of course, a spate of upsets leaves the aforementioned bracket wadded up and deposited in the nearest trash can. There are hundreds of factors that determine which programs succeed in the Big Dance, not the least of which is luck.

Still, we keep looking for that edge, trying to outsmart lady luck when we'd be better off just filling out the brackets with the favored team winning every game. Announcers tell us that teams with senior guards win at tournament time, so we favor teams with senior guards. Dick Vitale and Digger Phelps tell us the Big East is the greatest conference in the history of mankind, so we pick Big East teams to win in the tournament. Columnists tell us that coaches like Izzo just know how to prepare their teams for tournament play, so we pick teams with coaches like Izzo.

When it comes to evaluating coaches, however, there is always a chicken-and-egg conundrum. Where does the effect of the coach wear off and the effect of the players take hold? In other words, are the familiar faces we seem to see each April winning because they're such great tournament coaches, or are these guys merely capitalizing on past successes by collecting the best talent?

It's an interesting question, but difficult to define. At what point do we deem a coach "proven"? How do we divide coaching from other factors, such as quality of talent and luck?

Let's deal with the first question. In a sense, all college coaches are proven. That is to say, other than

Isiah Thomas, a coach isn't going to land a Division I job without some sort of track record, be it at a lower level as a head coach, or as an assistant coach. In this instance, we know we're dealing with tournament success, so we can narrow our group down to coaches that have won in the tournament. For our present purposes, we want to figure out if coaches have the ability to learn how to coach in the NCAA tournament. We also want to know if even after they've had some tournament success they're able to sustain that success regardless of the quality of their team.

The simplest way to do this is to tag a coach with the "proven" label after he has led a team to the Final Four. So that's what I've done. Using Calhoun as an example, he didn't make his first Final Four appearance until 1999, when he broke through with the national champion Huskies. At that point he was 26 years into his Division I coaching career, the first 14 of which were at Northeastern. Obviously, Calhoun was "proven" before winning the national title, but for our purposes here, he isn't labeled as proven until that 1999 tournament. What we're interested in finding out is how he's done since.

And how do we go about determining that?

Thankfully, the NCAA tournament provides us a handy little proxy for team expectation called seeds. A group comprised of university athletic directors and conference commissioners is locked up in a little room for several days each March. Not only do they decide who gets to play in the tournament, they also assess the relative merits of the teams they select. Generally speaking this selection committee does a remarkably good job on both counts, though they are far from perfect.

The results of the selection committee's efforts are four 16-team brackets, with teams matched up according to seed. What we're going to do here is measure how well our group of proven coaches is able to "play to seed." For example, a one-seed is expected to win at least four games. A two-seed is expected to win three, presumably losing in the regional final when they run up against the top seed. Seeds nine through 16 are all expected to lose in the first round. Their win expectation is zero. Here is our simple chart showing expected wins (eW) by seed:

NCAA Tournament Win Expectation By Seed

Seed	eW	Seed	eW	Seed	eW	Seed	eW
1	4	5	1	9	0	13	0
2	3	6	1	10	0	14	0
3	2	7	1	11	0	15	0
4	2	8	1	12	0	16	0

We're now going to count up how many wins above or below expectation each of our proven coaches has compiled in the era of 64-team tournaments. We do have one complicating factor. The win expectation for a one-seed is actually more than four. They're supposed to win four games to escape their region, but then they confront the Final Four. While the committee does rank the one-seeds relative to each other, the public isn't privy to those rankings. We can usually figure out who was slotted where, but there is a certain amount of guesswork involved.

I've decided to let coaches keep any Final Four wins as wins above expectation. Based on what we know, the win expectation for a team once they reach the Final Four is zero. (Assuming that the bracket holds form and they play a fellow top seed, which in reality doesn't happen that often.) Since winning a Final Four game or two is a good thing, it would seem that giving the coaches credit for winning those extra games is the right way to go.

After counting up all of these extra wins (or lack thereof) for proven coaches, what do we expect to find? That's simple. If beating your seed in the tournament is a sustainable skill for proven coaches, we'd expect them to end up with positive wins-above-expectation totals.

Is that how it turns out? I'll let you decide.

Our group of 58 coaches has accounted for 402 tournament appearances subsequent to their initial Final Four showings. Here's how they fared:

Coaches vs. Coaches: NCAA Tournament Performance Of 58 Final Four Coaches In 402 Tournament Appearances

Category	Number	Percentage
Worse than seed	155	38.5%
Exactly to seed	149	37.1%
Better than seed	98	24.4%

Performance measured relative to "expected wins" according to seed.

Whether or not these numbers suggest some degree of skill is open to interpretation. On one hand, proven coaches match or beat their seed 61.5 percent of the time. On the other hand, they are 14.1 percent more likely to fall short of their seed than they are to beat it. The aggregate wins-above-expectation figure for our group is -51. Just 16 of our 58 coaches finished with a positive figure. Based on this methodology, it'd be tough to argue that, in general, coaches have the ability to consistently beat the seed the NCAA assigns them.

That is not to say that there aren't some interesting stories here, not the least of which involves one Tom Izzo.

Izzo was something of an unknown quantity when he first took Michigan State to the Final Four in 1999. Since then his Spartans have earned a spot in each of the last ten NCAA tournaments. Only twice has Izzo failed to match or exceed his team's seed. Six times he's beaten it and never has he fallen more than one win short of expectation. In total, Izzo has compiled nine wins above expectation since he became a proven coach. It seems likely that either the Spartans have been consistently under-seeded, which is a possibility, or that Izzo really knows what he's doing when it comes to winning in the tournament.

On the other end of the spectrum, we have Lute Olson and Mike Montgomery, who are on the bottom of our list with -11 wins above expectation. Olson earned his proven stripes by leading Iowa to the Final Four in 1980, so all of his Arizona appearances count in our study. That's 23 appearances in the 64-team era before his last one in 2007. That span saw four more Final Four appearances and the 1997 national championship. Yet even with all those wins, in the aggregate his Wildcats were as likely to get knocked off in the early rounds as they were to advance deep into the bracket. Olson lost in the first round as a two-seed in 1993. He lost in the second round as a one-seed in 2000.

Meanwhile, Montgomery took three-seed Stanford to the 1998 Final Four, but after that the Cardinal was a consistently bad bet. In six subsequent NCAA tournament appearances under Montgomery, Stanford failed to exceed their seed. Only once did they match it. Twice the Cardinal lost in the second round as a top seed. Last season, Montgomery got back into the tournament as the head coach of California. The Golden Bears were seeded seventh, which means they should have won at least one game. They lost in the first round to Maryland.

None of this is conclusive, of course, but the results are interesting. The ability of a proven coach to help his team overachieve relative to its seed does not seem to be a consistent trait. However, at the extremes, there does seem to be a pattern of coaches who are and who are not good tournament coaches. We'll give you a chart of all 58 coaches and let you decide if you want to factor it in the next time you fill out a bracket for the office pool. If it doesn't work out, we only ask that you don't tear it out and deposit in the trash alongside your forsaken bracket.   *Bradford Doolittle*

Coaches By NCAA Tournament Wins Over Expectation

Coach	Wins above expectation	Coach	Wins above expectation
Tom Izzo	9	Jim Calhoun	-1
Larry Brown	5	Eddie Sutton	-1
Denny Crum	4	John Thompson	-1
Steve Fisher	4	Gene Bartow	-1
Dale Brown	4	Dick Bennett	-1
Rollie Massimino	4	P.J. Carlesimo	-1
Don Haskins	3	Bobby Cremins	-1
Rick Pitino	2	Clem Haskins	-1
Jerry Tarkanian	2	Dana Kirk	-1
Joe B. Hall	2	Rick Majerus	-1
Nolan Richardson	2	Thad Matta	-1
Gary Williams	2	Roy Williams	-2
Ben Howland	1	John Calipari	-2
Bill Guthridge	1	Hugh Durham	-2
Johnny Orr	1	Rick Barnes	-2
Jim Valvano	1	Tom Crean	-2
Jim Boeheim	0	John Thompson III	-2
Billy Donovan	0	Bruce Weber	-2
Terry Holland	0	Lou Carnesecca	-3
Mike Davis	0	Jud Heathcote	-3
Jim Harrick	0	Jim O'Brien	-3
Paul Hewitt	0	Kelvin Sampson	-4
Lon Kruger	0	Tubby Smith	-5
Jim Larranaga	0	Lou Henson	-6
Digger Phelps	0	Bobby Knight	-7
Bill Self	0	Billy Tubbs	-8
Norm Sloan	0	Bob Huggins	-10
Dean Smith	-1	Lute Olson	-11
Mike Krzyzewski	-1	Mike Montgomery	-11

he NBA draft has become a serious business. Like Mel Kiper did for the NFL, ESPN Insider's Chad Ford and Web sites DraftExpress.com and NBADraft.net have popularized NBA mock drafts. Even before last June's draft was complete, those sites were already preparing new projections—for 2011.

Aside from rare exceptions like Brandon Jennings and Jeremy Tyler, virtually every American prospect plays college hoops, thanks to the NBA's recently-enacted age limit. Meaning pro fans can now enjoy NCAA basketball on multiple levels, both for the pageantry and tradition of the college game and to watch tomorrow's NBA stars today.

Naturally, Basketball Prospectus has lent a level of statistical sophistication to the scouting process by translating college stats to their NBA equivalents. Our translations utilize a database of more than 200 players from the 2000-2008 NBA drafts to model how players' tempo-free statistics have carried over from their final season in the NCAA to their first in the NBA, accounting for strength of schedule (as measured by Ken Pomeroy's SOS ratings).

To represent the scouting perspective, we've used the 2010 mock drafts from DraftExpress.com (DX) and NBADraft.net (NBAD), as well as Chad Ford's top 100 list (ESPN) to rank both the consensus top ten returning prospects and the five incoming freshmen with the highest draft stock. To highlight the places where the scouts apparently disagree with the stats, we also look at five players rated more highly by the numbers and five players projected to go earlier than their numbers would suggest.

For each returning player, we've listed some key translated statistics. Most notable is Win%, the estimated winning percentage of a team made up of the player in question and four average teammates. Also note that "BS%" is the player's combined rate of blocks and steals per possession.

The Consensus Top Ten Returning Prospects

1. Ed Davis, PF, North Carolina (Sophomore)										
Height	Weight	DX	NBAD	ESPN	Avg.	Win%	TS%	Usg	Reb%	Ast%
6-9	215	6	2	3	3.7	.453	.455	.127	.182	.014

During his freshman campaign, Davis played off the bench in a complementary role. With the departure of the veteran core of the Tar Heels' championship squad, Davis will be a star as a sophomore, making it easier to determine whether he is worthy of the hype. Right now, Davis' rebounding and shot blocking are NBA-caliber. However, he will have to improve as a finisher, having shot a mediocre 52 percent on twos despite his low usage rate last season.

2. Cole Aldrich, C, Kansas (Junior)										
Height	Weight	DX	NBAD	ESPN	Avg.	Win%	TS%	Usg	Reb%	Ast%
6-11	250	4	4	7	5.0	.556	.547	.157	.191	.014

Think of Cole Aldrich as Ed Davis, a year later. Aldrich saw even less action as a first-year reserve for a championship team before emerging as the Jayhawks' go-to player last season. Aldrich's combination of size and strength makes him a probable top-five pick, and his sophomore numbers suggest he's already capable of stepping into an NBA rotation. Aldrich is an outstanding defensive rebounder and shot blocker who has shown the ability to score down low and even step outside at times.

3. Willie Warren, SG, Oklahoma (Sophomore)										
Height	Weight	DX	NBAD	ESPN	Avg.	Win%	TS%	Usg	Reb%	Ast%
6-4	200	3	11	6	6.7	.342	.522	.167	.036	.042

The scouts came to see Blake Griffin, but they also fell in love with Warren. He served as the perimeter counterbalance to Griffin's dominant paint presence as a freshman, and this year he will be the go-to guy for the Sooners. If Warren can maintain his efficiency inside the arc (57 percent on twos), he'll be a top-10 pick. The biggest concern is that Warren is on the smaller side for an NBA two-guard and could end up in a combo role. He's also a very poor rebounder.

4. Greg Monroe, C, Georgetown (Sophomore)										
Height	Weight	DX	NBAD	ESPN	Avg.	Win%	TS%	Usg	Reb%	Ast%
6-11	240	10	13	4	9.0	.517	.523	.171	.128	.039

Many of last year's highly-touted freshmen struggled to convert potential into production. Monroe was an exception, even on an underwhelming Hoyas squad. His 58 percent two-point accuracy was augmented by his ability to get to the free throw line and convert there at a solid 70 percent clip. Defensively, Monroe was as good at collecting steals as blocks, unorthodox for a Georgetown big man but impressive nonetheless. The lone statistical Achilles' heel is Monroe's poor rebounding. Despite that, by the numbers Monroe has more upside than either Aldrich or Davis.

5. Al-Farouq Aminu, F, Wake Forest (Sophomore)										
Height	Weight	DX	NBAD	ESPN	Avg.	Win%	TS%	Usg	Reb%	Ast%
6-8	210	8	14	5	9.0	.383	.479	.161	.135	.020

For a player considered to be a project, Aminu wasn't bad as a freshman, using his athleticism to post solid defensive numbers. At the offensive end, he is something of a tweener. Aminu might not have enough size to play power forward in the NBA, but he has yet to demonstrate perimeter skills, making just seven three-pointers all season long. In terms of that development, Aminu's poor free throw shooting (67 percent) is not encouraging.

6. Devin Ebanks, F, West Virginia (Sophomore)										
Height	Weight	DX	NBAD	ESPN	Avg.	Win%	TS%	Usg	Reb%	Ast%
6-8	205	12	5	12	9.7	.440	.462	.146	.148	.038

Like Aminu, Ebanks will likely have to spend more time on the perimeter as a professional. He was even less effective from beyond the arc, making five of his 40 three-point attempts, but his superior ballhandling ability will aid that transition. The lanky Ebanks rebounds well enough to hold his own in the post and could play as a four-man in an up-tempo system, a la Earl Clark. He developed as a scorer over the course of the year, which he capped with consecutive efforts of 20-plus points in the Big East tournament.

7. Solomon Alabi, C, Florida State (RS Sophomore)										
Height	Weight	DX	NBAD	ESPN	Avg.	Win%	TS%	Usg	Reb%	Ast%
7-1	230	14	8	10	10.7	.422	.474	.155	.141	.007

The native of Nigeria flashed potential as a redshirt freshman, ranking 16th in the nation—and third among first-year players—in block rate. At 7-1, Alabi has legit center size to go along with strong athleticism. Typical of a young big man, Alabi remains a work in progress at the other end. He was second on the Seminoles in usage after NBA-bound Toney Douglas, but could stand to improve his accuracy around the rim. This year's performance will be telling.

8. Evan Turner, G/F, Ohio State (Junior)										
Height	Weight	DX	NBAD	ESPN	Avg.	Win%	TS%	Usg	Reb%	Ast%
6-7	205	7	15	11	11.0	.455	.498	.213	.116	.053

The best all-around prospect in the country, Turner can contribute to an NBA team in a variety of ways. A fine rebounder from the wing, Turner also can help out with ballhandling and has potential as a shutdown defender. Offensively, Turner could stand to become more efficient, but did reasonably well given that he used more than 25 percent of the Buckeyes' possessions as a sophomore. Regular trips to the free throw line—nearly seven a night—helped in that regard.

9. Craig Brackins, PF, Iowa State (Junior)										
Height	Weight	DX	NBAD	ESPN	Avg.	Win%	TS%	Usg	Reb%	Ast%
6-10	230	20	9	13	14.0	.349	.443	.256	.147	.019

As a sophomore, Brackins *was* the Cyclones' offense, using 34 percent of the team's possessions—the fifth-highest total in the nation and second among players returning for 2009-10 (behind only Luke Harangody). Naturally, a role that large limited Brackins' efficiency, and his translated True Shooting Percentage of .443 is lowest among the top ten prospects. Another concern is that Brackins is old for his class—he turned 22 in early October because he spent a year in prep school.

10. Patrick Patterson, PF, Kentucky (Junior)										
Height	Weight	DX	NBAD	ESPN	Avg.	Win%	TS%	Usg	Reb%	Ast%
6-8	223	13	17	15	15.0	.499	.530	.168	.143	.024

Patterson is the only returner from last year's list, where he ranked...tenth. He took a nice step forward as a sophomore, especially on the glass. Patterson improved his defensive rebound percentage from 15.6 to 20.3 percent, addressing his biggest statistical weakness. Another solid season of development, especially on the defensive end, could make Patterson a lottery pick.

The Stats Like ...

Trevor Booker, PF, Clemson (Senior)										
Height	Weight	DX	NBAD	ESPN	Avg.	Win%	TS%	Usg	Reb%	Ast%
6-7	215	23	28	45	32.0	.552	.511	.161	.164	.023

Booker could be this year's version of Paul Millsap (his best comparison in our database of translated college stats). Undersized for the post at 6-7, Booker was highly productive as a junior nonetheless. His 57 percent shooting led the ACC, as did his 9.7 rebounds per game. Equally intriguing is Booker's defensive versatility. He's a fine shot-blocker and comes up with plenty of steals for a big man, a promising indicator as far as quickness. NBADraft.net and DraftExpress both have Booker as a first-round pick, but they still could be understating his ability to contribute right away.

Kenneth Faried, F, Morehead State (Junior)										
Height	Weight	DX	NBAD	ESPN	Avg.	Win%	TS%	Usg	Reb%	Ast%
6-8	215	37	65	55	52.3	.557	.461	.157	.203	.020

Even accounting for the weak level of competition, Faried put up eye-popping numbers for the OVC champs. His translated 20.3 rebound percentage is better than any of the consensus top 10 prospects, and only Monroe can match Faried's combination of blocks and steals. Also note that Faried backed up the numbers on the floor in the NCAA tournament, when he had 14 points and 11 boards in a competitive loss to Louisville. His athleticism makes him an intriguing second-round possibility.

Luke Harangody, PF, Notre Dame (Senior)										
Height	Weight	DX	NBAD	ESPN	Avg.	Win%	TS%	Usg	Reb%	Ast%
6-8	251	45	46	29	40.0	.468	.439	.262	.176	.026

The Fighting Irish had a disappointing season in 2008-09, but don't blame Harangody. He was asked to shoulder an enormous load, using over a third of Notre Dame's possessions while on the floor. That hampered Harangody's accuracy, as he shot just 47 percent from the field, but he was amazingly sure-handed. Harangody's turnover rate ranked sixth in the nation. As a pro, Harangody's strength and physicality will help him make up for shortcomings in size and speed. The similar Jon Brockman ended up going early in the second round in June.

Manny Harris, G, Michigan (Junior)										
Height	Weight	DX	NBAD	ESPN	Avg.	Win%	TS%	Usg	Reb%	Ast%
6-5	170	38	32	65	45.0	.479	.471	.232	.130	.065

Like Turner, Harris is a multi-skilled Big Ten wing who took a major step forward in his sophomore season. So why is Turner a possible lottery pick while Harris is projected to go in the second round? Size has something to do with it, as Turner is two inches taller. However, Harris' assist rate suggests he might even be able to play some point in the NBA, which would enhance his value.

Jarvis Varnado, F/C, Mississippi State (Senior)										
Height	Weight	DX	NBAD	ESPN	Avg.	Win%	TS%	Usg	Reb%	Ast%
6-9	210	35	23	24	27.3	.525	.482	.163	.152	.012

Nobody in the country blocks shots like Varnado, which will be his ticket to the NBA. He enters his senior season as a possible late first-round pick after he was not on any draft boards this time a year ago. Varnado improved on the offensive end in 2008-09, increasing his usage rate from 13.7 to 22.2 percent without sacrificing any of his accuracy from the field. If Varnado can contribute on offense, his shot blocking is strong enough to make him an NBA starter.

The Scouts Like ...

William Buford, SG, Ohio State (Sophomore)										
Height	Weight	DX	NBAD	ESPN	Avg.	Win%	TS%	Usg	Reb%	Ast%
6-5	85	27	3	40	23.3	.321	.458	.166	.076	.019

Opinions on Buford's draft prospects are mixed. Only Ford has him listed this year, as a second-round pick, but NBADraft.net projects him as a top-three pick in the 2011 Draft. To justify that, Buford will need to significantly broaden his game. As a freshman, he was largely a three-point specialist, attempting more than twice as many triples (119) as free throws (53). Creating his own shot remains a work in progress.

Malcolm Lee, SG, UCLA (Sophomore)										
Height	Weight	DX	NBAD	ESPN	Avg.	Win%	TS%	Usg	Reb%	Ast%
6-5	190	11	5	43	19.7	.292	.461	.143	.091	.025

Lee spent most of his freshman season as a spectator, even when he was on the court, but his time is now: Darren Collison and Jrue Holiday both went to the NBA as first-round picks. Lee will start at shooting guard and be asked to be the Bruins' go-to guy on the perimeter. Like predecessors Holiday and Russell Westbrook, Lee is an excellent defensive player with the ability to match up with either guard position. A red flag: 42 percent shooting from the line is unacceptable for a guard.

Kemba Walker, PG, Connecticut (Sophomore)										
Height	Weight	DX	NBAD	ESPN	Avg.	Win%	TS%	Usg	Reb%	Ast%
6-0	180	20	24	22	22.0	.346	.464	.144	.070	.045

Putting Walker on this list might not be fair, since the biggest problem with his stat line as a freshman was a distinct lack of assists. That shortage is explained in large part by the fact that Walker played heavily alongside fellow point guard A.J. Price in an undersized backcourt, especially after Jerome Dyson was lost with a torn meniscus. Price now plays for the Indiana Pacers, so Walker will run the UConn offense this season and can demonstrate that he deserves to be a first-round pick.

Terrico White, SG, Mississippi (Sophomore)										
Height	Weight	DX	NBAD	ESPN	Avg.	Win%	TS%	Usg	Reb%	Ast%
6-5	211	21	7	30	19.3	.290	.437	.176	.058	.033

White put himself on the map by winning SEC Newcomer of the Year honors, but his season was not nearly as impressive when viewed through the prism of advanced statistics. White struggled to finish, shooting less than 50 percent on two-pointers, and rarely got to the free throw line. To make a living as a perimeter specialist, he's going to need to shoot better than last year's 35 percent from three-point range.

Tony Woods, F/C, Wake Forest (Sophomore)										
Height	Weight	DX	NBAD	ESPN	Avg.	Win%	TS%	Usg	Reb%	Ast%
6-10	234	29	28	28	28.3	.267	.469	.114	.115	.002

There is no question that Woods is a major project, but one with enough potential that all three sites see him going late in the first round—though more likely in 2011 than 2010. For an athletic 6-10 big man playing limited minutes off the bench, Woods' defensive numbers were unimpressive. He grabbed just 13.2 percent of available defensive rebounds, below average for a center, and blocked 3.9 percent of opposing two-point shots—fewer than teammate Aminu.

Top Five Freshmen

1. John Wall, PG, Kentucky					
Height	Weight	DX	NBAD	ESPN	Avg.
6-3	175	1	1	1	1.0

Entering what is sure to be his lone season of college basketball, Wall is the only prospect with a blog devoted to his NBA prospects—DraftJohnWall.blogspot.com. Barring something disastrous, he will be the top overall pick. The question is what Wall can accomplish, individually and on a team level, before heading off to the NBA.

2. Derrick Favors, PF, Georgia Tech					
Height	Weight	DX	NBAD	ESPN	Avg.
6-9	215	2	4	2	2.7

If anyone is to push Wall for the right to be the No. 1 pick next June, it's Favors, a powerful, athletic big man. Before Wall blew up in the spring, Favors was the consensus top prospect in the class. He and Wall are the lone freshmen considered certain lottery picks after one year of college.

3. John Henson, F, North Carolina					
Height	Weight	DX	NBAD	ESPN	Avg.
6-10	200	9	4	8	7.0

The jewel of the defending champs' incoming class, the lanky forward should be a lottery pick in either 2010 or 2011. The biggest determining factor in when Henson reaches the NBA might be how quickly his body develops.

4. Avery Bradley, G, Texas

Height	Weight	DX	NBAD	ESPN	Avg.
6-3	180	17	6	20	14.3

Bradley heads to Austin as ESPNU's top-rated college prospect. His reputation as a lockdown defender precedes him, and Bradley is also a creative offensive talent. The big question from an NBA perspective is whether Bradley can ultimately play the point. At 6-3, he's undersized as a two-guard.

5. Xavier Henry, SG, Kansas

Height	Weight	DX	NBAD	ESPN	Avg.
6-6	210	24	19	14	19.0

The biggest thing that might hold Henry back as an NBA prospect is the depth of talent around him at Kansas this season. With Aldrich, Sherron Collins and Tyshawn Taylor also potential first-round picks next June, Henry may not play a featured role as a freshman.   *Kevin Pelton*

The Damage Done

The phrase "man among boys" was never more apt than when watching Greg Oden play high school basketball. The seven-footer looked like he was 35 the day he stepped onto a court as a sophomore. He went on to be one of the most-watched players in the storied history of basketball, but injury problems have derailed his pro career thus far. One factor cited by NBA insiders is not his size, but his usage. Like many elite players, Oden and his teammate, Mike Conley Jr., played nearly year-round as part of AAU basketball. Does the structure of youth basketball have a negative impact on the game?

College basketball has long used the "travel team" and AAU system as a feeder, one that has become nearly as important as state-organized high school basketball. The advent of elite camps has added to the ability of college coaches to see potential players against elite competition in limited locations, cutting the time and cost of recruiting. But there may be a hidden cost. By playing so much, are gym rats turning into training room residents?

Any activity is going to be negatively impacted by fatigue, but basketball is a unique sport in that practice often takes the form of a game. Legendary coach John Wooden said that one of the biggest challenges of coaching is that "practice is often the part of the game that is hardest for players. They have always 'just played' and never learned the skills necessary to improve, only to play." Whether that takes the form of AAU tournaments or a run at Rucker Park, it's hard to say that playing basketball is a negative.

These elite tournaments—organized under the auspices of the AAU, but in actuality run by anyone willing to put together a tournament schedule, find a site, and put up with the headaches—have become the preferred venue for college recruiters. That convenience has a price however. Bringing eight, 16, and in some cases even more teams together in one places has a tendency to create a frenetic pace. Playing two and three games in a day is common, plus one coach says "You put that many kids in one place and you know what they do in their down time? Play more basketball. Put on their own dunk contests." There are injuries, but anecdotal evidence shows that despite the pace, the injuries tend to happen at a rate similar to that of high school basketball.

"There's a survivor effect, but it's not as visible as you'd think" said one NCAA Division I head coach who spoke anonymously due to recruiting restrictions. "We see these kids virtually year-round and some of them wear down. I want to see kids who love the game, but there are kids who start breaking down instead of improving. This isn't buckling under pressure, but is usually sloppy play or even injury." That injury problem is exacerbated by the lack of quality care available.

While it would be impossible and impractical to have Athletic Trainers at every gym run, it would surprise many fans to learn that aside from elite camps, there's seldom any qualiified medical personnel available. "I've never seen a Trainer or doctor at one of these things," said a D-I recruiter. "I'm at all of these things and you see kids taping their own ankles sometimes, but that's it. A lot of kids don't even tie their shoes right, but I've seen kids roll their ankle in a morning game and then come back that afternoon hobbling, but playing. They want to be seen as tough, but it's really hard to get a read when they're playing like that."

The sheer volume of games is a significant problem. Weekend tournaments can involve as many as six or seven games with limited recovery time. Players pile into vans, drive hours, pack into cheap hotel rooms, run up and down the court, eat fast food, and seldom do more than a shootaround for warmups. Is it any wonder that there aren't more significant injuries here? The biggest issue may be reporting. The insidious nature of fatigue-based injuries makes it difficult to say "it happened here." Outside of the inevitable traumatic injuries—sprained ankles, fractures, serious muscle strains—most of the kids will vanish back into their daily routine, taking any minor injuries with them.

It may seem obvious that a fatigued player is more susceptible to injuries, but in fact the relationship is more subtle. According to Jinni Frisbey, the Head Athletic Trainer at the University of South Alabama, fatigue shows up most often in coordination. "Muscles are the major support system for ligaments and tendons," she explained, "so when muscles get tired, things break down behind that. Most of the basketball problems we see are legs—ankles, knees, hamstrings. I really worry when I see hamstrings because that's more from running than the type of accidental sprains you see in normal basketball. A sprained ankle can be dumb luck in landing wrong, but there's also a factor that a healthy, well-conditioned athlete is able to adjust and maybe not sprain it as much."

The easiest way to note fatigue as a factor is to watch the timing of injuries. "It's exactly when you'd expect it. Injuries happen more often at two key times in the season for most athletes—early or late," Frisbey explained. "Early usually means the start of camp in basketball or football, when the body is ramping up and is susceptible to simple fatigue. It's being asked to do something it's not used to and the body hasn't adjusted yet. At the end of the day, the worn-down athlete or the one that hasn't recovered from yesterday is going to end up on the sidelines with me."

"At the end of the season, we're seeing something of a survivor's effect, but we also see a new set of injuries," Frisbey continued. "That long wear-down really taxes recovery. For high school and college aged kids, nutrition is a huge factor. We're not talking about a training table for most of these kids, we're talking about a Big Mac or a Whopper. We're talking cafeteria food and maybe a Powerbar. They eat at weird intervals and often not only have the normal demands on the body, but are also growing, which creates a need for extra nutrients to support that."

It's quite possible that the fatigue factor that appears to come from an extended, often year-round schedule is actually just the absence of quality support from a physical and medical standpoint. It surprises many fans to find out that few high schools, especially in rural areas, have access to Athletic Trainers. This is at the scholastic level and the access is even worse for even elite travel and AAU teams. A quick survey of coaches and recruiters asking if any of these teams travelled with an Athletic Trainer brought laughter. At many elite tournaments, the host will provide access to a Training Room, but even then there's very limited interaction. One Athletic Trainer who has worked at elite tournaments and camps suggested that many athletes equated any treatment as weakness. "They all think that a recruiter is around every corner and that if they're seen in the Training Room, that scholarship is going to someone else."

That cultural attitude is strong not only on the elite circuit, but on the playgrounds as well. Brandon Rush, who played on the hard courts of Kansas City, said he had never been injured before tearing his ACL at Kansas in 2007. "Maybe rolled an ankle," he told me early in the 2008 season, after he signed with the Indiana Pacers. A couple questions later, he admitted that he was often sore, fatigued, and could remember his knee being "loose" as far back as high school. While Rush certainly had quality care at Kansas, the initial reluctance to discuss any physical limitations speaks as much to the culture as the reality.

There's one other concern, one that slides past most observers but could be the most costly of injury issues. With the modern NCAA and NBA player, there's an increase in the number of what Trainers call "insidious injuries." This type of injury doesn't announce its arrival with a single discrete and visible cause like a rolled ankle or a knee that gives way. These are instead the injuries that happen little by little, as time and fatigue slowly sap the player's ability in a way that is invisible even to the player and coach. Oden's microfracture surgery in what would have been his sophomore year of college is a perfect example. The surgery didn't happen because he was drafted, but rather because of countless trips running up and down the court on knees that were tested by his weight and the hard surface. (And before you ask, no, the shoes don't help.)

Dr. Daniel Kharrazi, team physician for the Los Angeles Lakers, has seen hundreds of players as the team prepares for the draft and he sees a difference in players today. "They're breaking down," he says. "It has to be the pace of play, because I see Kareem Abdul-Jabbar and he looks like he could play now. Wilt Chamberlain was in his sixties before he passed, and he ran marathons. He had no knee, hip or back problems at all. Now, I can't find a kid coming out as a one-and-done without some sort of consultation in his records." Dr. Kharrazi raises an interesting question—are these kids overplaying or is there some other significant change that's breaking players down?

There's no good solution here. Players are going to play while chasing a scholarship. Elite tournaments and camps exist to make life easier on everyone and their benefit far outweighs any fatigue concerns for players that may not end up under the control of any particular recruiter. Cuts in scholastic programs make it impossible to require the presence of a Certified Athletic Trainer, though it would solve many problems. The final line of defense, however, seems to have abdicated its responsibilities, as parents push their talented progeny into a system that seems purpose-built to wear them down, to break the weak, and leave only the best standing.

There's a teenager somewhere, his ankles swollen and his legs tired, sitting on the curb and looking up at the basket. He is in pain and breaking down physically. That's some hoop dream.   *Will Carroll*

2010
Previews

Atlantic Coast Conference
Life Beyond Chapel Hill?

The national championship won by North Carolina last April was widely viewed as a tribute to persistence. Tyler Hansbrough, Ty Lawson, and Wayne Ellington chose to put off their entrance into the NBA for one more year, it was said, in order to return to school and pursue the title that had thus far eluded their grasp.

If the Tar Heels' ascent of that mountain was an ordeal comprised of setbacks at progressively more tantalizing termini (the second-round loss to legend-in-the-making George Mason in 2006; the strange second-half drought leading to the Elite Eight loss in OT to Georgetown in 2007; the strange first-half blowout inflicted by Kansas in the 2008 Final Four), the actual culmination of all that effort proved to be something of a serene escalator ride to the summit. True, LSU kept things interesting for about 30 minutes in the second round, but otherwise the Tar Heels were never seriously threatened, certainly not by Michigan State in UNC's 89-72 title game victory. In the case of Roy Williams' team, persistence led to a remarkably drama-free tournament, followed by those ubiquitous trappings of success: T-shirts, ball caps, and cutting down the nets

The persistence displayed by the conference's other 11 teams, however, has yet to yield any such reward. In fact for ACC programs outside Chapel Hill the past few seasons, the drama has been continuous and inescapable. Chalk it up to the high expectations engendered by membership in one of the nation's elite conferences.

Note for example that unless you had the good sense to emblazon "NORTH CAROLINA" on your jersey, success in the NCAA tournament has remained stubbornly elusive for conference teams over the past five years. No ACC team besides Carolina has advanced to the Elite Eight since 2004, when both Duke and Georgia Tech made it that far. Over the past three NCAA tournaments, non-UNC conference teams have posted a disappointing 13-21 record when their respective seeds would have been expected to yield a 19-15 mark. Winning the ACC/Big Ten Challenge every November is nice, but some more success in March for coaches not named Roy Williams would be nicer still.

Not that the ACC's glass need be seen as half-empty, of course. This season the conference welcomes no fewer than nine McDonald's All-Americans to the league, more by far than any other conference and indeed as many as the Big 12 (five), SEC (three), Pac-10 (one), and Big Ten (zero) combined. The ACC has never lacked for talent. They certainly won't in 2010.

ACC PROSPECTUS			
	2009 Record	Returning Minutes (%)	2010 Prediction
North Carolina	13-3	27	12-4
Duke	11-5	61	11-5
Maryland	7-9	84	9-7
Boston College	9-7	84	9-7
Florida St.	10-6	71	9-7
Georgia Tech	2-14	73	8-8
Virginia	4-12	89	8-8
Wake Forest	11-5	63	8-8
Clemson	9-7	60	7-9
Virginia Tech	7-9	66	7-9
Miami	7-9	49	5-11
NC State	6-10	47	3-13

Which brings me to my fearless predictions. What happens when 12 talented teams play each other 96 times? I think we'll see a lot of records around .500, with North Carolina and Duke being a little better than that and NC State and Miami being a little worse. In between that top and bottom I foresee an eight-team scrum.

Only the Tar Heels could be named a favorite, albeit a slim one, to repeat as conference champions when returning just 27 percent of their minutes. For that they can thank Ed Davis, Marcus Ginyard, and four (yes, four) incoming McDonald's All-Americans. No, the Heels won't be as good as they were last year, or for that matter as they were the last couple years. I just think they'll be good enough this year.

If you think Georgia Tech and Virginia look surprisingly robust in my predictions, I have my reasons. In the case of the Yellow Jackets, credit my bullish outlook to a per-possession performance last year that was much better than a 2-14 record would suggest and to the arrival of Derrick Favors, not necessarily in that order. And in the case of the Cavaliers, teams that were bad but not DePaul-bad the previous year and that return this many minutes simply tend to get a lot better. Ask South Carolina about last year or Baylor about their 2008. So I think new UVA coach Tony Bennett is well positioned to extend and embellish his reputation as a worker of relative miracles in bucolic campus towns with fewer than 50,000 inhabitants.

One final housekeeping note. The 16-game schedule is here to stay in the ACC for the foreseeable future. Coaches voiced *unanimous* opposition to an 18-game conference schedule at the conference's annual spring meeting in May. The coaches cited a fear that locking in a strenuous conference schedule would make ACC programs less likely to play top-quality non-conference opponents.

Fair enough. But henceforth any continued scheduling of cupcakes to an egregious extent, particularly if your team returns a lot of minutes, will be dealt with harshly by me. You have your 16 games, coaches, just . like you wanted. Now, go schedule UConn instead of Marist. You are on notice. *John Gasaway*

Boston College ou†

2009: 22-12 (9-7 ACC), lost to USC 72-55, NCAA First Round
In-conference offense: 1.08 points per possession (3rd)
In-conference defense: 1.11 points allowed per possession (11th)

What Boston College did well: *Score.*

I realize you probably didn't spend a lot of time last year telling your friends about the unusually efficient Boston College flex offense.

Well, you should have. Al Skinner may not have the name recognition of a Krzyzewski or a Williams, but say this for the Eagles' head coach: The man has shown beyond a doubt that he can generate some points.

Little noticed but consistently quite good: Boston College offense, 2006-09		
	PPP	ACC avg.
2009	1.08	1.04
2008	1.04	1.04
2007	1.10	1.05
2006	1.10	1.04
Conference games only PPP: points per possession		

Granted, there was a dip to merely "average" on offense in 2008, as BC coped with the departure of mainstay Jared Dudley. Still, it's an impressive record overall. Last year the key to the Eagles' scoring was their offensive rebounding, as Skinner's team secured a notably robust 41 percent of their own misses in conference play. Give much of the credit there to 6-6 Corey Raji, who posted an offensive rebounding percentage that was second only to NC State's Tracy Smith among ACC players.

What we learned in 2009: *You can get an NCAA bid despite having an exceptionally bad defense.*

It's not too much to say that Boston College shocked the college basketball world with their 85-78 win at North Carolina on January 4. Prior to that game the Tar Heels were undefeated and ranked number one in the nation, while BC had already lost to a not terribly impressive St. Louis team. Be that as it may, Tyrese Rice carved up the UNC defense to the tune of 25 points, thanks in large part to 9-of-10 shooting from the line. The Eagles accomplished just about the most impressive feat the sport has to offer: Beating the top team in the nation on its own floor.

That win, quite rightly, proved to be a huge bullet point in BC's favor when March rolled around. The NCAA selection committee not only saved a spot for the Eagles but even gave them a seven-seed. Not bad for a team that followed up its win at Chapel Hill by dropping a 12-point decision at home to Harvard.

If the committee had looked a little closer, though, they might have found cause for giving Skinner's team a less lofty seed. Specifically they might have seen a defense that was a hair's breadth away from being the most permissive such unit in the ACC. (Instead that distinction went to NC State. Barely.) In fact, BC's was the worst major-conference defense to appear in an NCAA tournament in at least four years.

Boston College's problem on D was simple: Opponents were treated to way too many shots. Teams facing the Eagles found they had little problem holding on to the ball and, what's more, were given large numbers of offensive boards. (You're reading that correctly. Boston College games last year featured tons of offensive rebounds for both teams.) Small wonder, then, that BC lost to "underdog" USC in the first round of the NCAA tournament, allowing the Trojans to score 72 points in just 63 possessions. Had Skinner's defense been merely average, who knows what might have been?

What's in store for 2010: Rice, a scoring point guard who was the focal point of last year's very good offense, is now gone. But pretty much everyone else returns, many of them as juniors. This will be an experienced team that nevertheless sports a very large question mark on defense.

Prospectus says: According to ESPN.com, there's "a real sense [at BC] that the Eagles can be contenders for the ACC title in 2010 and 2011." Three years ago I saw a very mediocre Virginia team share the conference regular-season championship with an outstanding North Carolina team, so I never say never. But before they can talk realistically about an ACC title in 2010, Boston College needs to talk about defense. Conference champions don't allow opponents to score between 1.08 and 1.11 points per trip, as the Eagles have now for four years running in ACC play.

Meet the Eagles

Joe Trapani (6-8, 225, Jr.). Trapani was the closest thing Skinner had to a pure shooter last year, making 79 percent of his free throws and 36 percent of his threes. He was also this team's best bet to secure a defensive rebound, which speaks volumes because Trapani's performance here was merely average.

Rakim Sanders (6-5, 230, Jr.). In his last two games of 2009—a one-point loss to Duke in the ACC tourna-

ment and the 17-point first-round loss to USC—Sanders went a combined 6-for-23 from the field. Suffice it to say he can't wait for the new season to start. Those two outings notwithstanding, Sanders was an effective presence on offense last year as a wing, particularly inside the arc.

Corey Raji (6-6, 220, Jr.). As noted above, Raji functioned something like a mini DeJuan Blair for BC last year, hauling in offensive rebounds at a prodigious rate. (He recorded seven in just 24 minutes, for example, against Duke in the ACC tournament.) That was huge for a team that achieved above-average results on offense despite average shooting from the field.

Josh Southern (6-10, 250, Jr.). A big man this foul-prone (5.5 fouls per 40 minutes) usually blocks more shots than Southern did last year. Then again any defensive boards that he can furnish this year could have a profound impact on this team's fortunes.

Biko Paris (6-1, 200, Jr.). Where Rice was a scoring point guard, Paris served strictly as a pass-first point guard in limited minutes as a sophomore. Skinner has been quoted as expecting Paris to be more Rice-like this year.

Reggie Jackson (6-3, 200, So.). Jackson averaged 20 minutes a game as a freshman coming off the bench for Skinner in 2008-09. He couldn't find the range from beyond the arc, but decent two-point shooting (52 percent) suggests Jackson could someday take on a larger role in the offense.

Tyler Roche (6-7, 220, Sr.). One of those proverbial "glue guys," albeit one who made a very respectable 36 percent of his threes.

Evan Ravenel (6-8, 260, So.). Ravenel is being talked up by the BC coaching staff as a player to watch this year. That's interesting in as much he'll face the exact same competition for minutes as last year, when he didn't see the floor at all after mid-January.

Cortney Dunn (6-8, 240, Jr.). Perhaps the player who should feel most directly challenged by preseason praise from the coaching staff about Ravenel.

Clemson

P:
W: Booker
B:
Press

2009: 23-9 (9-7 ACC), lost to Michigan 62-59, NCAA First Round
In-conference offense: 1.09 points per possession (2nd)
In-conference defense: 1.01 points allowed per possession (5th)

What Clemson did well: *Force turnovers.*

Opponents facing Clemson last year coughed up the ball quite often: 23 percent of the time, in fact, in ACC play. That was important because when those same opponents succeeded in holding on to the rock, they actually fared pretty well against the Tiger defense. Among the ACC's five best defenses, Clemson's stood out for its reliance on creating turnovers.

Feast or famine: Top ACC defenses, 2009		
Team	Opp. PPP	Opp. PPep
Florida St.	0.98	1.27
Duke	0.98	1.28
Wake Forest	1.01	1.25
North Carolina	1.01	1.24
Clemson	**1.01**	**1.32**

Opp. PPP: opponent points per possession
Opp. PPeP: opponent points per effective (TO-less) possession
Conference games only

Opponents shot very well on their threes against the Tigers and had a good deal of success on the offensive glass. The turnovers those opponents committed, then, were all that stood between Clemson and a much less effective defense.

What we learned in 2009: *When NCAA tournament upsets become rarer, they become more prominent.*

You've probably heard that Clemson has "underachieved" the past two years, now that the Tigers have lost consecutive NCAA first-round games to lower-seeded opponents (12-seed Villanova in 2008 and 10-seed Michigan last year).

In the literal sense of the term, of course, that's an accurate description. Clemson didn't achieve as much as they were expected to in either year's tournament. No one knows that better than their fans. But I get a little tired of "underachievement" being tossed around with descriptive finality when it's based almost entirely on 40 (or perhaps, in this case,

80) minutes of basketball.

The Tigers lost by three points to Michigan because the Wolverines succeeded—as the slower-paced team almost always will—in creating a tempo to their liking and because Clemson couldn't score against UM's 1-3-1 zone. K.C. Rivers and Terrence Oglesby, who together made 39 percent of their threes last year, went 2-for-12 from outside the arc against the Wolverines.

That's life in the NCAA tournament. Have an off day and you're done. Whether or not this off day speaks to something more enduring and systemic about Clemson in particular, however, is another matter entirely. In fact before you write off the Tigers as doomed, just remember how authoritatively and insistently observers used to speak of Bill Self's allegedly genetic inability to get to the Final Four. Until 2008.

What's in store for 2010: Oglesby surprised pretty much everyone on May 27 by announcing his intention to play professionally in Europe, rather than return to Clemson for his junior year. His unscheduled departure, along with the more traditional exit made by Rivers after his senior year, left Purnell with a huge hole on the perimeter. The good news for Tiger fans is that their coach has brought in two highly-touted freshmen, Milton Jennings and Noel Johnson. Both are billed in advance as having good range from outside.

Prospectus says: Trevor Booker is a known quantity, but how Clemson fares as a team will depend in large part on how well the freshmen—Jennings, Johnson, and/or Donte Hill—perform. The departures of Oglesby and Rivers mean there's a huge chunk of possessions and shots there for the taking. The newcomers don't have to be All-ACC right from the start, mind you. They just need to make opposing defenses respect them enough to not collapse on Booker.

One early indicator should be how well the new guys fare against teams like Texas A&M and, perhaps, West Virginia at the 76 Classic in Anaheim over Thanksgiving weekend. Grab a turkey leg and tune in.

Meet the Tigers

Trevor Booker (6-7, 240, Sr.). You could make a case that this is your preseason ACC player of the year. Booker upped his game across the board as a junior last year, taking on a larger role in the offense while at the same time becoming more efficient in his production. Though listed at just 6-7, he made twos with a frequency and at a rate (58 percent) more commonly associated with taller players. Booker even blocked a respectable number of opponents' shots. He did it all for Clemson last year and, with his team having lost three starters, he'll want to keep that going in 2010. Also note that Booker is far and away this team's most effective presence on the defensive glass. That's important because this is not a very good defensive rebounding team.

DeMontez Stitt (6-2, 175, Jr.). Functioned as a pass-first point guard last year, one who was a smidge too turnover-prone.

Milton Jennings (6-9, 225, Fr.). A McDonald's All-American from Summerville, SC, Jennings is reportedly a somewhat slender power forward with excellent perimeter skills.

Noel Johnson (6-6, 190, Fr.). Virtually as highly regarded as Jennings, Johnson is a shooting guard from Fayetteville, GA, who was released from his prior commitment to USC in the wake of Tim Floyd's resignation.

Andre Young (5-9, 170, So.). Purnell has made a point of saying the only guaranteed starter is Booker, meaning, one might venture to say, that the coach would like to see Young push Stitt for the starting point guard spot.

Devin Booker (6-8, 235, Fr.). Trevor's younger brother.

David Potter (6-6, 215, Sr.). Being both foul- and turnover-prone has limited Potter's playing time. Nevertheless, he does give indications of being a nascent perimeter threat, having hit 37 percent of his rare threes last year.

Tanner Smith (6-5, 220, So.). Like Potter, Smith committed too many fouls and turnovers in too few minutes last season. Then again Smith was a freshman.

Jerai Grant (6-8, 220, Jr.). In limited minutes as a sophomore in 2008-09, Grant showed that he can certainly block shots and get offensive rebounds.

Bobo Baciu (7-2, 245, So.). After sitting out the first five games of his freshman year (due to having played professionally in his native Romania), Baciu couldn't get on the floor. He underwent arthroscopic shoulder surgery this past June.

Duke

P: Nolan Smith
W: Scheyer, Singler
B: Zoubek, Plumlee x2
+ size

2009: 30-7 (11-5 ACC), lost to Villanova 77-54, NCAA Sweet 16
In-conference offense: 1.08 points per possession (4th)
In-conference defense: 0.98 points allowed per possession (2nd)

What Duke did well: *Change—abruptly and dramatically.*

The numbers above suggest that Duke played very good defense last year. The truth is that over their first seven conference games they played extraordinary defense. (Think Memphis-in-C-USA-good.) Then, on February 4, the Blue Devils lost at Clemson by the score of 74-47. From that point on their defense was terrible (NC State-bad).

It was if one team played the first seven conference games and an entirely different team played the last nine:

Remarkably bipolar: Duke defense, 2009		
	Opp. PPP	W-L
First 7 games	0.80	6-1
Last 9 games	1.12	5-4
Overall	0.98	11-5
Conference games only		
Opp. PPP: opponent points per possession		

Part of this, as one might guess, was simply scheduling. For example the back half of the conference slate included two games against eventual national champion North Carolina. Still, the magnitude of the difference here can't be explained away entirely by the schedule. Duke changed, and for the worse.

What happened, quite simply, was that opponents' shots started going in. Bear in mind that the Blue Devils have long exhibited a near-obsession with minimizing the number of threes that opposing teams attempt. Last year that obsession persisted but the consequences from February on were little short of disastrous, as opponents quite happily feasted on the Blue Devils' suddenly woeful interior D.

You Want Us To Shoot Twos? Works For Us. Two-Point Accuracy Of Duke's Opps., 2007-09	
	Opp. 2FG%
2007	48.2
2008	49.6
First 7 games, 2009	40.8
Last 9 games, 2009	54.0
Conference games only Opp. 2FG%: opponent two-point FG percentage	

Granted, Duke's offense over this same nine-game span was very good (1.08 points per trip), allowing Mike Krzyzewski's team to finish tied for second in the ACC along with Wake Forest. How odd, then, that it was in fact the usually reliable offense that let the Blue Devils down in their 77-54 Sweet 16 loss to Villanova. Against the Wildcats Jon Scheyer and Gerald Henderson were a combined 4-of-32 from the floor.

What we learned in 2009: *Jon Scheyer can get to the line.* Scheyer is an excellent pure shooter who merits close guarding on the perimeter. Much more baffling, however, is opposing teams' manifest willingness to send Scheyer—an 84 percent foul shooter—to the line. The senior from Northbrook, Illinois, went to the line last year at a far higher rate than the dynamic and NBA-bound Henderson, for example. It's all very intriguing. In 2008-09, Scheyer was a notably ineffective source of made shots inside the arc, making a paltry 41 percent of his twos. Ineffective, that is, unless he drew a foul, which he did quite often.

Note to Duke opponents: Make Scheyer prove he can make that two.

What's in store for 2010: Offensive mainstays Scheyer and Kyle Singler return; otherwise, this is going to be a dramatically different Duke team now that Henderson is a Charlotte Bobcat, 2009 late-season freshman mini-sensation Elliot Williams is a Memphis Tiger, and Greg Paulus is, of all things, the quarterback at Syracuse.

Prospectus says: If Mike Krzyzewski has shown one quality of late, it is a willingness to change styles. We are likely to see that quality displayed again this year. With Ryan Kelly, two Plumlees (Miles and Mason), and old standby Brian Zoubek on hand, this is suddenly a much bigger Blue Devil team than in years past, one that has four players listed at 6-10 or taller. On offense Coach K's group may look less like the perimeter-oriented Dookies of old and more like, say, Kansas. If the relatively inexperienced big men can take care of the boards on both ends, Singler and Scheyer have shown they can score from outside. (Maybe Andre Dawkins will show the same ability as well.) Indeed, offense is a relative constant in Durham. The question facing this team is how well it will defend in its new taller yet more youthful configuration.

Meet the Blue Devils

Kyle Singler (6-8, 230, Jr.). Last year Singler was the beneficiary of no small measure of analytical sympathy, as it was said that he was forced to play out of position in the post and that he "wore down" as the year progressed. He most certainly played out of position and who's to say what we'll see when he plays his more natural face-the-basket role. He may just go nuts. In defense of Singler's conditioning, however, let the record show that in 2008-09 he did not wear down, at least not on offense. In fact his efficiency was remarkably stable, starting with Presbyterian in early November and running all the way through Villanova in late March. I think there's a lesson there for us all. Just because a player's cheeks get red, it doesn't mean he's "wearing down."

Jon Scheyer (6-5, 190, Sr.). See above for my thoughts on Scheyer's curious ability to convince opponents and, not least, refs that he is in fact Dwyane Wade. Note additionally that with the departure of Gerald Henderson, a large chunk of possessions and shots has suddenly become available. Watch for a goodly portion of these to fall to Scheyer, as he looks to become more of a scoring point guard in 2009-10 after being moved to the point in mid-February last year.

Nolan Smith (6-2, 185, Jr.). Smith famously displaced Greg Paulus as the starting point guard in the preseason last year, only to lose that job in the wake of Duke's 27-point loss at Clemson in early February. Note however that Smith continued to get quality playing time, averaging 22 minutes a game in the NCAA tournament. Also remember that, at least last year, "point guard" was a highly relative term in an offense that spread assists around to a striking degree.

Ryan Kelly (6-10, 220, Fr.). A McDonald's All-American from Raleigh, Kelly is reported to be a skilled big man with excellent range on his shot.

Andre Dawkins (6-4, 190, Fr.). Dawkins chose to skip an available senior year of high school athletic eligibility and instead complete some summer coursework in order to proceed directly to Durham. He is a highly-regarded shooting guard (past comparables in terms of high-school renown would include McDonald's All-Americans like Ohio State's William Buford and Georgetown's Austin Freeman) who has the very good fortune of joining an elite team that is nevertheless thin on the perimeter.

Brian Zoubek (7-1, 260, Sr.). Used by Coach K largely as an instant size fillip off the bench, Zoubek has been dependably foul-prone in each of the past two seasons, averaging well over six whistles per 40 minutes both years. I maintain that when a seven-footer doesn't start, refs, like the rest of us, just assume the big guy must be there to foul. If he can stay on the floor, however, Zoubek gives hints of being an excellent offensive rebounder.

Lance Thomas (6-8, 225, Sr.). A role player who never shoots and doesn't leave much of a trail in the areas of rebounding, steals, or blocks, Thomas nevertheless receives significant playing time (drawing 16 starts and averaging 19 minutes a game last year). In each of the past two years opponents have been notably content to foul this career 55 percent FT shooter.

Miles Plumlee (6-10, 240, So.). Plumlee couldn't get on the floor as a freshman in 2008-09, but he's being talked up in the preseason by the coaching staff.

Mason Plumlee (6-10, 230, Fr.). Still another McDonald's All-American and the younger brother of Miles, Mason is said to be a strong rebounder, something his new team could definitely use. (Duke was almost exactly average on both the offensive and defensive glass in ACC play last year.)

Florida State

2009: 25-10 (10-6 ACC), lost to Wisconsin 61-59 (OT), NCAA First Round
In-conference offense: 1.00 point per possession (9th)
In-conference defense: 0.98 points allowed per possession (1st)

What Florida State did well: *Force missed shots.*

The Seminoles' field-goal defense in-conference last year was, by a hair, the best such performance seen in the ACC over the past four seasons.

Stingy Seminoles: Best ACC FG Defenses, 2006-09		
Team	Year	Opp. eFG%
Florida St.	2009	46.0
Virginia	2007	46.1
North Carolina	2006	46.3
Duke	2006	46.9
Maryland	2008	47.4
Conference games only		
Opp. eFG%: opponent effective FG percentage		

To earn this distinction, FSU had to be both lucky and good. They were lucky in the sense that how well your opponents shoot threes is only partly (see below) within your defense's control. And the Seminoles' conference opponents were terrible at shooting threes last year, making a woeful 32 percent of their attempts. Then again, maybe the fact that Leonard Hamilton was able to put such a tall lineup on the floor had something to do with all those misses from beyond the arc. That size definitely made life miserable for opposing offenses in the paint, where ACC foes made just 45 percent of their twos. One big factor here was plainly the arrival of 7-1 redshirt freshman Solomon Alabi, who personally swatted away more than one in every ten two-pointers attempted by foolhardy opponents during his minutes.

What we learned in 2009: *Better defense alone can propel you from the NIT to an NCAA five-seed.*

Last year the effectiveness of the Florida State offense was virtually unchanged from what we saw from this team in 2008: In both years the Seminoles scored almost exactly a point per trip in ACC action. But, as we've seen, the defense was a different story. FSU went from below-average to outstanding on D in just one season, improving from 7-9 in-conference in 2008 to 10-6 last year.

The clear improvement displayed by this team, however, was somehow misconstrued nationally. (Perhaps in part because FSU triumphed over a North Carolina team without Ty Lawson in the ACC tournament semifinals.) A mistaken impression gained unmistakable credence: It was widely assumed that the high-scoring and athletic teams of the Al Thornton era had returned. In fact they had not. This offensively-challenged team was a little over-seeded as a five in the NCAA tournament, and the Seminoles were edged in overtime in the first round by (under-seeded) 12-seed Wisconsin.

What's in store for 2010: The relative struggles of Florida State on offense last year merit our notice looking ahead, because the Seminoles no longer have Toney Douglas. In 2008-09 Douglas was not only far and away Hamilton's most prominent weapon on offense, he was also, much more importantly, the team's most efficient option for scoring. His absence leaves a very large hole. Then again the defense figures to again be a strength, thanks to Alabi.

Prospectus says: Leonard Hamilton seems oddly optimistic for a coach who didn't have a very good offense last year and since that time has lost his best offensive weapon. Credit the optimism not only to the new five-year contract he signed in August, but also to the potential that observers see in Alabi, Chris Singleton, and Michael Snaer. I see the same potential, I just don't know when the Seminoles will deliver on it. I suppose it comes down to this: With Alabi as its anchor, the defense should be fine. So watch Singleton and Snaer. If their shots go in and if they can hang on to the ball, this team can meet its expectations.

Meet the Seminoles

Solomon Alabi (7-1, 250, So.). As a freshman Alabi was largely a shot-blocking specialist on defense who provided little in the way of rebounding on that end of the floor. No shame in that: Defenders as valuable as Hasheem Thabeet and Jarvis Varnado had similar profiles as freshmen. Not to mention Alabi made a decent 54 percent of his twos while assuming a much larger role in the offense than either Thabeet or Varnado did as first-year players in 2006-07. Also note that for a seven-foot freshman shot-blocker, Alabi was remarkably foul-free. The young Seminole would appear to be on a nice trajectory—and apparently I'm not the only one who thinks so. Alabi is currently projected as a lottery pick on more than one mock draft for 2010.

Chris Singleton (6-9, 225, So.). Singleton struggled to make the jump last year from McDonald's All-American to consistent performer in the ACC. His shooting, both inside and outside the arc, was below-average, while his turnovers were a little too numerous. And while Singleton did get the line with regularity, even this was a mixed blessing for the 'Noles as he made just 61 percent of his free throws. On the other hand, it's probably not entirely a coincidence that opposing teams struggled so mightily to hit threes in 2008-09, considering the 6-9 Singleton played a significant portion of his minutes as the "3" in Hamilton's D.

Michael Snaer (6-5, 200, Fr.). The freshman from Moreno Valley, CA, might be walking into a situation not unlike that confronting Sylven Landesberg at Virginia last year. Not only are Snaer and Landesberg both the same size, more or less, they're also both McDonald's All-Americans who joined ACC teams that had just said goodbye to their star players on offense: Douglas in the case of FSU, Sean Singletary in the case of the Cavaliers. Landesberg immediately established himself in his first season as his team's primary weapon on offense. The good news for Snaer is that doing the same at Florida State this year may be neither so easy nor so necessary, given the talent of his teammates. We shall see.

Derwin Kitchen (6-4, 205 Jr.). A Jacksonville product who arrived in Tallahassee last year by way of Iowa Western Community College, Kitchen became a starter in the backcourt alongside Douglas in January and achieved his best results outside the arc (where he hit 37 percent of his infrequent threes) and, more surprisingly, on the defensive glass (where he posted a higher rebound percentage than the 6-9 Singleton). Like Singleton, however, Kitchen struggled with turnovers.

Ryan Reid (6-8, 240, Sr.). Reid started 16 games early in the season in 2008-09 and for the year averaged 19 minutes a game. He is oddly proficient at getting himself to the line, considering he is hardly the focal point of Hamilton's offense.

Deividas Dulkys (6-5, 195, So.). Though he had an absolutely abysmal freshman season in terms of shooting the rock, Dulkys did lead the team in scoring during their three-game August trip to Spain.

Jordan DeMercy (6-7, 215, Jr.). DeMercy saw regular playing time for Hamilton last year thanks primarily to his defense.

Luke Loucks (6-5, 205, So.). Another option at point guard, though a surprisingly foul-prone one, given his position and relatively normal steal rate.

Georgia Tech

[handwritten: P: W: Lawal B: Favors]

2009: 12-19 (2-14 ACC), lost to Florida St. 64-62, ACC Quarterfinals
In-conference offense: 0.92 points per possession (12th)
In-conference defense: 1.02 points allowed per possession (6th)

What Georgia Tech did well: *Force missed shots.*

Yes, I know I just finished saying the exact same thing about Florida State. Bear with me.

For a team that finished just 2-14 in-conference, Georgia Tech was surprisingly stingy in terms of field-goal defense last year:

Tech's Weirdly Tough FG Defense: Best ACC FG Defenses, 2009	
Team	Opp. eFG%
Florida St.	46.0
Wake Forest	47.5
Georgia Tech	**48.0**
North Carolina	48.8
Boston College	48.9
Conference games only Opp. eFG%: opponent effective FG percentage	

So if the Yellow Jackets were this good at defending the goal (which is, after all, the nominal purpose of basketball defense), how come theirs was merely the sixth-best defense in the ACC? Well, for one thing the Ramblin' Wreck was incredibly foul-happy, sending opponents to the line far more often than any other D in the conference. (ACC opponents averaged 25 freebies a game against Georgia Tech.) Otherwise this could have been a very different defense and, indeed, a very different team.

"In spite of our record," Paul Hewitt has said, "we weren't far off." I know that sounds like standard coach-speak after a tough season, but in this case the standard coach-speak is in fact correct.

What we learned in 2009: *Scoring requires not only made shots but also, more fundamentally, attempted shots.*

Tech may have been better than their record (they were 0-3 in OT games in-conference), but let's not kid ourselves about this offense. As indicated above it was indeed the worst offense in the ACC. More worrisome for Hewitt, it was sub-standard across the board, particularly in holding on to the ball (last in the conference) and in two-point shooting (again, last). Nor were there many made free throws (last) or offensive boards (11th).

This offense needs help.

What's in store for 2010: Help is on the way, in the form of 6-10 big man Derrick Favors and his fellow illustrious freshmen.

Prospectus says: After DeAndre Jordan in 2008 and B.J. Mullens in 2009, I've become a little gun-shy about very highly-touted big men coming out of high school. (Both young men may well turn out to be ten-time All-Stars and first-ballot Hall of Famers. I don't say they won't. I am speaking only of the impact each player had during his one season of college ball.) That being said, Derrick Favors looks like someone who can anchor his team's defense while challenging the opponent's. With Gani Lawal freed up and a more experienced Iman Shumpert picking his spots and delivering the ball, this promises to be a much improved offense, not to mention a much improved team.

Meet the Yellow Jackets

Gani Lawal (6-9, 235, Jr.). Lawal worked out for some NBA teams after last season before eventually deciding to return to Atlanta for his junior year. The young man had good reason to think the next level might be interested in him, for he had in fact improved markedly over his sophomore year. Last year Lawal was the best defensive rebounder in the conference not named Jimmy Graham or Ed Davis. More importantly he was equally strong on the offensive glass and made 56 percent of his twos, qualities that made Lawal a very precious commodity on this offensively challenged team. Note however that he really has a tough time at the line, where he's a career 54 percent shooter. Even so, Lawal is currently projected as a first-round pick in 2010 on a number of mock boards.

Derrick Favors (6-10, 245, Fr.). A McDonald's All-American from Atlanta, Favors does Lawal one better in the hype department. (No small feat, that.) The freshman is currently projected as a top-five pick in the 2010 draft on more than one mock. Favors is reported to be an outstanding defender and rebounder who can finish in the paint.

Iman Shumpert (6-5, 210, So.). Good grief, according to Georgia Tech's official 2009-10 roster, Shumpert has grown an inch and gained *25 pounds* since last year. (He must like The Varsity in Atlanta as much as I do!) Anyway, note that Hewitt prefers a point-guard-by-committee approach, one where whoever gets the outlet pass on a break should do whatever needs to be done without worrying too much whether there's a "PG" or an "SG" next to his name. On that basis Shumpert functioned as something of a combo guard last year, one who recorded a lot of assists and notched some steals but nevertheless struggled (committing many turnovers, missing many shots, etc.). The coach is on the record as absolving his young guard of any blame here, saying Shumpert was simply thrown into an untenable situation as a freshman. If so, Shumpert's role model this year should be Manny Harris last year. Harris suffered through a similarly rough freshman campaign at Michigan in 2008 but improved significantly as a sophomore. I would only add one very small advisory label here: Shumpert's 66 percent accuracy from the line in 2008-09 may not preclude great things to come in the area of perimeter shooting, but it doesn't exactly make it a sure thing, either.

Moe Miller (6-2, 190, Jr.). Miller finished last season as a starter alongside Shumpert. Aside from the fact that he shoots less often, Miller is a virtual Shumpert end-result clone, recording scads of assists but really fighting the turnover bug.

D'Andre Bell (6-6, 220, Sr.). A defensive specialist who started 22 games in 2008, Bell missed all of last year due to back surgery. Prior to his injury he occasionally filled in at point guard while displaying very good shooting from the line.

Zachery Peacock (6-8, 235, Sr.). In Bell's absence last year, Peacock logged a lot of minutes guarding, chasing, and often fouling smaller opposing players.

Mfon Udofia (6-2, 185, Fr.). The highly touted point guard from just outside the Perimeter (Stone Mountain) could challenge Miller for minutes in the backcourt alongside Shumpert.

Nick Foreman (6-3, 210, So.). It is physically impossible to shoot less often than did Foreman last year—just 46 times in 397 minutes—but the otherwise enigmatic young lad does give Hewitt some experienced backcourt depth.

Lance Storrs (6-5, 220, Jr.). Storrs averaged 21 minutes a game last year but his playing time might diminish with the return of Bell and the arrival of various highly touted freshmen.

Various highly touted freshmen. Say this for Hewitt, he brought in one impressive recruiting class. In addition to Favors and Udofia, the freshmen include: **Brian Oliver**, a 6-6 wing from Delaware; **Glen Rice Jr.**, a 6-4 shooting guard from nearby Marietta, GA; and **Kammeon Holsey**, a 6-8 power forward who was lost for the year due to a torn ACL in August. At this writing it's unclear—between players like Foreman, Storrs, Oliver, and Rice—who will receive minutes and who will never be seen (or possibly even redshirt).

Maryland

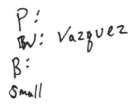

P:
BW: Vazquez
B:
Small

2009: 21-14 (7-9 ACC), lost to Memphis 89-70, NCAA Second Round
In-conference offense: 0.99 points per possession (10th)
In-conference defense: 1.06 points allowed per possession (7th)

What Maryland did well: *Persevere.*

It's easy now to forget how dire things looked in College Park nine months ago. On the morning of January 28, for example, the Terrapins were coming off a 76-67 loss at home to Boston College, a game that marked the Terps' fourth loss in five games. Gary Williams' team stood at 2-4 in the ACC, 13-7 overall. Four days earlier Maryland had been humiliated at Duke by the score of 85-44, the worst defeat the school had suffered in 46 years.

Nor were the problems restricted to matters on the court. Williams was embroiled in a nasty (and needless) public squabble with his own athletic department over what he considered to be the botched enrollment of former recruit Gus Gilchrist. Five days later Williams even received the dreaded vote of confidence from AD Debbie Yow: "He has my personal full support."

Then on February 12 the Washington Post published the first installment in its three-part 10,000 word series on Maryland basketball, "Missed Shots." The first article was headlined simply, "A Shell of Its Former Self." (Sub-head: "Mostly Because of Recruiting Missteps, Gary Williams Has Presided Over a Steady Decline Since the Terrapins' 2002 NCAA Championship.") It would have been all too easy to envision things spinning off from there in a very familiar and grim direction.

Instead, something more surprising happened. Thanks largely to a much improved offense, Maryland won five of their next eight, including an 88-85 win at home on February 21 over eventual national champion North Carolina. It was enough, barely, to get the Terps back to the NCAA tournament.

Every time a coach is fired (and I do mean literally every single time), there will be columns the next morning saying everyone knew this was coming, it had to happen, etc. Had Williams been let go last February the same exact thing would have been said of him and his program. Yet here he is, back at the old stand, with a team that reached the second round of the tournament last year and now returns four starters.

So exactly how inevitable is the next coach-firing, really?

What we learned in 2009: *You can score far fewer points than your opponents and still get an NCAA at-large bid.*

That being said, I wouldn't recommend that Williams try to pull that particular rabbit out of his hat again. In fact, just about everything had to break in the right direction after January 30 for this team to get into the NCAA tournament.

For instance, note that Maryland in 2009 was easily the least effective major-conference team, on a per-possession basis, to receive an at-large bid over the past four years.

Tiny Dancers: Least Efficient Major-Conference Teams To Receive At-Large Bids, 2006-09		
Team	Year	EM
Maryland	**2009**	**-0.07**
Boston College	2009	-0.03
Indiana	2006	-0.03
Seton Hall	2006	-0.03
Oklahoma	2008	-0.02
Michigan	2009	-0.02
Conference games only		
EM: efficiency margin (points per possession – opponent PPP)		

The Terrapins were very fortunate to have the eventual national champions in their conference. Their three-point victory at home over the Tar Heels gave Williams' team its best argument for an NCAA bid. Had Maryland lost that game, conversely, they would have finished the year 6-10 in the ACC, beyond the reach of even the most sympathetic member of the selection committee. As it was, the 10-seed Terps made the committee look good, trouncing seven-seed Cal in the first round, 84-71, before falling to Memphis. All things considered it was a strong showing by Maryland, one few could have foreseen just seven weeks earlier.

What's in store for 2010: If you saw this team in action last year, the 2010 Terrapins are going to look very familiar: Dave Neal is gone but the other four starters have returned. This continuity in personnel should mean improvement—and there is certainly room for improvement, particularly on offense.

Prospectus says: Gary Williams is going to put a Maryland team on the floor this year that is long on experience, takes excellent care of the ball, and is next to automatic from the line. On the other hand that same team is going to be really small. They will almost certainly be at a disadvantage on the boards against the majority of their ACC opponents. And they might not shoot all that well from the field. I think Maryland will improve in 2010 because: a) they actually weren't as good last year as commonly believed; and b) most everyone's back. There's a limit, though, to how much improvement we should expect from an undersized team that struggles to put the ball in the basket.

Meet the Terrapins

Greivis Vasquez (6-6, 190, Sr.). Vasquez submitted his name for the NBA draft last April but pulled out in June. With the departures of James Gist and Bambale Osby in 2008, the young man from Venezuela fairly took over the Maryland offense last year, absorbing possessions and attempting shots at a rate that far exceeded that of any other Terrapin. Vasquez actually didn't shoot terribly well from the field (45 percent on his twos and 33 percent on his threes), but he piled up assists while being remarkably trustworthy with the ball. Simply holding on to the rock is easily overlooked, of course, but for Maryland last year it was crucial: This poor-shooting team won games against superior-shooting opponents largely by not committing turnovers. The lion's share of the credit there goes to Vasquez. Note as well that he shot 87 percent from the line in 2008-09.

Landon Milbourne (6-7, 205, Sr.). On a team with no starters taller than 6-7, Milbourne shot more twos than anyone except Vasquez and made half of them. Like Vasquez, he's excellent (83 percent last year) from the line. Unlike Vasquez, Milbourne never records assists. Ever: He bumped into just 21 of the things in 1014 minutes last year.

Adrian Bowie (6-2, 190, Jr.). For a player listed at 6-2, Bowie exhibited some very good skills inside the arc in 2008-09, making more than half of his twos and getting to the line quite often. Given his 22 percent three-point shooting, he might want to focus even more of his energy down low in 2010.

Sean Mosley (6-4, 210, So.). Mosley's most effective play last year was to be fouled, which he was more often (per FGA) than any other Terp. Otherwise Mosley really struggled as a freshman to get the ball in the basket.

Eric Hayes (6-4, 185, Sr.). Still another outstanding free throw shooter (86 percent in 2008-09), Hayes should probably consider letting 'er rip more often from the field. No other player in a Maryland uniform shot as well as Hayes last year.

Dino Gregory (6-7, 225, Jr.). Gregory earned 16 minutes a game last year and was far more likely than any of his teammates to block an occasional shot. He is, as one might expect, foul-prone.

Jerome Burney (6-9, 220, Jr.). Last November Burney showed promise when he blocked two shots and hauled down four boards in eight minutes against Georgetown. Alas, the young man from Atlanta suffered a stress fracture and missed most of 2008-09.

Jordan Williams (6-9, 245, Fr.). Williams is billed as a proficient low-post scorer, perhaps because he averaged a notably robust 35.7 points a game last year as a senior at Torrington HS in Connecticut.

Miami out

2009: 19-13 (7-9 ACC), lost to Florida 74-60, NIT Second Round
In-conference offense: 1.06 points per possession (6th)
In-conference defense: 1.07 points allowed per possession (9th)

What Miami did well: *Showcase Jack McClinton.*
  McClinton entered his senior year with as much fanfare as anyone who plays basketball at Miami can reasonably hope to attract. He was a preseason All-ACC pick and the acknowledged focal point of every opposing defense.

So it's a credit to McClinton that he actually improved last year, taking on an even larger role in the Miami offense and making no less than 45 percent of his numerous threes. Granted Dwayne Collins is no slouch (OK, when he goes to the line he is a slouch), but it's not too much to say that McClinton was the alpha and omega of a very good Hurricane offense. During one three-game stretch in the heart of the ACC season, he scored 32, 34, and 35 points against NCAA tournament-bound opponents (Wake Forest, Duke, and North Carolina) and did so efficiently.

Whatever his future may bring (he was drafted with the 51st pick by San Antonio), McClinton put on quite a show during his last season as a Hurricane.

What we learned in 2009: *Losing several close games doesn't necessarily make you "unlucky."*

Miami fans will be forgiven for thinking that last year represented a tremendous missed opportunity. A year ago at this time the Hurricanes were ranked in the preseason top 25 for the first time in nine years. Four starters returned from a team that had made it to the second round of the NCAA tournament in 2008. Big things were expected in 2009.

What unfurled instead might be termed a series of unfortunate events, most of them concentrated in a 25-day period spanning January and February. In those 25 days the 'Canes went 1-6, effectively putting their NCAA tournament hopes on life support. Those hopes would linger a bit longer before finally being extinguished by a late-season road loss to last place Georgia Tech.

During their 1-6 stumble, Miami lost no fewer than three games that went to overtime. Had even one of those OT decisions gone the other way, the 'Canes would have finished 8-8 in the ACC and, most likely, received an NCAA bid. How fickle is fortune, right?

Maybe not. Keep in mind that Miami did in fact finish 8-8 and did get to the tournament in 2008. Then, in a rare instance of convenient statistical coincidence, the Hurricanes went out in 2009 and recorded the exact same levels of per-possession efficiency on offense and on defense. In both years the 'Canes scored 1.06 points per trip in conference play while allowing 1.07. A team that performs at that level "should" go 7-9, where "should" is defined by what has in fact happened over the past 292 team-seasons in the six major conferences since 2006.

Yes, Miami lost some heartbreakers. Then again they won one (a two-point win at home over Mary-

land). And, of course, not every loss went down to the last possession: The Hurricanes fell by ten at Georgia Tech, by 19 at home to Clemson, and by 13 at Florida State. Indeed one could see the luck glass as half-full and say that a team with a defense this suspect was in fact fortunate to have gone to the tournament at all in 2008 and to have been so very close again in 2009.

What's in store for 2010: Now that McClinton is gone there will be no shortage of headlines proclaiming that this is Dwayne Collins' team. That may well be the case in the locker room and even in the popular perception. Just keep in mind, though, that Collins has never accounted for more than 22 percent of his team's shots during his minutes on the floor. It may indeed be his team but Collins is going to need some help to continue Miami's high-scoring ways.

Prospectus says: For four years in a row Miami has allowed ACC opponents to score at least 1.07 points per trip. In other words the Hurricanes have always had to score a lot of points to be competitive. With McClinton's departure, that will likely prove more difficult.

Meet the Hurricanes

Dwayne Collins (6-8, 245, Sr.). Collins' free throw rate went through the proverbial roof last year, as he attempted a virtually identical number of shots from the line (192) and from the field (193). Whether this was due to more aggressive play on offense from Collins, a collective realization on the part of opponents that he was shooting just 58 percent from the line, or a little of both is open for discussion. One thing is certain: If Collins were merely adequate from the line he would be one of the most efficient little big men in the country. He is a beast on the offensive glass and makes 56 percent of his twos.

Malcolm Grant (6-1, 185 So.). A transfer from Villanova, Grant is expected to serve as Frank Haith's starting point guard. During limited minutes with the Wildcats in 2007-08, Grant gave indications of being an excellent pure shooter, hitting 47 percent of his threes and 84 percent of his free throws. Then again the fact that he made just 27 percent of his twos doubtless contributed to his minutes being so limited.

Durand Scott (6-3, 190, Fr.). Scott played on the same NYC high school team as Connecticut's Kemba Walker. No one player this year is going to take on a McClinton-sized role in this offense, but Scott will likely have every opportunity to pick up his fair share of that slack.

James Dews (6-4, 205, Sr.). Last year Dews appeared to suffer from a rare and unusually comprehensive form of shooting slump, one that drove down his effectiveness in all three shooting categories (threes, twos, and free throws). In particular his fall from a sterling 91 percent to a merely very good 76 percent at the line seemed to indicate that the young man had come down with the hoops equivalent of the yips. Be that as it may, a return to 2008 form for Dews would be most welcome for a team seeking made shots in the absence of McClinton.

Adrian Thomas (6-7, 225, Sr.). Thomas is something of a rarity: The foul-prone three-point specialist. Averaging 17 minutes a game in 2008-09, Thomas hit 37 percent of his threes. He also averaged almost exactly five fouls per 40 minutes.

Cyrus McGowan (6-9, 235, Sr.). For whatever reason—maybe due to sub-40 percent two-point shooting—McGowan's minutes went down late in the season last year. He does, however, give Haith another Collins-level performer on the defensive glass.

DeQuan Jones (6-7, 215, So.). Jones arrived last year as a highly-touted freshman wing, but, like McGowan, his minutes diminished as the year progressed.

North Carolina

2009: 34-4 (13-3 ACC), beat Michigan State 89-72, National Championship Game
In-conference offense: 1.16 points per possession (1st)
In-conference defense: 1.01 points allowed per possession (4th)

What North Carolina did well: *Maintain their excellence.*

I'm going to go out on a limb here and say that this Roy Williams guy has worked out pretty well in Chapel Hill.

In the six seasons since he was hired in April of 2003, UNC has been to four Elite Eights, three Final Fours, and won two national championships. Closer to home, the Heels have now claimed three consecutive regular season ACC titles, the last two of which were outright.

Which is to say North Carolina has been the best program in the nation over the past six years.

The program Williams left behind hasn't fared too badly either.

What we learned in 2009: *When "everyone's back" from what was already an elite team, simply maintaining your current level of performance is sufficient.*

There was a lot of talk a year ago about the 2008-09 Tar Heels possibly going undefeated, potentially

Success, 2004-09							
Team	Conf win%	Conf titles	NCAA bids	Sweet 16	Elite 8	Final Four	NC
North Carolina	.750	4	6	4	4	3	2
Florida	.635	1	4	2	2	2	2
Kansas	.812	5	6	4	3	1	1
Connecticut	.730	1	5	3	3	2	1
UCLA	.704	3	5	3	3	3	0
Michigan St.	.680	1	6	3	2	2	0
Louisville*	.710	2	5	3	3	1	0
Memphis**	.872	5	5	4	3	1	0
Duke	.729	2	6	4	1	1	0

* Louisville competed in Conference USA in 2004 and 2005, winning the conference the latter year.
** On August 20, 2009, the NCAA ordered Memphis to vacate its Final Four appearance and C-USA title from 2007-08. Memphis is appealing.

being the greatest team of recent years, maybe even being the greatest team "ever," whatever that means. After all, everyone was back. When everyone's back teams improve, right? Just imagine how far these Tar Heels can go!

Well, they won the national championship, which is as far as any team can go. I wish I could remember the precise date and context now (it was likely right after the Heels, playing without Ty Lawson, had lost to Florida State in the ACC tournament semifinals), but I have a clear memory of a radio interview last March where I was asked why North Carolina's season had been such a "disappointment." At the time I probably said something along the lines of: Just you wait, they can win it all if they can get Lawson healthy.

What I should have said, of course, is that no sane person could possibly brand going 28-4 (as UNC had, heading into Selection Sunday) and having a lock on a one-seed in the NCAA tournament as a "disappointment." No, Carolina didn't run the table. But neither did Florida in 2007 and those Gators had all five starters back from a national championship team. The Heels, in light of Marcus Ginyard's near-total absence due to injury, returned "just" four starters from a Final Four team. In retrospect this team was pretty much as good as they should have been. In other words they were the best team in the country.

What's in store for 2010: We've been here before, of course. In 2005 North Carolina won the national championship, donated the core of the team to the NBA, and then said hello to a flock of highly-touted freshmen. How do the two situations compare?

Observing Precedent: North Carolina Metrics In Years Following National Championships				
	2005	2006	2009	2010
Returning minutes (%)		12		27
Offense (PPP)	1.14	1.11	1.16	?
Defense (Opp. PPP)	0.91	0.98	1.01	?
Record	14-2	12-4	13-3	?
NCAA result	NC	2dRd	NC	?
Conference games only				
PPP: points per possession				
Opp. PPP: opponent points per possession				

This year's team will be more experienced than the group that Williams put on the floor in 2005-06. On paper the Heels return just 27 percent of their minutes from last year, but that figure understates the reality,

of course. Ginyard played a mere 37 minutes last year, but he started all 39 games in 2007-08 and will be available this year. With Ginyard, Deon Thompson, and Ed Davis on hand, Williams can call upon a level of experience he simply didn't have four years ago.

And, anyway, this year's freshman class is pretty good, too.

Prospectus says: An unnamed coach at another program told ESPN.com: "This is the first time North Carolina hasn't had a speed guard under Roy Williams. Raymond Felton and then Ty Lawson really had Williams' break going. How much Larry Drew can get the Carolina secondary break going will be the biggest question going forward in the ACC." The anonymous coach needs to brush up on his recent history. In 2006 Felton was a Charlotte Bobcat, Lawson was a high school senior at Oak Hill Academy, and North Carolina scored 1.11 points per trip in conference play. No, that's not as good as what the Heels did the year before or as good as what they've accomplished in the years since. But it's an absurdly good worst-case scenario for any offense. (No team other than the Heels scored that efficiently in the ACC last year.) More importantly, with an on-ball defender like Ginyard and a rebounding and shot-blocking hybrid like Davis, this 2010 team has it within its power to be excellent on defense. Don't cry for Carolina just yet.

Meet the Tar Heels

Deon Thompson (6-9, 245, Sr.). The lone returning starter from the national championship team, Thompson took the shots that were left over inside the arc after Tyler Hansbrough and Wayne Ellington had had their fill. In addition to making half his twos, Thompson also pitched in on the defensive glass, although his numbers here are likely to dip as he plays more of his minutes alongside the beastly Davis.

Marcus Ginyard (6-5, 210, Sr.). Ginyard's an excellent example of a defensive specialist (Williams refers to him simply as "our best defender"), one who will guard the ball and shoot less often than any of his fellow starters. He effectively missed all of last year due to a stress fracture in his left foot and was given a medical redshirt, enabling him to return for a fifth season. Carolina could have used Ginyard last year in their losses to Boston College (Tyrese Rice scored 25 points) and Wake Forest (Jeff Teague scored 34).

Ed Davis (6-10, 225, So.). For purely selfish reasons I'm really glad Davis chose to return for his sophomore season. I just want to see what he can do with a starter's minutes. Coming off the bench last year Davis gave every indication that he can both dominate the defensive glass and block shots. For any player to do that is rare enough. For a freshman to do that really makes me want to see that player start for at least one season before moving on to the next level.

John Henson (6-10, 195, Fr.). Yes, you're reading that correctly. Henson is listed by his own school as 6-10, 195. Then again Kevin Durant wasn't built like Rainier Wolfcastle, either, and he did OK. A McDonald's All-American from Tampa, Henson is billed as having the ability to blend in perfectly with UNC's up-tempo approach to offense.

Tyler Zeller (7-0, 240, So.). Zeller broke his left wrist in the second game of the year, against Kentucky on November 18. He returned exactly three months later and averaged six minutes a contest over the Heels' last 13 games, giving the frontcourt a blow until the next TV timeout. Zeller arrived in Chapel Hill with a recruiting profile eerily similar to Henson's. Both players are slim bigs praised for their athleticism and versatility.

Larry Drew (6-2, 180, So.). This season's presumptive starting point guard, Drew saw spot duty last year as Lawson's back-up and dished a laudable number of assists. However he also committed turnovers with troubling frequency.

Dexter Strickland (6-3, 180, Fr.). A McDonald's All-American from Rahway, NJ, Strickland is touted for his scoring and ability to attack the basket.

David (6-10, 225, Fr.) and Travis (6-10, 235, Fr.) Wear. Twin brothers and, like Thompson and Drew, products of southern California. Both are McDonald's All-Americans.

Will Graves (6-6, 240, Jr.). Graves was averaging 11 minutes a game through late January, but was subsequently suspended for the remainder of the season by Williams for an unspecified violation of team rules.

North Carolina State ~~out~~

2009: 16-14 (6-10 ACC), lost to Maryland 74-69, ACC First Round
In-conference offense: 1.05 points per possession (7th)
In-conference defense: 1.11 points allowed per possession (12th)

What North Carolina State did well: *Shoot.*

No ACC team was more accurate from the field during conference play last year than was NC State. Whatever struggles the Wolfpack has endured the past few seasons—and those struggles have been real enough—Sidney Lowe's team has at least continued the Herb Sendek-era tradition of filling up the basket.

Apparently Really Good Shooting Is Irrelevant: Most Accurate ACC Shooting, 2006-09		
Team	Year	eFG%
NC State	**2006**	**55.7**
Duke	2006	55.4
North Carolina	2006	54.1
NC State	**2009**	**53.4**
NC State	**2007**	**53.1**
Conference games only		
eFG%: effective FG percentage		

Indeed, a list of the best shooting performances by Atlantic Coast teams over the past four seasons is unmistakably Raleigh-centric.

Note that over that same span the Wolfpack is 25-39 in the ACC. (Yes, the defense during that same time has been somewhat less impressive than the shooting. See below.)

That 2006 team, the last that Sendek coached in Raleigh, shot—and, obviously, made—a ton of threes. Under Lowe, conversely, NC State has been much closer to the conference average for attempts from beyond the arc. The two things that have stayed constant across the two regimes have been accuracy and pace: NC State is consistently more deliberate in their tempo than your average ACC team. Lowe's team is not achieving these glittering numbers with lots of easy looks off of fast breaks.

What we learned in 2009: *You need to stay flexible with that starting lineup.*

The year that Tracy Smith had as a sophomore for NC State last year reminds me a little (repeat, a little) of Luke Harangody's freshman campaign for Notre Dame in 2006-07. Both players started their seasons as reserves, both would nevertheless shoot with the frequency of preseason All-Americans whenever they got in the game, and both saw enough of those shots go in to make their way into the starting lineups by mid- to late-year.

What's interesting about Smith in particular is that once he started getting heavy minutes, from about late January on, his game calmed, statistically speaking. (For the most part. He did, however, cough up five turnovers in a regular-season-ending loss at Miami.) Once he knew he was going to get minutes, it was if Smith didn't feel like he had to squeeze all his production into each possession. And having Smith on the floor was a clear benefit to the offense, for the sophomore was emerging as the best offensive rebounder in the ACC, indeed one of the best in the country.

It was a wise lineup shift during a challenging season for Lowe.

What's in store for 2010: Since you saw them last NC State bid farewell to seniors Ben McCauley and Courtney Fells, while Brandon Costner, who played last season as a redshirt junior and had a year of eligibility remaining, chose to play for pay in Belgium. Meanwhile the Pack's most highly-decorated incoming recruit, Lorenzo Brown, failed to qualify academically and will play this season instead at a prep school.

Prospectus says: This will be an inexperienced team unburdened by high expectations. Lowe's men will have to improve on last year's league-worst defense to have any chance of moving up in the standings. Last year conference opponents simply ate NC State alive on the interior, making twos virtually at will. Job one is to stop that particular bleeding.

Meet the Wolfpack

Tracy Smith (6-8, 240, Jr.). As noted above, Smith was a force of nature on the offensive glass last year. Nevertheless his overall offensive efficiency is hurt by the fact that he's a bad free throw shooter who's fouled often. In fact he's almost as successful from the field (54 percent on his twos) as at the line (59 percent). Keep in mind that Smith took on the starring role in the NC State offense even when he was a sophomore playing alongside upperclassmen like Costner and McCauley. To say he's likely to take a few shots and absorb a few possessions this season, then, would be a gross understatement.

Javier Gonzalez (5-11, 170, Jr.). A pass-first point guard who nevertheless hit 43 percent of his infrequent threes in 2008-09, Gonzalez had real problems with turnovers as a sophomore. In fact his travails here were emblematic: NC State gave the ball away on 22 percent of their possessions in ACC play. An inability to hang on to the ball was the only limiting factor on an offense blessed with both excellent shooting and the conference's best offensive rebounder.

Farnold Degand (6-3, 185, Sr.). Like Gonzalez, Degand gave the ball away too often while functioning as a point guard creating shots for others rather than looking for his own.

Dennis Horner (6-9, 220, Sr.). Horner apparently swallowed an accuracy pill last fall. After a sophomore campaign that can be charitably described as "uneven," he emerged last year as a prototypical highly efficient role player, one who shot rarely but very effectively from both sides of the arc. This year he may well have an opportunity to take more of those shots.

C.J. Williams (6-5, 205, So.). As a freshman wing Williams deferred to his elders and shot next to never during his limited minutes. The time for that degree of deference is likely past. Williams can now show what he's got.

Richard Howell (6-7, 215, Fr.). With Lorenzo Brown's detour to prep school, Howell becomes arguably the top freshman prospect on the roster. Then again....

Deshawn Painter (6-9, 220, Fr.). Maybe Painter can share that "top freshman prospect" honor with Howell, or even wrest it away.

Virginia

2009: 10-18 (4-12 ACC), lost to Boston College 76-63, ACC First Round
In-conference offense: 0.96 points per possession (11th)
In-conference defense: 1.06 points allowed per possession (8th)

Bennett

What Virginia did well: *Present their next coach with a situation tailor made for instant karma.*

Virginia will almost certainly improve this year, for two reasons wholly unrelated to their new coach. First, the Cavaliers were bad but not unspeakably so last year. Second, almost everyone's back. Regression to the mean and a team's level of experience are tidal forces in this here sport. Tony Bennett will have both working in his favor this season, and not for the first time.

A team that performed this poorly the previous year but that returns this many minutes has, of course, happened before. Take Bennett's first season as a head coach. His 2006-07 Washington State team had gone 4-14 in the Pac-10 the year before under Dick Bennett but returned Derrick Low, Ivory Clark, Aron Baynes, Robbie Cowgill, and Kyle Weaver. The Cougars vaulted all the way to 13-5 and Tony Bennett, not without reason, was widely hailed as a miracle-worker. (Improvement in Pullman that year was very likely. Improvement all the way to 13-5, however, was undeniably impressive.)

Nevertheless, the two closest recent analogues for Virginia this year are arguably Baylor in 2008 and South Carolina last year. Both of those teams should give Cavalier fans cause for hope in 2010. Two years ago the Bears reached their first NCAA tournament in 20 years; last year the Gamecocks very nearly reached the dance as well, as first-year coach Darrin Horn was widely hailed in Columbia as a miracle-worker.

Their Past, Virginia's Future? Similarities In Year-Before Performance And Returning Minutes					
Team	Year	EM yr. Before	Returning minutes (%)	EM	Conf. W-L
Baylor	2008	-0.11	89	0.01	9-7
South Carolina	2009	-0.09	87	0.03	10-6
Virginia	2010	-0.10	89	?	?
Conference games only					
EM: efficiency margin (points per possession – opponent PPP)					

Coincidentally, Baylor and South Carolina both improved their performance by the exact same amount (0.12 of a point per possession). If Virginia does like-wise this season, they should be right around .500 in the ACC. Note the "should." The past does not mandate the future, nor does efficiency margin translate seamlessly into wins and losses. Luck and happenstance will play their part. In November all any of us can do is traffic in likelihoods. And the likelihood is that Virginia will be much improved in 2010.

What we learned in 2009: *Life on the road is tough for a young team.*

The Cavaliers were 1-9 on their opponents' home floors last year, a record that very easily could have been 0-10. Virginia's lone win was an 88-84 decision in OT at Georgia Tech on December 28.

What's in store for 2010: If the Cavaliers are anything like Bennett's teams at Washington State, the pace in Charlottesville will be more deliberate this season, while offensive rebounds become much less numerous (so that fast breaks by the opponent can be challenged with all available personnel). Then again, the new coach may choose to introduce his system in increments rather than all at once. In an April interview with the Richmond Times-Dispatch's Jeff White, Bennett had this to say: "I think people think we're going to walk it down the floor every single play, we're going to make ten to 12 passes, and then we're going to be allowed to shoot with under eight seconds on the clock. I certainly hope that's not the case."

Prospectus says: The primary weakness with this team last year was simply that they couldn't get the ball in the basket, either from in close or beyond the arc. You know Bennett will do his part and that this team will at least be taking good shots. If maturation and coaching are enough to improve this team's accuracy, Virginia may live up to the total-makeover examples set by teams like South Carolina last year and Baylor in 2008, if not Washington State in 2007.

Meet the Cavaliers

Sylven Landesberg (6-6, 205, So.). With the departure of Sean Singletary after the 2008 season, Landesberg was effectively handed the keys to the Cavalier car last year as a freshman. And while his shots didn't always fall (he made 46 percent of his very frequent twos and 31 percent of his rare threes), Landesberg did demonstrate that he was already quite capable of taking care of the ball. This has led Bennett to muse aloud about Landesberg taking on more minutes as a point guard this season (a scoring point guard, one presumes). Note as well that Landesberg got to the line far more often than any of his teammates and made 80 percent of his freebies.

Calvin Baker (6-2, 185 Sr.). Baker played all of last year with a stress fracture in his left foot and his performance—particularly his outside shooting—suffered accordingly. Bennett hopes Baker can turn back the clock to 2008, when the former William & Mary standout made 37 percent of his threes in his first season as a Cavalier.

Mike Scott (6-8, 235, Jr.). An excellent offensive rebounder, Scott was his team's lone bright spot in terms of shooting from the field. All those offensive boards helped him make 55 percent of his twos in 2008-09.

Assane Sene (7-0, 235, So.). Sene was spectacularly foul-prone last year, averaging well over six fouls per 40 minutes. When he could stay on the floor, though, he was an effective shot-blocker. Sene started 16 games as a freshman.

Sammy Zeglinski (6-0, 180, So.). As a redshirt freshman Zeglinski recorded more than his fair share of assists while mirroring Landesberg's level of success from the field, for good or ill, with eerie precision (albeit while shooting less often). Nevertheless by early February he'd lost his job as the starting point guard, in large part because of a propensity to commit turnovers.

Jeff Jones (6-4, 200, Jr.). Jones had an absolutely brutal year shooting the rock as a sophomore. Say this for the young man, he was undeterred. During his (limited) minutes on the floor, Jones was almost as likely as Landesberg to launch a shot.

Jamil Tucker (6-9, 240, Sr.). In each of his three seasons as a Cavalier Tucker's minutes have increased and he's shot more threes than twos. Last year that shot selection paid off, as Tucker hit 40 percent of his threes. Note also that he was limited in 2008-09 with an injured right shoulder.

Tristan Spurlock (6-8, 215, Fr.). Spurlock is a wing from Springfield, VA, who committed to Virginia when Dave Leitao was still in residence and then chose to honor the commitment after meeting with Bennett. He's billed as a versatile and athletic player who attacks the basket.

Virginia Tech

2009: 19-15 (7-9 ACC), lost to Baylor 84-66, NIT Second Round
In-conference offense: 1.04 points per possession (8th)
In-conference defense: 1.08 points allowed per possession (10th)

What Virginia Tech did well: *Hang in there.*

It's very hard for me to believe that Virginia Tech has been to just two NCAA tournaments (1996 and 2007) in the past 23 years. They seem so much more competitive than that.

Take last year. Aside from a disastrous conference opener (where they lost by 25 points at Duke), the Hokies were in just about every game they played, up to and including their three-point loss to eventual national champion North Carolina in the ACC tournament quarterfinals. (Granted, the Tar Heels played that game without Ty Lawson.) This is after all the team that knocked then-number-1-ranked Wake For-

est from the ranks of the unbeaten—and did so in Winston-Salem. Alas, the heroic wins came too early and the competitive losses were too numerous: Tech finished the year losing eight of its last 11 before once again heading off to the NIT.

When the USC job came open over the summer, Seth Greenberg's name figured prominently in the speculation on Tim Floyd's replacement. (Greenberg formerly coached at Long Beach State and knows the southern California hoops landscape.) It was speculation the Hokies' coach was quick to downplay, however, as he told all who would listen that he's content with his gig in Blacksburg. Apparently he means to see this thing through and get the Virginia Tech program to a place beyond merely "competitive."

What we learned in 2009: *Deron Washington was apparently a very important defender in 2008.*

A year ago at this time it was generally acknowledged Tech was losing a tough defender in the 6-7 Washington. What few foresaw, however, was that his departure after the 2008 season would coincide with what can only be termed a total defensive collapse in Blacksburg.

Life Without Deron Washington: Virginia Tech Defense, 2008 vs. 2009			
Year	Opp. PPP	Conf. rank	Conf. W-L
2008	0.98	1st	9-7
2009	1.08	10th	7-9
Conference games only Opp. PPP: opponent points per possession			

What's really unfortunate is that the Hokies' struggles on D masked and indeed negated a significant improvement on offense. It's not too much to say, then, that bad defense torpedoed Virginia Tech's season in 2009. What happened?

It turns out the problem was larger than merely Washington's absence. (Sorry, Deron.) ACC opponents shot a little better on their twos and did a much better job hanging on to the ball. Where Tech really suffered, though, was on the defensive glass. A team that rebounded an absurd 73 percent of their conference opponents' misses in 2008 suddenly found it could get to just 65 percent of those boards in 2009. That's about average for the ACC in general but it represented a major set-back for this team in particular, one they were unable to offset with above-average performance elsewhere. Virginia Tech's season was deflected into a NIT path by the sheer number of shots opponents were able to attempt.

What's in store for 2010: The work load in this offense was strikingly bifurcated last year. Players were either featured performers or they were role players—there was no in between. Featured performer A.D. Vassallo is gone, but his co-equals Malcolm Delaney and Jeff Allen return, along with a full supporting cast.

Prospectus says: Delaney and Allen give Virginia Tech an experienced nucleus, one that powered an of-

fense that was right at the ACC average last year. Seth Greenberg's team is a few defensive stops away from winning some of the close ones.

Meet the Hokies

Malcolm Delaney (6-3, 190, Jr.). I don't use the b-word often, but once could certainly make a case for hauling it out here: Delaney blossomed at point guard last year, becoming more efficient at the same time that he took on a much larger role in the offense. It was a particular kind of efficiency, though, one that wasn't always easy on the eyes. His shooting inside the arc was largely ineffective, for example, but those frequent forays into the paint did net him a good many trips to the line, where he shot 87 percent.

Jeff Allen (6-7, 230, Jr.). Defensive rebounding in Blacksburg last year began and ended with Allen. There was no one else. Allen personally hauled in one in every five opponent misses during his minutes on the floor. (For a player tasked with cleaning the glass, Allen has also posted an admirably robust steal rate in each of his first two seasons.) If he can get some help on the boards this year, this defense can improve. On offense Allen was the anti-Delaney. He was dependable from the field but shot just 61 percent at the line, a figure that hurt his overall effectiveness because Allen was fouled quite often. He's also had a colorful disciplinary history, earning suspensions for bumping an official as a freshman and for offering a notably vivid hand gesture to a Maryland fan in College Park as a sophomore.

J.T. Thompson (6-6, 210, Jr.). Thompson missed the first ten games of the season last year recovering from surgery to correct a hernia. Upon returning to action he steadily increased his production and by the end of the year it appeared that Greenberg was auditioning Thompson for a larger role in 2010. (See for instance Thompson's 21-point effort against Duquesne in the first round of the NIT.) To assume that larger role, however, Thompson will have to cut down on his fouling.

Dorenzo Hudson (6-5, 220, Jr.). Greenberg clearly likes the intangibles supplied by Hudson, for last year the sophomore made 24 starts and averaged 20 minutes a contest even as he continued to struggle with his shot for a second consecutive season.

Victor Davila (6-8, 245, So.). Davila started ten games as a freshman but his minutes declined noticeably late in the year, perhaps in part because of a lack of production on the glass. Nevertheless, Greenberg has been talking up Davila, saying he's counting on the sophomore making "a huge jump" in 2009-10.

Cadarian Raines (6-9, 240, Fr.). An in-state product from Petersburg, Raines arrives in Blacksburg billed as a very good shot-blocker.

Terrell Bell (6-6, 205, Jr.). Like Hudson, Bell has met with little success while shooting from the field during his first two seasons. Unlike Hudson his minutes have been limited.

[handwritten: P W: Amino B]

[handwritten: 8-4 on 2/19]

Wake Forest

2009: 24-7 (11-5 ACC), lost to Cleveland State 84-69, NCAA First Round
In-conference offense: 1.07 points per possession (5th)
In-conference defense: 1.01 points allowed per possession (3rd)

What Wake Forest did well: *Surprise.*

Wake Forest entered last year ranked somewhere between number 21 and 24 in the nation, depending on which preseason poll you were using. If there were a mantra for this team it was watch out for 2010, when players like Jeff Teague, James Johnson, and Al-Farouq Aminu would match their obvious talent with a just a little more experience. Such was the consensus a year ago.

Whereupon Teague, Johnson, and Aminu promptly set out to prove that experience is overrated. The Demon Deacons sprang out of the gate and went 16-0, a record which included a memorable 92-89 win over eventual national champion North Carolina in Chapel Hill. Their efforts were rewarded a week later with a number 1 ranking nationally.

The surprises were just getting started, however. What had been a very good defense in December and January (bearing in mind that UNC scored its points in a remarkably up-tempo 88-possession game) became much less so in February and March. While Wake posted triumphs against the Carolinas and Dukes of the ACC world, they dropped games to the likes of Georgia Tech and North Carolina State. The struggles against inferior opponents proved to be prophetic, for the Deacons ended their year with an 11-point first-round ACC tournament loss to Maryland and a 15-point first-round NCAA loss to 13-seed Cleveland State.

Nor will the mantra about 2010 hold true, at least not in its original form. Teague and Johnson are gone, both having been selected in the first round of the draft. This team was surprising from start to finish.

What we learned in 2009: *Young teams can improve all of a sudden.*

The Deacons returned virtually all of their minutes last year from 2008 and it showed. Though Wake certainly had their peaks and valleys, this team was indeed dramatically improved, particularly on offense.

Taking a page from North Carolina's book, Dino Gaudio's team put a less effective but stylistically identical offense on the floor last year, upping their tempo noticeably (though a goodly portion of this was in fact attributable to an increase in turnovers) and decreasing their attempts from beyond the arc drastically. As a result the Deacons got to the line much more often and hauled in significantly more offensive boards.

Most importantly, in the span of one season this team went from "average" to "best in the league by far" in two-point percentage. Leading the charge on this front were two pretty good NBA prospects:

Improvement In Close: Two-point FG Percentage, 2008 & 2009		
Player	2007-08	2008-09
Jeff Teague	44.8	50.2
James Johnson	57.4	59.8

Not to mention Teague and Johnson were joined last year by Aminu, who made 57 percent of his twos as a precocious freshman. When your team suddenly shoots twos this well, you should indeed cut down on the shots from outside. Dino Gaudio, take a bow.

What's in store for 2010: The departures of Teague and Johnson would leave a hole for any program. And the fact that Teague and Johnson left earlier than anyone could have anticipated only adds to Gaudio's challenge. When this year's recruiting class was being signed, its players were likely envisioned as a supporting cast. Aminu better be prepared for his close-up.

Prospectus says: When you lose Jeff Teague and James Johnson, your offense is going to take a step back. That being said, this is a really big team, one that can certainly equal or even exceed what Wake accomplished last year on D.

Meet the Demon Deacons

Al-Farouq Aminu (6-9, 215, So.). The fact that he projects as a wing "at the next level" may explain why Aminu keeps launching an occasional three, despite the fact that he made just 18 percent of the darn things in 2008-09. Otherwise he had precisely the freshman year you'd like to see from a player this talented on a team where he didn't have to be the main weapon. He was very good on the defensive glass, he made his twos, and he got to the line consistently. Speaking more aesthetically, if you saw him run the floor last year alongside Teague and Johnson and finish on the break, you've seen exactly what the NBA likes about Aminu.

L.D. Williams (6-4, 210, Sr.). Williams started all 31 games last year and invariably shadowed the opposing team's main scoring threat on the perimeter.

Chas McFarland (7-0, 235, Sr.). While his playing time was limited by his frequent fouling, McFarland earned his starting job last year by being the best offensive rebounder on a much improved offensive rebounding team.

Ishmael Smith (6-0, 175, Sr.). Longevity has its advantages: Smith was actually Wake's starting point guard his first two seasons, before losing that spot last year to Teague. Now the job is his once again. He posted an astonishing assist rate as a freshman, but in each of his previous three campaigns Smith has presented the appearance of a pass-first point guard who struggles with turnovers.

Gary Clark (6-4, 200, Jr.). Clark couldn't get on the floor last year but during the odd random moments when he did appear he evinced a notable willingness to shoot the rock, something that sets him apart from everyone listed here except Aminu.

Ari Stewart (6-7, 190, Jr.). Another potential newcomer to playing time who might be willing to take some of the pressure off Aminu, Stewart is a highly-regarded wing from greater Atlanta.

Ty Walker (7-0, 215, So.). Walker arrived last year with heavy advance billing (by some recruiting lights he was as big a catch for Wake as Aminu) but he played a total of just 42 minutes as he sought to bulk up his frame. Nevertheless he is being talked up by the coaching staff coming into this year. (Unrelated: In September Andy Katz wrote a great story for ESPN. com on how, despite his meager freshman totals, Walker has already been contacted via Facebook by at least one agent looking to represent the young man at the next level.)

Tony Woods (6-11, 245, So.). Woods' lone start last year was against Cleveland State. Hopefully the coach doesn't hold that against him.

David Weaver (6-11, 240, Sr.). Still more frontcourt depth. This team will not lack for size.

Since the turn of the millennium Kansas and Texas have been remarkably consistent and reliable presences near or, more often, at the very top of the Big 12. They're the only two teams from the conference who've made the NCAA tournament in each of the past ten seasons. (The Longhorns started their current streak of tournament appearances in 1999; the Jayhawks began theirs in 1990.) KU has been to three Final Fours and won one national championship since 2000, while the Horns have made it to three Elite Eights and one Final Four in that time. Both Kansas and Texas reached the 2003 Final Four (and both lost to Carmelo Anthony and Syracuse).

And, perhaps not coincidentally, the programs in Lawrence and Austin have both been remarkably stable over that span. Texas has employed Rick Barnes since 1998. Kansas plucked Bill Self from Illinois to replace Roy Williams in 2003. The average tenure of the other ten Big 12 coaches now stands at 2.6 years, and keep in mind that is with the league welcoming no rookie coaches this season. (Three-fourths of the conference's coaches have been hired since March 1, 2006.) The Jayhawks and the Longhorns quite simply stand out from the rest. They should do so again this season.

Kansas is a near-unanimous pick of pundits and fans alike to win the 2010 national championship. While I try to dissent from near-unanimity whenever possible—it's more fun—I find that in this instance I must march with all you other lemmings. Meaning the only mode of iconoclasm available to me with this team will have to go something like this: Kansas is in

fact even better than everyone says. Look at Michigan State. A few months after the Spartans made it to the national championship game, everyone has Tom Izzo's team ranked in the top five nationally—and yet they lost two starters. But the Jayhawks return every starter and indeed every player who appeared in their five-point loss to that beefed-up version of Michigan State in the Sweet 16. That doesn't mean MSU isn't truly a top-five team going into this year, of course. But it does say to me that Sherron Collins and Cole Aldrich are leading a team that is everyone's favorite for good reason.

If any Big 12 team can hope to make Kansas sweat even a little this year, it figures to be Texas. The Longhorns look like they'll have their deepest and most talented roster since the LaMarcus Aldridge-led 2006 team that lost in OT in the Elite Eight to Tyrus Thomas, Glen Davis, and LSU. In addition to returning starters like Damion James, Justin Mason, and Dexter Pittman, Barnes will have Mc-Donald's All-American shooting guard Avery Bradley on hand to extend and embellish Austin's tradition of precociously talented underclassmen in burnt orange.

Not that either Kansas or Texas will be handed anything by the rest of the league, of course. After all, last year two Big 12 teams reached the Elite Eight and neither the Jayhawks nor the Longhorns were anywhere to be seen amidst that august octet. Oklahoma and Missouri crashed that party in rather convincing manner in 2009. The Sooners only had one of the most dominant players of the decade in Blake Griffin. Now they have "only" one of the best players in the

BIG 12 PROSPECTUS

	2009 Record	Returning Minutes (%)	2010 Prediction
Kansas	14-2	97	15-1
Texas	9-7	72	12-4
Oklahoma	13-3	42	10-6
Texas A&M	9-7	72	9-7
Oklahoma St.	9-7	57	9-7
Kansas St.	9-7	65	9-7
Missouri	12-4	63	8-8
Baylor	5-11	47	7-9
Iowa St.	4-12	65	6-10
Texas Tech	3-13	66	5-11
Nebraska	8-8	40	3-13
Colorado	1-15	89	3-13

country in Willie Warren—along with a couple fancy new McDonald's All-Americans, Tiny Gallon and Tommy Mason-Griffin. Don't sell OU short in 2010. As for the Tigers, they will likely take a step back this year after losing a good deal of their offense in the departures of DeMarre Carroll, Leo Lyons, and Matt Lawrence. Nevertheless, Mike Anderson still has J.T. Tiller, meaning opposing offenses will still feel like hell for 40 minutes.

Meantime in College Station fans have quickly come to regard NCAA tournament wins as a divine right. And why not? Texas A&M has won at least one game in each of the last four tournaments, a claim Kansas, for one, can't match. For the second consecutive year Mark Turgeon has seen a raw post player leave early and be selected in the second round of the NBA draft. It will therefore be up to Donald Sloan and Bryan Davis to extend this quiet streak into its fifth year.

There was nothing quiet about Travis Ford's arrival at Oklahoma State last year. The new head coach energized the air around Gallagher-Iba Arena with a faster pace, lots of threes, and, most importantly, more wins. The Cowboys reached their first NCAA tournament in four years in 2009 and won a squeaker against Tennessee before falling to one-seed Pitt by eight points in the second round. This year Ford will want to encourage James Anderson to take on a larger role in the offense. Anderson brings together three modifiers I don't believe I've ever seen in one player: "McDonald's All-American," "underrated," and "efficient."

At Kansas State Frank Martin hopes that newly minted McDonald's All-American Wally Judge possesses that most precious of skills in Manhattan: Accurate shooting. No Big 12 team shot worse from the field last year in conference play than did the Wildcats. Nevertheless, K-State returns four starters this season, including YouTube sensation Denis Clemente. If their shots start to fall they could really surprise some people.

Misses weren't a problem last year for LaceDarius Dunn at Baylor. Dunn simply makes every kind of shot there is in this sport, be it twos, threes, or free throws. I think he deserves a little more attention, but of course he probably wouldn't have this problem if not for the fact that misses weren't a problem

for the Bears' Big 12 opponents in 2009, either. Just one season removed from making their first NCAA tournament in 20 years, Scott Drew's team fell all the way to 5-11 because they couldn't stop the other team from scoring.

Every time I think Dunn's location in Waco, Texas, explains his relative obscurity, I remind myself that Iowa State's Craig Brackins is himself far from the madding crowd (in Ames, Iowa), yet somehow he managed to get our attention in 2009. Funny how recording a 42-14 double-double against Kansas will do that for a player. Brackins will continue to score points in abundance for the Cyclones this year but a more hopeful development for Greg McDermott's offense would be if someone else would step forward and take some of that load off Brackins.

Then again having a 6-10 star who shines a little too brightly is a worry Pat Knight wouldn't mind having at Texas Tech. After taking over for his father in February of 2008, Knight has searched in vain for a starting five that will stay healthy and win some games. Lacking that kind of stability, the Red Raiders went 3-13 in the Big 12 in 2009. I never thought I'd say this of a Knight coaching in what might be the most conservative campus town outside of Provo, Utah, but: Defense is the problem for this markedly up-tempo team.

Which leaves Nebraska and Colorado, near-unanimous choices to finish at the bottom of the conference in 2010. The Cornhuskers have at least had recent success (relatively speaking): Doc Sadler's team went .500 in the Big 12 last year. This season, however, no team in the conference returns fewer minutes than the Huskers.

At the opposite end of that spectrum, only Kansas returns a higher percentage of its minutes than Jeff Bzdelik does this year at Colorado. The Buffs will indeed be better than last year (and Cory Higgins surely merits a special award for unbelievably efficient production achieved with little or no help). But until this team can stop turning the ball over and starving itself of chances to score, CU will remain very much a work in progress, seeking stability in a conference where that quality has adhered stubbornly to the traditional powers.

John Gasaway

Baylor

[handwritten: P: Carter (C)]
[handwritten: W: Dunn]
[handwritten: Big 2] *[handwritten: Slow 264]* *[handwritten: B: Udoh]*

2009: 24-15 (5-11 Big 12), lost to Penn State 69-63, NIT Championship Game
In-conference offense: 1.05 points per possession (7th)
In-conference defense: 1.10 points allowed per possession (11th)

What Baylor did well: *November, December, and March.*

You don't often run across a team that wins 24 games but goes just 5-11 in their conference. Baylor did it by sandwiching a miserable January and February (5-10) in between a strong start (12-1) and a surprising stretch run in March (7-3). The varying records weren't solely a function of the competition, either. In November Scott Drew's team beat Arizona State on a neutral floor; in March they took down Kansas and Texas on consecutive days at the Big 12 tournament.

Going into last year there were big expectations for this roster—big by Waco standards, at least—as Drew brought back four starters from the program's first NCAA tournament team in 20 years. The Bears were picked to finish third in the Big 12, and at the time I wondered if I was being unduly skeptical when I picked Baylor to finish a mere fourth: "There is likely to be a ceiling on how good this team can really be. The ceiling is defense."

I was not being unduly skeptical. Drew's team finished ninth in the Big 12, allowing conference opponents to score 1.10 points per trip. Only Texas Tech had a worse defense. Baylor was particularly vulnerable on the road, going just 2-7 all season on an opponent's home floor.

What we learned in 2009: *If you're hiring someone with a connection to a recruit, make sure you can live with the hire even if you lose the recruit.*

In the summer of 2008 Baylor hired Dwon Clifton to be the Bears' director of player development, a position that had not previously existed. The fact that Clifton was the AAU coach of the nation's top high school player, John Wall, was, in Drew's telling, purely coincidental. The coach told Gary Parrish of CBSSports.com, "We hired Dwon and his resume speaks for itself."

It better. Drew now has Clifton (since promoted to coordinator of operations) but no Wall, who announced in May of 2009 that he would follow John Calipari to Kentucky. At the time of Clifton's hiring, Drew's rival coaches were variously bemused or upset

and, to his credit, Texas head coach Rick Barnes went on the record. "We don't believe in doing that," he told the New York Times.

Well, I suppose Barnes and his fellow coaches are happy now. The presence of Wall's AAU coach wasn't sufficient to lure the young man to Baylor. There's risk involved in making a recruiting-driven hire. Caveat emptor: Hiring a coach may just net you one new coach, and nothing more.

What's in store for 2010: Drew enters the new season having lost leading scorer Curtis Jerrells and two other starters, Kevin Rogers and Henry Dugat. In their place the Bears will trot out not only returnees like LaceDarius Dunn and Tweety Carter, but also at least one new arrival: Michigan transfer Ekpe Udoh.

Prospectus says: After watching his man defense be gutted like a fish over the course of the conference season, Drew went with a surprise zone in the Big 12 tournament against heavily favored Kansas. It worked, and the Bears improbably came within 40 minutes of making it to the NCAA tournament, falling to Missouri by 13 in the tournament title game. I wonder if we might see some zone from Baylor in 2010. If your man defense is giving up points and not creating turnovers, what have you got to lose? After all, Dunn and Carter are going to make some threes this year. The defense in Waco doesn't have to be outstanding for this team to win some games. (More to the point, the defense in Waco won't be outstanding.) Just adequate will do.

Meet the Bears

LaceDarius Dunn (6-4, 205, Jr.). Dunn had his second consecutive outstanding season last year, but amidst the din and clamor of a team's crashing expectations no one really noticed. I realize that he wasn't even regarded as the best guard on his own team (Jerrells made third-team All-Big 12; Dunn was honorable mention), but to be perfectly honest I'm a little unclear on why this guy is still laboring in such obscurity. A 6-4 scorer with undeniable perimeter range who makes 54 percent of his twos while functioning as his major-conference offense's co-star really should be generating more buzz by now. Dunn's effectively the same size as Terrico White of Ole Miss, yet it's the latter that's projected as the first-rounder in 2010. Why? I have no idea.

Take Your Pick: LaceDarius Dunn vs. Terrico White						
Player	School	%Poss.	3FG%	2FG%	TORate	ORtng.
Dunn	Baylor	24.4	38.8	54.1	14.9	114.8
White	Miss	23.3	35.4	49.5	14.8	107.2

True, Dunn's indifferent on defense and famously averse to assists, but when has either of those features been a disqualifier for the NBA? (They're practically mandatory! Just kidding.) Not to mention his production has been preternaturally steady the past two seasons. The only thing that changed last year was that Dunn got a lot more minutes. Is he being overlooked simply because Waco's off the beaten hoops track? I'm at a loss. In a conference with Willie Warren the title of best shooting guard is already spoken for, but Dunn's right there with James Anderson for second place.

Tweety Carter (5-11, 185, Sr.). Strange but true: Since arriving in Waco as a McDonald's All-American in 2006, Carter's share of the shots in the Baylor offense has gone down slightly each year that he's played. Yet all the while he's become more and more accurate. Last year as the lethally efficient fifth option behind Dunn, Jerrells, Dugat, and Rogers, Carter made 40 percent of his threes. Give him the rock, coach!

Ekpe Udoh (6-10, 240, Jr.). As a sophomore at Michigan in 2007-08, Udoh served notice that he was an outstanding shot-blocker, one who could swat the ball away multiple times a game without getting into foul trouble. He also, however, had the good hoops sense to realize that an offensively-limited shot-blocker was not going to mesh real well with a John Beilein system. (To be fair Udoh gave it a try, even attempting 16 threes that year.) He therefore transferred to a program closer to his Oklahoma roots.

Nolan Dennis (6-5, 180, Fr.). Dennis is a highly-touted shooting guard from Richland Hills, Texas, who was bound for Memphis until John Calipari went to Kentucky.

Quincy Acy (6-7, 225, So.). Acy began his college career in memorable fashion, setting a Big 12 record for consecutive made field goals by making his first 20 shots over four games. And while he did finally miss a shot, the freshman started ten games and showed some promise as a shot-blocker. By late in the year, though, he'd largely fallen out of the rotation, logging just 50 minutes over the Bears' final 11 games, a stretch that included trips to the Big 12 tournament and NIT title games.

Josh Lomers (7-0, 280, Sr.). Last year Lomers split time with Acy and the now-departed Mamadou Diene, as together the three players comprised what might be called this team's size squadron. Whichever squadron member was on the floor at a given time would play until he got into foul trouble, a process that usually took about 12 seconds.

Anthony Jones (6-10, 195, So.). Though he arrived with a bit of fanfare last season as a freshman (he was about as highly rated coming out of high school as Dunn had been the previous year), Jones found he couldn't get many minutes on a roster that already had plenty of good three-point shooters. Maybe that dynamic will break in Jones' favor this season, now that the 323 attempts launched from beyond the arc last year by Jerrells and Dugat are up for grabs.

Colorado *out*

2009: 9-22 (1-15 Big 12), lost to Texas 67-56, Big 12 Tournament First Round
In-conference offense: 0.92 points per possession (12th)
In-conference defense: 1.10 points allowed per possession (10th)

What Colorado did well: *Bottom out.*
Last season marked Jeff Bzdelik's second year at the helm in Boulder, but in terms of the program's arc 2008-09 actually represented the effective reboot of

the Buffs' roster. Richard Roby, Marcus Hall, Marcus King-Stockton, and Xavier Silas had all departed, and Bzdelik brought back just 43 percent of the roster's minutes from 2007-08.

The results were predictable: A 1-15 record in the Big 12, an offense that ranked last in the league by far, a defense that wasn't much better, and the insidious presence of absence in the form of empty yellow seats at the Coors Events Center.

And yet CU fans, even the absent ones, have more grounds for confidence in their coach than do the supporters of any other last place team in the country. (How's that for faint praise?) In addition to his extensive NBA coaching experience, Bzdelik directed one of the best offenses in the nation at the Air Force Academy in 2006, one powered almost exclusively by X's and O's. But clearly the Colorado job would present any coach with some formidable challenges in 2009. Bzdelik's contract reportedly requires the University to start construction on a practice facility by year three of his tenure. It is now year three, with no such facility in sight. Nor are the salaries paid to Bzdelik and his staff comparable to what most of their peers in the conference earn.

Little wonder that Bzdelik reportedly entertained overtures over the summer from the Minnesota Timberwolves. Had the T-Wolves moved with a little more alacrity, the coach may have made that jump. Instead, Bzdelik is returning to Boulder for year three of the rebuild.

What we learned in 2009: *Players on a last-place team can have outstanding individual seasons.*

As a sophomore newly elevated to the role of featured scorer for a hopelessly overmatched team last year, Cory Higgins really should have had an ugly year statistically, one filled with turnovers and missed shots. Instead he excelled, taking very good care of the ball while attacking the rim relentlessly and making 83 percent of his ostentatiously frequent free throws. True, his assists were notably less numerous, but as Northwestern coach Bill Carmody once memorably said of leading scorer Kevin Coble, with the teammates Higgins had his assists should be infrequent. Purely in terms of the scoring efficiency delivered by a featured player, Higgins' stats compare very favorably with the likes of Michigan's Manny Harris or Duke's Kyle Singler.

Apparently I'm not the only one who noticed Higgins' year. Bzdelik has said that after last season his star player was approached by other coaches who offered to rescue Higgins from the somnambulant Coors Center and get him in front of some packed houses.

What's in store for 2010: It's not too much to say, then, that this program was on a knife-edge over the summer, with both the head coach and the star player coming very close to leaving. If Bzdelik and Higgins had walked, Colorado would have been sent back to square one and in effect the last two years would have been wasted. Instead, the coach and the star are back, along with three other starters. So the Buffs will be better, especially if their role players can learn to hang on to the rock. Last year Colorado committed a turnover on 23 percent of their possessions in Big 12 play, the worst mark in the league.

Prospectus says: Colorado lost some close games last year—in overtime to Texas and Kansas State; by two to Nebraska and by five to Kansas—but in truth there was justice in their last-place finish. When you're outscored by 0.18 points per trip over the course of 16 games, the most common result will be 1-15. (After all, the Buffs' lone win—by six over Iowa State—was a close game, too.) So CU bottomed out last year and, with four starters returning, they will improve this year. It's just that there's a lot of distance for this team to cover between where they are now and mere respectability. They'll draw nearer to that destination in 2010, but it's going to take more than one season to get there.

Meet the Buffs

Cory Higgins (6-5, 190, Jr.). See above. As a freshman Higgins had played a supporting role behind Richard Roby and Marcus Hall. As a sophomore he carried his team.

Dwight Thorne (6-3, 185, Sr.). Similar to Higgins, Thorne had a surprisingly good year considering his team had the worst offense in the Big 12. The junior functioned as a viable dual-threat wing, making 41 percent of his threes and 53 percent of his twos, albeit in a supporting role.

Austin Dufault (6-9, 230, So.). Dufault struggled from beyond the arc as a freshman but his value to Bzdelik was plain: The young man from Killdeer, North Dakota, was usually the tallest Colorado player on the floor.

Nate Tomlinson (6-3, 185, So.). In his freshman year Tomlinson took his lumps as a pass-first point guard, committing a goodly number of turnovers. It was a rough welcome to the States for the native of Australia, but he does appear to have range from the perimeter.

Casey Crawford (6-9, 245, Jr.). A transfer from Wake Forest, Crawford started four games in 2008-09 and showed signs of being a perimeter threat, but his slight frame was adjudged by Bzdelik as not Big 12-ready and the young man's minutes dwindled accordingly as the season progressed. This year, as is customary for these cases, Crawford is reportedly bulked up and ready for action.

Alec Burks (6-6, 185, Fr.). Burks has been compared to former Buff Richard Roby by Bzdelik.

Shane Harris-Tunks (6-11, 225, Fr.). An Aussie like Tomlinson, Harris-Tunks is reportedly ready to contribute right away on defense for CU.

Levi Knutson (6-4, 200, Jr.). Despite the fact that three starters had just left, Knutson's minutes actually went down last year, perhaps in part because of poor three-point shooting.

Trey Eckloff (6-10, 235, So.). In limited minutes as a freshman Eckloff was both foul- and turnover-prone.

Iowa State *out*

2009: 15-17 (4-12 Big 12), lost to Oklahoma State 81-67, Big 12 Tournament First Round
In-conference offense: 0.95 points per possession (11th)
In-conference defense: 1.07 points allowed per possession (8th)

What Iowa State did well: *Be dull for a change.*

I mean "dull" in a good way and, believe me, Greg McDermott would understand exactly what I'm talking about. During McDermott's first two seasons in Ames, countless players came and just about as many went, up to and including Wesley Johnson (now at Syracuse and expected to step into the void left by the departures of Jonny Flynn and Eric Devendorf). Over the past 12 months, however, pretty much everyone has stuck around, most notably Craig Brackins, who surprised many observers by not entering last summer's NBA draft.

Very often the key condition that has to be met before a team turns around—post-Snyder Missouri and post-Keady Purdue come to mind—is mere roster stability. For the first time in McDermott's tenure, Iowa State has that.

What we learned in 2009: *Even with Brackins' emergence, the issue in Ames is still offense.*

Ordinarily a team presenting Iowa State's particulars would give me sufficient grounds to zero in on their defense. After all, said defense got worse last year, thanks in no small measure to the fact that opponents never (and I do mean never) turned the ball over to the Cyclones.

Pay No Attention To This Table About Defense: Iowa State Defense, 2008 vs. 2009		
Year	Opp. TO%	Opp. PPP
2008	17.1	1.02
2009	15.0	1.07
Conference games only		
Opp. TO%: opponent turnover percentage		
Opp. PPP: opponent points per possession		

So, yes, ISU's defense took a step back last year. But it's actually their offense that's the problem. On paper the Cyclones were an average three-point shooting team in 2008-09, but in Big 12 play McDermott's team made just 32 percent of its attempts from beyond the arc. Only Texas fared worse from the perimeter.

This team badly needs some accurate perimeter shooting, both to alleviate the pressure on Brackins and, at the risk of belaboring the obvious, to score three points at a time. In McDermott's perimeter-oriented offense there will never be offensive boards and Iowa State's already doing a pretty good job taking care of the ball. We also know that Brackins will shoot 400-plus twos this season and make 200-some. So the wild card here is threes.

What's in store for 2010: Did I mention Brackins is back? Among major-conference players last year, only Notre Dame's Luke Harangody played a role in his offense as outlandishly predominant as the one Brackins fulfilled for McDermott. This season there is much talk in Ames that Brackins' supporting cast has been strengthened. Note however that a second scorer of even average efficiency and ordinary second-scorer-level assertiveness would be a huge benefit for this offense. Iowa State doesn't need to find another Willie Warren in its midst to put alongside Brackins. More like another Kim English: Just a regular hoops Joe who will, you know, attempt shots on occasion.

Prospectus says: Last year under "Prospectus says," I wrote: "Until Iowa State can make some of those threes, points will be scarce." This is still true, even with Brackins' rather spectacular emergence. If there's hope to be had for Cyclone fans here, it's that the ISU offense did improve over the back half of the Big 12 slate last year, scoring almost a point per possession in the Cyclones' last eight conference games. The schedule this season will give us ample opportunity to see if McDermott's team has carried that improvement forward. Before they reach conference play ISU will already have gone up against either Notre Dame or Northwestern, as well as Cal, Bradley, and Duke. Tune in to see how many points are scored—heck, even how many shots are taken—by players not named Craig Brackins. As that number goes, so goes this team's ceiling.

Meet the Cyclones

Craig Brackins (6-10, 230, Jr.). Brackins became a mortal lock for the NBA on the afternoon of January 24, 2009, when he recorded 42 points and 14 boards against far and away the best defensive team in the Big 12, Kansas. I can't think of another example where a relatively overlooked player more or less instantly became universally acknowledged as NBA material. It was like Brackins was the Beatles and that game was his Ed Sullivan Show. So his decision to stay put at Iowa State caught a lot of people off guard, but I for one think he'll look a lot more impressive at the end of his junior year than he did after his sophomore season. The points explosion against the Jayhawks notwithstanding, the one facet of Brackins' game that he demonstrated beyond doubt last year was his defensive rebounding. It's superb, though in a conference with

Blake Griffin and Cole Aldrich it was all but impossible to stand out in that department. And on offense Brackins will likely improve on his 51 percent two-point shooting. More help from his teammates could help that along, as well.

Lucca Staiger (6-5, 220, Jr.). As the Cyclones' main perimeter threat, Staiger made 39 percent of his threes as a sophomore. Sounds great, but in truth a lot of those makes came in calendar 2008. Against Big 12 opponents Staiger made just 34 percent of his threes. He had surgery on his knee just before the season last year and the dip in his shooting hardly assuaged concerns regarding his durability. Nevertheless he's kept up an active hoops schedule: In the offseason Staiger represented Germany at the World University Games.

Diante Garrett (6-4, 190, Jr.). Garrett is a pass-first point guard who committed fewer turnovers last year. That was little noted but it was important. Had Garrett merely duplicated his turnover-intensive freshman year as a sophomore, this below-average offense could have tumbled down toward Colorado territory, even with Brackins.

Justin Hamilton (6-11, 260, So.). Earning 18 starts as a freshman, Hamilton was the nominal center for the Cyclones while Brackins was the power forward. Hamilton's involvement in the offense was largely limited to rebounding his teammates' misses. (He was pretty good at it.)

Marquis Gilstrap (6-7, 215, Sr.). Gilstrap is an eagerly awaited junior college transfer who Cyclone fans hope will take some of the scoring load off of Brackins.

Jamie Vanderbeken (6-11, 250, Sr.). In this case, at least, the advance billing was on target. Vanderbeken, who arrived last year as a junior college transfer touted for his three-point shooting, hit 41 percent of his treys in 2008-09.

LaRon Dendy (6-9, 230, Jr.). Still another junior college addition to this year's frontcourt rotation.

Chris Colvin (6-3, 195, Fr.). Colvin is a highly-rated point guard from Chicago.

Kansas

[handwritten: P: Collins W: Henry B: Aldrich, Morris x2]

2009: 27-8 (14-2 Big 12), lost to Michigan State 67-62, NCAA Sweet 16
In-conference offense: 1.09 points per possession (2nd)
In-conference defense: 0.94 points allowed per possession (1st)

What Kansas did well: *Fool me.*

A few hundred days have now passed since Kansas lost to Michigan State in the Sweet 16, and I still feel like people didn't really understand how good this Jayhawk team was, how it just as easily could have been KU that survived that day (see below) and made it all the way to the national championship game where, almost certainly, Bill Self's team would have met the same fate as did the Spartans.

The prevailing assumption with last season's Kansas team was always that they were a year away. I know that was my initial assumption, anyway. Last year in this space I picked the Jayhawks to finish third in the Big 12. And goodness knows this team certainly looked a year away at times. A Kansas team that's truly arrived probably shouldn't lose to UMass by one at the Sprint Center in Kansas City (as the Jayhawks did last December), or get blown out at Texas Tech by 19 (as KU did on March 4). After the nets are cut down in Indy in 2010, maybe we'll look back on that 2008-09 team and say they really were a year away.

All I know is I've now seen North Carolina, Florida, and Kansas all try to put good teams on the floor the year after the bulk of their rosters departed in the wake of a national championship. Last year's Jayhawk team, warts and all, was the class of that bunch.

Starting Over: North Carolina, Florida, and Kansas The Year After A National Championship			
	UNC 2006	FLA 2008	KU 2009
Returning minutes (%)	12	18	15
Offense (PPP)	1.11	1.11	1.09
Defense (Opp. PPP)	0.98	1.10	0.94
Efficiency margin	0.13	0.01	0.15
Record	12-4	8-8	14-2
NCAA result	2ndRd	no bid	Swt16

Conference games only
PPP: points per possession
Opp. PPP: opponent points per possession
Efficiency margin: PPP – Opp. PPP

I had been conditioned by the earlier examples provided by Carolina and the Gators to think I knew what

to expect from Kansas the year after they won it all and said goodbye to pretty much everyone. I was wrong. Last year's team wasn't as good as the 2008 edition, of course, but the fall-off was much smaller than I and everyone else expected. This team was much better than I anticipated and, more to the point, much better than people realize even today.

The true worth of last year's Kansas team is worth measuring, of course, because this year everyone's back. To be sure the Jayhawks aren't exactly being overlooked this season. Pretty much everyone and their cousin has KU as the favorites to win the national championship in 2010. I just happen to think Kansas might in reality be a little bit better than a team that everyone already expects to win it all.

Put it this way: North Carolina triggered a lot of "can they run the table" talk a year ago at this time. The Tar Heels returned all five starters from a team that reached the Final Four and outscored ACC opponents by 0.14 points per trip. (We know now, of course, that UNC never really did return all five starters, that Marcus Ginyard was fated to miss all of last year with an injured foot. We didn't know that then, however.) So why am I not hearing more "can they run the table" talk about Kansas this year? The Jayhawks return all five starters (or will, when Brady Morningstar returns from his suspension) from a team that reached the Sweet 16 and outscored Big 12 opponents by 0.15 points per possession.

I'm not saying Kansas will go undefeated. (Obviously. I have them going 15-1 in the Big 12.) The chances of any team doing so any year are very small. What I am saying is this team has as good a shot at it as Ginyard-less Carolina had last year.

What we learned in 2009: *Sherron Collins giveth, and Sherron Collins taketh away.*

Kansas wouldn't have won the national championship in 2008, of course, without the three that Mario Chalmers made against Memphis to tie the game in the final seconds of regulation. We'd do well to remember, though, that just to get the Jayhawks to that point in the game took a lot of work. And arguably the biggest single play leading up to Chalmers' heroics was Sherron Collins' steal and ensuing three with 1:46 left in regulation, a basket that drew KU to within 60-56. The hoops world but little remembers what Collins did that night, but Kansas fans do. Had Collins not made that play, there would have been no opportunity for Chalmers at the end. It was that simple.

How ironic, then, that in 2009 Collins would be cast in the Chalmers role, as the KU player thrust center-stage at the decisive moment of the season's final game. Unfortunately for Jayhawk fans, heroics in the clutch this time came from the player facing Collins, as Michigan State's Kalin Lucas completed a three-point play with 49 seconds remaining in what had previously been a tie game in the Sweet 16. Tom Izzo, showing total confidence in Lucas, called a clear-out for his point guard. Collins, as if offended by this kind of naked disrespect, checked over both shoulders for a Spartan about to set a ball-screen on him. None was forthcoming. Izzo thought Lucas could simply take Collins one-on-one, and it turned out Izzo was correct. Lucas drove Collins down into the paint, gave him a ball-fake, and then waited for the airborne Jayhawk to come back down, so as to be jumped into. Whistle, swish, and-one. To that point in his college career, Collins, listed at 5-11, had played 2,883 minutes and recorded three blocks. Nevertheless he left his feet in the final minute of a Sweet 16 game tied at 60.

Last year whenever Lucas ventured inside the arc, the only danger that he presented to opposing defenses was that he was very good at drawing fouls. Otherwise he was just another Jon Scheyer: Don't foul him. Simply enjoy watching him miss that two, six out of every ten times.

No wonder Collins decided to return for his senior season. He's a much better player than Kalin Lucas has reason to think.

What's in store for 2010: The only players who left after last year were either walk-ons or new arrivals who didn't get many minutes and therefore decided to transfer (Quintrell Thomas and Tyrone Appleton). When you say goodbye to just 239 minutes and welcome back 6,786 of them, though, I think you're justified in saying "everyone's back." Not only that, KU will also have all-everything freshman Xavier Henry in the fold this season.

Prospectus says: Run for your lives, rest of the nation. Yes, Kansas turns the ball over too much, and

they don't really try to make the other team cough it up. But this team is dominant in literally every other facet of the game. How dominant? Ponder this combination of finesse and defense: Last year a still-young Jayhawk roster came scarily close to shooting a better percentage on their threes in conference play (40.3) than Big 12 opponents shot on their twos against this defense (42.0). Assuming they can just stay out of fights with their football team, KU should win the national championship.

Meet the Jayhawks

Sherron Collins (5-11, 205, Sr.). Last year Collins had to navigate what might be the toughest transition of all in this sport, going from part-time supporting player on offense to full-time featured scorer. The fact that he was able to do so while retaining almost all of his previous efficiency speaks volumes about him. In 2008-09 Collins put a young team on his back offensively and the results, both individually and collectively, speak for themselves. No Big 12 team without the number one overall pick in the 2009 NBA draft had a better offense in conference play than did Kansas, which scored 1.09 points per trip against league opponents. Most of the credit there goes to Collins, who made 38 percent of his threes and 47 percent of his twos while functioning as both the team's go-to guy and its point guard.

Cole Aldrich (6-11, 245, Jr.). I made something of a pest of myself over the course of the season last year, hollering and waving my arms as best I could in a largely futile attempt to point out that Cole Aldrich plays basketball very well. I didn't have much luck, though, because there was this other guy in the conference who was getting most of the attention. Maybe now that the other guy's moved on Aldrich can get some love. He should. As a sophomore he personally hauled in almost 29 percent of opponents' missed shots during his minutes on the floor, a level of defensive rebounding that was exceeded only by that other guy, aka Blake Griffin, among major-conference players. Unlike Griffin, though, Aldrich is also a formidable shot-blocker (not to mention one who, for the most part, stays out of foul trouble). What Collins was to this team's offense, Aldrich was to its defense. Still, what the big guy was able to do on offense was almost as impressive, especially when you consider last year was the first time he'd received regular minutes. In

2008-09 Aldrich made 60 percent of his twos, drew fouls on the opposing team with the exact same (high) frequency as Collins, and, also like Collins, shot 79 percent at the line. Georgia Tech freshman Derrick Favors is currently receiving a good deal of advance praise and is even projected to go earlier in the 2010 draft than Aldrich. If Favors really is better than Aldrich right now, though, the praise being showered on the freshman is in fact woefully insufficient. Let us then say simply that among returning players, Aldrich is easily the best big man in the country.

Tyshawn Taylor (6-3, 180 So.). Taylor suffered a dislocated thumb in a September 22 altercation that involved several members of the KU basketball and football teams. At this writing, however, it appears that he won't miss any time due to the injury (which should heal in time for the season) or because of any disciplinary action by Self. As a freshman Taylor was superb on offense in a supporting role, if—and it was a huge if—he didn't cough up the ball. Taylor made an outstanding 56 percent of his twos, but more than any other Jayhawk who saw regular minutes he struggled with turnovers.

Xavier Henry (6-6, 220, Fr.). A McDonald's All-American from Oklahoma City, Henry originally committed to play for Memphis, but ended up in Lawrence when John Calipari took the Kentucky job. At least Henry ended up in Lawrence eventually. There was much drama along the way, however, and if Self looks a little grayer this season I won't be surprised. For one thing, Henry reportedly wavered in his commitment to KU over the summer and even mused about following Calipari to Lexington. If you're thinking to yourself that "reportedly" is a squishy term, keep in mind the reports here were coming from Henry's own father, Carl. And that was *before* a story by Brady McCollough appeared in the Kansas City Star in late June that, it would appear, had the temerity to quote Carl Henry correctly. ("If [Xavier] didn't have to go to college, he wouldn't do it." Surely this was the college hoops equivalent of a Kinsley gaffe, a recruit or someone in their family caught telling the truth.) The Henry family—Xavier's older brother C.J. is also joining the Jayhawks this year—was not happy with the story and Self flew to Oklahoma City to make sure Xavier was still coming to campus. After visiting with the coach, the freshman-to-be reiterated that he would indeed play for the Jayhawks.

Still think you might like to be a D-I coach?

Marcus Morris (6-8, 225, So.). Morris started 22 games as a freshman and while his minutes were limited by a combination of his team's depth and his own fouls, he did make half his twos while drawing almost as many fouls as he committed.

Brady Morningstar (6-3, 185, Jr.). On October 3 Self suspended Morningstar for the first semester, after the junior was arrested for suspicion of driving while intoxicated. Last year Morningstar started all but one game and while he logged more minutes than anyone but Collins, he surfaced in the offense only in rare cameo roles as a three-point specialist, one who made 42 percent of his attempts from beyond the arc.

Thomas Robinson (6-9, 230, Fr.). Robinson arrives as a freshman from Washington, D.C., via Brewster Academy in New Hampshire. He is billed in advance as an athletic and fearsome rebounder.

Tyrel Reed (6-3, 185, Jr.). Kansas in the Self era doesn't shoot many threes, of course, but last year the Jayhawks were nevertheless very accurate on the rare occasions when they pulled that trigger. Along with Collins and Morningstar, Reed helped make that happen, making 39 percent of his threes while averaging 21 minutes a game.

Markieff Morris (6-9, 230, So.). His twin brother Marcus may be more assertive on offense, but to date Markieff is the better defender, pulling down more boards and blocking more shots. Then again Markieff gives new meaning to the term "foul-prone," often earning two whistles just by walking from the bench to the scorer's table.

Mario Little (6-5, 210, Sr.). Arriving in Lawrence last year as a junior college transfer, Little missed KU's first seven games with a stress fracture in his right foot. No sooner had that healed than he broke a bone in his left hand at practice. Self clearly sees potential here, however, because he did give Little three starts when the young man finally managed to get healthy and stagger onto the court.

Travis Releford (6-5, 205, So.). Though he struggled to earn minutes on a team this deep, Releford would appear to excel at getting to the line. Only problem there being he made just 53 percent of his free throws as a freshman.

Kansas State

Furst 16

2009: 22-12 (9-7 Big 12), lost to San Diego State 70-52, NIT Second Round
In-conference offense: 1.02 points per possession (8th)
In-conference defense: 1.05 points allowed per possession (6th)

What Kansas State did well: *Recover.*

Late on the afternoon of January 24, 2009, things didn't look very good for post-Michael Beasley Kansas State. The Wildcats were already 0-4 in the Big 12, and now they were on-track to lose on the road to Colorado, of all teams. KSU had blown a ten-point second-half lead to the Buffs and been forced into overtime.

Fortunately for Frank Martin, however, Jacob Pullen scored five of his 17 points in OT to lead the Wildcats to the 77-75 win. After their 0-4 start Kansas State finished the conference season on a 9-3 run. In fact the win in Boulder was followed by this team's two most impressive games of the season: A shockingly easy 16-point victory in Manhattan over Elite Eight-bound Missouri, and another OT squeaker that went KSU's way, this time at Texas (a game in which Denis Clemente made 6-of-6 threes and 12-of-12 free throws on his way to 44 points). From late January on, this was a solid team, one that outscored its conference opponents by 0.04 points per possession over its last 12 games.

What we learned in 2009: *Officials working games in Manhattan suffer from frequent-whistle syndrome.*

According to ESPN.com, Kansas State has earned "kudos from Big 12 coaches for their defensive intensity," a sentiment the website passed along without further comment or notice. Dig a little deeper, however, and one wonders if "defensive intensity" in this instance may have been a pointed euphemism: This is one hack-tastic team.

The Wildcats' fouling went through the roof last year, as Big 12 opponents averaged more than 26 free throws per game. No other major-conference team in 2009 could match the Wildcats in terms of frequent fouling.

The officials in Manhattan may have been kept busy, but it was the purple-clad fans who really suffered here. These were flagrantly ugly games in 2009: Kansas State fouled a lot on their defensive end and then came down and missed a ton of shots on offense (a shortcoming they were able to offset to an extent thanks to ferocious offensive rebounding).

Note as well that being the most hack-happy team

So Many Whistles:
Most Foul-Prone Major-Conference Teams, 2009

School	Opp. FTA/FGA	School	Opp. FTA/FGA
Kansas St.	0.52	Georgia Tech	0.42
Texas Tech	0.49	Colorado	0.42
Oregon	0.47	Ole Miss	0.41
Oklahoma St.	0.45	Indiana	0.41
Seton Hall	0.43	Cincinnati	0.40
Baylor	0.43	Texas	0.40

Conference games only
Opp. FTA/FGA: opponent FT attempts divided by FG attempts

in this conference was no small feat. Indeed six of the 12 most foul-prone teams in all of major-conference hoops last year were Big 12 teams. That could be a passive reflection of on-court reality, of course— maybe the conference simply happened to be home to a lot of deep frontcourts that could spare the fouls. But this kind of lopsided concentration of fouls within one league suggests a far more likely possibility. Big 12 commissioner Dan Beebe really needs to consider telling his refs to dial it back a little this season. He should remind his officials they're not being paid by the whistle.

What's in store for 2010: Four starters return and Wally Judge arrives.

Prospectus says: In each of Martin's first two seasons in Manhattan, Kansas State has run hot and cold. With Beasley on hand in 2008, the Wildcats in January looked like a threat to reach the Final Four, only to lose six of their last 11 regular-season games. Last year, conversely, K-State opened Big 12 play by dropping their first four games, before turning things around in OT in Boulder. So don't be too quick to either champion or dismiss this team based on what you see in January alone. The one constant over those two seasons has been outstanding offensive rebounding. That will continue in 2010, and Kansas State has the experience to improve on last year's performance, especially if they stop sending opponents to the line so often.

Meet the Wildcats

Denis Clemente (6-1, 175, Sr.). Clemente became a YouTube sensation in the offseason with that shot he made off the scoreboard during practice. (Whereupon he was promptly displaced by the video of those guys allegedly making a shot from the upper deck of Kyle Field at Texas A&M. All glory is fleeting, especially on YouTube.) But the young man from Puerto Rico is more than a trick shot artist. Arriving in Manhattan last year as a transfer from Miami, Clemente hit the ground running as Martin's scoring point guard (or co-scoring point guard—see below), dishing assists and making 37 percent of his threes. He was notably less effective inside the arc, however.

Jacob Pullen (6-0, 200, Jr.). The impact of Clemente's arrival on Pullen was pretty interesting to watch last year. When Beasley was still around Pullen had functioned as the point guard who was nevertheless happy to look for his own shot. With Clemente in the lineup, however, Pullen shared these duties even as he rushed into the Beasley-less void and upped his number of shots significantly. The results were a mixed bag. Pullen's an active defender who improved to average from beyond the arc, but his turnover rate stayed right where it was (a little too high) and his two-point accuracy took a big hit with Beasley no longer around to occupy opposing defenses. (Not to put too fine a point on it, but K-State was an atrocious two-point shooting team last year in Big 12 play. The 'Cats made just 44 percent of their twos, the worst figure in the league.)

Wally Judge (6-9, 250, Fr.). Judge is a McDonald's All-American from Washington, D.C., whose "natural" position is apparently still up for discussion. Is he a power forward? Is he a wing? Wherever he finds himself, it is said that he can score.

Dominique Sutton (6-5, 210, Jr.). While he started all but two games last year, Sutton averaged just 23 minutes a game, as his playing time was limited by foul trouble and by Martin in more or less equal measure. If he can stay on the floor, though, Sutton can help this team as a solid defensive rebounder and as a fourth option on offense who makes more than half his twos.

Luis Colon (6-10, 265, Sr.). Colon fouled out of six games last year and the odd part about that is he's not a shot-blocker. Nevertheless the big guy earned his starting spot and scant minutes (18 per game) by virtue of being Martin's best defensive rebounder.

Jamar Samuels (6-7, 215, So.). Off the top of my head I can't think of another player I've run into who actually grew shorter the way Samuels apparently has, going from a listed height of 6-8 in 2008 to today's 6-7. Assuming he can overcome this rare affliction and remain over six feet tall, Samuels should continue to excel as both a shot-blocker and an offensive rebounder. And while you've probably already guessed that he's yet another foul-prone Wildcat, Samuels' biggest drawback is actually the fact that he is himself fouled with frightening regularity yet shoots just 57 percent from the line.

Curtis Kelly (6-8, 250, Jr.). Speaking of adventures in listed heights, I have seen Kelly listed variously as 6-8 and 6-10. At Connecticut in 2007-08 he appeared in 23 games as a role player without settling on a stylistic identity, be it rebounding, shot-blocking, or what have you.

Rodney McGruder (6-4, 205, Fr.). A high school teammate of Judge's, McGruder is billed as a slasher who can get to the tin.

Missouri

2009: 31-7 (12-4 Big 12), lost to Connecticut 82-75, NCAA Elite Eight
In-conference offense: 1.08 points per possession (5th)
In-conference defense: 0.96 points allowed per possession (2nd)

What Missouri did well: *Sow confusion, both on and off the court.*

When Mike Anderson was hired at Missouri in 2006, it was understood that the new coach would bring with him his up-tempo pressing style of full-court defense, a scheme that had enabled his last UAB team to force opponents into turnovers on 29 percent of their possessions. Instead of the instant arrival of "40 minutes of hell," however, what ensued was more like 24 months of annoying delay, as players were variously suspended before returning (Leo Lyons, Jason Horton, Darryl Butterfield, and Marshall Brown), suspended only never to return (Stefhon Hannah), or arrested only never to return (Kalen Grimes).

Then, finally, came last year. The turmoil subsided, the roster stabilized, and what do you know: Big 12 opponents were forced into turnovers on 26 percent of their possessions.

When 40 Minutes Of Hell Finally Arrived: Missouri Defense, 2008 Vs. 2009		
	Opp. TO%	Opp. PPP
2008	19.5	1.10
2009	25.6	0.96

Conference games only
Opp. TO%: opponent turnover percentage
Opp. PPP: opponent points per possession

To be sure, Missouri's offense also improved last year, but the magnitude of the change on that side of the ball came nowhere near the total makeover that occurred on defense. Little wonder, then, that this team's signature victory is so often misunderstood: Anderson plays 40 minutes of hell, Missouri upset Memphis in the Sweet 16, therefore 40 minutes of hell must have been what knocked off Memphis.

Certainly the pace of that 102-91 triumph, clocking in at 83 possessions, testified to a frenetic atmosphere. But the notion that Missouri was getting lots of easy baskets off of turnovers in that game just isn't true and, worse, it diminishes Anderson's feat. In fact Memphis committed just 14 turnovers in those 83 possessions. The truth is Missouri scored 102 points straight up against one of the best defenses in the country. They did it by driving the ball into the teeth of that defense over and over and over again.

It worked. Mizzou shot 45 free throws. (They made just 30, otherwise this game would have veered toward a total blowout). Leo Lyons alone went to the line 18 times. In John Calipari's last game at Memphis he looked on helplessly as Shawn Taggart, Antonio Anderson, and Roburt Sallie all fouled out.

During the Big 12 regular season Missouri didn't even rise to the level of average when it came to getting to the line. Tell that to Calipari. Anderson scouted his opponent, made his plan, got his team to buy in, and pulled it off beautifully.

What we learned in 2009: *It doesn't matter if he was the boss's nephew, DeMarre Carroll was a beast.*

I have a soft spot for players that become absolute monsters as seniors. Such players can never get the attention that their monstrosity would have earned them as freshmen, of course, but that doesn't make them any less effective during that one season.

DeMarre Carroll was one such monster last year. He paid some serious dues on his way to an unbelievable senior campaign on behalf of his uncle, Mike Anderson. Carroll had to sit out a year after transferring in from Vanderbilt, and before he ever saw a minute of floor time for the Tigers he was shot in the ankle while standing outside a Columbia nightclub in July of 2007. And while he was very good as a junior in 2007-08, it would have taken a leap of faith to expect what in fact came to pass in 2008-09.

As a senior, Carroll made 58 percent of his twos while taking as large a share of the shots in his offense as did A.J. Abrams, Willie Warren, or James Anderson. He never turned the ball over, and among Tigers who saw regular playing time he was the best defensive rebounder Mike Anderson had.

Then again maybe a senior season this good can attract some notice. Carroll was selected at number 27 by the Memphis Grizzlies in the first round. At 6-8 he's not going to dominate the NBA with his size, but if you saw him play last year you know better than to doubt his motor.

What's in store for 2010: On paper Missouri loses three starters, which sounds weighty enough. In fact the loss is much bigger, for Carroll, Leo Lyons, and Matt Lawrence by themselves constituted most of the offense for a team with a good offense and an excellent defense. The possessions absorbed by last year's seniors are now up for grabs.

Prospectus says: Missouri will continue to force opponents into turnovers as long as J.T. Tiller is still here, but the Tiger defense is nevertheless likely to take a step back this season. Likewise, it's hard to envision this year's offense being as efficient as it was in 2008-09, now that the bulk of the possessions will go through players new to regular minutes and/or featured roles. So while Missouri may not make it to the Elite Eight again this year, the program has secured its future in a more durable and meaningful way by signing Anderson to a new seven-year contract virtually the moment he left the floor after the Connecticut game. History is likely to show that was a good move on Mizzou's part.

Meet the Tigers

J.T. Tiller (6-3, 200, Sr.). Tiller is a notoriously disruptive defender (he was named co-defensive player of the year in the Big 12 along with Cole Aldrich) but, unlike some other players renowned for their D, he more than pulls his own weight on offense. As a junior Tiller posted the highest assist rate on the team while taking pretty good care of the ball and making 51 percent of his twos. Last year he injured his wrist in Missouri's win at Texas on February 4 and had surgery immediately following the season—which is pretty incredible when you realize that he led his team with 23 points in the Memphis game.

Zaire Taylor (6-4, 190, Sr.). A combo guard who became a starter last year after transferring from Delaware, Taylor played a supporting role on offense while giving Anderson still another creator of chaos on defense. It's hard for Missouri defenders to get out from behind Tiller's shadow, but on just about any other team Taylor would be the designated perimeter stopper.

Kim English (6-6, 200, So.). Last year was something of an apprenticeship for English. He was highly touted coming out of high school but Anderson had the good fortune not to need the young man's production as a freshman. Averaging 14 minutes a game, English made some threes, missed a lot of twos, and generally displayed an assertiveness that should serve him and his team well this year in the post Carroll-Lyons-Lawrence era.

Marcus Denmon (6-3, 185, So.). Denmon's pure 60-foot buzzer-beating swish to end the first half against Memphis in the Sweet 16 was the most spectacular shot of the NCAA tournament, if not the entire season. When he wasn't sinking amazing shots from the other side of the court, Denmon gave hints that his 30 percent three-point shooting may have an upside, as he made 79 percent of his free throws.

Keith Ramsey (6-9, 210, Sr.). Arriving last year as a junior college transfer, Ramsey gave Anderson a good defensive rebounder to back up Carroll and Lyons. He was also the Tiger most likely to block a shot.

Miguel Paul (6-1, 170, So.). As a freshman Paul gave indications he could develop into a dependable point guard, recording an assist rate that was second only to Tiller's. Then again Paul's turnover rate was the highest on the roster.

Justin Safford (6-8, 230, Jr.). Whatever else he accomplishes in his career, Safford now has a story to tell the grandkids, about the time he made Hall of Fame coach Jim Calhoun switch Connecticut's defensive assignments specifically to stop Safford in an Elite Eight game. And unlike most such stories from grandparents, this one will be true. So never mind the scarce minutes during most of the season last year. Safford's got game.

Laurence Bowers (6-8, 205, So.). See "Kim English," above. Bowers last year was still another talented and confident freshman that Anderson had the luxury of working into the lineup at his leisure. He got fewer minutes than English, but if Bowers can score as effectively and rebound as well on defense as he did during spot duty in his first season, he'll go a long way toward filling the hole left by Carroll's departure.

Mike Dixon (6-1, 175, Fr.). A point guard from Kansas City, Dixon has been praised by Anderson for his ability to both score and deliver assists.

Nebraska *out*

2009: 18-13 (8-8 Big 12), lost to New Mexico 83-71, NIT First Round
In-conference offense: 0.97 points per possession (10th)
In-conference defense: 0.98 points allowed per possession (3rd)

What Nebraska did well: *Go .500 in the Big 12.*
Nebraska went 8-8 in the Big 12 last year, marking the first time since 1999 that the Cornhuskers won at least as many as they lost in league play. Doc Sadler's team was thoroughly respectable, notching wins at home over NCAA tournament teams like Missouri

and Texas, while winning on the road at places like Colorado, Texas Tech, and Baylor. It was a solid year, one that ended in the first round of the NIT.

One can reasonably ask, however, if "solid" is as good as it can get at Nebraska, where "Nebraska" is understood to be a program where an ever-revolving cast of junior college transfers comprises a goodly portion of the roster. I'm not saying that particular understanding of the program can't change, of course. In fact that's one of the beguiling things about this here sport. Just one or two recruiting slam dunks can turn things around. (After all, if not for a bizarre enrollment snafu Roburt Sallie, last seen single-handedly saving Memphis from a first-round tournament disaster, would currently be draining his threes in Lincoln.) I never say never.

What I am saying is that the Huskers have been well-coached and undermanned for a decade now. They will be again in 2010.

What we learned in 2009: *Even the shortest team in the nation can play D.*

The season that Nebraska had in 2009 was like a perfectly designed experiment conducted by a council of curious hoops gods. The question under consideration was this: What's the absolute ceiling for a really short team in terms of defense?

Now we know. According to the effective height statistic created by my colleague Ken Pomeroy, the Huskers were the shortest D-I team in the nation last year. And yet they played excellent defense, allowing Big 12 opponents to score just 0.98 points per trip. Only Kansas and Missouri were stingier on D.

Sadler's team certainly wasn't achieving these results with blocked shots and defensive boards. Instead, Nebraska went the Missouri route, albeit the slow-tempo version thereof, and forced their opponents into a lot of turnovers. Big 12 teams playing the Huskers gave the ball away on one in every four trips last year. Creating turnovers, along with baiting opponents into shooting threes instead of twos, constituted the entirety of the Nebraska defense. And it worked. Defense alone carried the Huskers to an 8-8 record.

(Mark me down as mystified, however, as to why this team didn't shoot more threes. Clearly Nebraska's only hope on offense was to be a perimeter-oriented team, much like the one that Sadler put on the floor in 2007. After all, the Huskers were decent from beyond the arc last year, making 36 percent of their threes in conference play. Moreover Sadler's team was already forfeiting the offensive glass entirely, just as one would expect from a team shooting a lot of threes. Surely the only way for Nebraska to lift their ghastly two-point percentage even a little would have been to establish the threes first, just as Travis Ford did with his similarly undersized Oklahoma State team last year. I don't get it.)

What's in store for 2010: Point guard Cookie Miller announced after last season that he would transfer to be closer to his family. (He ended up at Miami of Ohio.) And Christopher Niemann, a 6-11 sophomore from Germany who sat out last year to meet eligibility requirements, tore his ACL in August and is out for the season. So in 2010 Nebraska will rely on returnees like Sek Henry and Ryan Anderson, along with a full kit of new arrivals.

Prospectus says: Some things from last year won't change for Nebraska in 2010. The Huskers will again play fundamentally sound defense at a slow tempo while forcing opponents into a lot of turnovers. Likewise the offense will again score points at a rate below the league average. The one thing that is likely to change, however, is the overall result: Nebraska right now doesn't look like a team that's going to get to .500 in the Big 12 like they did in 2009.

Meet the Cornhuskers

Sek Henry (6-3, 200, Sr.). Throughout his career in Lincoln, Henry has functioned as a secondary option on offense, first behind Aleks Maric, then last year behind Ade Dagunduro and Steve Harley. All of the above are now gone, and it may be time for Henry to absorb some more possessions in this attack. Last year he showed real improvement on both sides of the arc while taking more shots in the wake of Maric's departure.

Ryan Anderson (6-4, 205, Sr.). While alternating between being a starter and a sixth man, Anderson has made a career out of helping his team on defense in ways that few 6-4 players can match. Last year was no different: Anderson was often the best defensive rebounder on the floor for Sadler. He also posted the highest steal rate among Huskers who saw regular minutes. This activity on D does lead to fouls, to be sure, but Anderson is a key component of Nebraska's defense.

Lance Jeter (6-3, 230, Jr.). Jeter started his career in college athletics as a wide receiver on the Cincinnati football team. Now he's a point guard for Nebraska, having arrived in Lincoln this season as a junior college transfer.

Toney McCray (6-6, 205, So.). McCray averaged 16 minutes a game coming off the bench as a freshman, but they were assertive minutes, as he launched shots with the confidence of a featured scorer. He also blocked shots with surprising regularity for a 6-6 freshman. McCray injured his elbow in September, but is said to be doing OK.

Brandon Richardson (6-0, 190, So.). Though he was sidelined for four games by a shoulder injury, Richardson averaged 15 minutes a game last year as a red-

shirt freshman and proved to be an excellent perimeter defender, recording 25 steals in just 414 minutes.

Quincy Hankins-Cole (6-8, 240, Jr.). A junior college teammate of Jeter's, Hankins-Cole is billed as a strong rebounder.

Ray Gallegos (6-3, 175, Fr.). Gallegos is a combo guard from greater Salt Lake City who will see some minutes this season coming off the bench and playing point guard, according to Sadler.

Brandon Ubel (6-10, 220, Fr.). Praised as a "true" power forward (meaning he's 6-10), Ubel hails from Overland Park, Kansas, and could see immediate minutes in Niemann's absence.

Oklahoma ᴼᵘᵗ

2009: 30-6 (13-3 Big 12), lost to North Carolina 72-60, NCAA Elite Eight
In-conference offense: 1.13 points per possession (1st)
In-conference defense: 1.02 points allowed per possession (4th)

What Oklahoma did well: *Ride Blake Griffin all the way to the Elite Eight.*

The Big 12 has produced three exceptional underclassmen in the last three years: Kevin Durant, Michael Beasley, and Blake Griffin. You could make a case that of those three players Griffin put together the best season.

True, the erstwhile Sooner has an advantage in this comparison, in that he was in his second year as a college player. Who knows what Durant or Beasley might have done if, for some insane reason, they got it into their heads to stick around? Be that as it may, Griffin was the lone sophomore here and the havoc he wreaked in 2008-09 was nothing less than a throwback to the Bill Walton/Lew Alcindor days of total domination by a post player—on offense. (Those other guys blocked shots. Duly noted.)

When your featured scorer makes 66 percent of his twos and takes reasonably good care of the ball while drawing eight fouls for every 40 minutes he plays, a couple of impolitic but nevertheless insistent truths arise. Your team is going to be really good, no matter how bad they are on defense. And your offense is going to be outstanding, no matter how bad the other four players are at offense.

Fortunately for Jeff Capel, Oklahoma was in fact OK (har!) at defense, in large part because Griffin was the best defensive rebounder in major-conference basketball. And the Sooners were, of course, excellent on offense because Griffin had an incredibly talented sidekick named Willie Warren (see below).

Yes, Griffin misses two out of every five free throws, and that is no minor detail when you attempt 324 of them over the course of a season. Still, in basketball's curiously punitive world fouls are both an incentive for the offense and a disincentive for the defense. (When I'm made hoops czar they will just be the former. I hate seeing foul trouble intrude on great collisions of like talent.) Griffin failed to gather all the points available to him, but the fouls he drew still depleted the personnel available to the opponent.

So while a Griffin who was merely adequate at the line would indeed have summed to something even more spectacular, we shouldn't lose sight of what actually took place in Norman last year. After all, it took the best team in the country to end Blake Griffin's superb season.

What we learned in 2009: *It's possible for coaches to speak in something other than coachspeak.*

Going into the 2008-09 season, Capel was quoted as saying his team would be able to play at a faster tempo now that his roster had some depth. Coaches pretty much always promise to go up-tempo, of course, but this was one instance where the man behind the microphone was actually telling the truth. While the Sooners didn't suddenly become North Carolina or anything, the difference was still clear.

Capel Delivers More Possessions: Oklahoma Tempo, 2008 Vs. 2009		
	Pace	Big 12 rank
2008	63.6	10th
2009	68.8	5th
Conference games only Pace: possessions per 40 minutes		

Oklahoma's turnover rate increased at the higher pace (while that of their opponents actually went down), but Capel was right to step on the gas. In 2008 his team was outscored in Big 12 play; the Sooners' chances of winning decreased the more possessions they played. Last year, by contrast, Capel had the benefit of one of the most dominant offensive players of recent years. It was the coach's job to see that said player got as many chances to score as possible. And Capel didn't allow mere stylistic inertia to get in the way of accomplishing that task. Well done, Coach.

By the way, Capel's saying much the same thing this year, that his sassy new-look no-Griffin team will play faster. My advice is to be skeptical this time. Two consecutive accelerations of the magnitude that we saw with this team last year would be highly unusual. More likely the Sooners will pretty much stay where they are, give or take a couple possessions.

What's in store for 2010: Willie Warren will take a lot more shots. And he should.

Prospectus says: The Sooners should be fun to watch this year. I don't foresee a lot of defense in Norman this season, but then again with Warren and a precociously talented freshman class, OU should score a lot of points in 2010. Opponents might find it difficult to keep up.

Meet the Sooners

Willie Warren (6-4, 205, So.). One website is telling me that Warren needs "to become smarter with his shot selection," but I confess I have no idea what this means or which player the website could possibly have been watching last year. As a freshman Warren was virtually the Platonic ideal of a true dual-threat shooting guard, making 37 percent of his threes and 57 percent of his twos while attempting equal numbers of both. Yes, he compiled those glittering numbers against defenses that had to account for a certain Blake Griffin, but that's the only context in which we can judge Warren right now and his performance was magnificent. He needs to become smarter with his shot selection about like John Calipari needs to become a better recruiter. The sophomore that Bill Self has called the best offensive player he's ever recruited (alas, Self didn't get him) is projected as a high-lottery pick next summer. In this instance the NBA and I are in perfect perceptual accord.

Tiny Gallon (6-9, 295, Fr.). One suspects that in this case "295" is a polite euphemism, because in truth Gallon is a movable beast. A McDonald's All-American from Vallejo, California, by way of Oak Hill Academy, Gallon is reputed to be a skilled post scorer. However the fact that this fall Capel's been glimpsed fretting in print about his team's rebounding even though he's just signed a "295"-pound McDonald's All-American might suggest Gallon needs to improve that part of his game. Or it might suggest simply that coaches like to fret, which they certainly do. More importantly from my chair, you can blame Gallon for at least part of the never-ending Renardo Sidney saga at Mississippi State. A year ago at this time Gallon had narrowed his list of schools down to a final two: Oklahoma and MSU. He visited both campuses and then chose to sign with Capel. Had Gallon ended up instead in Starkville, I doubt Jarvis Varnado would be paying his own way right now to free up a scholarship for Sidney.

Tommy Mason-Griffin (5-11, 205, Fr.). Still another McDonald's All-American, Mason-Griffin is a point guard from Houston praised for both his perimeter range and his ability to penetrate.

Tony Crocker (6-6, 210, Sr.). Crocker went nuts against Syracuse in the Sweet 16, hitting 6-of-11 threes and scoring 28 points. Up to that point he'd been a solid third option behind Griffin and Warren, making 35 percent of his threes.

Cade Davis (6-5, 200, Jr.). Averaging 15 minutes a game on a roster where the starting five monopolized the playing time to an unusual extent, Davis functioned almost entirely as a three-point specialist and, like Crocker, made 35 percent of his attempts from beyond the arc.

Andrew Fitzgerald (6-8, 260, Fr.). Fitzgerald is a highly-rated big man from Baltimore by way of Brewster Academy in New Hampshire.

Steven Pledger (6-4, 215, Fr.). If Capel is correct and

the Sooners do speed up, it could mean more minutes right away for the likes of Pledger, a shooting guard from Chesapeake, Virginia, who's reputed to be an excellent perimeter shooter.

Ryan Wright (6-9, 240, Sr.). Wright arrived last year as a transfer from UCLA who'd fled the logjam in Ben Howland's frontcourt (Alfred Aboya, Luc Richard Mbah a Moute, Lorenzo Mata, et al.). Unfortunately he didn't fare much better securing playing time in Norman, averaging just eight minutes a game in support of the Griffin brothers.

Oklahoma State

2009: 23-12 (9-7 Big 12), lost to Pitt 84-76, NCAA Second Round
In-conference offense: 1.09 points per possession (3rd)
In-conference defense: 1.07 points allowed per possession (9th)

What Oklahoma State did well: *Finish.*

You likely remember the 2008-09 Oklahoma State team as a fast-paced three-point-shooting bunch that gave DeJuan Blair and Pitt everything they could handle before falling to the Panthers in the second round of the NCAA tournament. With first-year coach Travis Ford at the helm, the Cowboys made their first appearance in the dance since 2005. That kind of respectable denouement looked a very long way away for this team in mid-February, however.

The Pokes started Big 12 play 3-6, a record that in part reflected a schedule front-loaded with games against the league's four best teams (home losses to Missouri and Oklahoma, road losses at Kansas and Texas). Still, schedule-skewed records have been known to sap a team's confidence to the point where they start losing the games they should win. To Ford's credit, that didn't happen with the Cowboys.

OSU played its best basketball in February and March, improving markedly on defense (there was room to) and avenging an 0-2 showing against archrival Oklahoma during the regular season with a thrilling 71-70 win in the Big 12 tournament quarterfinals.

What we learned in 2009: *Taking over a team that returns most of its minutes is a sweet gig.*

Oklahoma State showed clear improvement last year and to me the really interesting question is how much of that was specifically Ford's doing and how

much would have happened anyway. Keep in mind it's an open question whether Sean Sutton would have been retained as head coach had officials in Stillwater known in April 2008 that OSU alum Bill Self wasn't going to go anywhere, no matter how much money the Cowboys put on the table.

Sutton was sent packing after Oklahoma State endured three consecutive below-.500 seasons in the Big 12, the first of which included a mid-season passing of the torch from Eddie Sutton to his son. In last year's book I noted that the similarity in records over those three years (6-10, 6-10, and 7-9) masked the fact that the Cowboys actually improved markedly in what proved to be Sutton's final season. Indeed, viewing the two full seasons of Sutton's tenure alongside year one of the Ford era suggests that the upward trend displayed by the program as a whole spans the two coaching regimes rather seamlessly.

Cowboys Up : Oklahoma State Improvement, 2007-09			
Year	Returning minutes (%)	EM	Improvement over previous year
2007		-0.09	
2008	48	-0.01	+0.08
2009	**75**	**+0.02**	**+0.03**

Conference games only
EM: efficiency margin (points per possession – opponent PPP)

In other words Sutton took a roster that returned just 48 percent of its minutes and somehow got that team to improve its per-possession performance significantly. Ford then took a roster that returned 75 percent of its minutes and piloted it to a moderately improved performance.

Give Ford full credit. He had the good sense to say yes when a major-conference program with a veteran roster came knocking at his door. Much like Darrin Horn at South Carolina last year, Ford took over a team returning the lion's share of its minutes, delighted the players by upping the tempo, and then reaped the rewards. On the other hand I have to wonder: Could Sean Sutton have taken this same team to 9-7 last year? I think the answer is yes, he probably could have. Certainly that's where the trend line was pointing. In retrospect you'll forgive Sutton for wishing Self had received his diploma from OU instead of OSU.

What's in store for 2010: Despite losing point guard Byron Eaton, Ford is fairly exuding optimism, saying that a deeper roster will allow the Pokes to operate at a faster pace while improving on both offense and defense. Down, coach, down!

For reasons outlined in the preceding Oklahoma preview, I think it best to take Ford's words about a faster tempo this season with a grain of salt. (Significant accelerations in each of two consecutive years, which is what we'd be talking about if the Sooners and/or the Cowboys go faster this year, are rare.) But the good news is this team is already playing fast enough.

Keep in mind OSU doesn't go up-tempo to force opponents into turnovers. Stretching back to UMass and including his first year in Stillwater, that's not Ford's shtick. Instead, Ford likes a fast tempo because it's a really good platform from which to launch a lot of threes: You get open looks and you don't (have the chance to) commit many turnovers. That approach suits his personnel very well.

Prospectus says: This season Oklahoma State will again be working at a size disadvantage and opposing offenses may therefore continue to shoot quite well from both sides of the arc. Still, Ford has a full supply of good three-point shooters on hand to run his perimeter-oriented offense, one that will constantly be seeking to turn the size disparity to their own advantage: A team this quick operating at a pace this fast is tough to guard for 40 minutes. More specifically, James Ander-

son has proven himself to be a threat from anywhere on the floor. So, yes, the Cowboys have the personnel and the scheme to score more points than the other team. With their defense they'll probably need to.

Meet the Cowboys

James Anderson (6-6, 210, Jr.). Considering there were no true shooting guards on the All-Big 12 team last year (it was Sherron Collins and four bigs: Blake Griffin, Cole Aldrich, DeMarre Carroll, and Craig Brackins), this league certainly has no shortage of excellent shooting guards. I know I've already held forth about how great Willie Warren and LaceDarius Dunn are, but James Anderson is right there with them. Last year Anderson's game went from good to excellent, as he riddled opponents with made shots from quite literally everywhere on the floor, making 41, 55, and 83 percent of his threes, twos, and free throws, respectively. Only quibble: He needs to shoot more. Not that he has to get all Craig Brackins about it. More like Sherron Collins, I should say.

Obi Muonelo (6-5, 220, Sr.). On offense Muonelo functions almost exclusively as a spot-up shooter, one who's notably more effective outside the arc (making 40 percent of his threes) than inside of it (hitting just 44 percent of his twos). During any given minute of playing time, Muonelo is almost as likely to shoot as is Anderson. Then again Muonelo's arguably more valuable to his team on defense: Last year he personally pulled down 22 percent of opponents' missed shots during his minutes. Muonelo's heroics in this department went a long way toward explaining how a decidedly undersized team was able to achieve results on the defensive glass that put the Cowboys right at the conference average in Big 12 play.

Keiton Page (5-9, 170, So.). At the risk of sounding repetitive, Page is a very good three-point shooter, one who made 40 percent of his threes as a freshman. Don't be fooled by the point-guard looks and demeanor. Shooting is what he does, rarely but well.

Marshall Moses (6-7, 240, Jr.). As a sophomore Moses made 15 starts but averaged less than 20 minutes a game in part because he's so foul-prone. When he's in the game he supports the gang of perimeter shooters surrounding him primarily by rebounding their misses, which he does quite well.

Matt Pilgrim (6-8, 235, Jr.). Pilgrim played two seasons at Hampton before transferring to Kentucky and redshirting last year. Last spring when it became plain Pilgrim wasn't going to figure prominently in John Calipari's plans, the well-traveled player transferred yet again, this time to Oklahoma State. He's been granted a waiver by the NCAA and is eligible to play this year.

Ray Penn (5-9, 165, Fr.). Penn is billed as a scoring point guard who's fearless in attacking the rim and drawing contact.

Roger Franklin (6-5, 220, Fr.). A wing from Duncanville, Texas, Franklin turned down Michigan State and Arizona, among others, in favor of Ford and Oklahoma State.

P: Lucas Bilbay?
W: Bradley (S)
B: Pittman, Damien James

Texas

Disfunctional — bad guards, no set rotation. Fast 8

2009: 23-12 (9-7 Big 12), lost to Duke 74-69, NCAA Second Round
In-conference offense: 1.07 points per possession (6th)
In-conference defense: 1.03 points allowed per possession (5th)

What Texas did well: *Display a very high programmatic "floor."*

What we saw from Texas in 2009 might be about as "bad" as it can get under Rick Barnes: A 9-7 record in the Big 12, a seven-seed in the NCAA tournament, and a second-round exit at the hands of two-seed Duke. Know what? That's really not all that bad.

Barnes arrived in Austin in 1998 and he's taken each of his 11 Texas teams to the NCAA tournament. No Longhorn team has won fewer than nine games in conference play under his watch. In 2009 he took a team that was merely average when it came to shooting twos and downright awful at shooting threes (worst in the conference) and still produced an offense that outperformed the Big 12 average. How did he do it?

What we learned in 2009: *The "barrage index" is alive and well in Austin.*

Last year I cooked up a stat I called the barrage index to explain how Texas can score points without, you know, actually putting the ball in the basket (an activity many close observers of the game regard as essential). I'll admit it's a goofy name, but then again a really good barrage index helped North Carolina win the national championship last year.

A high barrage index shows that a team combined very good offensive rebounding with very few turnovers. Most often those two qualities are more or less antithetical: A team that's beastly on the offensive glass usually doesn't fuss too much about something as dainty as the occasional turnover. (See Michigan State.) On the other hand a team skilled enough on the perimeter to never turn the ball over usually isn't beastly enough in the paint to get offensive boards. (See Northwestern.)

On those rare occasions, however, when a team does combine those two abilities, they get *a lot* of chances to score. There's still no one who can touch what Texas did in this department in 2008, but a list of top performing teams in terms of the barrage index over the past four seasons shows two things. The year 2009 was a very good one for this particular goofy stat. (Maybe teams are catching on!) And clearly Barnes, along with Roy Williams, has something consistent going on here.

Beware The Barrage: Best Teams In Terms Of "Barrage Index," 2006-09				
School	Year	TO%	OR%	Barrage Index
Texas	**2008**	**14.5**	**37.6**	**259**
Pitt	2009	17.9	43.2	241
North Carolina	2009	17.8	41.4	233
Texas	**2009**	**17.0**	**37.9**	**223**
Connecticut	2009	17.5	39.0	223
North Carolina	2008	19.4	43.0	222
Conference games only: ACC, Big 12, Big East, Big Ten, Pac-10, SEC TO%: turnover percentage; OR%: offensive rebound percentage				

The Longhorns' very good offensive rebounding has remained almost literally unchanged the last two seasons. And while D.J. Augustin's departure did result in a few more turnovers in 2009, keep in mind that the average Big 12 team gave the ball away on 20 percent of its possessions in conference play last year. Meaning Texas was still excellent at taking care of the rock post-Augustin. As a result, a team that ranked next-to-last in the Big 12 in shooting from the field (only Kansas State was worse in league play) and that attempted an average number of free throws nevertheless scored 1.07 points per trip. Coach Barnes, take a bow.

What's in store for 2010: We have seen not only this program's very high floor, but also this offense's very respectable "rock bottom." Points will be more plentiful at the Frank Erwin Center this season. Shooting from the field will be better. And, not least, the backcourt depth will be ridiculous.

Prospectus says: Perimeter defense was an issue for Texas last year, as Big 12 opponents made 39 percent of their threes. That percentage should drop significantly this year, however, as Barnes now has entire platoons of talented guards to throw at opposing teams. Fresh legs should not be an issue—along with Kansas this is the deepest team in the conference. Speaking of Kansas, I'm on the record as thinking the Jayhawks will win the national championship. That being said, if the Longhorns' youth lives up to its clippings Texas should be more than capable of beating KU when Bill Self's team comes to Austin on February 8. Circle your calendar.

Meet the Longhorns

Damion James (6-7, 225, Sr.). Never mind last year's "leading scorer" A.J. Abrams, a player who earned that distinction in part by simply playing more minutes than any other major-conference player in the nation besides Chase Budinger. No, James was the actual workhorse in this offense in 2008-09. He made half his twos and, as noted above, on this team that made James a valuable player indeed. Where James really stands out, though, is on the defensive glass, where last year he pulled down 23 percent of opponents' missed shots during his minutes. Sure, that was overshadowed by the close proximity of some of the best defensive rebounders in the country last season (namely Blake Griffin, Cole Aldrich, and Craig Brackins), but James was doing it at a listed height of 6-7.

Justin Mason (6-2, 195, Sr.). A defensive specialist who guards the opponent's best perimeter player, Mason pitched in on offense last year by upping his assists significantly in Augustin's absence. Note however that Mason is a career 59 percent free throw shooter.

Avery Bradley (6-2, 180, Fr.). Bradley is a McDonald's All-American from Tacoma by way of Findlay Prep in greater Las Vegas. Rated by at least one service as the top prospect in the nation last year, he's a shooting guard who's renowned for his ability to attack the rim. Barnes has also said that Bradley is "further along defensively than anybody we've ever had." When a coach says that in October about a freshman, that kid stands to get big minutes right away, even on a team this deep.

Dexter Pittman (6-10, 290, Sr.). Though he started 24 games last year, Pittman was limited to just 17 minutes a game by three factors: Barnes' stated belief that Pittman takes the occasional play off, particularly early in the year; conditioning; and foul trouble. What's interesting is that during those 17 minutes each game, the Texas offense would stop whatever it had been doing previously and go through Pittman—with great results. After all, a player that makes 61 percent of his twos and is easily the best offensive rebounder in the Big 12 is a handy guy to have around. So if Pittman can stay on the floor, he bids fair to be the closest thing to DeJuan Blair we get this season: An offensive-rebounding man-weapon who single-handedly destroys opposing defenses from within.

Dogus Balbay (6-0, 175, Fr.). Last year Balbay started 13 games as a pass-first (really, pass-always) point guard but struggled with turnovers and for the year averaged just 21 minutes a game.

Gary Johnson (6-6, 240, Jr.). Johnson's a player who was very highly touted coming out of high school but, due to various health issues (namely a heart condition and a broken nose), he didn't really get his first crack at quality minutes until his sophomore season. The results were mixed: Johnson can certainly get himself to the line, but once there he shoots just 67 percent and his two-point accuracy (45 percent) is likewise eminently improvable.

Jai Lucas (5-10, 150, Jr.). A 2007 McDonald's All-American, Lucas is unquestionably a big-name transfer for the 'Horns. He's also a bit of a mystery, however. At Florida in 2007-08, Lucas functioned as a 5-10 shooting guard next to 6-6 point guard Nick Calathes. Not that there's anything wrong with that, of course. Texas fans just spent four seasons watching a 5-11 shooting guard named A.J. Abrams. It's just that, at least as a freshman, Lucas was a shooting guard who never shot. Calathes and Marreese Speights carried the Gator offense that season—everyone else was a role player. Lucas therefore remains something of an unknown quantity.

Varez Ward (6-2, 190, So.). On paper Ward is both turnover- and foul-prone and played a small role in the Longhorn offense during limited minutes as a freshman. But anyone who saw this team play Duke in the second round of the tournament last year has vivid memories of Barnes repeatedly calling clear-outs for Ward in the second half of that game. Though his team lost to the Blue Devils by five, Ward scored a career-high 16 points that day. Maybe that game was the start of something for Ward. We'll see.

Jordan Hamilton (6-7, 225, Fr.). Virtually as highly regarded out of high school as Bradley, Hamilton's a wing from southern California that Barnes says "knows how to score" but needs to work on his D.

J'Covan Brown (6-1, 185, Fr.). Brown was to have arrived on campus last year but failed to qualify academically. He was cleared for this season by the NCAA in August. Nevertheless it sounds like he has some work ahead of him if he wants to crack this rotation. "Not being here this summer set him back," Barnes has said.

Texas A&M

2009: 24-10 (9-7 Big 12), lost to Connecticut 92-66, NCAA Second Round
In-conference offense: 1.08 points per possession (4th)
In-conference defense: 1.05 points allowed per possession (7th)

What Texas A&M did well: *Groom still another raw talent for the second round of the draft.*

In 2008 seven-footer DeAndre Jordan finished up his freshman year at Texas A&M, declared for the draft, and was selected early in the second round by the L.A. Clippers. As a rookie last season Jordan came close to averaging as many minutes per game in the NBA (15) as he had in the Big 12 (20).

Then in 2009, 6-10 starter Chinemelu Elonu surprised many observers by following Jordan's example and declaring for the draft after his junior year. He was selected with the next-to-last pick in the draft by the Lakers.

This second consecutive early departure has led to some commentary suggesting that Mark Turgeon's Texas A&M team will be depleted this season. It would of course be a deeper (not to mention much taller) roster if it included Jordan as a junior and Elonu as a senior this year. But we'd do well to remember exactly what A&M is doing without here. Neither Jordan nor Elonu played featured roles in the offense, and the Aggies actually improved significantly last year in Jordan's absence. That's not to say the improvement was caused by Jordan leaving, of course, or that they might not have done even better had Jordan stuck around. It is merely to say that there's no reason why this team can't do very well this season without Elonu.

While the A&M defense took a noticeable step back last season (Big 12 opponents were suddenly more accurate from both sides of the arc and took better care of the ball), the regression on D was offset entirely by a much larger improvement on offense. This was mainly fueled by better three-point shooting, as the Aggies' in-conference accuracy from beyond the arc improved from 33 all the way to 39 percent. Josh Carter and B.J. Holmes proved to be a very productive duo on the perimeter, albeit in support of a team that doesn't shoot too many threes.

It's true that Elonu helped this surge in scoring along with excellent offensive rebounding. Still, don't be surprised this year if his shoes are filled—almost—by some combination of Bryan Davis (defensive rebounding) and a still burgeoning David Loubeau (offensive rebounding).

What we learned in 2009: *You can do a pretty fair imitation of Connecticut, until you run into Connecticut.*

Last year Connecticut won well-deserved notoriety for putting up some truly ridiculous numbers where free throw disparities are concerned. Thanks to an offense that made a lot of trips to the line and a defense that absolutely never fouled, Jim Calhoun's team enjoyed a big advantage in free throw attempts game in and game out in 2009.

No team was going to match the Huskies in that department, of course, but let it be said that Texas A&M wasn't too shabby here either.

Charity Is Uneven:
Largest Disparities In Free Throw Rates, 2009

School	FTA/FGA	Opp. FTA/FGA	Disparity
Connecticut	0.42	0.18	+0.24
Texas A&M	**0.49**	**0.30**	**+0.19**
North Carolina	0.38	0.24	+0.14
Oklahoma	0.43	0.29	+0.14
Washington	0.48	0.34	+0.14
Providence	0.40	0.28	+0.12

Conference games only: ACC, Big 12, Big East, Big Ten, Pac-10, SEC
FTA/FGA: FT attempts divided by FG attempts

Note that what was a nifty little added benefit for UConn, however, was much more important for the Aggies. Manufacturing free throw attempts was the strength of the A&M offense, while Turgeon's defense was better at not fouling than they were at any other single facet of the game on that side of the ball.

As it happens Connecticut and Texas A&M ended up colliding in the second round of the NCAA tournament, where the Huskies proved to be superior at this whole FTA disparity thing. UConn shot 27 free throws to A&M's 17 on their way to an easy 92-66 win.

What's in store for 2010: Turgeon could use either a disruptive perimeter defender, some added backcourt depth, or both. As it stands now, opponents playing A&M never turn the ball over, and that comprises the largest single obstacle between this team and a better defense.

Prospectus says: A&M has an impressive streak going, having not only reached the NCAA tournament in each of the last four seasons but also having won at least one game each time. But the margin for error personnel-wise in College Station seems to be getting thinner with each passing season. A year ago Turgeon lost Jordan, Joseph Jones, and Dominique Kirk. This year he has to replace Elonu and leading scorer Carter. It will be up to the veterans, Donald Sloan and Davis, to see that the streak continues. It'll be close.

Meet the Aggies

Donald Sloan (6-3, 205, Sr.). Sloan has a blog on the official A&M site. "As you know," he writes, "last year I declared for the NBA Draft and it was a good learning experience for me. I had some really impressive workouts and left good impressions on people in high places." You would think the second-leading scorer on what was in fact a very good Big 12 offense would at least have some wares to hawk at the next level. (After all, that description fits players like Cole Aldrich and Willie Warren.) But Sloan's was a unique case. Though he entered 2008-09 as a career 51 percent two-point shooter, he suffered through a tough year of shooting inside the arc, making just 40 percent of his attempts from in close. In each of his three seasons in College Station, Sloan's role in the offense has expanded and his two-point accuracy has gone down. On the plus side he took excellent care of the ball while posting the highest assist rate of any Aggie starter. A 74 percent free throw shooter last year, Sloan also contributes to the FTA disparity cited above by getting to the line quite often.

Bryan Davis (6-9, 250, Sr.). Texas A&M was a very good defensive rebounding team last year and Davis contributed substantially to this result. Indeed in the wake of Elonu's departure Davis's defensive rebound percentage will likely go up this year. On offense he makes 54 percent of his twos and gets to the line even more often than Sloan, though Davis shoots just 64 percent when he gets there.

Derrick Roland (6-4, 190, Sr.). Roland is Turgeon's defensive specialist, one who made the Big 12's All-Defensive team last year. On offense Roland struggled with both turnovers and his shooting while playing a supporting role.

B.J. Holmes (5-11, 175, Jr.). A pure shooter and a three-point specialist, Holmes made 42 percent of his threes last year coming off the bench and averaging 22 minutes a game. Curiously, he too gets to the line on a regular basis (where he shoots 84 percent), even though he poses no scoring threat whatsoever inside the arc: Holmes made just 29 percent of his twos as a sophomore.

David Loubeau (6-8, 230, So.). As a freshman Loubeau averaged just 14 minutes a game but he gave indications of being still another Aggie who can get to the line. Loubeau also showed flashes of being an outstanding offensive rebounder. Anyway, he finished the year strong, shooting 5-of-5 from the field and scoring 11 points in 20 minutes against Connecticut.

Dash Harris (6-1, 175, So.). Harris posted the highest assist rate on the team as a pass-first point guard coming off the bench, but like Roland he too suffered from recurring bouts of the turnover bug.

Naji Hibbert (6-6, 200, Fr.). A shooting guard from Baltimore, Hibbert is expected to help replace some of the points that were lost when Carter departed last year.

Khris Middleton (6-7, 215, Fr.). Middleton is a wing from North Charleston, South Carolina, who's reputed to be an excellent perimeter shooter.

Texas Tech

fast 14

2009: 14-19 (3-13 Big 12), lost to Missouri 81-60, Big 12 Tournament Quarterfinals
In-conference offense: 1.02 points per possession (9th)
In-conference defense: 1.11 points allowed per possession (12th)

What Texas Tech did well: *Beat Kansas.*

There are expectations attached to going 3-13 in conference play, as Texas Tech did in 2009. Like the fact that such a team probably struggled mightily on the road. Check: Pat Knight's team was 0-8 on Big 12 opponents' home floors. Or the fact that the team's few wins likely came at home against opponents near the bottom of the standings. Well, yes and no. The Red Raiders notched their three W's in Lubbock against Colorado, Baylor, and...Kansas.

And of the three games the one against the Jayhawks was by far the easiest win, as Tech blew KU out 84-65. It was senior night and Alan Voskuil gave the home crowd something to remember him by, hitting 9-of-14 threes and scoring 35 points.

The Raiders haven't exactly been world-beaters of late—they last won an NCAA tournament game in 2005—but one thing they can lay claim to without fear of contradiction is mastery over Kansas within the city limits of Lubbock. Despite the fact that Kansas has consistently been one of the top programs in the country over the past decade, the Jayhawks haven't won a game at the United Spirit Arena since 2003. Too bad for Knight this year's game is in Lawrence.

What we learned in 2009: *The name "Knight" isn't necessarily synonymous with patient half-court sets.*

Travis Ford has earned a reputation as something of a speed merchant with his up-tempo teams at UMass and now Oklahoma State. And everyone knows that Missouri under Mike Anderson likes to force the pace and try to create turnovers with their pressing defense. But few realize that the third Big 12 team to average more than 70 possessions per 40 minutes last year was not Kansas, or Oklahoma, or Texas. It was Texas Tech, which has been speeding up significantly now for the past two years.

Pat Goes Faster Than Bob Texas Tech Tempo, 2007-09		
Year	Pace	Big 12 rank
2007	64.5	10th
2008	70.4	2nd
2009	**71.7**	**3rd**
Conference games only *Pace: possessions per 40 minutes*		

Last year marked Pat Knight's first full season at the helm in Lubbock, and he pretty clearly indicated a preference for a fast pace. He still runs his father's motion offense, of course, but Knight's certainly not averse to seeing if an open look can be created at the very beginning of the possession.

What's in store for 2010: Knight likely hopes that he can settle on a clear rotation this season, a wish that went largely unfulfilled last year as the coach found himself calling on John Roberson, the now departed Alan Voskuil, and a cast of thousands. Indeed no player outside that Big Two started more than 21 of the Raiders' 31 regular season games in 2008-09. Playing deep into your bench can be a sign of strength, of course, but for Texas Tech last year it indicated merely that the Raiders were overmatched. Big 12 opponents made a lot of twos, got a lot of offensive rebounds, and most especially shot a lot of free throws. It all added up to the worst defense in the conference. So watch for Knight to make improvement on D a point of emphasis in 2010. (Meaning, if he doesn't he should.) One big difference could be the return of a healthy Trevor Cook.

Prospectus says: Last year under "Prospectus says" I said 2009 would be a success "if the defense improves to the point where it allows fewer than 1.05 points per trip in the Big 12." That didn't happen, as the Red Raiders instead allowed conference opponents to score 1.11 points per possession, the worst mark in the league. I therefore find that my new "Prospectus says" for this year needs only slight modification. The 2010 season will be a resounding success for Texas Tech if Pat Knight's offense and defense can meet out there somewhere around 1.05, scoring and allowing that many points per trip in Big 12 play. It's possible, but it will require improvement on both sides of the ball.

Meet the Red Raiders

John Roberson (5-11, 165, Jr.). Roberson's been the starting point guard for Tech for two seasons now, and while his turnover rate is still a little high he upped his assists markedly in his sophomore year. Though he's not much of a threat inside the arc (unless he's fouled—he's an 83 percent FT shooter), Roberson made 36 percent of his threes last year. If he has more help on the floor this year we're likely to see Roberson play to his strengths, perimeter shooting and getting to the line, and leave the twos to his teammates.

Mike Singletary (6-6, 215. Jr.). Knight chose to use Singletary almost exclusively as a sixth man last year but in fact the sophomore was as integral to the offense as Roberson—when he was on the floor. (He averaged 23 minutes a game.) His mission is simple: To draw fouls on the other team. Singletary shot 187 free throws in just 700 minutes of playing time last year and made 73 percent of all those attempts. He also made half his twos and was his team's best defensive rebounder. Note as well that Singletary played his best ball late in the year. Against Texas A&M in the Big 12 tournament, he scored 43 points (again, off the bench) fueled by 12-of-14 shooting at the line.

Nick Okorie (6-1, 195, Sr.). Okorie arrived last year as a junior college transfer and launched shots with the assurance of a featured scorer, making 37 percent of his occasional threes. The weightier portion of his game, however, was the 43 percent shooting he recorded on his frequent twos. Okorie missed four games last year with an ankle injury.

Trevor Cook (6-9, 240, Sr.). A back injury sidelined Cook in January last year and he missed the Raiders' last 19 games. Before that he had shown himself to be a shot-blocker who made 60 percent of his twos and suffered from recurring foul trouble over 14 games.

Robert Lewandowski (6-10, 240, So.). Lewandowski started 19 games as a freshman and was one of a handful of players in D-I last year to shoot a higher percentage on his twos (58) than on his free throws (56). If he can cut down on his turnovers and avoid being fouled, however, a freshman big man who makes 58 percent of his twos while playing a normal-sized role in the offense during his minutes, as Lewandowski did, would typically be expected to progress nicely as a sophomore.

D'Walyn Roberts (6-7, 200, Jr.). He lost his starting job in late January, but Roberts appeared in every game and set screens, played D, and made 55 percent of his twos strictly as a role player on offense.

David Tairu (6-3, 180, Jr.), Brad Reese (6-6, 190, Jr.), and **Theron Jenkins (6-6, 210, Jr.)** Knight will have three junior college transfers available as shooting guards and/or wings to add to his backcourt depth this season.

Big East Conference
Time For An Encore?

Due to a slew of returning players such as Notre Dame junior Luke Harangody and Pittsburgh sophomore DeJuan Blair, as well as a number of highly ranked recruits such as Georgetown freshman Greg Monroe and Rutgers freshman Mike Rosario, the Big East was the preseason pick to be the deepest and strongest conference in the nation last year. But as the season progressed, the league sorted itself into haves and have-nots. While seven teams posted conference efficiency margins above +0.08 and made the NCAA tournament, the rest of the Big East struggled.

Of the teams that missed the NCAA tournament, some like Providence had great conference records, but not enough quality wins to make the field. Others like Notre Dame and Georgetown seemed to have the right pieces, but suffered long losing streaks that ended their chances.

But the seven teams that made the NCAA tournament left enough of an imprint that the 2008-09 season was clearly a success for the Big East. The conference earned three one-seeds in the NCAA tournament, notched 17 NCAA wins, placed four teams in the Elite Eight, and sent two teams all the way to the Final Four. And in the eyes of many, the Big East was the most dominant conference in the nation last year.

With all that success, the conference experienced a lot of turnover in the offseason. Six teams bring back 50 percent or fewer minutes from last year. What should we expect from all the new faces? Sprinkled throughout the team previews, I have information on how likely freshman are to produce and players are to improve from season to season. This should provide some information about what to expect, on average.

But what the numbers mostly show is that freshman performance has a lot of variance. And like most previewers, I struggle with where to rank Connecticut, Syracuse, Pittsburgh, Notre Dame, Marquette, and Providence. For now I tend to rank these teams based on historical coaching success and recruit quality. But given all the freshman variability, the upside and downside for these teams remains great.

Also, I want to note that while there are a lot of new players this year, there are no new head coaches in the Big East this season. Perhaps the economy has put the clamps on athletic budgets, or perhaps it was not the right year to make a change. But several coaches such as DePaul's Jerry Wainwright and St. John's Norm Roberts have earned a reprieve this year and have at least one more chance to turn things around. *Dan Hanner*

BIG EAST PROSPECTUS

	2009 Record	Returning Minutes (%)	2010 Prediction
Villanova	13-5	64	15-3
Connecticut	15-3	38	13-5
Louisville	16-2	55	13-5
West Virginia	10-8	83	13-5
Cincinnati	8-10	79	11-7
Syracuse	11-7	44	11-7
Georgetown	7-11	69	10-8
Pitt	15-3	35	10-8
Notre Dame	8-10	50	9-9
Seton Hall	7-11	76	9-9
St. John's	6-12	96	8-10
Marquette	12-6	42	7-11
Providence	10-8	37	6-12
Rutgers	2-16	52	4-14
South Florida	4-14	65	3-15
DePaul	0-18	68	2-16

Cincinnati

2009: 18-14 (8-10 Big East), lost to DePaul 67-57, Big East First Round
In-conference offense: 1.02 points per possession (11th)
In-conference defense: 1.10 points allowed per possession (15th)

What Cincinnati did well: *Build a core and wait for a star.*

Cincinnati won seven of nine games in the middle of their Big East schedule, but otherwise the Bearcats were dismal. Last year they were a dominant offensive rebounding team, but Mike Williams has now run out of eligibility. Mick Cronin's team was also good at defending the three-point line and held opponents to a relatively low effective FG percentage of only 47.3 over the course of the entire season. But the team collapsed defensively in the Big East and allowed eFG's of 72.8, 55.4, 55.0, 56.1, and 52.8 in late-season losses.

That's not much to get excited about, but to the Cincinnati fanbase, none of that is important. The key thing this team did in 2009-2010 was let Deonta Vaughn and Yancy Gates shine. And by emphasizing star players, making playing time available, and appearing to be only one star player away from the NCAA tournament, the Bearcats hit the jackpot. This summer Cincinnati announced the late signing of one of the most talked about recruits in the entire country, McDonald's All-American Lance Stephenson.

What we learned in 2009: *Mick Cronin's recruiting remains boom or bust.*

A lot of second-division teams in the Big East can argue that they've never had the talent to compete at the elite level, but Cincinnati has not been in that box. They've recruited some nationally recognized high school players over the past few years, but the team has never really come together.

In 2005, consensus top-100 recruit Devan Downey came to Cincinnati, only to transfer when Bob Huggins was forced out and former assistant Andy Kennedy was not given the job as head coach. Downey became a superstar at South Carolina and is a senior this season. Verdict: Bust.

In 2006, borderline top-100 recruit Deonta Vaughn joined the team. From his freshman season, Vaughn led the team in scoring and became the clear leader of the Bearcats. Verdict: Boom.

Also in 2006, former McDonald's All-American Mike Williams joined the team after transferring from Texas. Williams immediately tore his Achilles tendon, rehabbed, returned, and performed admirably, but could not get Cincinnati into the NCAA tournament. Verdict: Williams had an offensive rating of 113.5 last year and was a great offensive rebounder, but because of the injury he was a minor Bust.

In 2007, the team added the mammoth center and top-100 recruit, Anthony McClain. He is yet to find his way into the rotation, however. McClain played only 12.3 percent of his team's minutes last season. Verdict: Bust.

That same year the team also welcomed borderline top-100 recruit Alvin Mitchell. Mitchell was terrible in 2007-08, shooting just 26 percent from the floor on 80 shots before being suspended from the team. He improved significantly in 2008-09, but was eventually encouraged to transfer. Verdict: Bust.

In 2008, the team added consensus top-100 recruit Yancy Gates. He quickly became the team's second best player behind Vaughn and his offensive rebounding percentage was second best in the Big East last year, behind only conference co-Player of the Year, DeJuan Blair. And any time you're compared to Blair, that's a tremendous compliment. Verdict: Boom.

Also in 2008, the team added consensus top-100 recruit Cashmere Wright, who was injured before the regular season started and sat out the year. Verdict: Bust for now.

In 2009, the team will add borderline top-100 recruit Ibrahima Thomas. The 6-10 Thomas clashed with new coach Travis Ford at Oklahoma State last year before transferring to Cincinnati. He'll be eligible to join the Bearcats in the middle of the season. Verdict: Bust at OSU.

The track record is hit or miss, but Vaughn and Gates have become the Bearcats best players, and their development has left the team only a handful of wins away from the NCAA tournament. And in 2009 the team will add the biggest recruit in a decade, New York City superstar Lance Stephenson.

On paper Stephenson solves a lot of the Bearcats' problems. Scoring—check. Stephenson is New York state's all-time leading scorer. Turnovers—check.

Instead of teams double-teaming Vaughn (which led to the worst turnover rate of his career in 2008-09), Stephenson will keep the defense honest. Free throw attempts—check. Stephenson loved to drive to the basket in high school. And for those who believe in intangibles, Stephenson did win the city championship in all four years of high school.

What's in store for 2010: As the above list shows, recruits are often boom or bust. Looking at the total population of players in the Recruiting Services Consensus Index (RSCI) Top 100 over the last four years:
• 25 percent had offensive efficiency ratings above 107.5 as freshmen.
• 25 percent had offensive efficiency ratings below 92.9 as freshmen.

To put these numbers in perspective, a rating below 92.9 is going to drag down any offense: Meaning a substantial minority of even top-100 recruits do not play well immediately. And because the McDonald's All-American team often includes recruits outside the top 20, many members of that august roster are busts too. But at the very top the picture's much rosier: Top-ten recruits that enroll in college usually pan out. For freshmen in the top ten:
• 25 percent had offensive efficiency ratings above 116.0 as freshmen.
• 25 percent have offensive efficiency ratings below 105.2 as freshmen.

In the last four years, the worst offensive ratings for freshman top-ten recruits belonged to Stanford's Brook Lopez (98.2), and Duke's Gerald Henderson (96.7). But Lopez and Henderson were not only outstanding defensive players, they also both developed into stars in subsequent years.

Thus, barring something shocking, Lance Stephenson will contribute this season. Putting him alongside Vaughn and Gates should make Cincinnati good enough to compete with the best teams in the Big East.

Prospectus says: Based on talent, Cincinnati could compete for a Big East title, but the defense was terrible in Big East play last year. Indeed in view of their poor defensive performance, the Bearcats were probably lucky to win eight games last season. Concerns about their defense lead me to project Cincinnati as an NCAA tournament team, but not a competitor for the Big East title.

Meet the Bearcats

Deonta Vaughn (6-1, 190, Sr.). Vaughn has not only been a prolific scorer for three straight years, he also had one of the highest assist rates in the Big East last year. Still, many felt he was not a natural point guard; he should benefit from the debut of Cashmere Wright at the point.

Yancy Gates (6-9, 260, So.). Not only is Gates an elite offensive rebounder as mentioned above, he's also a presence in the paint defensively. He has a strong block rate and defensive rebounding percentage.

Lance Stephenson (6-5, 210, Fr.). His nickname is "Born Ready."

Cashmere Wright (6-0, 175, Fr.). Elite point-guard recruit who sat out last year due to injury.

Rashad Bishop (6-6, 225, Jr.). He led the team in steal rate and will continue to do a lot of the dirty work for this year's Bearcat team.

Larry Davis (6-3, 195, Jr.). It seems like every team has a streaky shooting guard whose best role is coming off the bench.

Dion Dixon (6-3, 195, So.). Although he was even less consistent at three-point shooting than Davis, his complementary skills such as offensive and defensive rebounding kept Dixon in the starting lineup last year.

Steve Toyloy (6-8, 255, Sr.). A reserve rebounder in 2008-09, Toyloy could fill a critical role now that Mike Williams is gone.

Ibrahima Thomas (6-11, 230, Jr.). At Oklahoma State Thomas had the best offensive and defensive rebounding rates of any rotation player in 2007-08, and the best block rate in 2008-09. But he clashed with Travis Ford and ultimately decided to transfer. He will provide some athleticism and some much needed size in the paint when he becomes eligible mid-season.

Connecticut

P:
W: Walker
B:

2009: 31-5 (15-3 Big East), lost to Michigan State 82-73, NCAA Final Four
In-conference offense: 1.10 points per possession (5th)
In-conference defense: 0.95 points allowed per possession (2nd)

What Connecticut did well: *Win on the details.*

With six years of tempo-free statistics now compiled at Kenpom.com, the numbers show clearly why Jim Calhoun is one of the most successful coaches in the nation. His teams have a distinctive style and a clear model for success:

1) Force missed shots. In every one of the last six years, UConn has been one of the top ten teams in the nation at forcing misses.

Denied: UConn Defense, 2004-09		
Year	Opp. eFG%	D-I rank
2004	41.5	1st
2005	42.9	3rd
2006	43.0	3rd
2007	41.9	1st
2008	44.2	8th
2009	42.4	2nd
Opp. eFG%: opponent effective FG percentage		

2) Intimidate with the block. Blocked shots not only cause misses, they discourage teams from going for future layups. In each of the last two years UConn has had one of the lowest foul rates in the country, suggesting strongly that teams are simply afraid to take the ball inside against the Huskies. And despite perennial cries that UConn's bigs may be giving opponents too many offensive rebounds by always going for blocked shots, last year's group was in fact the best defensive rebounding team Calhoun has had in the last six years.

3) Don't take chances defensively. With the exception of 2007, a Calhoun defense doesn't force turnovers. But that doesn't matter when you can force misses at the rate UConn does. Players stay on their man and don't allow open looks.

4) Don't take chances offensively. UConn is very conservative in that they attempt fewer threes than any other offense in the Big East. But three-pointers lead to streaky play. Certainly there are times when players like A.J. Price have taken over from deep, but the core philosophy is to only take threes when a better shot is not available.

5) Get offensive boards. In each of the last six years, Calhoun's teams have been in the top 20 nationally in offensive rebounding percentage.

6) Get to the line. The free throw rate at UConn has been at its best in recent years.

Free Throws Are Easy Points: UConn Free Throw Rate, 2004-09		
Year	FTA/FGA	D-I rank
2004	34.5	233rd
2005	41.3	60th
2006	41.9	35th
2007	45.5	15th
2008	48.1	4th
2009	46.4	6th
FTA/FGA: FT attempts divided by FG attempts		

And the beauty of these six factors is that all of them require hard work and effort. It's not simply elite talent and great shooting that leads to glory for UConn. It's great coaching from the staff and great effort from the players.

What we learned in 2009: *Hard work eventually pays off.*

In the wake of the Huskies' Elite Eight loss in OT against George Mason in 2006, some wondered if Calhoun had lost a step. The group that was once the most feared team in the Big East had become a secondary consideration. But 2009 proved that was not the case. Connecticut spent part of the season as the number one team in the country, earned a one-seed in the NCAA tournament, and made it to the Final Four.

What's in store for 2010: Connecticut lost much of its team to graduation or the NBA. But Calhoun returns one McDonald's All-American in Kemba Walker, and adds a new one in freshman Alex Oriakhi. There's simply too much talent here for me to predict a big drop-off this season.

Prospectus says: In 2006-07, UConn suffered a mass defection to the NBA and posted a 6-10 record in Big

East play. And while that's still a possibility with a young team, on paper this roster is loaded. Walker and Dyson will find the slew of talented big men and help them get better. And if the team follows Calhoun's core philosophies, it will win a lot of games. The Huskies may return only 38 percent of their minutes from last year, but they're still expected to challenge for the Big East title this year.

Meet the Huskies

Jerome Dyson (6-4, 190, Sr.). Connecticut has been so talented the last few years, I've often questioned Dyson's shot selection. But he was more efficient last year, raising his offensive rating from 100.7 to 106.2. With one of the roster's best assist rates and an even better steal rate, he is an important veteran presence on a young UConn team.

Kemba Walker (6-1, 170, So.). With Walker and Dyson, UConn will have two of the conference's best distributors on the floor. And that will be important with a young team. I'd like to see both Walker and Dyson improve their three-point accuracy, but we've seen that perimeter shooting plays a relatively small role in the UConn offense. As long as Walker and Dyson can drive and dish, this team will be in good shape.

Stanley Robinson (6-9, 220, Sr.). Robinson returned from a first-semester suspension and played a key role for the team down the stretch. For instance he scored 28 points in the heartbreaking six-OT loss to Syracuse in the Big East tournament. Robinson had a high block rate last year, but on a team that also included one Hasheem Thabeet, he was hardly noticed as a defensive stopper.

Gavin Edwards (6-10, 230, Sr.). Edwards was towards the back of the rotation last year, but he was highly efficient when he was in the game, posting an offensive rating of 120.9.

Ater Majok (6-10, 235, Fr.). Majok is eligible to join the team in December. He was not allowed to play last season due to academic eligibility issues, but is a highly-regarded recruit, and is expected to play well when he's allowed on the court.

Alex Oriakhi (6-9, 240, Fr.). The McDonald's All-American is expected to be an inside force for Connecticut, but even if he's not, the team has plenty of talent in Robinson, Edwards, and Majok to dominate in the paint. You know a team has a lot of talent when it doesn't need a McDonald's All-American to play well.

Jamal Coombs-McDaniel (6-7, 210, Fr.). The high-school team in Tilton, New Hampshire, produced a pair of top-100 recruits last year in Oriakhi and Coombs-McDaniel. Who knew there was so much hoops talent in the Granite State?

Darius Smith (6-1, 170, Fr.). The team hopes Smith can spell Dyson and Walker.

DePaul out

2009: 9-24 (0-18 Big East), lost to Providence 83-74, Big East Second Round
In-conference offense: 0.92 points per possession (15th)
In-conference defense: 1.17 points allowed per possession (16th)

What DePaul did well: *Improve offensively over time.*

There's no sugarcoating a team that went winless in Big East play and had the worst conference efficiency margin of any BCS school at -0.25 PPP, but there is hope for DePaul. In 2008 the worst efficiency margin in a BCS conference belonged to Oregon State and the Beavers improved from -0.30 PPP all the way to -0.13 last year, a change that resulted in seven more wins in the Pac-10.

To perform its own Oregon State-type turnaround, DePaul will need to improve substantially on both sides of the ball. The good news, if there is any, is that in 2009 the Blue Demons' offense did improve slightly as the season wore on. (See table, next page.)

On the flip side, DePaul had the worst defense in the Big East last year. The 1.17 points allowed per possession meant Jerry Wainwright's team in effect made its opponents look like UCLA, Pitt, and North Carolina

Sign Of Improvement?
DePaul Offense, 2009

Month	PPP
January	0.90
February	0.93
March*	0.95

PPP: points per possession
* Includes Big East tournament

on a regular basis. Not to mention the defense actually got worse as the season progressed and the losses mounted. In February DePaul gave up a whopping 1.25 points per trip.

Yet in a strange way, the defensive collapse may be the best sign of hope for this team. At times in his career Wainwright has shown he can coach an elite defense. In 2007 at DePaul the Blue Demons were 40th nationally in adjusted defensive efficiency, and in 2004 at Richmond, Wainwright's Spiders ranked 11th in the nation by the same metric. Assuming Wainwright can get his team to put in the effort they lost in February of last year, the defense will be better, even if questions remain (and they do) about whether the offensive turnaround can be sustained.

What we learned in 2009: *Dar Tucker is a symptom of a larger offensive problem.*

Dar Tucker has been labeled a "me-first" player, and the classic example of what went wrong with DePaul's offense last year. With his team struggling mightily, Tucker quickly became interested in padding his own stats instead of helping the Blue Demons get better. Tucker improved his points per game from 13.6 to 18.5, but saw his individual offensive efficiency fall from 107.4 to 95.0. And despite the fact that he was often double-teamed due to his high volume of shots, he had a relatively low assist rate. At the end of the season, Tucker declared for the NBA draft. (He went undrafted.)

The question in the data is whether this was a one-year aberration or a long-term trend for Jerry Wainwright's teams. Looking at Ken Pomeroy's tempo-free data for Wainwright's last six seasons (four at DePaul, two at Richmond), the following trends emerge:

• Wainwright's never had an elite shooting team. The 2007 season was the best year here, but even his NCAA tournament team at Richmond struggled to make baskets.

• Nor has the coach ever had a team that was able to

draw fouls. This has been particularly true at DePaul.

• Lastly, Wainwright has always had teams with low turnover rates.

Together this paints an unpleasant picture. While a low turnover rate is generally a good thing, it can also hint at a team that doesn't move the ball effectively to get easy shots. So while DePaul avoids the risk of forcing the ball inside to Mac Koshwal or throwing the ball away on a backdoor cut to Will Walker, Wainwright's teams have also gone without the reward of easy buckets and free throws. The team is therefore left to defer to players who can create their own shot.

Tucker was a player who could create his own shot last season. And while ultimately he may have been trying to pad his own stats, he was often the best option this offense had. As a player who could shoot without forcing the ball inside, Tucker was not only symbolic of last year's DePaul team, he also represented a recurring feature in Wainwright's career.

What's in store for 2010: With Tucker gone, the team will now look to Will Walker to take a lot of the shots, while also hoping that one of several new players, such as junior college transfer Mike Stovall, is prepared to play and score right away.

Prospectus says: There is good reason to believe Wainwright will get his team to play better defense in 2008-09. The 1.25 points allowed per possession in February was simply too extreme to recur. But the historical data pose serious questions about whether Wainwright's offense can create the type of easy baskets needed to succeed in a BCS conference. The improved defense should produce a couple of Big East wins this season, but DePaul may be in for another long year.

Meet the Blue Demons

Will Walker (6-0, 190, Sr.). Walker did everything for the Blue Demons last year and will be expected to do more in 2008-09. He was the team's second leading scorer, its best three-point shooter, and most efficient scorer overall. Walker also led the team in steal rate and almost never turned the ball over despite taking over a quarter of his team's shots while on the floor.

Mac Koshwal (6-10, 255, Jr.). An outstanding rebounder and the team's third leading scorer, Koshwal was the only effective post player for DePaul in 2008-09.

Eric Wallace (6-6, 215, So.). Wallace was part of an impressive 2007 Ohio State recruiting class that included Evan Turner and John Diebler. But those two players played essentially the same position as Wallace and he couldn't make it off the bench. So he transferred to DePaul and is now eligible to join the team. Normally if a player can't beat out the competition on the depth chart, I assume he won't be an impact transfer. Then again Turner and Diebler are star players, so there may be hope for Wallace.

Jeremiah Kelly (6-1, 170, So.). An inability to shoot limited Kelly's ability to drive and create last season. Defenders could stay back rather than challenge him on the perimeter, putting a ceiling on Kelly's effectiveness as a point guard.

Michael Bizoukas (6-1, 175, So.). Bizoukas could challenge Kelly for playing time at point guard, but his shooting was even worse than that of his classmate.

Devin Hill (6-9, 200, So.). Forced to play significant minutes as a freshman due to the limited post options on the team, Hill was not an effective offensive player. On the other hand he was an elite shot-blocker and important defensive presence.

Mike Stovall (6-5, 200, Jr.) Will the skills of this junior college transfer translate to the rugged Big East?

Tony Freeland (6-6, 200, Fr.). By simply chipping in as an offensive rebounder and athletic player, Freeland can play a role on this team. But no one in DePaul's freshman class is a sure thing.

Georgetown

2009: 16-15 (7-11 Big East), lost to Baylor 74-72, NIT First Round
In-conference offense: 1.01 points per possession (12th)
In-conference defense: 1.03 points allowed per possession (7th)

What Georgetown did well: *Convert easy buckets.*

Though doing so often results in a slow-paced game, John Thompson III's teams methodically try to get the ball inside, working backdoor cuts and looking for wide open post feeds to generate layups. Thompson's modified Princeton offense consistently puts players in position to make easy baskets. With the exception of his first year at Georgetown, his teams have always had one of the best two-point shooting percentages in the country.

Layups Are Good Shots: Twos Under John Thompson III			
School	Year	2FG%	D-I rank
Princeton	2004	56.0	4th
Georgetown	2005	51.8	41st
Georgetown	2006	53.5	15th
Georgetown	2007	57.8	2nd
Georgetown	2008	56.3	2nd
Georgetown	2009	54.8	7th

That continued in 2008-09 with players like Austin Freeman and Jason Clark posting two-point percentages of 57.3 and 61.5, respectively, on numerous cuts

to the basket. And Greg Monroe replaced Roy Hibbert in the post and was sensational from the start. Not only did Monroe come close to Hibbert's high shooting percentage, he was able to draw fouls at an even higher rate than Hibbert.

Despite the easy baskets and numerous free throws, however, the Princeton offense stalled in 2008-09. While Monroe was able to fill in for Hibbert, no one was able to replace the lethal three-point shooting of Jonathan Wallace. And without a consistent perimeter shooter besides DaJuan Summers, whose presence was often demanded in the paint, this offense struggled. Hoya opponents were not forced to play out on shooters and the cuts and drives to the basket were not as wide open as in past years. The team still worked the ball around for easy baskets, but with more congestion in the paint the team's turnover rate increased substantially. This was particularly true in the second half of the season: In the 15 contests after the Duke game in mid-January, Georgetown turned the ball over on 24 percent of their possessions. The net result was the Hoyas' worst adjusted offensive efficiency since Thompson's first year with the team.

The defense was also down across the board, proving what a huge role Hibbert had played. In the two years Hibbert started, the defense was in the top ten nationally in FG defense. But with the big guy gone, the defense was only 40th nationally at forcing missed shots. Not to mention there were times when Georgetown attempted to play elite defense without defensive rebounding. Against Memphis, for example, the Hoyas held their opponent to an effective FG percentage of 37.8—but allowed the Tigers to grab fully 47 percent of their own missed shots.

The defensive rebounding did improve slightly after 6-8 Nikita Mescheriakov was added to the rotation in late January. Prior to that time, Georgetown allowed opponents to grab 38 percent of their misses, but with Mescheriakov in the rotation this number dropped to 33.

What we learned in 2009: *Talent does not always ensure an NCAA tournament berth.*

In 2007-08 Wallace forced the other team to spread the floor and was a precision passer. Roy Hibbert was a great rebounder and the perfect defender to stop opponents from driving into the lane. Wallace and Hibbert were lesser known recruits, but the above stats suggest something else. They were a perfect fit for the system.

Last year Georgetown had three McDonald's All-Americans in Monroe, Freeman, and Chris Wright, as well as one of the most versatile forwards in the country in Summers. But the pieces didn't fit. It wasn't that Wright couldn't drive by his man on occasion. It wasn't that Monroe didn't require a double-team. It wasn't that Freeman couldn't finish when he caught the ball in traffic. But on a night-to-night basis, the errors in rebounding and turnovers were costly. At their best, the team had the talent to crush UConn and Syracuse. But at their worst, the small deficiencies led to a lot of close losses.

What's in store for 2010: In the offseason the team faced the prospect of losing both Summers and Monroe to the NBA draft. But while Summers did indeed take his game to the next level, Monroe eventually elected to stay in school. I think this was the best possible scenario for Georgetown. Summers always seemed out of place in John Thompson's system. He projected as a Jeff Green type, a versatile driving forward, but with the exception of an occasional monster dunk Summers was much more comfortable on the perimeter. It often seemed as if he were auditioning for a two-guard role in the NBA instead of playing in

the paint as his team needed. And in his final season, that translated to the defensive end as well. Summers' defensive rebounding rate fell from 17.4 percent two years ago to 11.5 last year.

Summers may find the NBA more to his liking, but Monroe is a perfect fit on any team. From holding his own against Hasheem Thabeet to scoring over ten points in all but four games as a freshman, Monroe excelled. Georgetown fans are lucky to get to see him play for another season.

Prospectus says: Based on some blow-out victories and close losses, the margin-of-victory statistics say Georgetown was better than a 16-15 team last year. And with three McDonald's All-Americans returning, particularly Greg Monroe, there is a lot to be excited about. But I think depth will remain the Achilles heel of this team. With Omar Wattad transferring, Jesse Sapp graduating, and DaJuan Summers departing for the NBA, the Hoyas have just ten scholarship players on the roster again the season. There is simply no room for injuries or players who need time to develop around the stars. Then again there are a lot of other teams in the Big East that lack depth this year, and Georgetown's core should be enough for this team to return to the NCAA tournament.

Meet the Hoyas

Greg Monroe (6-11, 245, So.). At times last season, he was listed as a top-five pick in the NBA draft. Besides his blocks, rebounds, and shooting percentage, he also led the team in steals.

Chris Wright (6-1, 210, Jr.). Wright is great in transition and great at creating for his teammates. But the methodical Princeton offense doesn't always complement his athleticism. He needs to improve his three-point shooting for the offense to produce at an elite level.

Austin Freeman (6-4, 225, Jr.). The team's most efficient scorer, Freeman lets the game come to him. He shoots three-pointers when wide open and takes layups when the cut to the basket is there. But given the team's limited depth, there are times when he needs to be more aggressive.

Hollis Thompson (6-7, 205, Fr.). Thompson may be expected to start right away. By enrolling last spring, he was able to get a head-start.

Jason Clark (6-2, 170, So.). A combo guard who plays a lot of roles on this team, Clark can score from three, cut to the basket, and bring the ball up the court. But he had too many turnovers last season.

Julian Vaughn (6-9, 245, Jr.). Vaughn struggled with turnovers at Florida State and that continued at Georgetown last year. That limits his ability as an offensive player, but he provides vital rebounds and blocks when Monroe takes a seat on the bench.

Nikita Mescheriakov (6-8, 215, Jr.). In January Mescheriakov joined the rotation as the team made a concerted effort to play a bigger lineup. Although he didn't get that many boards, the team's defensive rebounding did improve with more size on the floor. Other than an occasional three-pointer, he is not a star offensively or defensively, and the fact that he was regularly playing 20 minutes a game at the end of the year indicates the lack of depth on this team.

Henry Sims (6-10, 225, So.). Sims was a player who could have benefited from a redshirt year, but Thompson was forced to play him right away due to the team's limited depth.

Louisville

2009: 31-6 (16-2 Big East), lost to Michigan State 64-52, NCAA Elite Eight
In-conference offense: 1.06 points per possession (8th)
In-conference defense: 0.92 points allowed per possession (1st)

What Louisville did well: *Defend well enough to win a (conference) championship.*

Obviously under Rick Pitino the heart of Louisville has been its defense. With the exception of their first year in the Big East, Louisville has consistently had one of the best adjusted defensive efficiency ratings in the nation.

Defense Wins Games : Louisville Adjusted Defensive Efficiency, 2004-09			
Conference	Year	Adj Eff.	D-I rank
C-USA	2004	83.9	1st
C-USA	2005	88.7	14th
Big East	2006	92.8	36th
Big East	2007	88.4	16th
Big East	2008	84.1	5th
Big East	2009	84.2	2nd
All games			

Statistically, the team was not dramatically better in 2008-09. Yes, Louisville forced a few more turnovers, blocked a few more shots, and allowed a few less free throws. But the numbers were very similar to the previous year. The key in 2008-09 was that the team finally put it all together. It no longer let an unexpected loss (see Seton Hall 2007-08) or a slew of injuries derail the season. Whereas the previous two seasons had ended up one game short of the conference crown, the 2008-09 team delivered Louisville's first Big East title in only the school's fourth year in the league. And the team followed up the regular-season title with a Big East tournament title as well.

What we learned in 2009: *David Padgett isn't walking through the door, but when the players buy in, the offense can be elite.*

Despite the conference title, the offense took a minor step back in 2008-09. Statistically, the main difference was a drop in free throw attempts as Earl Clark became more of a jump shooter and a little less aggressive around the basket. And with David Padgett and Derrick Caracter gone, the net impact was a lower free throw rate for the team. But hidden in the overall numbers is the fact that the team struggled to find an offensive identity for much of last season.

It's clear that Padgett was the type of player you can never really replace. He was the perfect point forward for the Louisville squad and no one could match his incredible decision making. And during a four game stretch from January 31 to February 12, the team seemed to struggle to make good decisions and find good shots. During that stretch the team launched too many threes, missed too many shots and scored just 0.87 points per possession.

But something changed after Louisville was blown out by Notre Dame. Maybe the team finally bought in and realized they needed to run Rick Pitino's offense to be successful. Maybe things just finally started to click. But in mid-February, the team found the magic formula. Over the next 13 games, Louisville averaged 1.16 points per trip. And with an elite offense to match the elite defense, the Cardinals won their next 13 games, earned a one-seed in the NCAA tournament, and reached the Elite Eight.

What's in store for 2010: Admittedly with all the blogs and Twitter accounts, the world of sports information has changed dramatically. One positive aspect of this is that coaches can choose to talk about their teams directly and unfiltered by the media. And Rick Pitino does this better than anyone at his website. So while I can provide my analysis of the returning players, Pitino's blog has provided his first-hand thoughts. Some of these are referenced below.

In terms of departures, Louisville will miss Earl Clark's ability to score inside and outside, but Clark was not one of the team's most efficient scorers. And given the talent on this team, the Cardinals may be able to replace hiss production. The loss of Terrence Williams will be more critical as Williams did his best David Padgett impression down the stretch last year and was a key distributor during the team's amazing run.

Prospectus says: The X-factor this year for Louisville will be the off-court distractions. And there's no question that some exceptionally crude chants are going to be directed at Pitino this year. Add some recent off-court issues involving Terrence Jennings and Jerry Smith, and this is a team that is desperate to get on the court and play some actual games.

But from a basketball perspective, this team is as loaded as any team in the Big East. I see only two potential downsides for the Cardinals. First on offense, the lack of consistent distributors could lead to some ugly games early in the season. And on defense, the returning players will have to improve their defensive rebounding. But those are things that can be sorted out as the season progresses. And I fully expect this team to compete for a Big East title again.

Meet the Cardinals

Samardo Samuels (6-9, 260, So.). There's no question that Earl Clark will be missed, but Samuels is arguably the more indispensible offensive player. Skilled post players are simply impossible to find

and retain in college basketball and his 58 percent two-point shooting, high free throw rate, high block rate, and outstanding offensive rebounding put him on everyone's preseason watch list. One thing he needs to work on is his defensive rebounding. Clark and Williams were so good on the defensive glass that you might not have noticed Samuels' low production here last year, but he'll need to carry more of that load this season.

Edgar Sosa (6-2, 175, Sr.). A big component of the winning streak last year was Williams distributing the ball. But with Williams graduating, an even larger burden falls on Sosa to run the offense. A starter since his freshman year, Sosa's turnover rate has steadily increased the last two seasons and his shooting percentage, particularly from three-point range, reached a career low last season. The result is this statement from Pitino on his website: "It takes certain players longer to mature than others."

Jerry Smith (6-2, 190, Sr.). Smith on the other hand is everything you expect out of a Pitino player. His steal rate was one of the best in the Big East, and he can light it up on the offensive end where he made 54 threes last year, shooting 41 percent. That's the most three pointers of any returning player and a key reason why he was the most efficient individual scorer on the team last season.

Terrence Jennings (6-10, 240, So.). Jennings could have started for a lot of Big East teams last season. He shot almost 60 percent and really crashed the offensive boards.

Preston Knowles (6-1, 190, Jr.). According to Pitino, Knowles "is the best sixth man in the country." And I cannot argue with that. Knowles has the best steal rate of any returning player, he had the highest three point percentage on the team (shooting 43 percent with 48 made threes), and he had one of the lowest turnover rates in the Big East last year. If Smith weren't so darn consistent, Knowles would probably get a chance to start.

Peyton Siva (6-0, 175, Fr.). Pitino notes that Siva will see lots of playing time this season, and I wonder if he won't challenge Sosa for his starting job. Siva is a McDonald's All-American out of Seattle, the team's third McDonald's All-American in the last four years.

Jared Swopshire (6-8, 220, So.) Swopshire is the team's "most dedicated player," according to Pitino, but like Samuels and Jennings, he isn't a natural passer. And without anyone to play the Padgett/Williams role, I think the team may have to play three guards more frequently this season.

Reginald Delk (6-5, 200, Sr.). I might have picked Knowles to see more playing time, but Pitino sug-

gests Delk may be in position to win one of the starting spots. Part of having a great defense is having a tall lineup and Delk is a taller guard on the team.

Rakeem Buckles (6-8, 215, Fr.). Another consensus top-100 recruit who I would expect to get some playing time this year. But Pitino is more cautious, stating that Buckles will "need time to mature physically."

Marquette

P:
W:
B: Hayward

2009: 25-10 (12-6 Big East), lost to Missouri 83-79, NCAA Second Round
In-conference offense: 1.12 points per possession (2nd)
In-conference defense: 1.04 points allowed per possession (8th)

What Marquette did well: *Score.*

With three of the most productive four-year guards in NCAA history in Jerel McNeal, Wesley Matthews, and Dominic James, as well as one of the most versatile junior forwards in the game in Lazar Hayward, Marquette had one of the most dominating offenses in the Big East last year. New coach Buzz Williams seemingly had the talent to let the team play on autopilot, but he refined the offense and the team's offensive efficiency improved from 1.06 points per possession in conference play in 2008 to 1.12 in 2009. The improvements were mostly subtle things.

For example, Matthews had already been incredibly effective at drawing fouls and making free throws, and the team made sure he had the ball in his hands more often in 2009. He attempted 167 free throws and made 79 percent of those shots as a junior. As a senior those numbers jumped to 257 and 83 percent, respectively. And Haywood, who had always been pretty good at ball handling for a 6-6 forward, became more confident in his shot and lowered his turnover rate to one of the lowest levels in the Big East.

What we learned in 2009: *Marquette's year was a tale of two seasons.*

On February 25, Marquette was 23-4, on pace for a protected seed if not a one-seed in the NCAA tournament, and was hosting the number two team in the country in Connecticut. At the 8:41 mark of the first half against UConn, Marquette took the lead 28-22 and ESPN panned to the Marquette student section which looked like a mosh pit with joyous students jumping

up and down. Marquette was on top of the world.

But what the students didn't know at that point was that the season was about to take a turn for the worse. James broke a bone in his left foot in that game, and would miss most of the rest of the season. (He did appear briefly in the NCAA tournament.) And the dreams of a deep NCAA run came to an abrupt end. Marquette lost five of its final six games, and lost in the second round of the NCAA tournament to Missouri.

Missing Dominic James: Marquette 2009, Before And After The UConn Game		
	Before	After
Pace	68.9	65.6
PPP	1.14	1.07
eFG%	54.1	45.5

Conference games only
Pace: possessions per 40 minutes; PPP: points per possession
eFG%: effective FG percentage

Certainly Marquette may have struggled down the stretch even with a healthy James, as the schedule was back-loaded with the conference's toughest opponents. But it seems likely that the team would have won a few of the marquee matchups with James in the lineup, and been in a position for at least a Sweet 16 run. But the wonderful four-year journey did not have a happy ending for McNeal, Matthews, and James.

What's in store for 2010: In 2005 Marquette welcomed three consensus top-100 recruits that became some of the biggest stars in the program's history.

Now in 2009, the team hopes the formula works anew. The recruiting class once again includes three top-100 recruits in Junior Cadougan, Erik Williams, and Jeronne Maymon. Can lighting strike twice?

Although the loss of Tom Crean was painful, at least the timing was good. By departing when McNeal, Matthews, and James were returning as seniors, Buzz Williams had time to plan for their departure and build a solid recruiting class for the new season. Besides the three top-100 recruits, the school welcomes a freshman center from Senegal and two junior college transfers who are expected to contribute immediately. Unfortunately, Cadougan injured his Achilles tendon in September and is expected to miss the entire season. His loss will hurt, as Williams expects a lot from this freshman class.

The other concern for this season is that the Marquette defense was significantly worse under Buzz Williams than under Tom Crean. Obviously the team's lack of size may be responsible, but the tallest player on the roster, 7-2 Youssoupha Mbao, may be more of a long-term project and might not be ready to play extended minutes for the team from the beginning.

Prospectus says: Buzz Williams has spent a lifetime working his way up the coaching ranks and he's finally earned the opportunity to prove himself with a new set of players. No longer will he be inheriting Tom Crean's team, the time has come for Williams to show what he can do.

Like Providence, Marquette has a couple of efficient returning players, and a big recruiting class that is expected to perform right away. And while Marquette's recruiting class is rated higher than that of Providence, there are no guarantees. In fact, with Cadougan already injured, the dream that the top-100 trio will duplicate 2005-2006 is in doubt.

But my biggest concern this year is whether Marquette can play the kind of defense needed to stay in the Big East's upper division. The team made due with a smaller lineup last year, but they had a veteran team. And even with all those veterans, the two-point defense was still near the bottom of Division I. Can Williams bring the defense around enough to keep this young team in games? If not, it could be a long season.

Meet the Golden Eagles

Lazar Hayward (6-6, 225, Sr.). Already a 1,200-point scorer who was highly efficient inside and outside, Hayward will now be the focal point of opposing defenses' attention. His shooting percentage might fall and his turnover rate might increase somewhat, but he is simply too versatile a player not to be a star again in 2010. Not only does he do a great job on the offensive end, his defensive rebounding rate was one of the best in the Big East. In fact, his defensive rebounding percentage of 21.6 compared favorably to Hasheem Thabeet's 22.0 last season.

Jimmy Butler (6-6, 215, Jr.). Butler was extremely efficient on the offensive end, converting over 50 percent of his shots and virtually never turning the ball over. He had the fourth lowest turnover rate in the Big East which led to an offensive rating of 131.2. But he also almost never touched the ball, taking just 10.8 percent of his team's shots when on the floor. He basically only attempted wide open shots when one of his talented teammates drew the defense away from him. How will he perform without the senior trio to feed him the ball and draw the defense's attention? Butler's also part of a catch-22 for Marquette. Can the team really afford to play two undersized post players and still defend the paint?

Maurice Acker (5-8, 165, Sr.). After the injury to James, Acker jumped into the lineup. While his performance was passable, he struggled to score against the taller Big East guards and his overall efficiency numbers were not quite good enough. He will still have a role on the team, but Marquette may be better off with him coming off the bench again in 2009-10.

David Cubillan (6-0, 175, Sr.). A senior guard, Cubillan's seen his minutes steadily decline at Marquette. He will have to improve his play substantially to keep the incoming class from taking his already limited minutes.

Jeronne Maymon (6-6, 250, Fr.). One of a trio of top-100 recruits, Maymon will be expected to play and score right away for Marquette.

Junior Cadougan (6-1, 205, Fr.). Cadougan was expected to be the star point guard, but an injury has likely derailed his freshman season.

Erik Williams (6-7, 200, Fr.). The third of the three top-100 recruits, the key for the season may be how soon Williams learns to defend bigger post players.

Youssoupha Mbao (7-2, 215, Fr.). A freshman from Senegal who could provide some much needed size in the paint, but he may need some time to refine his game.

Darius Johnson-Odom (6-2, 200, So.). This junior college transfer should be able to drive and penetrate and provide some excitement with Cadougan out for the season.

Dwight Buycks (6-3, 190, Jr.). Another combo guard who will compete for playing time.

Notre Dame

P:
W:
B: Harangody

2009: 21-15 (8-10 Big East), lost to Penn State 67-59, NIT Semifinals
In-conference offense: 1.08 points per possession (6th)
In-conference defense: 1.09 points allowed per possession (13th)

What Notre Dame did well: *Avoid turnovers.*

Ken Pomeroy has been tracking adjusted offensive efficiency for six years, and Mike Brey's team has had a top 25 offense in five of those seasons. The formula has been simple. Limit the number of turnovers. By simply taking open shots, instead of forcing the ball into traffic, Notre Dame gets more shots per possession than most teams. And more shots leads to more points. Last year comprised the pinnacle of this philosophy as Notre Dame had the lowest turnover rate in Division I.

Statistically, Ryan Ayers led the way. Among players who were on the floor for at least 40 percent of their team's minutes, Ayers had the third lowest turnover rate in the country last season. But Ayers is a spot-up shooter who was not asked to do much with the ball. The real key was former Big East player of the year Luke Harangody who achieved the sixth lowest turnover rate in the nation despite taking almost 36 percent of his team's shots during his minutes. As a post player who operated in traffic on most occasions, Harangody's ability to avoid turnovers was truly spectacular.

The combination of Harangody inside and lethal sharpshooters Ayers and Kyle McAlarney—who made 94 and 124 threes, respectively, while each shooting over 40 percent—made Notre Dame a lethal offense at times. In 11 games the team scored better than 1.20 points per possession. And when the Fighting Irish were knocking down shots, the team was simply unbeatable.

What we learned in 2009: *Notre Dame did not get better.*

Most 2008-09 previews of the Irish went something like this: "Notre Dame loses only one rotation player in starter Rob Kurz. And with everyone else returning, including reigning Big East player of the year Luke Harangody, the Fighting Irish should compete for a Big East title."

But those title aspirations were soon crushed. A seven-game losing streak starting in mid-January relegated the team to the NIT. The losing streak was the product of an early four-game stretch where the team couldn't score and a late three-game slump where the defense was completely absent.

Let's start with the offense. While on average returning players get better each year, this effect is far from uniform. Looking at all returning D-I players over the last four years, the next table tabulates the likelihood their individual offensive efficiency rating increased or decreased.

Change In Offensive Efficiency: Returning Division I Players, 2006-2009			
Change in ORtg	Freshman to Sophomore	Sophomore to Junior	Junior to Senior
+10 or more	32.6%	23.0%	19.0%
0 to +10 points	32.1%	34.8%	36.0%
-10 to 0 points	24.5%	29.3%	33.0%
-10 points or less	10.8%	12.9%	12.0%
Minimum 10% of team's minutes played			

While the majority of players become more efficient over time, only one-third of freshman and less than a quarter of sophomores and juniors experience big leaps from year to year. And a surprisingly high number of players regress every season. (Note that these numbers are very similar even if I control for changes in team quality or changes in the percentage of shots taken by the player.) And at Notre Dame, this regression is exactly what we saw in 2008-09:

Change In Offensive Efficiency: Notre Dame 2007-08 Vs. 2008-09			
Player	2008	2009	Change
Ayers	123.3	122.2	-1.1
McAlarney	115.0	111.0	-4.0
Harangody	110.2	109.2	-1.0
Zeller	119.6	106.7	-12.9
Jackson	93.4	100.7	+7.3
Hillesland	104.2	98.5	-5.7
Peoples	114.5	97.5	-17.0
Minimum 10% of teams minutes played			

Only Tory Jackson's offensive rating went up from one year to the next, as he became a slightly better shooter. But while the overall offense took a tiny step back, it was still elite nationally.

The real problem was the defense. Many people asked the simple question: Could Rob Kurz really have meant so much to this team? Well, yes, it turns that Kurz meant a lot. In 2007-08 he had one of the top block rates in the Big East, and as a reliable defensive rebounder he was a key defensive presence in the paint for the Fighting Irish. Without Kurz, Notre Dame's adjusted defensive efficiency fell from 92.4 to 97.2.

But while the loss of Kurz hurt, I think the long term issue is that Brey's teams play a passive zone defense. In the six years Pomeroy has been tracking defensive efficiency, Brey's teams have never forced turnovers. In five of the six years, the team has ranked above 300 in D-I in turnovers forced. And in 2008-09 Notre Dame had the worst forced turnover rate in the country.

On defense, the Irish wait for the other team to take shots and hope that it's a miss. That strategy might have worked in some conferences in some years. But in 2009 the Big East was a talented veteran conference and the elite teams simply dissected and destroyed this passive zone.

With both the nation's lowest offensive turnover rate and its lowest defensive turnover rate, Notre Dame was truly an extreme statistical outlier in 2008-09.

What's in store for 2010: Ayers and McAlarney have graduated and the two highly efficient three-point shooters will be hard to replace. But the team does add Mississippi State transfer Ben Hansbrough, who is now eligible. Hansbrough shot 41 and 36 percent on his threes in two seasons in Starkville while making over 100 total threes. The incoming freshman class also brings a lot of size to the roster. To the extent that height predicts defensive performance, this could help Notre Dame defensively in the coming years.

Prospectus says: This team is hard to predict. On the upside, the college basketball world is blessed to get to see Harangody play another season, and Brey's track record as an offensive mastermind suggests this team will find ways to score. On the downside, a preseason injury to Purdue transfer Scott Martin limits the depth of this team, and with several key players leaving the offense may fade slightly. But the key downside is the defense. Until Notre Dame changes its defensive philosophy, the best-case scenario for 2010 remains an early NCAA tournament exit.

Meet the Fighting Irish

Luke Harangody (6-8, 245, Sr.). A dominant offensive and defensive rebounder, a solid shot-blocker, and a player who never turns the ball over, Harangody is a former Big East player of the year because of his prolific scoring. He remained an efficient scorer last season despite using 34 percent of his team's possessions, the most of any player in a BCS conference.

Tory Jackson (5-11, 195, Sr.). Jackson improved his shooting substantially in 2008-09, but with the rest of the team floundering, his assist rate fell last year.

Ben Hansbrough (6-3, 205, Jr.). The brother of Tyler, Ben Hansbrough is the best hope to replace the perimeter shooting that hitherto has been supplied by Ayers and McAlarney.

Jonathan Peoples (6-3, 205, Sr.). While his three-point shooting percentage has always been decent, Peoples has never taken a lot of shots and may be relegated to serving as the first guard coming off the bench.

Tyrone Nash (6-8, 230, Jr.). Nash earned more playing time as the season progressed last year and was an efficient finisher around the basket. But he doesn't have the outside touch of Harangody and he can disappear for large stretches of time on the floor. Nash will either improve this year or see the younger players pass him in the rotation.

Jack Cooley (6-9, 244, Fr.). Notre Dame brings in a large number of post players such as Cooley, hoping that Brey can work his offensive magic and bring them along right away.

Joey Brooks (6-5, 215, Fr.). Brooks and his fellow freshmen all have enough upside to project as Big East rotation players.

Mike Broghammer (6-9, 243, Fr.). Most of this year's new post players probably envisioned replacing Harangody after he left for the NBA. But with the big guy returning, Broghammer and his mates will get the opportunity to play with him instead.

Thomas Knight (6-9, 251, Fr.). Aside from scoring, Notre Dame hopes that Knight and/or another freshman can become a defensive stopper in the paint.

Pitt

Slow 3|7

2009: 31-5 (15-3 Big East), lost to Villanova 78-76, NCAA Elite Eight
In-conference offense: 1.17 points per possession (1st)
In-conference defense: 1.01 points allowed per possession (4th)

What Pitt did well: *Grab offensive rebounds.*

If you've read any statistical article about Pittsburgh in the past two years, you know that DeJuan Blair was a complete monster offensively, with the most dominating offensive rebounding stats imaginable. His 23.6 offensive rebounding percentage last season not only led the nation, it was the highest rate in the five years Ken Pomeroy has been tracking individual tempo-free statistics.

Normally offensive rebounding is of secondary importance. Shooting percentage is the most important component of total offensive efficiency. But Blair rebounded so well that while Pitt's effective FG percentage ranked only 42nd nationally, this was actually the second best offense in the country overall, behind only North Carolina.

What we learned in 2009: *Jamie Dixon is the best active coach who's never been to the Final Four.*

In six years at Pitt, Jamie Dixon has the best winning percentage in school history and his team has made the NCAA tournament every year. But once again in 2009, Dixon came up just short in his quest for his first Final Four appearance. In the Elite Eight Villanova's Scottie Reynolds made a layup with two seconds left and that was enough to overcome a herculean effort from Sam Young and give the Wildcats the 78-76 win. (See table.)

I like to call Pitt the "Wisconsin of the East" because Dixon really seems to get the most out of his players every year. The formula has changed over time, from dominating defense in 2004 to unstoppable rebounding and offense in 2009, but Dixon knows how to win.

An Elite Group, But No Final Four For Dixon: Most NCAA Tournament Wins Last Six Years			
Coach	**Current school**	**Wins**	**Final Four**
Roy Williams	North Carolina	21	Yes
Jim Calhoun	Connecticut	14	Yes
John Calipari	Kentucky	14	Yes
Bill Self	Kansas	14	Yes
Ben Howland	UCLA	14	Yes
Billy Donovan	Florida	13	Yes
Tom Izzo	Michigan State	12	Yes
Rick Pitino	Louisville	11	Yes
Mike Krzyzewski	Duke	11	Yes
Jay Wright	Villanova	11	Yes
Rick Barnes	Texas	10	Yes
Thad Matta	Ohio State	9	Yes
Jamie Dixon	Pittsburgh	9	No
Bruce Weber	Illinois	8	Yes
Bo Ryan	Wisconsin	8	No

His team is always in the hunt for the Big East title and a great NCAA tournament seed, and always seems to bring back a veteran group of players who are ready to dominate in November. But then each March the lack of five-star recruits and McDonald's All-Americans seems to make the difference as the Panthers come up just short of a deep NCAA tournament run, much like the Badgers under Bo Ryan.

What's in store for 2010: The formula is about to change. This year Pitt loses substantially all its veteran players and minutes, including its top three scorers, and four starters. But the Panthers have something they haven't had since 1987, a McDonald's All-American. Dante Taylor not only brings talent as one of the elite freshmen in the country, he brings hope that Dixon may now be able to attract the caliber of players needed to match his elite coaching ability. And if Dixon can bring the best talent in the country to Pittsburgh, the sky is the limit.

Prospectus says: Given all the injuries and players leaving, I cannot argue with people who pick Pittsburgh to finish under .500 in the Big East. But Jamie Dixon has proven he can develop players and find new ways to win, and I expect another remarkable season from one of the league's brightest coaches.

Still, get ready for a dangerous selection Sunday. With an easy non-conference schedule chosen to give the team time to develop, Pitt is probably going to be lacking quality wins on their resume at the end of the season. And even a 10-8 conference mark may not be enough to get the Panthers into the NCAA tournament this year.

Meet the Panthers

Dante Taylor (6-9, 240, Fr.). Many are hoping Taylor will be a taller version of DeJuan Blair, as his strength is his physical play and rebounding ability. But comparisons to Blair are not fair to the freshman. Blair was a true diamond in the rough who proved from his first big game against Duke that he was ready to dominate college basketball. Give Taylor a chance to develop his own signature style.

Jermaine Dixon (6-3, 200, Sr.). Dixon is recovering from breaking his foot a second time, and as the only returning starter, he'll definitely be missed. But the non-conference schedule is not very challenging. The earliest BCS opponents include Indiana and DePaul, both of whom struggled last season. The key is for Dixon to be healthy by January.

Gilbert Brown (6-6, 200, Jr.). Brown is academically ineligible for at least the first semester. Again, this is crushing to Pittsburgh given the lack of depth, but he may be back in time for the real tests in Big East play.

Brad Wanamaker (6-4, 210, Jr.). Many people hoped Wanamaker could replace Ronald Ramon as a three-point gunner, and while he was able to make 39 percent of his threes, he was so careful in his shot selection that he was not perceived as a true deep threat. The key this season will be how well he plays when he gets more minutes and more shots in the offense. Wanamaker is also a spectacular defensive rebounder for a player of his size.

Ashton Gibbs (6-2, 190, So.). Gibbs could be the break-out star on the team this year. He played fewer minutes than Wanamaker, but was aggressive in his time on the court. Gibbs made 36 threes while shooting 44 percent from beyond the arc. He was also one of the most efficient scorers on the team as a freshman.

Gary McGhee (6-10, 250, Jr.). I'm normally hesitant to predict big things for players who play as few minutes as McGhee played last year. But Dixon has shown an ability to develop veteran big men, and it may be McGhee's turn. Then again McGhee will have to improve his turnover rate, defensive rebounding, and finishing ability.

Nasir Robinson (6-5, 220, So.). Robinson's an undersized forward, and I have a hard time seeing how he'll fit into this year's rotation unless he suddenly develops a jump shot.

Talib Zanna (6-9, 225, Fr.). Another consensus top-100 post player, Zanna will get a chance to play right away.

Providence

2009: 19-14 (10-8 Big East), lost to Miami 78-66, NIT First Round
In-conference offense: 1.07 points per possession (7th)
In-conference defense: 1.10 points allowed per possession (14th)

What Providence did well: *Plan for the future.*
Somehow, despite no discernable improvement on offense or defense, Keno Davis managed to take Providence from 6-12 to 10-8 in the Big East last season. But there was indeed a key change. Davis installed an up-tempo system. The Friars sped up from the middle

of the pack to the 10th fastest adjusted tempo in Division I. The faster pace had some positive and negative effects. While the increase in transition layups led to a higher percentage of two-pointers made and a higher number of free throw attempts, the per-possession defense sagged.

But the high-tempo attack was not just about winning games in 2008-09. Unlike other bright young coaches like Iowa coach Todd Lickliter, Davis seems to realize that part of building a program is selling recruits on an exciting style of basketball. And if Davis did nothing else last year, the most important thing he did was hit the recruiting trail. With no fewer than eight players graduating, including four starters, his top priority was to start building for the future. He inked six freshmen and two junior college transfers. Including two Friars who sat out last year, Davis now greets the 2009-10 season with ten new players and only three returnees.

What we learned in 2009: *Davis will adapt to the personnel he has on hand.*

As the son of a coaching legend, Davis appears prepared to play and win with different styles. In his one year as head coach at Drake, Davis slowed the Bulldogs down and played a methodical dissecting style. He didn't have Big East caliber athletes, but he had some shooters, and by working a precision half-court attack, the Bulldogs improved from second-to-last in the Missouri Valley to a five-seed in the NCAA tournament. Now that he's at Providence, however, Davis has installed a high-octane attack.

At Drake Davis also developed a classic perimeter-oriented team that was heavily dependent on three-point shooting. In 2007-08 fully 46 percent of the Bulldogs' shots were from beyond the arc, up from just 33 percent the previous year. But in his first season at Providence, Davis seemed to move the team in the opposite direction, perhaps by necessity. The Friars fell to near the bottom of D-I in three point accuracy last season.

While junior Sharaud Curry was a pleasant surprise, shooting 39 percent with 57 made threes, Providence was worse as a whole. Junior Brian McKenzie fell from a 41 percent three-point shooter with 56 makes as a sophomore to a 27 percent shooter with just 25 made threes as a junior. McKenzie's struggles combined with the transfer of Dwain Williams (a 41 percent shooter with 48 made threes in 2008) left the Friars with limited options from the perimeter last

season. But even without reliable three-point shooting, Davis found ways for his team to win. In Providence's biggest triumph of the season, an 81-73 win over then-number one Pitt, the Friars attempted just 12 threes. Thus whether slow or fast, inside or outside, Davis has shown an ability to adapt to his personnel and win games.

What's in store for 2010: According to the official Providence season prospectus, the faster tempo is here to stay in 2009-10. Alumni remembering the early days of Rick Pitino would love to see the return of a high-octane, three-point shooting attack. But whether Davis emphasizes the three this year will likely depend on the performance of the ten newcomers, particularly eligible transfer Kyle Wright who shot 42 percent from beyond the arc and made 94 threes at Monroe College last year.

In terms of offensive efficiency, no team is harder to predict given all the newcomers. Looking across all D-I teams, freshman performance is a mixed bag. Looking at players with a minimum of ten percent of their team's minutes:
- 25 percent have offensive ratings above 102.3.
- 25 percent have offensive ratings below 84.6.
- In the BCS leagues, however, the freshmen do a little better.
- 25 percent have offensive efficiency ratings above 105.7.
- 25 percent have offensive efficiency ratings below 89.8.

Some may pick Providence for last place in the Big East based on all the new players, but I think that's unlikely. Last year DePaul and South Florida had zero players with offensive ratings above 105.7 and Rutgers had only one rotation player above 105.7. If only a few of the new Friars pan out, Providence should perform above this level. And since this team already returns two efficient players in Sharaud Curry (111.9) and Marshon Brooks (107.9), I think it's unlikely PC will fall to the cellar in 2010. Furthermore, if Davis hits the jackpot with the new talent, Providence could be a real sleeper team this season.

Prospectus says: If as expected only two or three of the newcomers pan out, Providence should have a similar offense to last season's, perhaps taking a slight step backward. But what concerns me is that Davis has yet to establish himself as a defensive coach at either Providence or Drake. Despite pressing at times, the Friars forced turnovers at a lower rate than the year before, and did not increase their steal rate. I like Providence as a sleeper team this year, but based on my concerns about the defense, I can't pick them higher than 13th in the Big East.

Meet the Friars

Sharaud Curry (5-10, 170, Sr.). Curry's quickness is a perfect match for the up-tempo system, and he'll be the leader in 2009-10. But who will take the tough shots when he's double-teamed?

Marshon Brooks (6-5, 190, Jr.). Last year's scoring sixth man: Brooks' overall efficiency hides the fact that he was a relatively poor three-point shooter as a sophomore. He took 128 threes, but made just 31 percent of those attempts.

Brian McKenzie (6-4, 205, Sr.). As both a spot-up shooter without a shot and a player that did not adapt well to the up-tempo system, McKenzie lost his starting job and a good deal of his playing time last season. Based on his mediocre free throw shooting (69 percent), I don't expect his perimeter shooting to bounce

back substantially. McKenzie may start early in the season, but I'd expect the newcomers to replace him sooner rather than later.

Johnnie Lacy (6-0, 170, Fr.). Though not a consensus top-100 recruit, Lacy is considered an elite point guard who should fit in well with the up-tempo attack.

Vincent Council (6-2, 180, Fr.). Yet another strong point guard prospect, Council can be expected to run with the Friars.

Jamine Peterson (6-6, 200, So.). Peterson was red-shirted his sophomore year. While Davis claims he did this to give Peterson more time to develop, it's certainly disconcerting that Peterson couldn't distinguish himself enough as a sophomore to earn playing time.

Russ Permenter (6-9, 230, Jr.). Since there are no returning post players on the team, Permenter's junior college experience may give him the edge for a starting job.

Kadeem Batts (6-8, 235, Fr.) Batts is another candidate for a starting job in the post.

Rutgers

2009: 11-21 (2-16 Big East), lost to Notre Dame 61-50, Big East First Round
In-conference offense: 0.92 points per possession (16th)
In-conference defense: 1.06 points allowed per possession (10th)

What Rutgers did well: *Force missed shots.*

The addition of 6-9 freshman Gregory Echenique, paired with 7-0 junior Hamady Ndiaye, gave Rutgers two of the Big East's best shot blockers in 2008-09. In fact, Ndiaye and Echenique posted the conference's second- and third-highest block rates, behind only co-Big East Player of the Year Hasheem Thabeet.

Echenique was more than just another intimidator in the paint. His presence meant the guards no longer had to sag back into the paint on a regular basis. Instead, the Scarlet Knights' guards stayed out on shooters, and Rutgers' three-point defense improved substantially from allowing opponents to make 40 and 37 percent of their threes in Fred Hill's first two years, to just 31 percent last season.

The Achilles heel of the defense remained a lack of turnovers, but since opponents' shooting is the most important component of defense, Rutgers' ability to force misses led to its best defensive performance in Hill's three years as head coach. Obviously, the defensive performance was best in the non-conference schedule, but the team improved significantly as conference play progressed:

Sign Of Improvement? Defense (Opponent Points Per Possession)	
Month	Opp. PPP
January	1.11
February	1.04
March*	0.97
* Includes Big East tournament	

What we learned in 2009: *Turnovers can hold back talent.*

Rutgers hasn't been to the NCAA tournament since 1991, but there was palpable excitement about the team last year. The excitement was sparked by the first McDonald's All-American in school history, Mike Rosario. The Knights also returned two prolific senior scorers in JR Inman and Anthony Farmer. And as a whole, the team had five top-100 recruits on the roster for possibly the first time ever. With Rosario, Inman, Ndiaye, and Echenique, as well as Corey Chandler, Rutgers figured to have the talent to compete with anyone. Add the fact that borderline top-100 recruit Earl Pettis improved his offensive rating by over 20 points, and the Knights also had some depth.

But a funny thing happened on the way to an NCAA or NIT bid. Rutgers won just two Big East games. The obvious problem was that the offense never clicked. The lack of shooting touch was the biggest problem, but the shooting percentage was actually up from previous years. The new problem was turnovers:

Change In Turnover Rate: Returning Rutgers Players, 2007-08 Vs. 2008-09			
Player	2008	2009	Change
Farmer	17.4	19.6	+2.2
Inman	19.3	26.0	+6.7
Chandler	23.1	26.5	+3.4
Coburn	22.2	34.0	+11.8
Pettis	30.4	24.4	-6.0
Ndiaye	25.2	27.3	+2.1
Minimum 10% of minutes played			

As a group, Rutgers had the fourth-highest turnover rate of any BCS team. Only Earl Pettis was able to substantially improve his turnover rate in the off-season.

What's in store for 2010: Following a 2-16 season a team will almost always experience some changes. In the case of Rutgers, not only did JR Inman and Anthony Farmer graduate, the team's most improved player, Earl Pettis, chose to leave the team in the spring. More recently Corey Chandler, who sparred with the head coach and was suspended briefly last season, was dismissed from the team.

But in this case change is expected to be a good thing. The team not only returns its three most important players—Rosario, Echenique, and Ndiaye—it also adds two transfers and four solid freshmen. Moreover,

a raw statistical argument can be made that the team will be better off without Chandler and Inman, two of the worst shooters in the Big East.

Prospectus says: On paper I see four top-100 recruits including a McDonald's All-American and some nice defensive statistics and I think Rutgers might finally be ready to take that step this year. All they need is for a few of the new players to develop a reasonably efficient scoring touch. But I thought that last year and the team continued to be one of the worst-shooting teams in the nation. Until Rutgers shows some scoring touch, it is hard to move them up from the bottom of the Big East standings.

Meet the Scarlet Knights

Mike Rosario (6-3, 180, So.). The biggest recruit in Rutgers history made a dent on the international stage this summer, playing well for Puerto Rico's FIBA Under-19 team.

Gregory Echenique (6-9, 265, So.). Not only is he a force defensively, Echenique was the team's most efficient scorer in 2008-09.

Hamady Ndiaye (7-0, 235, Sr.). Inevitably when Echenique and Ndiaye go for so many blocks, they are also going to be out of position and give up some easy baskets. But both remain a force on the defensive glass.

Mike Coburn (6-0, 185, Jr.). Coburn posted best assist rate on the team, and he could get more playing time due to the departure of the team's other two primary distributors, Farmer and Chandler. Then again his high turnover rate suggests otherwise.

James Beatty (6-2, 195, Jr.). A junior college transfer who might jump ahead of Coburn on the point-guard depth chart.

Jonathan Mitchell (6-7, 225, Jr.). The former top-100 recruit transferred from Florida and is eligible to play this season. In 2007-08 he watched a host of freshmen jump ahead of him on the Gators depth chart and read the writing on the wall, but prior to that he was an effective scorer in non-conference action for Billy Donovan. Mitchell should have enough experience to play right away, and if he can produce some scoring punch it will do wonders for his new team.

St. John's

2009: 16-18 (6-12 Big East), lost to Richmond 75-69, CBI First Round
In-conference offense: 0.95 points per possession (13th)
In-conference defense: 1.07 points allowed per possession (11th)

What St. John's did well: *Grab offensive rebounds.*

Perhaps supplying the polar opposite to Georgetown's attempt to play defense without defensive rebounding, St. John's attempted to play offense last year with only offensive rebounding. Of course depending on offensive boards can be ugly. Against Marquette in the Big East tournament, the poor shooting was overwhelming and the Johnnies scored just ten points in the first half. But that same offensive rebounding led to a win against Notre Dame, a pair of wins against Georgetown, and a nice comeback against Duke.

St. John's offensive rebounding was shared across the board. While Pitt's amazing results here were led by DeJuan Blair's individual dominance, the Johnnies' dominance on the offensive glass was a team strategy. The team decided that to score they would need to crash the boards. And while this helped the offense, the defense appears to have given up more transition baskets. In 2009 St. John's had its worst defensive performance under Norm Roberts.

The Decline Of The St. John's Defense: Adjusted Defensive Efficiency

	Adj.Def.Eff.
2005	91.8
2006	89.8
2007	95.2
2008	93.2
2009	96.5
All games	

As a former Bill Self assistant, Roberts knows the importance of hard-nosed defense. And in a summer interview with ESPN's Andy Katz, he admitted that re-creating that swarming Kansas/Illinois/Tulsa defense is his primary goal this season.

But 2009-10 brings with it a series of questions for St. John's. Can the defense be improved while maintaining the same high level of offensive rebounding? Will a team that returns virtually every meaningful contributor and adds the injured star Anthony Mason Jr. finally reach .500 in Big East play? And will Roberts be able to keep his job?

What we learned in 2009: *Freshmen often get better.*

In Roberts' tenure St. John's has never had a defense ranked better than 150th in Division I. But many believe that might happen in 2009-10. Arguably, Mason's injury last year was the key. Mason took over 30 percent of the team's shots during his abbreviated minutes in 2007-08, and while he was clearly a capable scorer, he was often asked to do too much. His absence allowed a team comprised mostly of sophomores to gain playing time and develop their skills.

Sophomoric Efficiencies: Offensive Ratings Of Returning St. John's Players, 2007-08 Vs. 2008-09

Player	2008 Freshman	2009 Sophomore	Change
Rob Thomas	N/A	108.8	N/A
DJ Kennedy	98.4	106.1	+7.7
Paris Horne	90.8	105.8	+15.0
Sean Evans	74.5	96.7	+22.2
Justin Burrell	84.4	90.5	+6.1
Malik Boothe	76.9	81.8	+4.9
(Note: Rob Thomas played very few minutes as a freshman.)			

Few players in the country made a bigger jump last year than Sean Evans. A 51 percent free throw shooter, Evans will never be confused for a jump shooter, but in 2009 he discovered how to use his size to score around the basket. His two-point percentage rose from 43 as a freshman to 51 as a sophomore. He also improved his rebounding rate on both ends of the floor along with his turnover rate. The result was one of the biggest overall improvements in offensive efficiency in D-I.

More importantly, both Paris Horne and D.J. Kennedy developed into quality scorers. And if these players continue to develop while Mason becomes more judicious in his shot selection, St. John's might finally field a dangerous offensive team under Roberts in 2009-2010.

What's in store for 2010: The problem of course is that development is far from uniform. While on average players will improve every year, as noted in the Notre Dame and Seton Hall previews, the biggest offensive improvement is usually from freshman to sophomore year. The key to the season will be whether a team of sophomores can improve again.

Prospectus says: St. John's is still a long way from having an elite offensive team. But if Norm Roberts can get the defensive effort to return and if as expected the offense makes a modest improvement, the team can finish near .500 in the Big East.

Meet the Red Storm

Anthony Mason Jr. (6-7, 215, Sr.). After missing last year due to injury, Mason returns to the lineup—at least he will eventually. In October he re-aggravated a hamstring injury and is expected to miss the proverbial four to six weeks. When Mason's healthy his three-point shooting is a threat, something you couldn't say for the rest of the team last year. But his ability to create shots for himself and his high assist rate without turnovers are what promise to make him a key addition.

Paris Horne (6-3, 190, Jr.). Last year's leading scorer, Horne was the Red Storm's best three-point shooter at

only 33 percent last season. He should benefit tremendously from Mason's return. Horne also had the highest steal rate on the team.

D.J. Kennedy (6-6, 215, Jr.). Kennedy is quite effective at rebounding and drawing fouls despite being undersized for a big man.

Sean Evans (6-8, 255, Jr.). As noted above, almost no one improved more from 2008 to 2009 than Sean Evans.

Malik Boothe (5-9, 185, Jr.). Boothe couldn't shoot and he turned the ball over too much, but he was the only creator on the team last year, sporting one of the better assist rates in the Big East.

Justin Burrell (6-8, 235, Jr.). The team's best shot-blocker, Burrell was the rare player on the team who was not particularly adept at offensive rebounding.

Quincy Roberts (6-5, 195, So.). The team's best free throw shooter last year at 78 percent, Roberts needs to develop a consistent shot from the field.

Seton Hall

P:
W: Harell
B:

2009: 17-15 (7-11 Big East), lost to Syracuse 89-74, Big East Second Round
In-conference offense: 1.03 points per possession (10th)
In-conference defense: 1.08 points allowed per possession (12th)

What Seton Hall did well: *Avoid turnovers.*

We now have six years of tempo-free data on Bobby Gonzalez—three at Manhattan and three at Seton Hall—and his teams always have one of the lowest turnover rates in the country. As noted in the DePaul and Notre Dame previews, I actually have mixed feelings about teams with low turnover rates. In the case of a team like the Fighting Irish that has dynamic scorers at multiple positions, cutting down on the turnover rate creates more shots and can improve the chances of winning. But in the case of a team like the Blue Demons that's struggling to find good shots, the team may be better served to take more chances and try to get easier shots.

In the case of Seton Hall, the team's effective FG percentage ranked only 177th in Division I last season, suggesting to me that taking more chances might

be a good idea. But the strength of the Pirates is in its guard play. John Garcia is the only reliable post player, and while he's been effective (shooting a remarkable 61 percent on his twos last year) he can only do so much for the team. With a team built around solid guard play, a low number of turnovers is ideal.

Interestingly, Gonzalez has built guard-oriented teams in the past that are not highly reliant on three-point shots. The 2006 Manhattan NIT team with Jason Wingate, Devon Austin, and eventual Providence transfer Jeff Xavier was probably the prototype of what Gonzalez would like to see this year. All three guards could score from three-point range, on intermediate shots, and by drawing fouls in the paint. And because the Jaspers didn't turn the ball over, that team had one of the better offenses among the mid-majors.

If Seton Hall wants to build that type of low-turnover

team, the key will be whether the offense can emulate Wingate, Austin, and Xavier and convert more of those varied scoring opportunities. And the numbers do indeed suggest we should see some improvement in individual offensive efficiency this year. Let's look at the average improvement for returning players at Division I schools. I control for team quality and the percentage of shots taken by the player in these results.

Average Change In Offensive Efficiency: All Returning Division I Players, 2006-2009	
Period	Improvement
Freshman to Sophomore year	+4.32
Sophomore to Junior year	+2.17
Junior to Senior year	+1.46

With a lot of returning minutes and some scorers who are already capable, the Pirates have reason to believe they could have some very efficient players in the lineup this season.

What we learned in 2009: *Defensive rebounding hurt the team.*

In the last five years Gonzalez has not had an elite defensive rebounding team. But 2008-09 was the worst season on this particular record, with the Hall's opponents grabbing a ridiculous 40 percent of their own misses.

Part of the problem was that Gonzalez never felt comfortable with the reserve big men on this roster. At 6-9 and 6-11 respectively, Brandon Walters and Mike Davis each saw some playing time early, but neither could stay in the primary rotation and, not coincidentally, both players have since transferred. Furthermore 6-11 Melvyn Oliver never got a chance to see the court, due to academic issues.

Robert Mitchell worked incredibly hard on the boards, but he's listed at 6-6 and this team was in desperate need of a role player who could intimidate in the paint. The Pirates actually improved their FG defense substantially, but without grabbing the resulting boards there was little reward: Seton Hall's defense overall was near the bottom of the Big East.

What's in store for 2010: Paul Gause is gone and he was the team's best defensive player last year with the fifth highest steal rate in D-I. But as long as Melvyn Oliver, freshman Ferrakohn Hall, or New Mexico State transfer Herb Pope can stay on the court and provide some additional size, there is reason to believe the defense will be better.

Prospectus says: With so many returning minutes and some interesting options among the transfers, Seton Hall should see at least some improvement on offense. But the season will hinge on the Pirates' defense. If Bobby Gonzalez can turn one of the new post players into an effective defensive option, the Hall could take a big jump in 2010. If the defense remains the same, however, an NCAA bid is unlikely.

Meet the Pirates

Jeremy Hazell (6-5, 185, Jr.). With 105 made threes and an ability to drive and draw fouls, Hazell is an absolutely lethal offensive player. Along with Eugene Harvey and Mitchell he formed a trio that almost never left the court for Seton Hall last season, as the Pirates had one of the lowest bench utilization rates in the country.

Eugene Harvey (6-0, 165, Sr.). The team's point guard has proven he cannot make the three-point shot, shooting 23 percent two years ago and 20 percent last season. At some point Harvey needs to stop taking those shots. If he would just focus on his ability to drive, draw fouls, and create, he could still be a solid offensive player.

Robert Mitchell (6-6, 180, Sr.). No one can question Mitchell's effort on the boards, but the Pirates probably need to field a bigger lineup in the post to have success defending the better Big East teams.

John Garcia (6-9, 265, Sr.). With a high block rate, accurate shooting, and strong rebounding on both ends of the floor, Garcia's everything you want in a post player.

Keon Lawrence (6-2, 175, Sr.). The kind of dynamic inside and outside guard that Gonzalez covets, Lawrence transferred from Missouri and is eligible this year.

Jeff Robinson (6-5, 230, Jr.). He was recruited as a guard for Memphis, but Robinson ended up playing at the forward spot for the Tigers and eventually decided to transfer. He hopes that Gonzalez can find a better role for him when he joins the team at mid-season.

Herb Pope (6-8, 235, Jr.). Pope struggled to get minutes on a New Mexico State team that won the WAC title in 2008. There are questions about whether he'll be able to score in the Big East, as his offensive rating was only 88.4 for the Aggies. But he has had an additional year to develop.

Jordan Theodore (6-0, 170, So.). Theodore played substantial minutes last season as a freshman, but he'll need to become a more efficient scorer if he wants to hold off Lawrence for a spot in the rotation.

South Florida

2009: 9-22 (4-14 Big East), lost to Seton Hall 68-54, Big East First Round
In-conference offense: 0.93 points per possession (14th)
In-conference defense: 1.05 points allowed per possession (9th)

What South Florida did well: *Continue building a BCS-caliber program.*

South Florida's strength last year was clearly their ability to force missed shots, but I have trouble complimenting a defense that's actually been on the decline.

South Florida Defense Since Joining Big East: Adjusted Defensive Efficiency By Year		
Year	Coach	Adj.Def.Eff.
2006	Robert McCullum	94.6
2007	Robert McCullum	96.9
2008	Stan Heath	97.4
2009	Stan Heath	98.1

Is this a trend or a pattern for Stan Heath? The truth is it's hard to tell. Despite several years of data on Heath at Arkansas and USF, the numbers are inconclusive because the coach has been saddled with two huge rebuilding projects. First in Fayetteville and then in Tampa, the talent on hand when Heath started his job was simply not of the caliber needed to reach the NCAA tournament. In both cases he's been forced to adapt to the players he has and to try to find a formula to take a leap up to a competitive level of play. Heath brings in yet another large recruiting class this season.

What we learned in 2009: *Heath will play slow if needed.*

The progress at South Florida has not been what Heath would like at this point, but he's adapted to the team he has on the floor. In 2009 he brought the pace down to the point where his team was the slowest group in the Big East. This limited the number of possessions and gave his team a chance to stay in games. It also allowed Heath to keep his best player, Dominique Jones, on the court at all times. No Big

East player logged a higher percentage of his team's minutes than Jones, whose presence was critical because he was the only USF player with an offensive rating above 100.

What's in store for 2010: If Arkansas is any indication, South Florida may be ready to make a substantial jump in Heath's third year with the team.

Third Year's The Charm? Stan Heath's Record		
Year	Arkansas	South Florida
1	9-19	12-19
2	12-16	9-22
3	18-12	
4	22-10	
5	21-14	

The Bulls have a clear star and they're adding four freshmen and two transfers, so there's reason for optimism if the new players can step in and play well right away. But while Heath was able to bring Arkansas back to a winning record in his third year, it wasn't until his fourth season in Fayetteville that he had a winning SEC record and got the team into the NCAA tournament.

Prospectus says: Unlike Arkansas, which won a national championship just 15 years ago, South Florida can't use history as a recruiting tool. Despite Stan Heath's best efforts he is simply not bringing in the top-100 recruits that he landed when he was with the Razorbacks. I still believe Heath is the perfect hire to build USF up to a competitive level in the Big East, but this is a very difficult job and, in the short term, the Bulls bring back too many inefficient players on offense to predict much improvement this season.

Meet the Bulls

Dominique Jones (6-4, 205, Jr.). Last year Jones maintained his high offensive efficiency despite a large number of shots, all the while using more of his team's possessions than almost anyone in the Big East. Only Luke Harangody and Dar Tucker absorbed a larger fraction of their team's offense. And Jones is not just a scorer. He also had wonderful assist and turnover rates last season. On a team that struggles offensively, Jones is the clear star.

Gus Gilchrist (6-10, 235, So.). At 6-10 Gilchrist has to become a more physical player. First, he needs to get closer to the rim. His 42 percent two-point shooting is simply not going to win games in the Big East. And Gilchrist used almost as many possessions during his minutes as did Jones, suggesting the team will be much better off if he's more judicious in his shot selection. Gilchrist also has the potential to be a dominant rebounder given his athleticism, but he didn't show it as a freshman.

Chris Howard (6-3, 200, Sr.). A highly effective point guard, Howard is great at drawing fouls or dishing the assist. If he could improve his shooting it would help the offense immeasurably, because he's expected to be on the floor a lot for this team.

Alex Rivas (6-10, 230, Sr.). His rebounds and blocked shots were important for the team, but 57 percent shooting at the line prevented Rivas from becoming a key offensive piece.

Jarrid Famous (6-11, 240, Jr.). A junior college transfer who some expect will start right away for the Bulls.

Anthony Crater (6-1, 170, So.). The Ohio State transfer struggled to get minutes as a Buckeye, but USF hopes that when Crater becomes eligible midseason he can spell Howard at point guard.

Mike Mercer (6-4, 190, Sr.). Mercer arrived last year as a transfer from Georgia but appeared in just four games before he and Crater were arrested in January for possession of marijuana. It was Mercer's second arrest in four months and Heath kicked him off the team before reinstating him in the offseason.

Justin Leemow (6-1, 175, So.). Leemow was not ready to contribute last year, but the leap from freshman to sophomore year is the biggest one of all.

P: Jardne
W: Johnson, Rautins
B:

Pae 52 # Syracuse

2009: 28-10 (11-7 Big East), lost to Oklahoma 84-71, NCAA Sweet 16
In-conference offense: 1.10 points per possession (4th)
In-conference defense: 1.02 points allowed per possession (6th)

What Syracuse did well: *Score in the paint.*

The Big East tournament may never be as big as the NCAA tournament, but Syracuse has done everything in their power to make it just as exciting. With three of the last five conference tournament MVPs (Hakim Warrick, Gerry McNamara, and Jonny Flynn) and more buzzer-beaters and dramatic games than any other team, the Orangemen have proven that you can make a name for yourself in March even without a deep NCAA tournament run.

Last year the game that captured the collective imagination of sports fans everywhere was the six-overtime thriller between Syracuse and Connecticut. Incredibly the Orangemen never led at any point in the first five OTs. Not until 1:22am ET did Jim Boeheim's team finally pull ahead, on their way to a 127-117 win. This incredible battle (and slight upset) was perhaps the signature moment of the college basketball season.

Jonny Flynn and Paul Harris carried the load for the Orange in that game. Flynn had 34 points and made all 16 of his free throws, while Harris added 29 points on 13-of-14 shooting from the line. With clutch performers like Flynn and Harris slated to return, many prognosticators were ready to anoint Syracuse as the Big East favorites heading into this season. But it was not meant to be. Flynn and Harris declared for the NBA draft.

Before we write Syracuse off, though, remember that last year's success wasn't all about three-point shooting and magical guard play. In 2008-09 the Orangemen did one thing better than at any point in the last six years: Make inside buckets. Syracuse shot 55 percent on two-pointers last year, and that domination in the paint gave the team its best adjusted offensive efficiency since their national championship in 2003.

What we learned in 2009: *Syracuse can replace its good players.*

The loss of Donte Greene was viewed by many as the NBA defection that would keep Syracuse out of contention last season. But while his 90 made threes and prolific inside scoring were indeed hard to replace, the Orangemen not only replaced his shooting, they improved without him. Andy Rautins returned from injury to make 102 threes on 37 percent shooting, and Rick Jackson stepped up in the paint, making 63 percent of his twos. The Syracuse offense that looked like it might take a step back was actually better last season.

What's in store for 2010: Thus the key question in 2010 is a simple one. Can Syracuse replace Jonny Flynn? Now a member of the Minnesota Timberwolves, Flynn had the second best assist rate in the Big East last year (behind Pitt's Levance Fields) and was a key factor behind the huge seasons enjoyed by Boeheim's big men. Arinze Onuaku led the Big East with a 67 percent shooting on his twos last year, largely because Flynn kept getting him the ball in a position where he could record yet another dunk. Onuaku, however, is a terrible free throw shooter (29.8 percent last year), suggesting he's not going to become the next Luke Harangody and start making seven-foot jumpers. If he and his frontcourt mates are going to have another big season, someone is going to have to get them the ball inside.

Can anyone on the roster do that? Rautins is the only returning guard in the rotation, and he hasn't been a traditional ball-handler. And while Syracuse does welcome 6-3 freshman Brandon Triche this year, the biggest key here will likely be the return of Scoop Jardine, who missed all of last year due to injury. Jardine may not be as efficient as Flynn, or even a natural point guard, but he was an effective distributor as a freshman, one whose assist rate exceeded what Rautins and Eric Devendorf posted last year.

Prospectus says: Jim Boeheim loses his top three scorers from last year, and all three were highly efficient guard/wing players. But Syracuse does return a lights-out three point shooter in Rautins and two very effective post players in Onuaku and Jackson, as well as adding a versatile scorer in Wesley Johnson. That

makes the key to this season the point guard role. If Jardine and Triche can distribute effectively, Syracuse has the tools and the talent to compete for a Big East title. But if they struggle, this could be an ugly offensive year with too many forced shots. I'll cautiously project the Orangemen as an NCAA tournament team, but no higher at this point.

Meet the Orangemen

Arinze Onuaku (6-9, 260, Sr.). Onuaku's two-point shooting not only led the Big East, it gave him the best effective FG percentage of any player at a BCS school. He's also a tremendous rebounder who posted a high block rate last year.

Andy Rautins (6-5, 195, Sr.). Under no circumstances should a defender help off of Rautins. He took more than five times as many threes as twos last year and made 102 of them.

Rick Jackson (6-9, 235, Jr.). The most improved member of the team last season, Jackson actually had a higher defensive rebounding percentage and block rate than Onuaku.

Wesley Johnson (6-7, 200, Jr.). Optimists think Iowa State transfer Johnson will be the difference on this year's team. Certainly he's a versatile scorer who can create his own shot. Johnson can score from three-point range, the mid-range, and the paint, and many observers think he'll carry this team. But I'm not quite ready to anoint him the best player on the team, even if he may have the best NBA prospects. For one thing the 96.1 offensive rating he recorded in his last season in Ames was not that great. Johnson scored a lot of points that year, but he needed a lot of possessions to do it. Perhaps with a more impressive cast surrounding him he'll elevate his game, but he has some work to do this season to become an elite player.

Scoop Jardine (6-1, 190, So.). The season may hinge on whether Jardine can get Onuaku and Jackson the ball in position to be successful. But Jardine's turnover rate was way too high as a freshman.

Brandon Triche (6-4, 210, Fr.). Triche will fight Jardine for the starting point guard role. Although he was not a consensus top-100 recruit, there are many who think he can pass Jardine in the rotation.

DaShonte Riley (6-11, 200, Fr.). With Onuaku and Jackson in the paint, the team doesn't need huge production from Riley, and that's a great luxury to have with a consensus top-100 recruit. Perhaps the biggest reason Syracuse fans should like Riley is that he chose the 'Cuse after de-committing from archrival Georgetown.

Villanova

P: Reynolds Fisher
W: Stokes

Fast 12

2009: 30-8 (13-5 Big East), lost to North Carolina 83-69, NCAA Final Four
In-conference offense: 1.10 points per possession (3rd)
In-conference defense: 1.01 points allowed per possession (5th)

What Villanova did well: *Improve in virtually every statistical category.*

Last year Villanova returned every important rotation player and was a trendy pick for a team on the rise in the Big East. But as I noted in the Notre Dame preview, improvements among returning players are highly variant. Credit hard work and great coaching, then, for enabling all those returning Wildcats to improve Villanova substantially as a team.

First, Jay Wright's team improved its conference offense efficiency from 1.00 to 1.10 points per possession, the biggest improvement in the Big East. And the improvement was seen across the board, as Villanova bettered its three-point shooting, two-point shooting, and free throw percentage. At the same time the Wildcats forced opponents into more missed shots, both inside and outside the arc. You get the idea: Villanova improved its offensive and defensive rebounding, drew more fouls, committed fewer fouls, and gave away fewer turnovers. Basically the only one of the four factors on offense and defense where Villanova did not get better was forced turnovers, but given all the other improvements, that minor decline was hardly significant.

This team's success was also a product of almost every single member of the rotation becoming more efficient:

Change In Offensive Efficiency: Villanova 2007-08 Vs. 2008-09			
Player	2008	2009	Change
Reynolds	105.6	107.8	+2.2
Cunningham	104.1	108.3	+4.2
Fisher	94.1	106.4	+12.3
Stokes	101.8	115.3	+13.5
Redding	99.7	104.5	+4.8
Anderson	114.9	112.1	-2.8
Clark	111.1	113.8	+2.7
Pena	95.4	101.7	+6.3

The team even continued to get better towards the end of the season, beating UCLA, Duke, and Pitt en route to the Final Four.

What we learned in 2009: *Villanova does not have to live and die by the three.*

Most people remember Randy Foye, Allen Ray, and Mike Nardi, and tend to think that because Villanova is a guard-led offense, it must rely on three-pointers to win games. And certainly the three is an important part of Wright's arsenal. But the three was less critical in 2008-09 than at any point in recent memory.

So what was the wrinkle that allowed the Wildcats to make it to the Final Four? Villanova emphasized taking the ball to the basket, as the team used its quickness to get easy shots. This was apparent in Scottie Reynolds' driving layup to beat Pitt in earning a Final Four bid. But it was even more visible in the season-long statistics where Wright's team posted its best free throw rate in the past six years. Corey Stokes got all the headlines for his three-point shooting, but it was Corey Fisher's relentless efforts to take the ball inside and Dante Cunningham's ability to draw fouls that provided the key balance for the team last season.

What's in store for 2010: Contrary to popular belief, Villanova was not the most dominant team statistically last year. The 22nd ranked adjusted offense and 15th ranked adjusted defense were very good, but not quite what you would expect out of a national title contender. This year 'Nova loses most of its size inside with the graduation of Cunningham, Shane Clark, and Dwayne Anderson. That suggests it may be premature to anoint the Wildcats the conference favorites heading into 2010, even with the return of Reynolds.

Then again Villanova's freshmen have the rest of the country drooling. The Wildcats bring in a pair of McDonald's All-Americans in Maalik Wayns and Dominic Cheek, as well as consensus top-100 recruits Mouphtaou Yarou and Isaiah Armwood. Wright will also call upon Duke transfer Taylor King (another McDonald's All-American), who is now eligible to play. Quite honestly, Villanova is approaching the type of elite recruiting depth we come to expect from only Duke and North Carolina. And that talent, combined with experienced guard play, suggests a team that can not only compete for the Big East title this year but also make a deep NCAA tournament run.

Prospectus says: Villanova may never have this combination of experience and talent on the court again. There are enough young players to expect a few questionable losses, but on paper this team is the class of the Big East.

Meet the Wildcats

Scottie Reynolds (6-2, 190, Sr.). "You mean he hasn't graduated yet?!" Reynolds was actually able to take on a slightly smaller role in this offense last year, a development that was good for everyone involved. Most notably it meant that there was no shortage of good options on the floor for Wright. As a junior, Reynolds showed an admirable ability and readiness to do whatever the situation required, be it an assist, a two, a three, or a trip to the line. He still isn't a great finisher on paper (making just 45 percent of his twos)—at least not until the final seconds of the Elite Eight game against Pitt.

Corey Fisher (6-1, 200, Jr.). Reynolds gets all the attention, as he's a true scoring point guard who can do everything. But Corey Fisher has plenty of elite point guard talent as well. Fisher led the team in both assist rate and getting to the line.

Corey Stokes (6-5, 220, Jr.). Stokes struggled from deep his freshman year, but he found his shot last season, leading the team with 76 made threes on 42 percent shooting from beyond the arc.

Reggie Redding (6-5, 205, Sr.). Redding is the quiet glue guy. He can pass the ball with above-average results and he improved his ability to make tough shots in traffic last season.

Mouphtaou Yarou (6-10, 250, Fr.). Though not a McDonald's All-American, Yarou is believed by many to be the best recruit in this freshman class. The fact that there's so much talent around him should accelerate his development in the post.

Antonio Pena (6-8, 235, Jr.). Pena is a classic role player in the post, but on a talented team his ability to block shots and grab rebounds will be critical.

Dominic Cheek (6-6, 185, Fr.). Wright prefers to play a smaller lineup of talented players, so the key for Dominic Cheek may not be his scoring, but how quickly he can learn to defend the post. The team will play some zone when he's on the floor, so he won't necessarily have to defend big men one-on-one.

Maalik Wayns (6-1, 185, Fr.). Is it possible to redshirt a McDonald's All-American? Right now it's hard to see how Wayns will get much playing time with Reynolds and Fisher on the floor, but he's ready to make a difference.

Taylor King (6-6, 230, So). King gives Villanova five McDonald's All-Americans on its roster (Reynolds, Stokes, Cheek, Wayns, and King.) He was a tremendous scorer at Duke, making 43 threes in limited playing time as a freshman. But questions about his defense may have limited his playing time in Durham.

West Virginia

[handwritten: P: W: Ebanks, Butler B:]

[handwritten: Discipline Issues]   *[handwritten: Slow Pace]*

2009: 23-12 (10-8 Big East), lost to Dayton 68-60, NCAA First Round
In-conference offense: 1.06 points per possession (9th)
In-conference defense: 0.98 points allowed per possession (3rd)

What West Virginia did well: *Expose a weakness and win big.*

West Virginia was the team of the blowout win in 2008-09. They beat Ohio St. by 28, Providence by 27, Seton Hall by 26, St. John's by 23, Villanova by 19, DePaul by 19, Rutgers by 18, Iowa by 17, and

Georgetown by 17. But perhaps most impressively, they beat Pitt by 14 in the Big East tournament when many believed the Panthers were playing for a one-seed in the NCAA tournament.

Those huge margins of victory made the Mountaineers a computer rankings favorite, and the type of team most people felt was better than a 10-8 Big East team. The team was deemed "unlucky" to finish seventh in the Big East. And as if the committee wanted to test the computers, the Mountaineers were paired with a team with some of the weakest margin of victory numbers in the nation, the Dayton Flyers, in the first round of the NCAA tournament.

But a funny thing happened to heavily favored West Virginia. They lost. Dayton, which had struggled offensively for much of the season, posted its second best offensive efficiency rating since December and won. And the Mountaineers simply could not stop one of the best mid-major players in the country, Chris Wright.

Was Bob Huggins' team really "unlucky" last year? Or were they just good at exposing the weaknesses of certain teams? West Virginia went just 2-8 against the Big East's elite teams last year, suggesting that no matter how much the computers loved them, the Mountaineers have a ways to go to reach the top of the Big East.

What we learned in 2009: *Bob Huggins continues to craft the team in his image.*

This may have more to do with John Beilein than the current coach at West Virginia, but it is abundantly clear that since taking over as head coach, Huggins has remade the offense.

The Return To The Cincinnati Style					
School	Year	Coach	TO%	3PA/FGA	FTA/FGA
West Virginia	2007	John Beilein	17.0	49.0	28.2
West Virginia	2009	Bob Huggins	17.9	34.0	35.9
Cincinnati	2005	Bob Huggins	18.8	33.1	45.8
School	Year	Coach	OffReb%		A/FGA
West Virginia	2007	John Beilein	30.2		68.7
West Virginia	2009	Bob Huggins	40.8		59.8
Cincinnati	2005	Bob Huggins	38.7		59.1

While Beilein's last team in Morgantown was a true perimeter-oriented outfit that avoided turnovers and took numerous threes, Huggins would prefer his team to be more physical and dominate in the paint. West Virginia has therefore become much more aggressive at offensive rebounding and at drawing fouls. The Mountaineers' falling assist rate reflects the fact that Huggins also likes his players to go one-on-one and create their own shot when the match-up is favorable.

What's in store for 2010: Alex Ruoff has now graduated, and while he was an incredibly effective scorer, the reality is that he never seemed to fit into Huggins' system. With Ruoff gone, the coach now has a cast of players that can play his more physical style of basketball. And with every other significant rotation player returning, West Virginia is expected to be better in 2010. When you consider the elite margin-of-victory numbers from last season, just a little improvement might mean a Big East title.

Prospectus says: West Virginia returns the most minutes of any Big East team to make the NCAA tournament last year. And with one of the "unluckiest" seasons and best margin-of-victory stats, there are a lot of smart people who will pick this team to win the Big East title.

But I'm a little more cautious. What concerns me is that Alex Ruoff was the team's most efficient player last year. And even if he wasn't Huggins' style of player, he will be missed. Even if the rest of the team has the average one- to five-point improvement in efficiency margin that we might expect, the loss of Ruoff could mean the total offensive efficiency stays the same this year. That's why I think West Virginia will be one of the best teams in the Big East this year, just not the conference champs.

Ruoff's departure, along with the off-court issues and the lack of success against elite teams last year, prevents me from putting West Virginia at the top. But with a team now built in the style Bob Huggins wants, the Mountaineers will be in the hunt.

Meet the Mountaineers

Da'Sean Butler (6-7, 225, Sr.). Butler may be the most under-hyped player in the Big East. The problem is he keeps getting out-shined by his own teammates. First it was Joe Alexander, than Alex Ruoff, and now even Devin Ebanks gets more hype. But Butler is the team's leading scorer, a phenomenal inside-outside player, and, despite taking shots more frequently than any of his teammates, he remains one of the most efficient scorers on the team.

Devin Ebanks (6-9, 210, So.). Ebanks is just a sophomore and has yet to fully fill out as a big man. But he's already developed the inside presence that Huggins wants to see in his post players. Ebanks is the team's best offensive and defensive rebounder and he draws fouls at the highest rate of any rotation player.

Dalton Pepper (6-5, 215, Fr.). Likely in an off-guard role, Pepper will be expected to knock down three point shots. Given all the weapons on this roster, he should see a lot of open looks as a freshman and have a real chance to make an impact.

Darryl Bryant (6-2, 200, So.). Bryant was suspended for fleeing the scene of a traffic accident and may miss some games to start the season. But assuming he gets on the floor, he'll continue to play a key role. His combination of three-point touch and ability to distribute makes him an above-average point guard.

Joe Mazzulla (6-2, 200, Jr.). Mazzula had a higher assist rate than Bryant, and may have been in line for more playing time, but injuries and off-court incidents also make his status for the season questionable.

Wellington Smith (6-7, 245, Sr.). Smith's blocked shots and offensive rebounding provide another key presence in the paint.

Kevin Jones (6-8, 245, So.). Jones rarely touched the ball last year, but when he did he often finished. The result was one of the lowest turnover rates in the Big East.

John Flowers (6-7, 215, Jr.). This team is exceptionally deep at forward with five returning rotation post players (Butler, Ebanks, Smith, Jones, Flowers) with offensive efficiency ratings above 100.

Casey Mitchell (6-4, 220, Jr.). A junior college transfer who is expected to compete with Pepper for a role as a three-point gunner.

SLOW

Last year's All-Big Ten first team was comprised of five sophomores: Michigan State's Kalin Lucas, Ohio State's Evan Turner, Michigan's Manny Harris, Penn State's Talor Battle, and Purdue's JaJuan Johnson. All five players are back as juniors this year, as is fellow junior Robbie Hummel, Johnson's teammate and last year's preseason conference player of the year.

This rate of return on sophomore investments is most unusual. None of the above players were seen as quite sexy enough by the NBA to leave early. So the league's best players are back. All of them. So are 11 out of 11 coaches. That carryover from last year testifies to a conference that figures to be "improved," but here we run into a paradox. You can make a case that a clear majority of the league's 11 teams will be better this season, but there are still 99 losses that will have to be distributed in conference play.

I expect that very few of those losses will stick to Purdue and Michigan State. After a season in which he was slowed by a hairline fracture in his lower back, Hummel is reportedly healthy, meaning Matt Painter, incredibly, still has on hand the essential elements (Hummel, Johnson, E'Twaun Moore, Chris Kramer, and Keaton Grant) of a team that went 15-3 in the Big Ten in 2008.

The Boilermakers will likely be challenged every step of the way by a Michigan State team that lost Goran Suton and Travis Walton but returns a veritable human wave of long and athletic talent, a wave channeled by two leaders who have proven their worth in the crucible of March: Tom Izzo and Kalin Lucas.

Any roster that brings back three starters from a team that beat Kansas, Louisville, and Connecticut on its march to the national championship game is a force to be reckoned with.

Ohio State and Minnesota can't match the Spartans' record of success in the 2009 tournament, but they do return more minutes than any other teams in the conference. The Buckeyes hope David Lighty's return will bolster a defense that sabotaged what could have been a memorable season in Columbus, one in which Evan Turner, William Buford, and Jon Diebler hit an amazingly high percentage of their shots. And in Minneapolis Tubby Smith will likely use a rotation that goes even deeper than Izzo's, if such a thing is possible. With their unusual blend of shot-blocking and ball-hawking, the Gophers should again render opposing offenses uncomfortable and unproductive.

If Minnesota is a prime candidate to continue their excellence on defense, I think it likely that Illinois will slip a notch or two in this department, now that designated stopper Chester Frazier has departed. For Illini fans the countervailing good news is two-fold: Bruce Weber's outstanding D can slip a little and still be quite good, and there is more than enough room, goodness knows, for this team to improve on offense. Demetri McCamey, Mike Davis, Mike Tisdale, and a couple talented freshmen will do their best to make it so.

Shadowing or perhaps outpacing Weber will be those two idiosyncratic schemers up north, Michigan's John Beilein and Wisconsin's Bo Ryan. In Manny Harris and DeShawn Sims, the Wolverines return virtually

BIG TEN PROSPECTUS

	2009 Record	Returning Minutes (%)	2010 Prediction
Purdue	11-7	82	14-4
Michigan St.	15-3	67	13-5
Ohio St.	10-8	90	12-6
Minnesota	9-9	89	11-7
Michigan	9-9	73	10-8
Illinois	11-7	60	10-8
Wisconsin	10-8	67	9-9
Northwestern	8-10	78	9-9
Penn St.	10-8	46	6-12
Indiana	1-17	64	3-15
Iowa	5-13	52	2-16

the entirety of their offense in just two players—two very talented and experienced players. Harris and Sims will lead a group whose quickness will result in a lot of points and whose size will likely allow a lot of points. For their part the Badgers' veteran backcourt of Trevon Hughes and Jason Bohannon will head up a roster that's trying to regroup after the 2008-09 team gave rise to that oddest and most unprecedented of Madison occurrences, average defense.

Of course no occurrence is so odd or unprecedented as Northwestern making the NCAA tournament. The Wildcats almost did just that last year, as Bill Carmody's team came within a tip here or a rebound there of going .500 in-conference, traditionally a good barometer of a team's chances for a bid. This season Kevin Coble and three other starters return, but the 'Cats do lose Craig Moore, whose accurate three-point shooting almost single-handedly prevented opposing defenses from simply walling off Coble. If NU can find someone (John Shurna?) to fill that void and co-star alongside Coble on offense, it's at least possible that history could be made in Evanston on Selection Sunday.

Penn State's made the tournament before, naturally, but it's been a while (not since 2001), and, like Northwestern, the Nittany Lions came agonizingly close to getting a long-coveted bid in 2009. In the end Ed DeChellis's team had to be content with an NIT title and the knowledge that Talor Battle has shown he can pretty much do it all. With Jamelle Cornley and Stanley Pringle no longer in the lineup this year, he'll have to.

Indiana fans feel like they've seen it all over the past 22 months, everything from being ranked number 8 in the nation (January 2008), to the sudden departure of their coach amidst a cloud of NCAA infractions (February 2008), to, finally, a team that won just six games in five months of playing basketball (November 2008 to March 2009). Well, rejoice, Hoosier fans. Those pages have been turned and Tom Crean has brought in an outstanding recruiting class. The rebuild is in full swing.

That leaves Todd Lickliter's Iowa Hawkeyes, a team that badly needs the continuity so cruelly abundant elsewhere in the Big Ten. For Matt Gatens' sake I hope they find it.   *John Gasaway*

Illinois

P: McCamey
W:
B: Tisdale

2009: 24-10 (11-7 Big Ten), lost to Western Kentucky 76-72, NCAA First Round
In-conference offense: 0.98 points per possession (9th)
In-conference defense: 0.93 points allowed per possession (1st)

What Illinois did well: *Defend, as always.*

This defense thing with Illinois is getting monotonous.

Consistently Prohibitive: Illinois Defense, 2005-09		
Year	Opp. PPP	Big Ten rank
2005	0.94	2nd
2006	0.96	2nd
2007	0.92	1st
2008	0.99	5th
2009	**0.93**	**1st**
Conference games only Opp. PPP: opponent points per possession		

Bear in mind there are a lot of eras spanned there, everything from reaching the national championship game to not getting into the tournament at all. Come what may, the Illini simply refuse to allow opponents to score a point per trip. Bruce Weber deserves the credit here, of course, but he had help last year in the notably spindly forms of Mike Tisdale and Mike Davis.

While Tisdale and Davis will never be confused for NFL tight ends, they are, at the risk of belaboring the obvious, 7-1 and 6-9 respectively. They don't block many shots but they both have good wingspans and, anyway, Weber apparently arranges to have his players' arms surgically locked into the defensive "up" position as entering freshmen. As a result Big Ten opponents made just 44 percent of their twos last year. When the other team can't make twos, you have a chance to be really good on D, particularly when you cut down on your fouling as dramatically as the Illini did in 2008-09.

What we learned in 2009: *You can get back to the NCAA tournament without improving your weak offense.*

With Davis emerging, somewhat surprisingly, as a force to be reckoned with on offense for a team that was improving from 5-13 to 11-7 in the Big Ten, there was an unmistakable sense afoot last year that the Illini had somehow gotten their offense pointed in the right direction—relatively speaking. Obviously no team that loses to Penn State at home by the peach basket-era score of 38-33 is the second coming of North Carolina. Still, this offense had to have been better than that ghastly thing we caught occasional glimpses of when we weren't covering our eyes in 2007-08, right?

Well, no, actually.

Where Have You Gone, Deron Williams? Illinois Offense, 2005-09		
Year	PPP	Big Ten rank
2005	1.18	1st
2006	1.06	4th
2007	0.95	9th
2008	0.99	7th
2009	0.98	9th
Conference games only PPP: points per possession		

By 2009 the Illinois offense had reached the hoops equivalent of vapor-lock. For the first time in the Weber era, but for painfully obvious and indeed compelling reasons, the Illini were significantly less likely to shoot a three than your average Big Ten team. (Attempts from outside the arc comprised just 30 percent of Illinois' shots in league play.) But if you're going to be an inside-the arc team, you should be able to get some offensive boards or some free throws, perhaps even both.

Illinois got neither, and in rather spectacular fashion. In 2008-09 Weber's team came in at number 344 nationally in the frequency with which they attempted free throws. Yes, that's last in the nation, allowing Kennesaw State to say with justice: In your face, Illinois!

The team's weakness on the offensive glass last year was less egregious but perhaps more telling. Michigan State notwithstanding, a significant portion of the Big Ten continues to cling tenaciously to the coaching wives tale that says if you're getting a lot of offensive rebounds you must be giving up a lot of points in transition. The Illini are far from alone, then, in surrendering their offensive glass entirely. Indeed the fact that Illinois could rank a relatively robust sixth in the league in this department while getting to a paltry 28 percent of their own misses in conference play speaks

stylistic volumes about the Big Ten.

Weber's team was a hair more accurate from the field and took much better care of the ball in conference play last year than in 2008. The fact that the offense stayed mired in the league's lower tier was therefore directly attributable to a relative lack of offensive boards and a total lack of free throws.

What's in store for 2010: During the offseason I did some doodling on a team projection system that looks at a roster's returning possessions adjusted for playing time, as opposed to simply using returning minutes. To be honest, a lot of the time there's not too much difference between those two measures. But then a team like Illinois comes along: This year's Illini were made for my wacky new system. On paper they return merely 60 percent of last season's minutes. True enough, but the 2008-09 Illini featured two senior starters, Trent Meacham and Chester Frazier, who were always on the floor yet played either relatively (Meacham) or incredibly (Frazier) small roles in the offense. Yes, Frazier was the Travis Walton-variety perimeter stopper on D. Understood. I'm merely suggesting not all teams that return 60 percent of their minutes are created equal. Don't be surprised if Illinois looks less young and inexperienced on offense in 2010 than that "60" would suggest. We shall see.

Prospectus says: Replacing last year's seniors, Frazier and Meacham, with D.J. Richardson and a player to be named later would figure to help the Illinois offense at the expense of its defense. That's a trade most Illinois fans will take. Between the length provided by Tisdale and Davis and the Gene Keady-instilled emphasis on D furnished by Weber, the Illini defense still projects to be very good even if it slips a bit. The activity known as offense, on the other hand, presents Illinois with vast and untrammeled vistas for improvement.

Meet the Fighting Illini

Demetri McCamey (6-3, 200, Jr.). Bad three-point shooting (31 percent) marred what otherwise would have been a really nice sophomore year on offense for McCamey, one in which he showed that he can function as a scoring point guard for Weber without coughing up the ball. Not to mention last year's very good 52 percent two-point shooting suggests McCamey could be one assertive-on-offense backcourt mate away from taking a great leap forward.

24 **Mike Davis (6-9, 220, Jr.).** After a freshman year that can charitably be termed nondescript, Davis improbably but unmistakably barreled out of the chute last year and, along with McCamey and Mike Tisdale, became one of the three featured performers in this offense. Nor were his contributions limited to one side of the ball. Among the following three lottery picks and one collegian, who posted the highest defensive rebound percentage last year: Connecticut's Hasheem Thabeet, Arizona's Jordan Hill, North Carolina's Tyler Hansbrough, or Illinois' Mike Davis? Hint: Apparently the defensive glass doesn't care whether your physique is ripped or not. In fact Davis came within a whisker of knocking off Michigan State's Goran Suton for the title of best defensive rebounder in a league fairly obsessed with the things.

54 **Mike Tisdale (7-1, 235, Jr.).** Then again Davis's excellence in defensive rebounding was partly a function of the abundant opportunities that befell someone who played alongside Mike Tisdale, for the seven-footer was oddly averse to picking up boards on that end of the floor. Illinois was able to muddle through anyway because Tisdale more than earned his keep in defending opponents' two-point shots, because Davis proved quite capable of leading the charge on the defensive glass, and, not least, because Tisdale had the happy knack of making 54 percent of his twos.

1 **D.J. Richardson (6-2, 185, Fr.).** Richardson is a highly-touted shooting guard from Peoria who arrives in Champaign via Findlay Prep in greater Las Vegas, where his team won a mythical ESPN-administered high school national championship last year. (Richardson played in the same backcourt as McDonald's All-American Avery Bradley, now a freshman at Texas.) Signing Richardson along with Brandon Paul (see below) helped Weber assuage restless Illini fans who previously had faulted the coach's recruiting.

33 **Alex Legion (6-5, 200, Jr.).** Legion arrived a year ago as a transfer from Kentucky with the expectation that his offense would allow him to earn minutes on a team starved for points. Instead he struggled to score, thus insuring that the defensively questionable Legion would rarely see the floor on a Bruce Weber team. In offseason workouts Weber reportedly placed a one-month ban on Legion shooting threes in an attempt to prod the junior into rounding out his game.

3 **Brandon Paul (6-4, 195, Fr.).** The reigning Mr. Basketball in the state of Illinois, Paul is a shooting guard from Gurnee who's earning plaudits for his athleticism, to wit: "I don't even have an adjective for it." Thus Weber, to John Supinie of the Gatehouse News Service in September.

23 **Dominique Keller (6-7, 230, Sr.).** Though he played limited minutes last year, Keller was notably assertive in seeking out his shot and, truth be known, he did OK, hitting 54 percent of his twos.

Indiana *out*

2009: 6-25 (1-17 Big Ten), lost to Penn State 66-51, Big Ten First Round
In-conference offense: 0.93 points per possession (11th)
In-conference defense: 1.12 points allowed per possession (11th)

What Indiana did well: *Scare good teams.*
On paper there's no earthly explanation for how a team like Indiana could possibly have been competitive against a team like Michigan State on March 3, 2009, the day MSU eked out a 64-59 victory in Bloomington. The Hoosiers finished 1-17 in the Big Ten. The Spartans beat two one-seeds, Louisville and Connecticut, on their way to the national championship game. Be that as it may, IU had no fewer than four chances to tie or take the lead in this game's last three minutes. It was that close.

Nor was that the only close loss. The Hoosiers fell to eventual NCAA participants Michigan and Minnesota by six and four points, respectively. The game against the Wolverines went into OT. For a team that won just six times in five months of playing basketball, Indiana could be surprisingly competitive.

Then again you're never referred to as "competitive" if you win. If there's a lesson that IU's 2008-09 season brought home, it's that it's tough to win when you return four percent of your minutes. Yes, you're reading that correctly. Last year's Indiana roster, in the person of Kyle Taber, had just four percent of the minutes that had been played by the 2007-08 team led by Eric Gordon and D.J. White.

To sift the statistical rubble that ensued as a direct consequence of this startling number would of course be beside the point, which was this: Indiana was operating at a talent deficit in every conference game they played, including the one they won against Iowa on February 4.

And yet, taking the most cursory glance at said rubble, I have to admit that one fact stood out and gave me pause. Last year Indiana "led" the nation in the frequency with which their two-point shots were blocked. Tom Crean's first IU team saw more than 14 percent of its twos swatted away. It was as if his overmatched players had to go up against Mississippi State's Jarvis Varnado game-in, game-out, for the entire season.

What we learned in 2009: *Rebuilding after a programmatic nuclear winter takes time.*

There really aren't any recent parallels for what Indiana was forced to go through last year, but one rough guide would be Baylor's performance in the aftermath of their notorious scandal under Dave Bliss six years ago.

Obviously this isn't a perfect comparison: Indiana's a "brand" in college basketball terms that Baylor is five national championships away from equaling. Also note that the Bears' case involved actual criminal behaviors as opposed to Kelvin Sampson's mere NCAA violations, so what befell the Bears' program was justifiably far worse. Bliss was fired as head coach in August of 2003, but the investigations and penalties were just ramping up. As late as the 2005-06 season, Baylor was still paying a very severe price, operating under a penalty that in effect banned the team from playing games until the beginning of the conference season. Conversely the Hoosiers, though nominally still operating under NCAA probation for infractions committed on Sampson's watch, have managed to take their medicine and bottom out in a much more expeditious manner.

But what the Bears do provide is a recent instance where a program went from having a roster in ruins (much like Indiana in June of 2008) to putting a team into the NCAA tournament. If you start Baylor's clock on January 11, 2006, when they were allowed by the NCAA to play their first game of the 2005-06 season, the Bears were able to make that journey in a remarkably short time. Indiana hopes they can not only do the same, but also sustain that success better than Baylor did last year.

From Siberia to Selection Sunday Baylor's Recovery After Its Implosion			
Year	EM	Conf. W-L	NCAA result
2006	-0.15	4-12	no bid
2007	-0.11	4-12	no bid
2008	+0.01	9-7	1st round
2009	-0.05	5-11	no bid
Conference games only EM: efficiency margin (points per possession – opponent PPP)			

Note that Indiana, which won just one game while watching their opponents outscore them by 0.19 points per trip, fared worse in the Big Ten last year than did Baylor in the Big 12 in 2006. Then again IU appears to be rebuilding at a very rapid pace, having brought in a recruiting class for 2009-10 that's been rated as one of the best in the country.

What's in store for 2010: Crean had an irresistible product to offer on the recruiting trail this past season. Opportunities for immediate minutes at a legendary program just don't come around like this every day. As a result the coach has an impressive freshman class that should be able to help out right away.

Prospectus says: Are we seeing the first inklings of Marquette 2008 in the roster Crean is building in Bloomington? Could be. The coach's last team in Milwaukee was an up-tempo (69 trips per 40 minutes in-conference) guard-heavy group that forced opponents into a ton of turnovers. In fact the Golden Eagles led the Big East in that category in 2008, extracting a turnover on 24 percent of their conference foes' possessions. Not to mention the sound bites comparing current IU players to past Marquette players have already begun. (Jordan Hulls has been called a latter-day Travis Diener.) If you see a Hoosier squad this year that suddenly takes much better care of the ball, harasses the perimeter, and records a goodly number of steals (and, yes, commits the occasional foul), you'll know that Crean is on-schedule with his rebuild.

Meet the Hoosiers

Christian Watford (6-8, 215, Fr.). A long-ish wing from Birmingham, Watford is earning praise from Crean for his perimeter shooting and his versatility.

Maurice Creek (6-5, 200, Fr.). Creek was cleared academically by the NCAA at the end of August, giving Crean a prolific shooting guard who averaged 18 points a game last year for Hargrave Military Academy.

Jeremiah Rivers (6-5, 210, Jr.). The son of Boston Celtics head coach Doc Rivers, Jeremiah transferred to Bloomington from Georgetown, where in 2007-08 he averaged 19 minutes a game and functioned almost exclusively as a defensive stopper on the perimeter.

Jordan Hulls (6-0, 170, Fr.). The reigning Mr. Basketball in Indiana, Hulls is a point guard from Bloomington who's touted for his outside shooting and decision making.

Devan Dumes (6-2, 190, So.). If not for his struggles with turnovers last year, Dumes would have had a season that was shockingly close to "normal" for a talented freshman. Considering he played on a team that labored under markedly abnormal circumstances, that's high praise. Dumes made 38 percent of his threes while taking a larger share of the team's shots than any other player. (And, in Dumes's defense, the struggle with turnovers was a self-reinforcing team-wide affliction. Indiana gave the ball away on 26 percent of their trips in Big Ten play, far and away the worst mark in the conference.)

Verdell Jones (6-5, 175, So.). Though not as accurate from the perimeter as Dumes, Jones approximated his own turnover-heavy version of normalcy as a freshman. Specifically the point guard from Champaign, Illinois, made almost half his twos while functioning as a co-featured option on offense alongside Dumes.

Tom Pritchard (6-9, 240, So.). Pritchard's efficiency was hurt by the fact that he's a 58 percent foul shooter who was sent to the line more often than any other Hoosier. The good news is he was highly effective on the offensive glass. Among Big Ten players only Michigan State's Delvon Roe posted a higher rebound percentage on that end of the floor.

Derek Elston (6-9, 220, Fr.). A forward from Tipton, Indiana, Elston has earned laudatory quotes from Crean for his toughness.

Iowa

2009: 15-17 (5-13 Big Ten), lost to Michigan 73-45, Big Ten First Round
In-conference offense: 0.99 points per possession (8th)
In-conference defense: 1.07 points allowed per possession (10th)

What Iowa did well: *Wave goodbye.*

Every office has a support person who tirelessly and often thanklessly organizes the goodbye party when someone leaves. Whoever that person is in the Iowa basketball office, Todd Lickliter should give them a year off. Just look at all the goodbye parties this nameless staff member has had to make happen....

April 10, 2008: Reserve guard Dan Bohall, who started the first seven games of the 2007-08 season but subsequently saw little playing time, announces what can only be termed his retirement from college basketball. He doesn't transfer to a different program; the sophomore simply wants to "spend more time with my family and my girlfriend."

May 2, 2008: Starting guard Tony Freeman announces that he will transfer out of the program. Freeman eventually lands at Southern Illinois, where this year he will play his senior season.

Then came what I trust Hawkeye fans refer to as the Friday Night Massacre: March 27, 2009. On that day no fewer than four Iowa players made plain their intention to go elsewhere:

• Starting guard and leading scorer Jake Kelly, who tragically lost his mother in a plane crash, announced he would leave Iowa to be closer to his home in Carmel, Indiana. He ended up at Indiana State.

• Kelly's fellow starting guard, Jeff Peterson, also declared that he would depart. Specifically citing the Hawkeyes' slow tempo as a factor in his decision, Peterson eventually elected to transfer to Arkansas.

• Junior college transfer Jermain Davis, who started 11 games for the Hawkeyes in 2008-09, announced he would transfer yet again, this time to Division II Minnesota State. "The style that we play is just so slow," Davis was quoted as saying on his way out the door.

• Lastly, junior college transfer David Palmer declared that he too would leave Iowa. He ended up at Division II Southern Indiana.

The departure of these four players was announced in an official Iowa athletic department release under the headline "Lickliter Eyes Future, Likes What He Sees."

What we learned in 2009: *Not everyone's on the tempo-free bus yet.*

As a really slow-paced team with a really bad defense, Iowa in 2009 was pretty much the perfect test case to see how far the tempo-free paradigm had progressed in its tireless quest for world domination. Based on the discussion triggered by this struggling team the answer would appear to be: Not all that far. The Hawkeyes lost their fair share of games in the 50s and thus labored under a presumption that their offense was the problem. Said offense was no juggernaut, to be sure, but the D in Iowa City was even worse.

It's hard to discern bad defense, though, when it's embedded within the slowest major-conference team in four seasons.

Good Thing There's A Shot Clock: Slowest-Paced Major-Conference Teams, 2006-09		
Team	Year	Pace
Iowa	**2009**	**56.8**
Northwestern	2007	57.1
Washington St.	2009	57.4
Wisconsin	2009	57.8
Oregon St.	2009	58.2
Arizona St.	2007	58.2
Conference games only		
Pace: possessions per 40 minutes		

Note however that there's a certain injustice in Lickliter being criticized on purely tempo grounds. Craig Robinson played about as slowly last year at Oregon State and he's the toast of college hoops. So too did Tony Bennett at Washington State and he was able to land himself a new gig at Virginia. If Iowa were winning games and keeping players, no one would fret about the pace. The question is not why Lickliter goes so slow, but rather why it's not working for him the way it works for Robinson and Bennett and, indeed, the way it used to work for Lickliter himself at Butler.

What's in store for 2010: For the second consecutive season Iowa will start the year with a number for returning minutes that is well below the conference average. True, the same could have been said about Ohio State

two years ago. But where the Buckeyes at that time were losing players to the NBA, the Hawkeyes, as detailed above, have been losing them to the SEC, the Missouri Valley, Division II, and at least one girlfriend.

Prospectus says: Iowa is almost universally being picked to finish last in the Big Ten this season and on this point I am in accord with the universe. Still, a Hawkeye fan who wanted to manufacture some optimism could at least envision this offense being decent this year. If nothing else Lickliter would appear to have multiple shooters on hand for his perimeter-oriented style. The key will be whether the coach can at last find a point guard who will take care of the ball and perhaps even stick around a year or two.

Meet the Hawkeyes

Matt Gatens (6-5, 215, So.). Gatens was the undeniable bright spot of Iowa's season, one who more than delivered on the advance praise that hailed him as a pure shooter. As a freshman playing for a struggling team, the Iowa City product made 40 percent of his threes and 90 percent of his free throws. Gatens also carried on the Adam Haluska tradition of taking excellent care of the ball. In the absence of Kelly and Peterson he should absorb a lot more possessions in this offense.

Anthony Tucker (6-4, 200, So.). Before being ruled academically ineligible for the spring semester, Tucker started eight games and averaged 21 minutes per contest while functioning as an unbelievably quick-triggered three-point gunner. If that makes him sound one-dimensional, keep in mind he made 43 percent of those threes. He is being talked up as this year's point guard.

Aaron Fuller (6-6, 210, So.). Fuller started 19 games last year and scored a season-high 16 points against Penn State on January 24 in a 63-59 road loss that the Hawkeyes came surprisingly close to winning. (Iowa finished 0-9 on the road in the Big Ten.) Nominally one of those perimeter-savvy wings that Lickliter favors, Fuller actually struggled to hit his threes as a freshman, making just 30 percent of his attempts from beyond the arc.

Devan Bawinkle (6-5, 210, Sr.). Originally recruited to West Virginia by John Beilein, Bawinkle arrived last year as a junior college transfer and gave new meaning to the term "perimeter-oriented," hoisting just five two-point tries the whole year. On the other side of the arc he made 37 percent of his 139 attempted threes, many of them from the corner.

Jarryd Cole (6-7, 250, Jr.). Though he did record a few offensive boards, Cole was on the floor last year exclusively for defense—when he wasn't in foul trouble.

Devon Archie (6-9, 215 Jr.). Archie is a junior-college transfer from Vincennes CC in Indiana.

Eric May (6-5, 220, Fr.). A wing praised for both his outside shot and his ability to attack the rim, May is an in-state product from Dubuque.

Cully Payne (6-1, 190, Fr.). In June of 2005 Payne had just finished the eighth grade in suburban Chicago when he made headlines by committing to DePaul. Three years later, however, the point guard chose to "re-open" his recruitment and signed a letter of intent with Mark Gottfried at Alabama. When Gottfried was let go by the Crimson Tide in January, Payne was released from his commitment. He now finds himself in Iowa City.

Michigan

2009: 21-14 (9-9 Big Ten), lost to Oklahoma 73-63, NCAA Second Round
In-conference offense: 1.01 points per possession (6th)
In-conference defense: 1.03 points allowed per possession (6th)

What Michigan did well: *Make more shots.*

Last year was a long time coming for Michigan fans, but it finally arrived: The Wolverines returned to the NCAA tournament for the first time since 1998 and upset seven-seed Clemson before falling to two-seed Oklahoma in the second round.

The largest single difference between a team that was battling Blake Griffin in late March and one that went 10-22 the year before was accuracy from the field.

Shooting Cures All Ills Michigan Offense, 2009 vs. 2008			
Year	2FG%	3FG%	PPP
2008	45.3	30.0	0.96
2009	50.3	32.1	1.01
Conference games only			
PPP: points per possession			

When we say "Michigan" improved its shooting, we of course mean Manny Harris and DeShawn Sims improved their shooting, for together the two Detroit products took an unbelievable 46 percent of the Wolverines' shots last year.

What we learned in 2009: *DeShawn Sims is underrated.*

Sims is more likely to shoot during his minutes on the floor than any other Big Ten player.

He May Try To Shoot: Highest Shot Percentages Among Big Ten Players, 2008-09		
Player	Team	%Shots
DeShawn Sims	**Michigan**	**30.7**
Lawrence Westbrook	Minnesota	29.8
Devan Dumes	Indiana	28.6
Kevin Coble	Northwestern	28.4
Manny Harris	Michigan	28.2
Minimum 20 minutes per game		
%Shots: percentage of team's shots taken by player during his minutes		

You'd think a player carrying this large a load in the offense for a rapidly-improving team would receive no shortage of attention. Actually Sims was somewhat overlooked last year, possibly because he couldn't earn the "leading scorer" tag for this team with Harris getting an additional two games' worth of minutes over the course of the season.

By "somewhat overlooked" I mean Sims was relegated to third-team All-Big Ten along with Northwestern's Craig Moore, Penn State's Jamelle Cornley, Illinois' Demetri McCamey, and a hobbled Robbie Hummel from Purdue. Fine players all, particularly Hummel when he's healthy, but someone who makes 55 percent of his twos while shooting as often as the 6-8 Sims did, usually as the tallest player on the floor for his team, arguably deserves a higher profile.

Beilein made his bones at West Virginia thanks in

no small measure to the stellar offensive efficiency of Kevin Pittsnogle and Mike Gansey, as well as the subsequent, and surprising, emergence of Joe Alexander. In 2005-06 at the peak of Beilein's wizardry in Morgantown, Pittsnogle made 54 percent of his twos while taking 29 percent of the Mountaineers' shots during his minutes. Differences in physique and height notwithstanding, Sims is Beilein's current Pittsnogle. (Minus the perimeter accuracy, to be sure.)

What's in store for 2010: It may seem strange to say about a perimeter-oriented team, but watch the twos. Just like last year, Michigan will likely shoot more threes than any other Big Ten team while posting a below-average three-point FG percentage. That need not be a problem, however, as long as Harris and Sims continue to improve inside the arc, just as Pittsnogle and Gansey did as they became more acclimated to Beilein's system.

Prospectus says: It's not Michigan's fault that, for reasons that escape me, this team is being a little overrated in the preseason, with projected rankings as high as top-ten in the nation. I don't say such surprises are out of the question, but I do say it's premature to expect that particular surprise based on what we know now about a team that was outscored in Big Ten play in 2009. Harris and Sims developed by leaps and bounds last year, but it's also likely that opponents will again be able to make a lot of twos against this defense. They'll need to: Michigan figures to score a lot of points.

Meet the Wolverines

Manny Harris (6-5, 185, Jr.). Harris played virtually all of his minutes last year alongside a series of nominal point guards (Kelvin Grady, C.J. Lee, Stu Douglass, etc.), but in truth he himself functioned like a scoring point guard last year, posting far and away the team's highest assist rate. Make that an excellent scoring point guard, one who overcame iffy perimeter shooting (33 percent) with frequent trips to the line (where he knocked down 86 percent). He also played close enough to the basket in the 1-3-1 zone to emerge as the team's best defensive rebounder. As such Harris helped to puncture a hoary stereotype, one that says zone teams can't rebound. Actually Michigan did fine on the defensive glass last year, getting to 71 percent of opponents' misses in conference play, a figure that

was good for third in the league behind the usual carnivores (Michigan State and Wisconsin).

DeShawn Sims (6-8, 235, Sr.). See above: Sims was an underappreciated mensch on offense last year, albeit one who made just 32 percent of his threes. (Get used to it. He's a career 30 percent three-point shooter playing for John Beilein. There will be misses. Sims offsets this by shooting four twos for every three.)

Zack Novak (6-5, 210, So.). Novak may not look like much, either in person or on paper, but he clearly has what Beilein wants. In a season where the coach experimented at somewhat remarkable length with players not named "Harris" or "Sims," Novak emerged early on as a regular and indeed received more minutes than anyone outside the Big Two. His infrequent shot attempts were mostly threes and the results there were about average (34 percent). Novak is perhaps better remembered for being on the receiving end of a rather infamous poster-quality dunk by Blake Griffin in the NCAA tournament.

Stuart Douglass (6-3, 175, So.). In the third game of his college career, Douglass hit a three to put his team ahead of UCLA for good with four minutes left in the game. Delivering the dagger against the fourth-ranked team in the country at Madison Square Garden was an auspicious debut for a relatively unheralded freshman. He would figure to see quality minutes again this year, likely at the point.

Darius Morris (6-4, 180, Fr.). Morris is a highly-regarded combo guard from L.A. who apparently is going to be given every opportunity, whether sooner or later this season, to earn a starting job as more of a point guard.

Laval Lucas-Perry (6-3, 185, So.). Arriving last year as a transfer from Arizona, Lucas-Perry became eligible in December and averaged 13 points per contest over his first six games. After that his production trailed off, however, and he played just 16 minutes in two NCAA tournament games. Still, don't write off Lucas-Perry just yet. The hope in Ann Arbor is that he'll show the same improvement in his second year in the Beilein system that Sims and Harris displayed last year.

Zack Gibson (6-10, 220, Sr.). Though he would figure to supply his team with some badly needed size inside, Gibson averaged just 12 minutes per game last year as Beilein plainly preferred the matchup problems his team posed for opponents when the Wolverines "went small." That is one instructive preference. Gibson, whatever his limitations, is a good shot-blocker on a team that allowed Big Ten opponents to make 54 percent of their twos, meaning Michigan's was the most permissive interior D in the league. Nevertheless Beilein plainly believes that moving Sims from the 5 to the 4 on offense so Gibson can play some D would cost more points than it would prevent. (Yes, Gibson is foul-prone, but that's not what's limiting his minutes. Last year he wasn't on the floor long enough to get in foul trouble, earning four whistles just twice all season.)

Matt Vogrich (6-4, 180, Fr.). By some lights Vogrich would rank as the highest-rated recruit in Michigan's freshman class. That being said, he'd be well advised to hit his shots from day one to secure minutes as a freshman shooting guard on a veteran roster where even the "center" shot 80-plus threes last year.

Ben Cronin (7-0, 265, Fr.). Cronin underwent surgery on his left hip in January and was granted a redshirt year. He gives Beilein another option for minutes in support of Sims.

Michigan State

2009: 31-7 (15-3 Big Ten), lost to North Carolina 89-72, National Championship Game
In-conference offense: 1.06 points per possession (3rd)
In-conference defense: 0.93 points allowed per possession (2nd)

What Michigan State did well: *Render iffy shooting irrelevant.*

There were no fewer than eight Big Ten teams that shot better from the field than Michigan State did in conference play last year (Ohio State, Purdue, Northwestern, Iowa, Wisconsin, Illinois, Michigan, and Indiana). Which raises the following highly abstruse and devilishly sophisticated hoops analysis question: So what? You didn't see any of those eight teams in late March, did you?

Tom Izzo therefore deserves every bit of the credit he garnered last April for taking his fifth MSU team to the Final Four. (Yes, fifth. In 14 seasons. Not bad.) I just want to make sure the credit is forwarded to the correct portion of the coach's skill portfolio. He has received the most praise for his manifest and indeed dramatic success as a program-builder. Fair enough, but we shouldn't allow ourselves to think Izzo merely lands the blue-chippers and sends them out on the floor. When you have a team that goes 15-3 in the Big Ten even though it can't shoot as well as 1-17 Indiana, there's some heavy schematic lifting involved for the head coach.

The Spartans transcended their poor shooting in three ways. In order of importance they were: 1) defense (bet you didn't see that coming); 2) offensive rebounding; and 3) trips to the line. As bad as State may have been from the field in the Big Ten (posting a 48.6 effective FG percentage), their opponents were even worse (47.2). There were a lot of misses from both teams when Michigan State took the floor, but the Spartans made sure the other team had more of them. (And surely it need hardly be remarked of a Izzo team that it excelled at taking care of their defensive glass.) Not to mention misses matter a lot less when you rebound them yourself, as MSU did with very nearly 43 percent of theirs, far and away the highest mark in the league. Lastly, the Spartans were the best team in the Big Ten at getting themselves to the free throw line.

It's a little scary to ponder what this team might do in 2010 if these three factors stay unchanged but MSU improves in the areas of shooting and taking care of the ball. Even a little.

What we learned in 2009: *Goran Suton was underappreciated.*

I've been a bit surprised to see preseason forecasts that are breezily unconcerned about this team losing Goran Suton. In fact I've even seen the erstwhile Spartan termed a "role player." Wow. Calling Goran Suton a role player is like saying Rick Pitino's offseason was uneventful.

It's true Suton played a smaller role in the offense than just about anyone else on the floor at a given moment except Travis Walton. But in an offense where Walton—in the lineup solely and exclusively for D—was the fifth choice, the fourth option was actually required to take on a much larger role than is customary. And Suton was perhaps both the best and most prominent such option in the country last year. He was no slouch on D, either.

Start with the fact that this alleged role player was the best defensive rebounder in the Big Ten last year. Then consider that Suton was also an excellent offensive rebounder who made 44 percent of his rare threes and 54 percent of his frequent twos. Given those lofty precedents, chances are that his minutes will now fall to a combination of players who are both less robust on the defensive glass and less efficient on offense. That doesn't mean that Michigan State is doomed without Suton, of course. Merely that improvement will likely be needed somewhere else. Say, cutting down on turnovers.

What's in store for 2010: MSU must replace not only Suton but also Walton, whose mission statement was to remove the opposing team's best perimeter scorer from the equation entirely. No single player is going to fill that role for Izzo this year, so it's not unreasonable to expect a drop-off in the defense. The good news for Spartan fans is this offense can do better.

Prospectus says: Once again Michigan State will clearly be the deepest and most athletic team in the Big Ten. Their defense may well slip now that Walton's gone, but there's enough room for improvement on offense that the net result can be about what it was last year. The key numbers here are 48 and 22. Last year in conference play, perimeter-averse MSU made just 48 percent of their twos and gave the ball away on 22 percent of their possessions. If the Spartans can raise that first number and lower the second (while of course maintaining their Tasmanian devil-level offensive rebounding), they can indeed fulfill the towering expectations being placed upon them.

Meet the Spartans

Kalin Lucas (6-0, 180, Jr.). Arguably the single most decisive play in Michigan State's march to the Final Four was the and-one that Lucas laid down on Sherron Collins with 49 seconds to go in a 60-60 game against Kansas in the Sweet 16. Truly, Lucas has proven himself "in the clutch." Not to mention saying "Michigan State" was good at getting to the line can be rendered more precise by saying Kalin Lucas was *excellent* at getting to the line—and he shot 81 percent when he got there. Put that together with 39 percent three-point shooting from a scoring point guard with a superb assist-TO ratio and you have one exemplary player.

Before joining the swelling Lucas-for-national-POY chorus, however, I want to see a big improvement in the 40 percent two-point shooting of a featured performer whose coach discourages threes.

Raymar Morgan (6-8, 225, Sr.). Morgan started strong last year before being diagnosed in late January with some combination of mononucleosis and walking pneumonia. Not surprisingly his performance dipped markedly, but his team was able to get to the Final Four anyway thanks to the maturation and production of players like Draymond Green and Durrell Summers. Morgan did provide one glimpse of what might lie ahead, however, when he recorded 18 points and nine boards in the Spartans' national semifinal win against Connecticut. For what it's worth in 2007-08 a pneumonia-free Morgan posted a glittering two-point FG percentage but was branded (by Izzo, for one) as a player prone to sudden and inexplicable disappearances, particularly against quality defenders.

Delvon Roe (6-8, 225, So.). Izzo plainly believes Roe is the near-future—the coach gave his hobbled freshman 31 starts—but we are still waiting to see the healthy version of this highly-touted recruit, who spent his entire first year playing through the after-effects of microfracture surgery. Last year Roe's involvement in the offense was limited largely to rebounding his teammates' misses (at which he was superb). On D he was predictably strong on the glass while blocking an occasional shot. I am, however, obligated to pass along this late-game gray-hair alert: Roe shoots just 46 percent from the line.

Chris Allen (6-3, 205, Jr.). Heralded upon his arrival in East Lansing as a Drew Neitzel-level three-point threat who could also finish, Allen is still trying to find the range from outside. Last year he hit just 31 percent of his threes, but, notably, Izzo is obviously steadfast in his commitment to Allen, giving him both minutes and an unwavering green light. (No Spartan is more likely to shoot during his minutes than Allen.) After offseason surgery to repair a broken bone in his right foot, Allen is reported to be healthy and ready for his junior season.

Durrell Summers (6-4, 195, Jr.). The most important thing to remember about Summers is that the dunk he stapled on Stanley Robinson's forehead against Connecticut in the Final Four was really, really impressive.

As for the rest of the year, Summers developed into a solid dual-threat wing as a sophomore, sandwiching a somewhat lackluster February between an impressive early season and strong postseason.

Draymond Green (6-6, 235, So.). On paper Green averaged just 11 minutes a game as a freshman but that number is highly deceptive. The truth is by late March Izzo was giving Green 20-plus minutes against the likes of USC, Kansas, and Louisville. Against those big boys Green proved to be a tenacious, if undersized, presence on the defensive glass.

Korie Lucious (5-11, 170 So.). Lucious owes Kalin Lucas for life. If not for the Spartan star's heroics against Kansas in the Sweet 16, the lingering offseason memory that I would carry of Lucious would be his disastrous four-minute two-turnover cameo against the Jayhawks. Thanks to Lucas, however, State lived to fight another day and Lucious did hit two huge threes against Connecticut. He stands to inherit some big minutes this season in the wake of Walton's departure—if he's healthy. Lucious broke a bone in his right foot in the national championship game and has had two surgeries in the offseason. At last report he's said to be on-track for returning in time for the start of the season.

Derrick Nix (6-9, 285, Fr.). Billed as a classic post scorer with good hands, Nix is a graduate of the same Detroit high school (Pershing) that produced Michigan star DeShawn Sims.

Garrick Sherman (6-10, 235, Fr.). Sherman is a highly-touted post player from Kenton, Ohio. Along with Nix (and 7-0 junior **Tom Herzog**), Sherman will give Izzo frontcourt depth to backfill the departures of Marquise Gray and Idong Ibok.

Minnesota

2009: 22-11 (9-9 Big Ten), lost to Texas 76-62, NCAA First Round
In-conference offense: 0.98 points per possession (10th)
In-conference defense: 0.98 points allowed per possession (4th)

What Minnesota did well: *Share the minutes.*

Tubby Smith is clearly the best thing that's happened to Minnesota basketball since Kevin McHale. (I'm talking about *University of* Minnesota basketball here.) One aspect of Smith's phenomenally successful rebuild, however, has gone largely unnoticed. The coach is an egalitarian extremist when it comes to spreading the minutes around. No other Big Ten coach comes close to Smith in terms of rotating players in and out. In a conference with Tom Izzo that's saying something.

Just look at this rotation:

Fanfare For The Common Gopher: Minnesota Playing Time, 2008-09			
Player	**Min.**	**Player**	**Min.**
Johnson	26.7	Joseph	16.7
Nolen	26.5	Carter	16.0
Westbrook	24.1	Abu-Shamala	12.3
Hoffarber	22.0	Busch	11.1
Sampson	20.8	Bostick	11.0
Iverson	17.7		
Min.: minutes per game			

No fewer than 11 different players averaged double-digit minutes for the Gophers. Everyone except Jamal Abu-Shamala and Travis Busch returns this year.

What we learned in 2009: *Deep teams don't necessarily grow stronger as the season wears on.*

Minnesota started the year 16-1, but from mid-January on they lost ten of their last 16 games to finish 22-11. Partly that was scheduling, of course. Smith put together a very soft non-conference slate for his young team (though the Gophers memorably beat Louisville by six in Glendale, Arizona, in December). At first glance it appeared simply that reality hit Minnesota in the form of Big Ten opponents.

In fact even within the confines of the Big Ten season the Gophers' level of play declined markedly. At no point in the year was Minnesota what you'd call dynamic on offense, but on the back half of the conference schedule they were downright anemic.

Minnesota's shooting from February on was little short of ghastly, but note additionally how turnovers were a particular problem late in the year, as Smith's team gave

Peaking At The Wrong Time Minnesota Offense, 2009			
	eFG%	TO%	PPP
First 9 games	48.3	22.0	1.02
Last 9 games	45.1	26.7	0.94

Conference games only; eFG%: effective FG percentage; TO%: turnover percentage; PPP: points per possession

the ball away on a staggering 27 percent of their possessions. You can't score if you don't get to shoot.

What's in store for 2010: As noted above, Minnesota returns nearly 90 percent of the minutes from a team that went .500 in the Big Ten last year. Teams that finish around .500 and then bring just about everyone back the following season have been known to take a big step forward. Take Villanova. In 2008 they went 9-9 in the Big East, both scoring and allowing one point per possession in conference play. (Thus 'Nova, just like the Gophers last year, posted an efficiency margin of zero.) Last year pretty much everyone was back for the Wildcats and Jay Wright's team went all the way for the Final Four. Am I saying Minnesota is a lock to get to Indianapolis this April? No. Villanova had more talent. But I am saying the Gophers should be much improved in 2010.

Prospectus says: Even with everyone back and a year's development, Minnesota doesn't figure to win many shootouts this season. That being said, just a little improvement on offense will go a long way because the Gopher D should again be very good. There aren't many teams in the nation that can both defend the paint and harass the ball as well as Minnesota.

Meet the Golden Gophers

Lawrence Westbrook (6-0, 195, Sr.). Last year Westbrook responded to the departures of Dan Coleman and Lawrence McKenzie by upping his number of shots dramatically. If his results (48 percent on his twos, 36 percent on his threes) look merely "good," keep in mind that "good" was stellar by the lights of this struggling offense.

Damian Johnson (6-7, 210, Sr.). Here's what I wrote last year: "Johnson is a highly unusual force for good on defense, an undersized interior player who inflicts tangible and measurable pain on opposing offenses without getting many defensive rebounds. Last year

Johnson combined blocked shots and steals as well as any player in Division I. He's also a good offensive rebounder. On the other hand...he was somehow allowed to attempt no fewer than 40 threes last year. He made ten." With the possible exception of the part about offensive rebounding, it's all still true, right up to the fact that in 2008-09 Johnson was somehow allowed to attempt no fewer than 38 threes. He made ten.

Al Nolen (6-1, 180, Jr.). Nolen cleared a developmental hurdle as a pass-first point guard in 2008-09, proving he could run the offense without turning the ball over. At the same time he continued to drive opposing backcourts insane, posting one of the highest steal rates in the nation. He is as important to his team as any six-point-per-game player in the country, not least because any other option at point guard is much less attractive to Smith.

Ralph Sampson (6-11, 230, So.). Smith wasted no time with Sampson, for the freshman started 24 games for Minnesota and did his father and namesake proud, blocking nine percent of opponents' twos during his minutes on the floor.

Colton Iverson (6-10, 235, So.). Minnesota has three of the nation's 40 best shot-blockers on its roster in the form of Johnson, Sampson, and Iverson, who together accounted for 81 starts. No wonder Big Ten opponents made just 43 percent of their twos, making Minnesota's the best interior D in the league.

Blake Hoffarber (6-4, 200, Jr.). Few players nationally appeared to be more spooked by the new three-point line than Hoffarber. The Gophers' designated three-point specialist saw his accuracy fall from 43 to 34 percent in one season. Then again an ankle sprain suffered in December may have been a contributing factor here.

Devoe Joseph (6-3, 170, So.). Joseph would appear to be a little undersized for his job description (dual-threat wing), but he showed promise in that capacity as a freshman, hitting 37 percent of his threes. More than any other Gopher, however, Joseph struggled with turnovers.

Devron Bostick (6-5, 210, Sr.). Arriving last year in Minneapolis as a junior college transfer, Bostick was far more assertive than any other Minnesota reserve in seeking out his own shot and was particularly effective inside the arc.

Paul Carter (6-8, 205, Jr.). Though he averaged just 16 minutes a game and missed a lot of shots in 2008-09, Carter is being talked up by the coaching staff after his performance on a traveling team this summer in China. Then again everyone that Carter played behind last year is still here.

Royce White (6-8, 240, Fr.). A highly-regarded combo forward from the Twin Cities, White figured to represent just how far Smith has brought this program in a short time. After all, Minnesota didn't used to get local recruits who also had offers from the likes of Michigan State, Wisconsin, and Texas.

Too bad, then, that White's been suspended "indefinitely" due to an October arrest for shoplifting at the Mall of America.

Rodney Williams (6-7, 210, Fr.). Still another hometown recruit, Williams is billed as a prolific scorer. He was cleared to play academically by the NCAA over the summer.

Note that at this writing the status of junior college transfer **Trevor Mbakwe (6-8, 240, Jr.)** is still unknown. He is currently facing an assault charge in Florida.

Northwestern

2009: 17-14 (8-10 Big Ten), lost to Tulsa 68-59, NIT First Round
In-conference offense: 1.03 points per possession (4th)
In-conference defense: 1.07 points allowed per possession (9th)

What Northwestern did well: *Grow.*

Improvement on the scale of what Northwestern pulled off last year, going from 1-17 to 8-10 in the Big Ten, is very rare. The Wildcats might have garnered even more attention, however, if not for the fact that their very rare transformation turned out, coincidentally, to be not so rare last year.

The four biggest improvements in major-conference basketball over the past three seasons all took place last year. You couldn't swing a cat in 2009 without knocking over yet another incredible turnaround team: Missouri, LSU, Oregon State, and NU all improved their per-possession performances in league play more than had the previous record-holder in that department (Washington State, 2007). Make no mistake: Northwestern's improvement last year was dramatic, even if it occurred in the company of other uplifting dramas in Baton Rouge, Corvallis, and Columbia.

One key factor behind the Wildcats' growth was the fact that Bill Carmody's team also grew in the more literal sense: Northwestern was simply taller in 2008-09. Coach all you want, but that fact alone is going to help your zone defense. A lot.

Against Big Ten opponents in 2008, Northwestern had the most permissive two-point field goal defense I've yet seen in four seasons of tracking major-conference play. Last year the Wildcats brought that FG defense in line with the conference average. They were

A Long Road Up To 'Average': Northwestern Interior D, 2008 vs. 2009		
Year	Opp. 2FG%	Opp. PPP
2008	60.0	1.16
2009	49.3	1.07

Conference games only
Opp. 2FG%: opponent 2FG percentage
Opp. PPP: opponent points per possession

still pretty weak at defending threes but Carmody's team offset that liability to an extent by, as always, forcing a ton of turnovers.

What we learned in 2009: *Making more threes helps a perimeter-oriented team. (It's true!)*

Nor was the good news in Evanston restricted to the defense. Much like LSU last year, Northwestern improved significantly on both sides of the ball at the same time. This was a better offense in 2009 thanks primarily to more accurate three-point shooting and fewer turnovers.

The made threes were largely the doing of the now-departed Craig Moore. In his first two seasons Moore was a 34 percent three-point shooter—that's decent, sure, but throw a stick at the Big Ten and you'll hit 20 guys that can hit at that rate. In his last two seasons, though, Moore made 40 percent of his threes while taking on a much larger role within the Northwestern offense.

That was a big lift for this offense and, more particularly, for Kevin Coble. Opposing defenses concerned about limiting Coble's touches also had to respect Moore. That respect, in turn, created openings on offense for Coble. Which is another way of saying that Moore will be missed.

What's in store for 2010: Carmody is going to try to replace Moore with some combination of two freshmen, Drew Crawford and Alex Marcotullio. It is virtually foreordained, of course, that the first-year players won't be as efficient on offense as Moore was as a senior. However, the Wildcats can offset this with better defense, specifically better perimeter D and, dare I say it, rebounding. Yes, I realize Northwestern plays a zone. So what? Michigan plays a zone and last year the Wolverines did fine on the defensive glass, thanks in large part to Manny Harris. Carmody should refuse to accept the we-play-zone excuse any longer. He should tell his men to get after it and get some boards.

Prospectus says: Northwestern could make the NCAA tournament this year. I would rate it as something less than a 50-50 proposition, in large part because most of the teams that finished above the Wildcats in the Big Ten last year should be as good or better this season. Still, the 'Cats receiving their first-ever bid in 2010 has to be entertained as a real possibility. In the wake of Moore's departure this offense would figure to stay pretty much where it is, as opposed to showing the improvement you'd ordinarily expect from a team that returns four starters. On the other hand if Michael Thompson can stay accurate from outside while taking more shots, or if one or both of the freshmen can surprise us, that would be huge. All Coble needs is for his teammates to attract just a little attention and respect from opposing defenses.

Meet the Wildcats

Kevin Coble (6-8, 210, Sr.). Coble's defensive rebounding fell off last year (and it wasn't because taller teammates were suddenly taking those rebounds away—the other team was), but otherwise my annual pro-Coble rant still holds: It has been his fate to be systematically overlooked by the larger hoops world due in large part to pace-deflated per-game stats that look ho-hum. Well, let's put Coble alongside that portion of the All-Big Ten first team comprised of wings and guards and see how he fares.

Kevin Coble vs. All-Big Ten Wings and Guards						
Player	Team	%Poss.	3FG%	2FG%	TORate	ORtng.
Coble	**NU**	**24.5**	**39.5**	**50.8**	**10.9**	**110.6**
Lucas	MSU	25.4	39.0	39.6	16.2	110.4
Battle	PSU	27.0	33.9	47.7	15.4	109.9
Turner	OSU	29.8	44.0	50.7	20.9	107.5
Harris	UM	31.8	32.7	46.6	19.1	106.9

Great players all, and clearly Coble belongs in this company. (With regard to Turner's eye-popping three-point percentage, keep in mind he made 11 of the things all year.) I would additionally point out, however, that while Craig Moore was great and all, Coble plainly had less help than anyone else listed here. He makes shots from both sides of the arc. This is his last season. Give him the love, already.

John Shurna (6-8, 210, So.). It doesn't require too much imagination to envision Shurna making the whole enterprise of rating high-school recruits look really silly this season. He arrived last year for his freshman year with a rating so low that I didn't even include him in our season preview. (Put it this way: He was the lowest-rated recruit in his class at Northwestern, a program that hasn't exactly been going toe-to-toe with John Calipari for the one-and-dones lately.) And all he did was start all 31 games, play a larger role in the offense than anyone not named Kevin Coble (larger even than Moore's), make 55 percent of his twos and 35 percent of his threes, and, not least, spend his off-season as a member of the 12-player USA team that went to New Zealand and won the FIBA Under-19 championship in July. Not bad for a who-dat. And speaking of misleading per-game stats, Shurna was trapped in a rotation last year where Coble, Moore, and Thompson were the only players given big minutes. I trust Shurna will get more of those minutes this season. He's earned them.

Michael Thompson (5-10, 180, Jr.). To the extent that the five-headed assist hydra known as a Princeton offense has a point guard, Thompson fulfills that role for the 'Cats. He's a career 42 percent three-point shooter who in his first two seasons played a supporting role in the offense behind Coble and Moore. With the departure of the latter, Thompson may be called upon this year to absorb more possessions and take more shots.

Kyle Rowley (7-0, 280, So.). Rowley fractured his left foot in August and is out "indefinitely," which I suppose could mean anything from being out for the year to missing no games at all. (Sorry I can't be a little more definitive there.) As a freshman Rowley was the very essence of a ceremonial starter, always there at tip-off but averaging a mere 13 minutes a game. Sure, he was foul-prone, but even a designated hacker can't get into foul trouble that quickly. (Or can he? Rowley did foul out in 12 minutes at Penn State on New Year's Eve. Wanted to get to the punch bowl, I guess.) In any event, if Rowley can get healthy and stay on the floor this year Carmody may be able to find out what the space-eating native of Trinidad can do for him.

Jeremy Nash (6-4, 190, Sr.). He wasn't a starter but Nash was on the floor for more minutes last year than anyone outside the Big Three. Though he's merely part of the scenery on offense, Nash excels at forcing opponents into turnovers. Northwestern led the league in this department last year, getting Big Ten opponents to cough up the rock on 24 percent of their possessions.

Teams are really uncomfortable on a number of levels when they play Northwestern. Nash helps that along.

Drew Crawford (6-5, 185, Fr.), and **Alex Marcotullio (6-3, 180, Fr.).** Crawford and Marcotullio are shooting guards who will both be given long looks at replacing the minutes and shots that previously went to Moore.

Ivan Peljusic (6-8, 215, Jr.). Peljusic started nine games in 2007-08 as a redshirt freshman but last year he came off the bench for all of his appearances. Though he averaged just ten minutes a game, he did stand out as the only reserve who pitched in on offense, proving particularly adept at delivering assists to Coble and Moore.

Luka Mirkovic (6-11, 235, So.). Speaking of non-starters who saw a lot of playing time, Mirkovic actually logged more minutes in the paint last year than the nominal starter, Rowley. If either of these two can show some life on the defensive glass (and stay out of foul trouble), they'll help their team immensely.

Ohio State

2009: 22-11 (10-8 Big Ten), lost to Siena 74-72 (OT), NCAA First Round
In-conference offense: 1.07 points per possession (2nd)
In-conference defense: 1.05 points allowed per possession (8th)

What Ohio State did well: *Shoot.*

Sometimes I wonder if Thad Matta looks at the stats from last year and weeps. In conference play Ohio State made 55 percent of its twos and 41 percent of its threes. UCLA's insane shooting performance last year notwithstanding, that kind of accuracy simply doesn't happen in major-conference ball. It almost certainly won't happen again this year for any team in the ACC, Big 12, Big East, Big Ten, Pac-10, or SEC.

In fact, while I don't wish to be unduly gloomy about this, the strong likelihood is that Matta could coach until he's Joe Paterno's age without ever again having a team that shoots this well.

Ohio State was absurdly accurate last year because featured performers Evan Turner and William Buford both shot very well, while supporting players Jon Diebler and B.J. Mullens both shot incredibly well. (Not to mention Dallas Lauderdale would only attempt a

When You're Hot The Entire Year: Most Accurate Major-Conference Teams, 2006-09		
School	Year	eFG%
UCLA	2009	57.9
Ohio St.	**2009**	**57.2**
Florida	2007	56.9
Georgetown	2007	56.9
Kentucky	2007	56.0
Conference games only		
eFG%: effective FG percentage		

shot if it were, literally, a slam-dunk proposition. I don't want to get all technical and arcane on you, but making 72 percent of your twos is pretty good.)

There were two tremendous missed opportunities here. One was the offense the Buckeyes could have had if they'd simply resurrected the program's early-Matta excellence in taking care of the rock.

Good Ball-Handling Gone Bad: Ohio State Turnovers, 2005-09		
Year	TO%	Big Ten rank
2005	16.7	2nd
2006	16.8	1st
2007	17.1	1st
2008	20.8	6th
2009	**22.3**	**9th**

Conference games only
TO%: turnover percentage

Ohio State's offense was very good anyway, of course (second only to Wisconsin's in Big Ten play), but it's not too much to say that it was within the Buckeyes' reach to be incredible. Illinois in 2005 very likely had the best offense of the decade in the Big Ten and even that team didn't shoot as well from the field as OSU did in 2009.

The other missed opportunity was the year the Buckeyes could have had if they'd simply played D as well as they always had before under Matta.

Defense Has (Suddenly) Left The Building: Ohio State Defense, 2005-09		
Year	Opp. PPP	Big Ten rank
2005	0.97	4th
2006	0.97	3rd
2007	0.94	3rd
2008	0.95	3rd
2009	**1.05**	**8th**

Conference games only
Opp. PPP: opponent points per possession

Conference opponents killed Ohio State with threes last year, shooting a lot of them and making 38 percent of all those attempts. The absence of David Lighty definitely played a role here. Still, even without Lighty a defense that was merely average could have landed this team near the top of the Big Ten standings.

What we learned in 2009: *The one-and-done rule is costing really tall people some money.*

B.J. Mullens prefers to be called Byron now that he is in the NBA, having been drafted with the 24th pick by Dallas and subsequently traded to Oklahoma City. Only a tiny fraction of college players get to the NBA, of course, and of that tiny fraction only the elite of the elite get there after just one season of college ball. Clearly Mullens is a member of that most exclusive fraternity.

Still, as Mullens' agent is no doubt aware, a year ago the young man from Columbus was expected to be even *more* elite, as mock draft boards at that time without exception projected him as a lottery pick, usually as a top-five selection. Then the NBA got to see Mullens in action against players who were no longer in high school. They still like the kid's potential, to be sure, but what they saw was a player who at 7-0 doesn't rebound as well on defense as the 6-5 Manny Harris does in a 1-3-1 zone, and doesn't block shots as well as the 6-8 DeAngelo Casto. (Nevertheless NBA.com praises Mullens as an "excellent rebounder and shot-blocker." He likely will be someday but right now this is merely default prattle coughed up by some perplexed staffer in the league office who was confronted with a really big sixth man who scored nine points a game.)

At least Mullens went in the first round. Coming out of high school in 2007, DeAndre Jordan sported a reputation as large as the one Mullens carried a year later. After one season of coming off the bench for Texas A&M, though, the 6-11 Jordan didn't go until early in the second round, when he was picked up by the Clippers. (And, truth be known, Jordan actually got some PT as a rookie, averaging about 15 minutes a game off the bench.)

Of course not all one-and-done big men see their draft stock go down. Greg Oden, for one, seemed to fare pretty well. But the last couple drafts do give one pause. At this writing, Mississippi State freshman Renardo Sidney is expending a good deal of effort (more specifically, his lawyer is expending a good deal of effort) to have the NCAA declare him eligible so that he can play college basketball. In light of the examples offered by Mullens and Jordan, however, the 6-11 Sidney might want to reconsider. The best thing for his salary as an NBA rookie could well be that he remain a tantalizing enigma, visible only in YouTube clips where he's dominating hapless 18-year-olds.

What's in store for 2010: Ohio State's defense should be helped along considerably by the return of Lighty, who last season missed 26 games after injuring his left foot in December. Interestingly, Lighty is the only "new" addition to this team. There is not a single freshman on this roster. Then again next year Matta, as is his habit, is positioned to welcome what is already being called perhaps the best recruiting class in the nation.

Prospectus says: The task at hand for Ohio State this season is to continue the good work on offense but improve the defense dramatically. The return of David Lighty should help Matta carry out this task. Lighty will guard the opponent's best player, while Turner and Buford carry the load on offense. True, this is not the deepest roster you'll run across and last year Georgetown proved pretty memorably what can befall a very talented but very thin team. But this particular thin team can do a lot of good things: Block shots (Lauderdale, when healthy), hit threes (Diebler), harass shooters (Lighty), punish defenses that focus solely on Turner (Buford), and just about anything else you need (Turner). The ingredients are in place to go further than the first round in the NCAA tournament.

Meet the Buckeyes

Evan Turner (6-7, 205, Jr.). If you knew ahead of time that Turner, who was reluctant to shoot as a freshman wing, would respond to the departure of Jamar Butler by simply absorbing a goodly portion of the point guard duties for this team while simultaneously becoming the Buckeyes' featured scorer, please raise your hand. In a year of surprising sophomores in the Big Ten (including but not limited to the newly efficient Manny Harris and the newly prominent Mike Davis), the newly dominant Evan Turner was arguably the biggest surprise of all. He was Matta's best defensive rebounder, his best bet to record a steal, and, not least, a really efficient source of points. For instance last year Turner improved his free throw percentage from 70 to 79 percent—that was handy, because Turner made 150 more trips to the line than any other Buckeye. Call him a point forward, one who's currently projected to be a lottery pick in the 2010 draft.

William Buford (6-5, 190, So.). Last year I hazarded a prediction that even as a freshman Buford would be "fed shots in abundance." Hey, I got one right: Buford did indeed fling the rock up toward the basket over 300 times in 2008-09; holding minutes equal he was more likely to shoot than even Turner. What's more Buford did pretty well, making half his twos and 36 percent of his threes. He's excellent at the line (85 percent) and thus far, even on his twos, functions as more of a spot-up shooter than a slasher. In a year where the All-Big Ten first team was comprised entirely of sophomores, Buford was named the conference's Freshman of the Year.

David Lighty (6-5, 220, Jr.). Lighty is known as a defensive specialist with the versatility to guard multiple positions. True enough, but before his injury he was also showing signs of developing a trustworthy perimeter shot.

Jon Diebler (6-6, 205, So.). After a freshman campaign that could charitably be termed ugly in terms of perimeter shooting, Diebler got it going from outside as a sophomore last year, hitting 42 percent of his threes. Ohio State was easily the Big Ten's best three-point shooting team in conference play, and the lion's share of the credit there goes to Diebler.

Dallas Lauderdale (6-8, 255, Jr.). Lauderdale broke a bone in his hand on October 12 and is expected to miss four to six weeks. He may be listed at just 6-8 but last year, in one of the most basic yet instructive uses of TV I've ever seen, ESPN taped Lauderdale at practice simply standing under the basket next to his seven-foot teammate, B.J. Mullens. When both players then raised their arms you could see in an instant that Lauderdale's wingspan put his hands at the same height as that attained by his much taller teammate. No wonder Lauderdale blocked shots like a possessed fool last year, swatting away 12 percent of opponents' attempted twos during his minutes on the floor. In other words Lauderdale was a better shot-blocker than any major-conference player not named Jarvis Varnado or Hasheem Thabeet. I do wonder, though, how Matta will use Lauderdale now that there's no offensively-oriented one-and-done big man (cf. Mullens, Kosta Koufos) on hand to split the minutes at the 5 with the defensively-oriented Lauderdale.

Zizis Sarikopoulos (7-0, 265, So.). Sarikopoulos sat out last year after transferring from UAB. He may well begin the year in the starting lineup now that Lauderdale has been sidelined temporarily with a broken bone in his hand.

P.J. Hill (6-1, 165, Sr.). Matta is notably unafraid of late-season lineup shuffles. In his first season in Columbus he benched senior starters Tony Stockman and Brandon Fuss-Cheatham in February and replaced them with a junior (Je'Kel Foster) and a freshman (Jamar Butler). Last year he put Hill into the starting lineup as a nominal point guard for the first time on February 24, and the junior college transfer stayed there for the Buckeyes' last eight games.

Hill falls squarely under the pass-first heading where point guards are concerned, attempting just 55 shots in 469 minutes.

Jeremie Simmons (6-2, 170, Sr.). Simmons (also a junior college transfer) was Wally Pipp to Hill's Gehrig and his numbers are surprisingly inoffensive for a starter who was benched. He made 36 percent of his threes while carrying a normal load on offense and taking reasonably good care of the ball.

Kyle Madsen (6-9, 240, Sr.). Having arrived two years ago as a transfer from Vanderbilt, Madsen may see some minutes now that Lauderdale's injured and the NBA has thinned out OSU's frontcourt rotation for the third consecutive year.

Penn State

2009: 27-11 (10-8 Big Ten), beat Baylor 69-63, NIT Championship Game
In-conference offense: 1.00 point per possession (7th)
In-conference defense: 1.04 points allowed per possession (6th)

What Penn State did well: *Achieve respect—even without an NCAA bid.*

If you had told Penn State fans a year ago that their team would be 10-8 in the Big Ten in 2009, they would have taken that. Of course they also would have assumed that a record that good would get the Nittany Lions into their first NCAA tournament since 2001.

That did not turn out to be the case, however, as an RPI that started with the dreaded "7" (as in 70) went a long way toward deflecting Ed DeChellis's team into the NIT. (Which they won, by the way.) Hindsight is 20-20, but scheduling New Hampshire (RPI 201), Towson (219), William & Mary (245), Army (280), Hartford (299), Lafayette (308), and New Jersey Institute of Technology (343) all in the same year probably wasn't such a hot idea after all.

Because you see it turned out this edition of Penn State didn't need the seven easy wins. For the first time in the DeChellis era, there was something different about this team. Last year the Nittany Lions had a defense.

Long Time Coming
Penn State Defense, 2005-09

Year	Opp. PPP	Big Ten rank
2005	1.14	11th
2006	1.13	11th
2007	1.19	11th
2008	1.12	10th
2009	1.04	6th

Conference games only
Opp. PPP: opponent points per possession

Talor Battle garnered almost all of the headlines coming out of Happy Valley last year, of course, and he deserved to. His emergence as an All-Big Ten performer was not only a key ingredient in his team's successful season, it was also a welcome shot in the arm and advertisement for the program itself.

Nevertheless, even with Battle's heroics this was still fundamentally the same offense that you saw from this team in Big Ten play in 2008. What was dramatically different, what got the Nittany Lions over .500 in-conference for the first time since 1996, was defense.

If you watched a Penn State game last year what you were seeing for the first time in years was Big Ten opponents missing an average number of shots against the Nittany Lions. Give DeChellis full credit: Penn State played almost all of its minutes last year with no player taller than 6-9 on the floor, yet somehow they found a way to make the other team miss.

What we learned in 2009: *You can be on-track to win the Frances Pomeroy Naismith Award in two years and still be a beast on the defensive glass.*

Talor Battle was many things to many different Nittany Lion fans last year: Scorer, point guard, leader, clutch shooter, you name it. One aspect of his game that probably didn't earn enough recognition, however, was his prowess on the defensive glass, where he personally hauled in 15 percent of opponents' misses during his minutes on the floor. He was no Blake Griffin (32 percent) or anything, but in this area Battle was able to outperform taller players like 7-1 Mike Tisdale of Illinois, 6-10 JaJuan Johnson of Purdue, and 6-10

Zack Gibson of Michigan.

In the offseason Battle grew an official inch, according to Penn State, and is now 6-0, as opposed to last year when he was a mere 5-11. As long as his growth spurt is over, he would appear to be a leading candidate for next year's Frances Pomeroy Naismith Award, given to the nation's top senior who is no taller than six feet. At a minimum, Battle is almost certain to be the best defensive rebounder in that particular candidate pool.

What's in store for 2010: In theory Penn State returns three starters this year, but in fact this team was hit hard by departures after last season, losing starters Jamelle Cornley and Stanley Pringle, as well as three-point-shooting reserve Danny Morrissey. Last year the offense was run strictly through Battle, Cornley, and Pringle, all of whom logged many more minutes than any PSU player outside the Big Three. In fact, no Big Ten team returns a lower percentage of its minutes from 2008-09 than do the Nittany Lions. This will be Battle's team.

Prospectus says: Penn State this year is one of those teams where you can't tell where the shots are going to come from. Battle will, of course, be the star in this offense, but with Cornley and Pringle gone there are a huge number of shots and possessions up for grabs, even with an All-Big Ten point guard running the show. And while the Nittany Lions' newfound respectability on defense would appear to be here to stay, past history suggests that the players assuming new prominence in the offense this season will not be as efficient as were last year's seniors.

Meet the Nittany Lions

Talor Battle (6-0, 170, Jr.). You've probably heard that the biggest "jump" a player makes in his career is the one that takes place between his freshman and sophomore seasons. However the improvement that Battle displayed as a sophomore was less a jump than a rocket launch. There was little to suggest that the player who arrived in Happy Valley as a relatively unheralded recruit (Jeff Brooks was supposed to be the big-name player in Battle's class) and who missed a boatload of shots as a freshman would do what Battle did as a sophomore: He was a markedly better player last year in literally every facet of his game. Most no-

tably he became far more efficient in his scoring even as he took on a much larger role in the offense. In retrospect the 28-point, 13-rebound effort that Battle recorded as a freshman against Michigan was a harbinger and not the freakish aberration it seemed at the time. He's a scoring point guard who takes more shots than anyone else on his team, records assists in bulk, and gets to the line with regularity. He will never be Stephen Curry from the perimeter, but last year he achieved respectability on the far side of the arc, making 34 percent of his threes.

Andrew Jones (6-10, 245, Jr.). DeChellis rather shrewdly appeared to play the NIT with one eye on winning the thing (mission accomplished) and another eye on 2009-10. Thus Jones, strictly a role player on offense during last season, notched his season-high for points against Notre Dame in the semifinals, scoring 16 points on 5-of-6 shooting from the field and 6-of-7 shooting from the line. More of the same would be most welcome this year.

David Jackson (6-7, 210, Jr.). Jackson has earned his minutes (not to mention 25 starts last year) thanks primarily to the length he provides on defense. Limited to performing a supporting role on offense, Jackson somehow was nevertheless permitted to attempt 39 threes last year. He made eight.

Jeff Brooks (6-8, 200, Jr.). Speaking of length on defense, the likes of Jackson and Brooks didn't exactly set box scores on fire their first two years but, to be fair, that wasn't their role. They were there to support Battle, Cornley, and Pringle on offense, and to get their hands up on D. How they'll be utilized now that Cornley and Pringle have moved on is an open and interesting question.

Andrew Ott (6-10, 240, Jr.). Ott gives DeChellis his only bona-fide shot-blocker, however to date the junior has been both turnover- and foul-prone.

Chris Babb (6-5, 215, So.). Though he averaged just ten minutes a game as a freshman, Babb could well contend for a starting spot in the backcourt this season in the wake of Pringle's departure.

Tim Frazier (6-1, 160, Fr.). A point guard from Houston, Frazier will give DeChellis additional depth in the backcourt this year.

Purdue

[handwritten: P: / W: Hummel, Moore / B: Jackson / JaJuan]

2009: 27-10 (11-7 Big Ten), lost to Connecticut 72-60, NCAA Sweet 16
In-conference offense: 1.02 points per possession (5th)
In-conference defense: 0.95 points allowed per possession (3rd)

What Purdue did well: *Prevent points while forcing fewer turnovers.*

Two years ago Purdue surprised the Big Ten, the nation, and maybe even Matt Painter, posting a 15-3 mark in conference play a season after bidding farewell to the twin pillars of their offense, Carl Landry and David Teague.

But there were some extreme aspects of that surprising year, aspects that tend not to be repeated. For one thing Purdue couldn't miss on their threes, hitting 40 percent of their attempts from beyond the arc against Big Ten opponents that season. Not to mention the Boilermakers forced turnovers on an absolutely unheard of 26 percent of conference foes' possessions. Obviously Chris Kramer is a superb defender, but 26 percent? That simply doesn't happen year after year.

Sure enough, both figures plummeted back to earth in Big Ten play in 2009 (dropping to 35 and 21 percent, respectively). Last year showed that, while Kramer's steal rate will always rank near the top nationally (as indeed it did again in 2009), Purdue's opponents need not turn the ball over a lot just because Kramer's on the floor.

Nevertheless, Painter's team defended just as well last year as they had during their breakout surprise season in 2008, even though their opponents were getting a lot more shots at the basket. The sign in front of the Paint Crew student section at Mackey Arena says "Defense Lives Here." True enough. How did Purdue pull that off in 2009?

What we learned in 2009: *JaJuan Johnson is first-team All-Big Ten.*

The most important single negative factor in Purdue's season was of course Robbie Hummel's health. The Boilers' offense last year was worse than it was in 2008 because too often Hummel wasn't in the lineup. However, the most important single positive factor has received hardly any notice. It was JaJuan Johnson's remarkably rapid maturation and improvement.

Shot-blocking was the one part of Johnson's game that was in place as a freshman. He improved that aspect of his performance just a little last year but, much more importantly, he mastered the strange and quixotic Thabeet-esque art of blocking shots without committing fouls. With a newly emboldened and assertive Johnson on the floor for more minutes in 2009, Purdue's opponents had even less success in the paint than in 2008, making a puny 45 percent of their twos. Granted, part of the credit there goes to Kramer, the perimeter D equivalent of Gorilla Glue. Teams that play the Boilers are rarely given easy entry passes into the post. However, the presence of the long and athletic Johnson had a lot to do with it as well.

And that was just on defense. On offense Johnson went from a tentative freshman to a featured star, making 54 percent of his twos while carrying as large a load as Hummel and E'Twaun Moore. He even remade himself into a 74 percent free throw shooter.

The only discordant note in Johnson's profile is that he doesn't register at all on the defensive glass, in part because on this particular roster that's Hummel's assignment. Nevertheless, Johnson, already the best big man in the Big Ten, is getting better.

What's in store for 2010: Purdue returns its top six players in terms of minutes from last year and, much more importantly, Hummel is reportedly healthy, having played pain-free minutes alongside Evan Turner and Talor Battle for coach Bo Ryan at the World University Games in Belgrade this past July.

Prospectus says: Painter's first couple seasons at Purdue were programmatically bumpy, as injuries decimated his team and players came and went. (Nate Minnoy, Chris Lutz, and Johnathan Uchendu, we hardly knew ye!) In the more recent past, however, the Boilers have been a model of roster stability. The core of the team that went 15-3 in the Big Ten in 2008—Hummel, Moore, Kramer, Johnson, and Keaton Grant—is still around in West Lafayette. This is merely another way of saying that, if they're healthy, Purdue is the favorite to win the Big Ten in 2010.

Meet the Boilermakers

Robbie Hummel (6-8, 210, Jr.). The highest compliment to be paid to Hummel is that he played last year with a hairline fracture in his lower back and yet for the most part he was still effective, making half his twos and 38 percent of his threes while again serving as his team's best defensive rebounder. The problem wasn't that his production went down as much as that his minutes went down, as Hummel missed four conference games entirely. On paper his role in the offense appears smaller than Moore's or Johnson's, but this is highly deceiving. (The deception flows from the fact that Hummel's game does not include any of the following: Assists, drawing fouls, or offensive boards. He just shoots, accurately, from both sides of the arc.) There are times to look past the paper and onto the court, and this is one of those times: Hummel is the catalyst not just for this offense but indeed for this team.

JaJuan Johnson (6-10, 215, Jr.). See above. One cautionary note, however: Johnson better stay healthy. This roster is not blessed with inordinate depth in the frontcourt.

E'Twaun Moore (6-4, 185, Jr.). Moore earned leading-scorer honors for the second consecutive year simply by logging more minutes and shooting more shots than anyone else. Actually his efficiency took a big hit as a sophomore, as his three-point shooting nosedived from 43 to 34 percent.

Chris Kramer (6-3, 215, Sr.). With scorers like Hummel, Johnson, and Moore, Painter has the luxury (much like Tom Izzo last year with Travis Walton) of using a starter pretty much exclusively for defense. That starter is Kramer, who makes life absolutely miserable for opposing offenses. Not that Kramer's been neglecting the other half of the game entirely. Note that last year he improved his free throw shooting dramatically, transforming himself from a 62 percent adventure into a 77 percent (relative) sure thing.

Lewis Jackson (5-9, 165, So.). Jackson will miss Purdue's season-opener against Cal State Northridge on November 13, due to an arrest for speeding in April. He later pled guilty to illegal consumption of alcohol and possession of drug paraphernalia. Last year Jackson started 30 games as a freshman and functioned as a pass-first point guard in an offense that previously had been more accustomed to combo guards and wings sharing the assist load. He was, however, the only Boiler who struggled with turnovers and he was also curiously foul-prone. As a result, Jackson was a starter who averaged just 24 minutes a game.

Keaton Grant (6-4, 200, Sr.). In contrast to Jackson, Grant was a reserve who averaged 27 minutes a game. He's a wing who prefers threes; last year Grant hit 35 percent of his attempts from beyond the arc.

D.J. Byrd (6-5, 215, Fr.). A wing from Crawfordsville, Indiana, Byrd is recovering from a torn meniscus in his left knee and at this writing his health is still unclear. It's worth noting here that Painter's local recruiting efforts have been exhaustive. At the moment, eight of the nine players in this year's and next year's (projected) freshman classes are from the state of Indiana. The ninth is from far-flung and exotic Chicago.

Patrick Bade (6-8, 235, Fr.). Speaking of all those in-state products, Bade is a graduate of the same Indianapolis high school (Franklin Central) that produced Johnson. The freshman figures to see more playing time since another incoming big man from Indy, Jeff Robinson, was ruled academically ineligible and will not play for the Boilers for the foreseeable future.

Wisconsin

Superslow 341

2009: 20-13 (10-8 Big Ten), lost to Xavier 60-49, NCAA Second Round
In-conference offense: 1.08 points per possession (1st)
In-conference defense: 1.00 point allowed per possession (5th)

What Wisconsin did well: *Score points the Wisconsin way.*

I don't think many people realized that this was the best offense in the Big Ten last year. The Badgers certainly weren't the most talented of teams, nor were they what you'd call dazzling to the eye. No, they just scored points better than any other team in the conference. Yet even if you continually reminded yourself that this was the second slowest-paced team in the nation's slowest-paced conference, Wisconsin's offense was still easily overlooked if you watched them in action. Why?

The Badgers weren't a great shooting team and, as is the case in every Big Ten locale outside of East Lansing (and perhaps Minneapolis), they don't believe in offensive boards in Madison. Wisconsin didn't get to the line much, either.

This team scored points simply because they didn't turn the ball over. Bo Ryan teams are renowned for taking good care of the ball, of course, but last year the Badgers took this to a new level, giving the rock away on just 16 percent of their possessions in Big Ten play. This was the best mark posted by any team in the league last year and, indeed, the best figure attained by Wisconsin over the past five seasons.

Ryan's team needed to be careful with their possessions because shot-for-shot your eyes were onto something: Holding turnovers equal, this was far from the conference's most elite scoring unit.

Wisconsin Needed More Bites At The Apple: Big Ten Offenses, 2009			
School	PPeP	School	PPeP
Ohio St.	1.37	Indiana	1.25
Michigan St.	1.36	Michigan	1.24
Minnesota	1.30	Northwestern	1.24
Wisconsin	**1.29**	Penn St.	1.22
Iowa	1.28	Illinois	1.21
Purdue	1.26		
Conference games only			
PPeP: points per effective (TO-less) possession			

(Looking at this list it's worth noting that Michigan State reduced their number of turnovers when the Spartans reached the NCAA tournament. You know the rest.)

When was the last time you came away from watching a team run its offensive set saying, "Wow! Great job not turning the ball over!" We're simply not wired to observe the game in such a cumulative and quotidian manner. But that was precisely the manner in which Wisconsin scored their points in 2009.

What we learned in 2009: *It is indeed possible for Bo Ryan to put a defense on the floor that is merely average.*

Ryan has cultivated a reputation, wholly justified, for being able to maintain a level of play in Madison

that is untethered from irrelevant little details like who the players are. That run of consistency finally hit a bump last year, though, as Wisconsin's defense deteriorated noticeably, going from outstanding to average in one season.

Teams Scoring (Gulp) Points Against Wisconsin? Badger defense, 2007-09		
Year	Opp. PPP	Big Ten rank
2007	0.93	2nd
2008	0.91	1st
2009	**1.00**	**5th**
Conference games only		
Opp. PPP: opponent points per possession		

While it's customary to think of defensive rebounding and interior FG defense as more or less a package deal—teams that are good at the former tend to be good at the latter—that package came unwrapped for the Badgers last year. Their excellence on the defensive glass continued (UW fans can thank Joe Krabbenhoft for that), but opponents suddenly found that they were able to riddle this defense with made twos. As a result said opponents shot fewer threes and, as strange as it looked against a Bo Ryan team, even got to the line quite frequently.

One contributing factor here was simply that Wisconsin was a markedly shorter team in 2008-09. The fact that the shorter team was able to continue its dominance of the defensive glass was quite an accomplishment. Still, Brian Butch, of whom it seemed more was always expected, was sorely missed last year. In his absence Wisconsin's two-point FG defense collapsed.

What's in store for 2010: Krabbenhoft and leading scorer Marcus Landry are gone, but the backcourt returns intact in the form of Trevon Hughes and Jason Bohannon.

Prospectus says: I know he hasn't received a lot of attention so far in his career, but watch Jon Leuer. It's not too much to say that his development could be the pivot (pun intended) around which Wisconsin's season turns. On offense if Leuer can serve as a productive option for touches in the post, he'll free up space for threes by Bohannon and Hughes. And on defense the best thing that can happen for the Badgers is that Leuer reprises Brian Butch's performance as a hybrid shot-defender and defensive rebounder. We know Wisconsin will take care of the ball and get their share of rebounds on defense. The weightiest variable in the mix is the newly reconstituted frontcourt, Leuer in particular.

Meet the Badgers

Trevon Hughes (6-0, 195, Sr.). In Ryan's offense it falls to Hughes to serve as something of a point guard/wing hybrid, dishing assists, shooting threes, and slashing to the basket. He was fine at the first two activities (he made 36 percent of his threes), and when he drew a foul, which he did quite often, he shot 77 percent at the line. But for whatever reason Hughes' effectiveness inside the arc when he wasn't fouled dipped last year, as he made just 40 percent of his twos.

Jason Bohannon (6-2, 195, Sr.). Bohannon logged more minutes last year than any other Badger and functioned primarily as a three-point threat in support of Landry and Hughes, hitting 37 percent of his treys.

Jon Leuer (6-10, 230, Jr.). Leuer started 12 games as a sophomore and, while his minutes were limited by the seniors ahead of him in the rotation, he is plainly a featured scorer waiting to be unleashed. He couldn't make his threes last year, but he did sink 51 percent of his twos while distinguishing himself as the Badger most likely to shoot during his minutes. Leuer's defensive rebounding has been mediocre thus far, but then again so was Krabbenhoft's in 2007-08 while Butch was still around. With Krabbenhoft gone, Leuer will be expected to step forward and take care of business on the defensive glass.

Keaton Nankivil (6-8, 245, Jr.). Filling the Jason Chappell honorary-starter role last year, Nankivil was on the floor for the opening tip 20 times yet averaged just 14 minutes a game. That being said, Nankivil was actually much more assertive on offense as a sophomore than Chappell ever was. It would be worth Ryan's while to throw a few more possessions Nankivil's way this season, just to see what the junior can do for this offense.

Jared Berggren (6-10, 240, Fr.). Berggren redshirted last year and is being talked up something fierce by the coaching staff heading into this season, up to and including speculation that he could win a starting spot.

Tim Jarmusz (6-6, 210, Jr.). A wing who averaged 16 minutes a game, Jarmusz is one of those defense-first role players who never shoots—unless it's a three, in which case it seemingly always (42 percent of the time) goes in.

Jordan Taylor (6-1, 195, So.). Taylor saw limited minutes as a freshman in support of Hughes at the point and proved to be quite foul-prone, earning 67 whistles in just 437 minutes.

Rob Wilson (6-3, 200, So.). If you had to choose a way to introduce yourself to the ESPN-viewing nation as a freshman, you could do worse than driving to the hole on Hasheem Thabeet and drawing a foul, as Wilson did in the title game of the Paradise Jam in November. Unfortunately for Wilson that kind of activity was the exception and not the rule, as he made ten shots from the field all year.

On the surface, it appears there's a lot of continuity in the Pac-10 this season. And continuity usually means an upgrade in play. Nine of the conference's member teams return at least 40 percent of their minutes from last season and six return at least half. However, most of the lost minutes were quality minutes. In addition to a few sensational seniors, nearly everybody else who could go pro and reasonably expect to stick in the NBA left early.

Nine of the first 35 college players drafted last summer were from the Pac-10. Even some of the others that used up their eligibility—like UCLA's Josh Shipp, Washington's Justin Dentmon, and Stanford's Anthony Goods—may not be appearing on an NBA team near you, but they played a major role for their Pac-10 team last year. The result across the conference is that most teams have familiar names set to take the floor in unfamiliar situations.

The most extreme example of this is Arizona State. The Sun Devils' roster doesn't look that much different from last season—they return six players from their eight-man rotation. But the two players that aren't returning are James Harden and Jeff Pendergraph, the top two players in terms of both minutes played and possessions used. The rest of roster spent last season shooting the occasional open three-pointer while the two future draft picks did their thing.

As far as the macro view of the league goes, don't take my predicted records too seriously. Somebody is going to win fewer than five games and somebody is probably going lose fewer than four games. Only eight times in the last 30 years has 14 wins been good enough to win the conference. Determining which

team(s) will do that is the hard part. What's a bit more certain is that there appear to be two distinct groups of teams in the league this season.

The group of teams with the potential to make noise on CBS this March would appear to be limited to Washington, Cal, and UCLA. The Huskies suffer their own high-usage losses with Dentmon and Jon Brockman. But for the second consecutive season, they'll have a freshman guard that will make an impact. This time, his name is Abdul Gaddy. Cal is only squad that is truly in "everyone's back" mode. They figure to start four seniors after a successful '09 campaign in head coach Mike Montgomery's initial season in Berkeley.

UCLA is definitely not bringing everyone back, having lost four starters from last season, but they have a roster filled with mostly unproven five- and four-star recruits. They represent the team I'm most uncertain about. With so much potential talent, a few guys figure to have breakthroughs that keep UCLA in the national conversation. But potential is no guarantee of future results. Indeed, some of these recruits were expected to have an impact last season and we didn't hear much from them. But given that neither Washington nor Cal seems to represent the strength of a one- or two-seed, it seems reasonable that a team with this much talent will compete with them.

That leaves the "others." There are differences in this group for sure—Arizona figures to finish higher than Stanford—but the idea is that the main source of wins for this group will be among each other. Included in this collection are three programs with new coaches, although they all have previous head coach-

PAC-10 PROSPECTUS

	2009 Record	Returning Minutes (%)	2010 Prediction
Washington	14-4	70	14-4
California	11-7	91	13-5
UCLA	13-5	42	13-5
Arizona	9-9	51	9-9
Arizona St.	11-7	66	8-10
Oregon St.	7-11	83	8-10
USC	9-9	22	7-11
Oregon	2-16	85	7-11
Wash. St.	8-10	44	6-12
Stanford	6-12	47	5-13

ing experience. Sean Miller takes over at Arizona after the Wildcats spent two years with temporary head coaches. Kevin O'Neill begins his fifth D-I head coaching job and second in the Pac-10, taking over for a hastily-departed Tim Floyd at USC. Finally, the only job opening that was the result of a promotion of sorts occurred at Washington State, where former Portland State coach Ken Bone was hired.

The Oregon schools have much of their rosters back, but Craig Robinson is on decidedly more solid footing with his job than Ernie Kent is with his. Each program should be expecting improvement over last season. Stanford's holding up the bottom of the predicted finish, but it was all I could do to not add a sixth win to their total. However, they're another weak recruiting class away from a return to the pre-Mike Montgomery days.

The result of this distribution is the possibility of only three NCAA bids for the conference. Just as a quick refresher, the conference received a total of 11 bids over the last two seasons and three of the four teams with a .500 conference record got an invitation. But relative to the other power conferences, the Pac-10 is down from where it has been over the past two seasons, so fewer bids are to be expected.

Special circumstances are required for the three-bid scenario to play out, though. It's more than possible that someone from the "others" will rise up and force the nation to take a little bit of notice (most likely, Arizona). But because of the critical personnel losses across the league, it's highly improbable that a 9-9 record in conference is going to get the committee's attention this season.   *Ken Pomeroy*

Arizona

2009: 21-14 (9-9 Pac-10), lost to Louisville, 103-64, NCAA Sweet Sixteen
In-conference offense: 1.08 points per possession (4th)
In-conference defense: 1.08 points allowed per possession (9th)

What Arizona did well: *Succeed without a defense.*

Which is a backhanded way of saying that the Wildcat offense was very, very good. This is a case where the in-conference ranking doesn't do the on-court play justice because UCLA (especially), Arizona State and Cal each had outstanding offenses and just happened to reside in the same conference. Finishing a close fourth behind those three is a compliment to Arizona's scoring ability.

And Arizona needed all of those points to sneak into the NCAA tournament because their defense was a disaster. This coming from a program where the defense had been suspect in the first two years of the Chase Budinger/Jordan Hill era. But Russ Pennell's unique trapping zone defense brought the team D to new lows. The premise of the defense was to concede open threes (often from the corner) in exchange for lock-down defense elsewhere. It looks good on paper, but it didn't work well in games.

Pac-10 opponents took just over 40 percent of their shots from beyond the arc (most in the conference), making 38 percent of their attempts. That was expected given the defensive strategy, however the rest of the floor wasn't well defended either—opponents made 51 percent of their twos and committed turnovers on just 19 percent of their possessions. Both of those figures were fourth-worst in the league.

What we learned in 2009: *There's no definitive way to select the 34 best at-large teams.*

In a year of oddly memorable moments for Arizona, what fans outside Tucson may remember most about the 2008-09 team is the Wildcats' surprise invitation on Selection Sunday. Inevitably, analysts were split into two camps: "they deserved it," or "they didn't deserve it, Team X deserved it," with Team X replaced by San Diego State, Creighton or Saint Mary's (with a smattering of Penn State supporters for good measure).

All of the debate over the situation reinforced one problem that can never be solved by the selection process. It is impossible to accurately distinguish between the 49th and 50th best teams in the nation, whether you do it with humans or computers. And that's the job the committee faces when filling out the final at-large selection. The difference in quality between those teams will always pale in comparison to the error created by whatever system is used.

What's in store in 2010: From a trend perspective, it's simple to forecast what is going to happen to Arizona this season: The offense will get worse and the defense will get better. Losing Hill and Budinger makes the former virtually certain. And with Russ Pennell out and former Xavier head coach Sean Miller in, the oodles of open three-point shots that were available to opponents will vanish. Miller runs a cousin of Tony Bennett's pack-line defense that frustrated Pac-10 teams in recent years. Xavier's defense didn't have quite the same level of dominance in the A-10 (2009 notwithstanding), but it's safe to say that fewer points will be scored and allowed by Arizona in 2009-10.

Prospectus says: Arizona carries the longest active streak of consecutive NCAA tournament appearances into this season, and it's likely that in a weaker Pac-10, it will take a winning conference record for that to continue. Sean Miller is going to bring defense to Arizona, but let's be clear on this: He's not Tony Bennett. He can't simply take any five players off of a playground and make them into an elite brick-inducing squad. There's going to be improvement in 2010 due solely to an upgrade in scheme but this is a team that is still going to have to score points. Thankfully for Miller, he inherits Wise who is one of the best point guards in the country. But Wise is going to need some help to keep the streak intact.

Meet the Wildcats

Nic Wise (5-10, 180, Sr.) Wise will likely be at the top of opposing game plans. How he deals with that this season will go a long way towards determining if the Cats' offense can stay in the top half of the conference. From this vantage point he doesn't get nearly enough credit for his outside shooting (he's a 41 percent career shooter from deep) considering he also has the responsibility of running the offense (he assisted on a quarter of his teammates' made shots last season). Nic is going to need at least one other player to distract the defense if he's to keep his three-point shooting in the 40's.

Kyle Fogg (6-3, 185, So.) Arizona fans had to be happy with the performance of Fogg last season. He was a late recruit last spring when all of the following necessitated some backcourt insurance: Jerryd Bayless decided to go pro, Brandon Jennings was exploring his European options, and Nic Wise was mulling over a transfer. Ultimately, of course, Wise stayed, and Fogg was a good if quiet complement in the backcourt. When he asserted himself, he often contributed positively, posting the second best true shooting percentage on the team (59.4) while maintaining an acceptable turnover rate. He has the reputation as a lockdown defender, which is a trait that should be more noticeable in Miller's more conventional defense.

Jamelle Horne (6-7, 215, Jr.) What's amazing is that besides Wise, Arizona doesn't have a single player on the roster that had a usage rate of more than 15 percent last season. This should make one wonder if guys like Horne kept themselves out of the headlines simply because they understood that Jordan Hill, Chase Budinger, and (likely) Wise were future draft picks. (Yes, I realize that Horne found himself very much in the headlines for two late-game fouls that contributed to Arizona losses.) Or is Horne actually a life-long role player incapable of creating shots that just happened to provide a good fit to the high-usage trio? We should know the answer to this by the end of 2009.

Solomon Hill (6-6, 230, Fr.) Hill is the most highly regarded freshman of Miller's first class in Tucson. Given the offensive vacuum, if Hill shows a willingness to make plays he could find himself being the number two option on the team.

Derrick Williams (6-8, 235, Fr.) Williams landed at Arizona after getting out of his commitment at USC when Tim Floyd resigned.

LaMont Jones (6-0, 200, Fr.) Jones, too, was set to go to USC, but now will spend his freshman season as Wise's understudy.

Kyryl Natyazhko (6-10, 255, Fr.) Because of a lack of bodies that can possibly play center, Natyazhko will contribute. But don't be surprised if his rebound rates are ordinary and his shot attempts are rare. The consensus puts Natyazhko as about the 50th best prospect in his class. This sounds promising, and it does bode well for his long term progress, but big men in this range typically don't make a big splash as freshmen.

Garland Judkins (6-3, 200, So.) Judkins was a part of the phalanx of role players under Pennell. After averaging over 25 minutes over the first five games, he then ceded playing time to Fogg. His role was reduced further when he was suspended for the rest of the season in early February.

Alex Jacobson (7-0, 245, So.) By grabbing 16 offensive boards in 172 minutes of action, Jacobson shows hints of having a skill that would draw the envy of other Pac-10 centers. Unfortunately, there's much work to be done in other areas of his game.

Arizona State

2009: 25-10 (11-7 Pac-10), lost to Syracuse, 78-67, NCAA Second Round
In-conference offense: 1.09 points per possession (2nd)
In-conference defense: 1.00 point allowed per possession (3rd)

What Arizona did well: *Shoot three-pointers.*

In a year when the three-point line was moved back a foot, the Sun Devils defied conventional wisdom and significantly increased their volume of shots from beyond the arc. There were actually 128 other D-I teams that could say this, though, so that by itself wasn't unusual. What's odd is that ASU took a bunch of threes the year before and rule change or no, you'd expect some regression to the mean. Of the 51 teams that attempted three-pointers on over two-fifths of their field goal attempts in '07-'08, 40 reduced that percentage in '08-'09. In hoisting a whopping 45 percent of their shots from beyond the arc, the Sun Devils easily led the conference.

What we learned in 2009: *Remarkable improvement can occur even when the roster doesn't change.*

I assume most people are like me and have horrible memories so it's worth noting that in 2008 the Sun Devils had the worst non-Oregon State offense in the conference. The transformation to become the best non-UCLA offense in the league a year later with no difference in personnel bordered on spectacular. What changed was James Harden's involvement in the offense. He went from being merely the go-to-guy as a freshman to one of the most heavily used players in the nation as a sophomore.

Under different circumstances this might be viewed as a case of selfishness where a kid was trying to showcase his skills for NBA scouts in attendance. In this case, however, it was a necessary change given what happened in 2008. In that season Harden's individual efficiency was much greater than his team's, so why not use even more possessions and see what happens? Harden did that last season, and while his efficiency dropped slightly, he helped open up all of those quality long-distance looks for his teammates, who not only took more shots, but improbably made more as well.

What's in store in 2010: Take Harden and Jeff Pendergraph away from the '09 edition of the Sun Devils and the team is left with a bunch of players who each used less than 20 percent of ASU's possessions

when they played. In fact, it's not even close—of the returning bunch, only Derek Glasser had a usage that exceeded 17 percent. This group was able to pick their spots last season while defenders were chasing Harden around the floor. Now they'll have to figure out how to create their own shots more often.

Prospectus says: There figures to be a significant discovery period in Tempe this season. Mainly, discovering who will take the shots that were so often taken by Harden and to a lesser extent, Pendergraph in '09. Despite the slow pace, this was a team that excelled on the point-scoring end in the Harden era. I think the surest sign about how well this team does in '10 will be how long it takes for analysts to mention ASU basketball and not talk about James Harden. I haven't been able to do that for very long in this preview and I fear that the rest of the hoops world is going to need some time to make that adjustment as well.

Meet the Sun Devils

Derek Glasser (6-1, 190, Sr.) It's difficult to forecast who will be the face of Sun Devil basketball this season, but Glasser has as good of a case as any. He enjoyed his finest season in '08-'09, draining 41 percent of his three-point attempts and assisting on 28 percent of his teammates' shots. That assist rate was second on the team. (To Harden.) However, the high field goal percentage came with Glasser taking fewer than one in six of his team's shots and without much acumen for getting to the hole.

Ty Abbott (6-3, 207, Jr.) Abbott arrived in Tempe as the second-most heralded recruit in the Harden class. After a promising intro to his college career, the shooting guard struggled with his shot last season, hitting just 29 percent of his carefully selected three-point shots.

Rihards Kuksiks (6-6, 210, Jr.) Kuksiks is the prototypical shooting forward. He doesn't do the things you normally expect from a 6-6 player—things like rebounding, getting to the free throw line, or making around half of your twos. Kuksiks' specialty is taking a pass and draining the longball. The Latvian was last seen taking all 13 of his field goal attempts from beyond the arc and making six of those (all of which were assisted) in the first-round loss to Syracuse.

Jamelle McMillan (6-2, 180, Jr.) McMillan's a combo guard that battled Abbott for minutes at the 2 last season. With Glasser monopolizing time at the point, that script should repeat itself in 2010.

Jerren Shipp (6-3, 208, Sr.) This season will make 10 of the last 11 that a Shipp sees action for a Pac-10 team. Jerren's minutes slipped last season as Sendek opted to go with a bigger lineup.

Eric Boateng (6-10, 257, Sr.) Having been an understudy to either Shelden Williams or Jeff Pendergraph in his three seasons of eligibility, Boateng may actually see some time in the starting lineup. He has always put up gaudy rebounding figures on both ends of the floor in his limited time. He otherwise won't cause a whole lot of extra work for the scorekeeper, though.

Victor Rudd (6-7, 207, Fr.) The six guys that return from Sendek's eight-man rotation last season took a whopping 64 percent of their shots from three-point land. Point being, there are minutes available for someone willing to attempt shots inside 15 feet. Among the newcomers, Rudd is the most likely to fill this role.

Demetrius Walker (6-2, 195, Fr.) Walker is a shooting guard that has the ability to score off the dribble.

Brandon Thompson (6-0, 180, Fr.) The San Antonio product has received praise from Sendek for his shooting ability.

Trent Lockett (6-4, 211, Fr.) Lockett is expected to get a few minutes as a freshman, bringing badly-needed athleticism to the team.

California

2009: 22-11 (11-7 Pac-10), lost to Maryland, 84-71, NCAA First Round
In-conference offense: 1.08 points per possession (3rd)
In-conference defense: 1.06 points allowed per possession (6th)

What Cal did well: *Make Ben Braun proud.*

Ben Braun was relieved of his duties as Cal head coach shortly after the end of the 2008 season. But he had to be keeping tabs from his new job at Rice when the group that he recruited was able to do enough to earn a seven-seed in the NCAA tournament. The Bears are in good hands under Mike Montgomery, but keep in mind that the team that many are picking to be the best in the conference will feature a starting lineup with four seniors who committed to Cal when Braun was the coach.

What we learned in 2009: *A defense just doesn't go very far if it can't block shots or make steals.*

With a completely new coaching staff, it's amazing how little Cal's statistical profile changed last season. The biggest exception to this was three-point accuracy, where the Bears went from average to the best in the country, making 43 percent of their attempts (limited though they were). But just about everywhere else you look, if Cal did something well in Braun's last season, they did it well in Monty's first season, and likewise with their weaknesses. Most unusual among the weaknesses was an utter refusal to block shots or steal the ball, categories where Cal finished in the bottom 20 of D-I teams. To assess the combined effect of these categories, we can create a stat that sums block rate and steal rate. In doing so, Cal gets lumped in with some fairly bad defenses.

Passive Defenses: National Rank, Steals Plus Blocks		
Team	SBP	DE Rank
South Dakota St.	11.0	112
Sacramento St.	11.7	339
UNC Wilmington	11.8	329
Evansville	11.8	126
Southern Utah	11.8	136
California	12.0	101
SBP: Steal rate plus block rate		
DE Rank: National rank of adjusted defensive efficiency		

This shouldn't shock anyone but there's a correlation between shot blocking/steal forcing and the quality of one's defense. For instance Memphis and Louisville were ranked second and third (behind Minnesota), respectively, in this stat and had the top two defenses in the country. Cal will have a short front line, so blocks won't be their specialty, but if their defense is going to rise to a level that earns the team a top seed in March, it would help if they forced a few more turnovers.

What's in store in 2010: Cal has everyone back from last season except for reserve center Jordan Wilkes, who actually had one more year of eligibility but decided he'd had enough hoops. The Bears will trot out one of the most experienced lineups in the nation and one that has a proven track record of being able to score with the kind of regularity that few teams can match.

Prospectus says: Mike Montgomery made his mark in Berkeley by improving the defense in his first season. Sure, the offense was often excellent, but this was this case in Ben Braun's last season as well. The defense was upgraded from downright awful to occasionally passable. But it was also still occasionally awful—the Bears held just two opponents below a point per possession in regular season Pac-10 play.

We've seen this script play out before. You know, the team that can score at will but can't get stops. But they return everybody from the previous season...and this time they mean business! They've been thinking about defense all summer, blah, blah, blah. Last year at this time, these words were being spoken about Baylor, and to a lesser extent Notre Dame. Two years ago it was NC State. Each of those teams failed to improved their defense and fell short of lofty preseason expectations.

Cal is a good team that is going to win a lot of games this season and get a draw in the top half of the NCAA bracket. But they're also a team with a significant weakness. One that history says is very difficult to overcome, even with hard work.

Meet the Bears

Jerome Randle (5-10, 160, Sr.) The preseason favorite to win the Frances Pomeroy Naismith Award, Randle produces an eerily similar profile to Arizona's Nic Wise. Randle's stats were slightly better, but in a statistically insignificant way. A 5-10 player who is able to make 53 percent of his twos is usually a special player. Indeed, Randle has the total package and produced the highest true shooting percentage for any player under six feet last season. (Though this feat was also statistically insignificant—he beat Ty Lawson by a mere .003 percent.) Cal's transition efficiency is significantly above average and Randle probably deserves a lot of credit for that as well.

Patrick Christopher (6-5, 215, Sr.) Christopher can score from anywhere on the floor, but his overall impact is limited by his inability to get to the free throw line.

Jamal Boykin (6-8, 230, Sr.) While Cal's absurdly accurate three-point shooting helped propel the offense to greatness, Boykin contributed to the efficiency with his play inside. He had a microscopic turnover rate, a true shooting percentage of 56 percent, and the fifth-best offensive rebounding percentage in the league. You would think a power forward as active as Boykin would get to the line more than 80 times in 33 games, but that was his big weakness last season. With Jordan Wilkes deciding to forego his final year of eligibility and pursue a career in the real world, Boykin figures to see more of his minutes as a center this season.

Theo Robertson (6-6, 225, Sr.) Robertson's game is nearly identical to Christopher's, though Robertson may be a little more selective in his shooting. It's a plan that works out well—Robertson has made 43 percent of his three-point shots in his career.

Jorge Gutierrez (6-3, 185, So.) As a freshman, Gutierrez got his minutes either in rare moments when Randle was on the bench or as an uncomfortable two-guard next to Randle (one who was just 8-of-26 from beyond the arc). Gutierrez flashed the predictable freshman trait of turnover issues, but he also posted an incredibly high defensive rebound rate for a man of his stature. On that end of the floor, he was a more effective rebounder than Christopher, Robertson, and Harper Kamp, all of whom were listed as being at least two inches taller.

Omondi Amoke (6-7, 215, So.) Amoke figures to be the biggest beneficiary of Wilkes' decision. In about eight minutes a game, he showed promise as a rebounder. Whatever minutes he can offer will allow Boykin to play the four, where he blossomed last season.

Harper Kamp (6-8, 255, Jr.) Kamp was the sixth man on the team, although one without much of an identity beyond that. His role in the offense was reduced significantly under Montgomery, to the point where he took a shade under one of every nine Cal shots when he was on the court. Kamp has battled knee problems through most of his first two seasons and had offseason surgery as a result.

D.J. Seeley (6-4, 185, So.) Seeley's game follows the Christopher/Robertson formula. He takes a third of shots from beyond the arc and doesn't get to the line. He should get scattered minutes here and there when one of the wings gets in foul trouble.

Nikola Knezevic (6-3, 185, Sr.) One of the few D-I players that took more free throws (17) than shots from the field (16), Knezevic had his minutes essentially eliminated by the time Pac-10 play started.

Markhuri Sanders-Frison (6-8, 290, Jr.) An import from South Plains Community College, an institution that has placed a couple of starting backcourt players into power conference programs in recent years (Texas Tech's Nick Okorie and Nebraska's Steve Harley) but whose bigs have struggled to make the transition.

Oregon

2009: 8-23 (2-14 Pac-10), lost to Oregon State, 62-40, Pac 10 Tournament First Round
In-conference offense: 0.95 points per possession (9th)
In-conference defense: 1.14 points allowed per possession (10th)

What Oregon did well: *Break their freshmen in.*

The storyline for the 2008-09 season in Eugene was that freshmen played a lot of minutes but didn't play particularly well. In the youngsters' defense, they didn't just have to make the jump from high school to major college basketball. They had to play against arguably the toughest schedule in D-I. Between a tough Pac-10 and a non-conference slate that offered no breaks, Oregon was playing against competent or better opponents in each of their 31 contests.

What we learned in 2009: *You can go 2-16 in conference and be lucky.*

In most cases, when you see a team with a poor record in conference, you can at least find a game or two where a play here or there might have turned a loss into a win. Including their Pac-10 tourney game, the Ducks were outscored by 253 points in compiling a 2-17 record against conference opponents, with just four of their losses occurring by single digits. Their Pythagorean expectation estimates that their chances of winning just one game were slightly better than winning the two that they did. Unlike some other teams in the conference, Oregon's record was an accurate representation of their performance.

What's in store in 2010: Ernie Kent fired long-time assistant Mark Hudson and brought in former Arizona assistant Mike Dunlap in what was widely viewed as a job-saving move on Kent's part. Dunlap, you'll recall, was Arizona's first choice to run their program last year when Lute Olson retired in the fall and he comes into the program highly-regarded (and highly-compensated—he'll be one of the highest paid assistants in the nation). Needless to say, there's a lot riding on this season for Kent.

Prospectus says: There are a few notes for optimism. First, Oregon in 2009 was significantly better than Oregon State in 2008 and you saw how the Beavers recovered last season (with somewhat less talent than exists here). Second, considering the Ducks were woeful in conference play, their pre-conference work was remarkably competent. They had a home win over NIT-bound Kansas State and a convincing win in Maui against Alabama. It seems logical that a team with nearly the same group of guys facing somewhat weaker in-conference competition will improve its record a bit.

The pessimist would say that this is the same group of guys that weren't competitive in Pac-10 play last season. And furthermore, in what was advertised promising group of freshmen heading into last season, only Michael Dunigan wasn't overmatched by the jump to college. The fear has to be that the rest of Dunigan's classmates may be permanently left behind.

Both sides have their points. This team will improve, but there's so much improvement necessary just to get back to .500 that there should still be plenty of ugly games involving the Ducks. Dunigan getting more minutes should pay off and if Malcolm Armstead is an improvement over Garrett Sim at the point, Ernie Kent will put a starting five on the floor that will win a few games. The problem is that there's so little quality depth on this team that they're an injury or two away from another disaster.

Meet the Ducks

Tajuan Porter (5-6, 155, Sr.) Give the nation's shortest two-guard credit—he was immune to the implosion that went on around him last season. Porter did what we've seen from him for three seasons now, take and make a bunch of threes (hitting 38 percent of his 228 attempts last season). All of this took place while defenses knew he was the most effective offensive weapon for the Ducks.

Michael Dunigan (6-10, 242, So.) Dunigan's minutes were limited last season, and by March he found himself coming off the bench after starting up to that point. His two-point percentage (49.7 percent overall, 44.6 percent in conference play) is underwhelming for somebody who's 6-10 and spends all of his time in the post. However, given the other options that Kent had last season, Dunigan deserved better. He has decent block and steal numbers and gets to the line plenty. His rebounding has room for improvement, but with the possible exception of Joevan Catron, his work was the best on the team in this area. Dunigan has a propensity to commit fouls, though he could be expected to show more restraint if he knew he was going to get 30 minutes per game.

Joevan Catron (6-6, 237, Sr.) While each of the returning Ducks struggled to adjust to life without Malik Hairston, perhaps it was Catron who was affected most of all. He was a productive, yet undersized, power forward as a sophomore. Last season, Catron's effective field goal percentage tumbled from 53 to 38 without Hairston operating as a dynamic wing alongside him. The good news is that Catron continued to be one of the best rebounders in the country listed at 6-6.

Jamil Wilson (6-7, 209, Fr.) Wilson is the most heralded newcomer to the Ducks' roster. He appears to be versatile enough to make the wing position more difficult to defend this season.

LeKendric Longmire (6-5, 200, Jr.) Longmire found himself taking many more three-pointers during his sophomore season, and it paid off as he made 26 of his 61 attempts (42.6 percent).

Garrett Sim (6-1, 178, So.) Sim was the surprise starter at point guard for most of his freshman season, and his best moments came in a December 3 game at Utah when he recorded 28 points in 33 minutes on 10-of-14 shooting (5-of-6 from three-point range) and dished out four assists. His work outside the Beehive State was not quite as noteworthy.

Matt Humphrey (6-5, 185, So.) Along with Dunigan, Humphrey was the other promising freshman in Kent's '08-'09 class. Matt didn't disappoint as a pure shooter, taking two-thirds of his shots from beyond the arc and making 35 percent of them. However, Humphrey didn't shoot much and his 51 percent conversion rate at the free throw line indicates his three-point accuracy will suffer if he gets the idea to shoot more.

Malcolm Armstead (5-10, 204, So.) With the transfer of Kamyron Brown, Armstead will fill the role of backup point guard if he doesn't win the battle for the starting job.

Jeremy Jacob (6-7, 220, So.) Jacob was teammates with Armstead at Chipola College last season. Two years ago, Jacob saw 89 minutes of action in six games at Georgia before suffering a stress fracture in his foot which wiped out the rest of the year. Because of the circuitous route to Eugene (a year of prep school followed by the medical hardship at Georgia), Jacob will begin Pac-10 play as a 22-year old sophomore.

Josh Crittle (6-8, 250, So.) Crittle struggled as a freshman but gained Kent's favor as the season progressed. He's a good offensive rebounder and gets to the line quite a bit. Given his general reluctance to shoot the ball, he commits too many turnovers. However, all of these observations occurred in 15 minutes per game so it's too early to completely know what to expect from Crittle going forward.

Drew Wiley (6-7, 215, So.) Yet another Duck that prefers to hang out on the perimeter, Wiley took about three-quarters of his shots from long range and is in direct competition with Humphrey for minutes off the bench.

Teondre Williams (6-4, 199, So.) Williams struggled to find an identity last season while hurting the Ducks' efficiency with sub-40 percent shooting. Perhaps it should have been no surprise that he was arrested along with Dunigan and Crittle shortly after the season for trying to injure ducks (real ones) with a BB gun.

Oregon State

2009: 18-18 (7-11 Pac-10), beat UTEP, 81-73, CBI Championship Game
In-conference offense: 0.95 points per possession (10th)
In-conference defense: 1.07 points allowed per possession (7th)

What Oregon State did well: *Transform Roeland Schaftenaar into America's best passing center.*

A big man that doesn't much care for the post, Schaftenaar won the equivalent of college basketball's lottery last off-season. After going 6-25 in 2008, the Beavers hired the coach known for an offensive system that was most suited to utilize Schaftenaar's strengths. He has reasonable touch from distance and is a capable passer—the necessary skills for a big man to thrive in the Princeton offense. After assisting on just seven percent of his teammates' hoops in 2008, he helped 26 percent of made shots in 2009. That number led the team, and it wasn't even close. In fact, among big men that played at least 40 percent of their team's minutes, there was no competition from anyone in the rest of D-I.

Don't Pass On Roeland: Top Assist Rates, 2008-09, Players At Least 6-10		
Player	Team	ARate
Roeland Schaftenaar	Oregon St.	26.0
Greg Monroe	Georgetown	18.8
Blake Griffin	Oklahoma	16.3
Jeff Foote	Cornell	15.9
Mike Davis	Illinois	13.8
ARate: percentage of teammates' baskets assisted		

What we learned in 2009: *The 1-3-1 zone defense gets a heck of a lot of publicity for not being all that effective.*

Craig Robinson is another devotee to the 1-3-1, a defense that is often described as being difficult to play against. In joining Michigan and Northwestern as power conference teams that regularly use the defense, we've yet to see a version of it that is actually difficult to score against. That doesn't mean that it's necessarily bad strategy to use the 1-3-1. It's possible that these teams would have an even worse defense playing man or a more conventional zone. On the plus side, the 1-3-1 is scientifically proven to force more turnovers. But it's not very good at forcing missed shots.

What's in store in 2010: Technically, the Beavers lose a starter in Ricky Claitt, who averaged about 33 minutes a game last season. However, Claitt was one of the most timid shooters in the Pac-10. Every other player of note is back, and Robinson has brought in a couple of freshmen that could contribute right away as well.

Prospectus says: The combination of events surrounding Oregon State basketball in 2008 and 2009 has created unrealistic expectations for 2010. Consider the improvement in Pac-10 record from 0-18 to 7-11 which coincides with the hiring of a coach whose brother-in-law wins a rather historic election right before the season starts. The Beavers won nearly every close contest they were in last season after conference play started, thus milking every last W from a point differential that would have otherwise predicted them for three conference wins. The feel-good story continued when the Beavs got a bid to the CBI with a 13-17 record. They got to play their pre-championship games at home and eventually won the title with an impressive win at UTEP.

Robinson was able to upgrade the play on both ends of the floor last season, but still, this team had the worst offense in the league. Whether a team is coached by the brother of the First Lady or not, there are likely to be more heartbreaking losses than there were last season. Therefore, this team could be significantly better and not have a better Pac-10 record than last season. Robinson's got the program headed in the right direction, but I have to see another season of improvement before I start forecasting the Beavers to contend for a tournament bid.

Meet the Beavers

Calvin Haynes (6-2, 185, Jr.) For the first six games of last season, the Beavers' results weren't much different than the year before. They were 1-5, including losses at Howard and home defeats to Yale and Montana State. It's not a complete coincidence that Haynes missed those six games before becoming academically eligible after the fall semester ended. OSU beat NIT-bound Nebraska in his first game, and downed Howard by 36 in the return game a week later. No Pac-10 player took a higher percentage of his team's shots while he was on the floor, even though Haynes' role diminished down the stretch as he coped with hand and knee injuries.

Roeland Schaftenaar (6-11, 240, Sr.) Schaftenaar's resume was detailed above. There's nobody in the pipeline to compete with him for minutes this season.

Lathen Wallace (6-3, 200, Jr.) Voted "Least Suited to the Princeton Offense" in his senior year of high school, Wallace took 61 percent of his shots from beyond the arc, up from 42 percent as a freshman. He also made 39 percent of those attempts. So far, so good. However, Wallace only made 48 percent of his twos and it's extremely rare for him to set up his teammates, a couple of traits that generally don't mesh well with a cut-and-pass offense. After butting heads for most of the season, Robinson gave Wallace the keys to the car in the Pac-10 and CBI tournaments, playing him nearly wire-to-wire over those seven postseason games.

Daniel Deane (6-8, 245, Jr.) Considering how often each player shoots, Deane is the Beaver most likely to get to the free throw line, which is something Oregon State as a team struggled with. Actually, it's something that affects all Princeton-based systems. The notable exceptions to that were Robinson's Brown teams, which were consistently among the national leaders in free throw rate. I'm beginning to think that was simply due to Brown having better athletes than their Ivy League foes. That's a situation that despite Robinson's recruiting prowess is not likely to duplicate itself in the Pac-10.

Seth Tarver (6-5, 210, Sr.) Tarver was a season-long starter and made most of his noise on the defensive end, where he played at the top of the 1-3-1.

Omari Johnson (6-9, 215, Jr.) Johnson's a big wing that has decent ability to knock down open jump shots.

Josh Tarver (6-3, 190, Sr.) Josh is Seth's brother, and while not a twin, their games are very similar. Josh plays the point when he sees action, although that didn't happen often last season. The top reason cited by Robinson: turnovers. However, from a strictly statistical perspective his numbers don't give away any serious flaws in his game.

Jared Cunningham (6-3, 170, Fr.) Robinson brings in a recruiting class of five, and Cunningham would appear to be the most likely of the quintet to make an impact. While there's talk of him seeing major minutes at point guard, the bar to be reached for starting is going to be higher than one might believe based on Josh Tarver's extended stay in the doghouse last season.

Roberto Nelson (6-4, 190, Fr.) The other freshman with a chance to start at some point is Nelson, who's a combo guard that was on the national radar last summer when he surprisingly committed to the Beavers.

Stanford

2009: 20-14 (6-12 Pac-10), lost to Oregon State, 65-62, CBI Semifinals
In-conference offense: 1.03 points per possession (7th)
In-conference defense: 1.07 points allowed per possession (8th)

What Stanford did well: *Dominate non-conference opponents.*

Now it's true that Stanford didn't exactly sched-ule up, but the list of teams to go unbeaten against non-conference competition over the past decade is rather short:

- 2009 North Carolina (National Champion)
- 2009 Pittsburgh (Elite 8)
- 2009 Stanford (CBI Semifinalist)
- 2008 Kansas (National Champion)
- 2006 Florida (National Champion)

The way to join this list is to beat all of your regular season non-conference foes and (a) win a national title or (b) lose to a team from your own conference in the postseason. Stanford was able to sneak past the velvet ropes and into this exclusive club by not having to beat anyone better than Northwestern in the regular season, and then by getting to the semifinals of the CBI where they lost to Oregon State. So don't let history forget the 2009 Cardinal: 13-0 against non-conference teams, 7-14 against the Pac-10.

What we learned in 2009: *There is no difference between Johnny Dawkins' and Mike Kryzyzewski's defensive philosophies.*

Whenever a coach makes his debut, there's a fair amount of guesswork in what style he will impose on his new team. In the case of Anne and Tony Joseph Director of Men's Basketball Johnny Dawkins (that's his official title, we have to call him that), all we knew heading into last season was that his entire basketball life, at the collegiate level anyway, was spent working or playing for one person. So it figured that the statistical fingerprints found on last season's team might resemble some of what we've seen at Duke over the past decade. Indeed, on the defensive end this is exactly what happened.

Stanford's aggressive man defense resulted in a complete denial of opponents' three-point attempts. Conference opponents took just 22 percent of their shots from beyond the arc. The problem for Stanford was that Pac-10 opponents made about 52 percent of their two-point attempts, and even their rare threes were on target at a 41.5 percent clip. Stylistically the defense resembles a Coach K product, but not yet in terms of effectiveness.

What's in store in 2010: Stanford loses three starters and a top reserve from last year's team. The issue is not that there's a lot of talent going out the door (although Cardinal fans will miss the scoring ability of Anthony Goods and Lawrence Hill), but that there's just not much filling in behind the departures yet. Mainly what the Cardinal could use is some size to better deter the dribble penetration that regularly knifed through the Stanford D, and while the frontline will be marginally bigger this season, the bigger players don't have a history of blocking shots.

Prospectus says: It's year two of the Dawkins Era but you might as well reset the clock. In losing the remaining parts of the engine from the Trent Johnson regime, Dawkins now has to fend for himself in the Pac-10. Yes, Landry Fields and Josh Owens will lead this team, and Dawkins didn't recruit them either, but this is the first season they'll be the go-to-guys for Stanford. Unlike last season, Dawkins has a blank slate with a group of players that don't have much baggage under a previous system. Mission for this year: Finish putting your stylistic fingerprints on the Stanford program. Mission for next year: Bring in the talent to fit said fingerprints. This is year one of the rebuilding of Stanford basketball.

Meet the Cardinal

Landry Fields (6-7, 210, Sr.) We'll learn a lot about Fields' ability to take shots this season. He's been an active shooter during his career, taking more than 20 percent of the Cardinal's shots in each of his first three seasons. This is no small feat playing alongside Lawrence Hill and Anthony Goods during that time and Brook Lopez for two of those seasons. Last season Fields took a big step forward by hitting 55 percent of his two-point shots. This, after making just 40 percent of those attempts in the previous two seasons.

Jeremy Green (6-4, 190, So.) Green made the Pac-10's all-freshman team primarily on the strength of connecting on 46 percent of his three-point attempts. Warning to Stanford fans: That percentage is going to go down this season. Last season, Green did his work on 103 attempts. That's likely to double this season, if only because Green's playing time figures to double. Of the 131 players that took at least 200 three-point attempts last season, only one made at least 46 percent of his shots (Eastern Kentucky's Mike Rose).

Josh Owens (6-8, 220, Jr.) Owens' first season with serious minutes resulted in what we typically see for a big man in his first season of D-I ball. He doesn't shoot much, but is efficient when he does, and he doesn't rebound as much as one would like for someone with his size and athleticism.

Drew Shiller (6-0, 180, Sr.) Shiller was Mitch Johnson's backup last season and should take over starting chores in his senior year. Like Johnson, Shiller thinks pass long before he thinks shot.

Gabriel Harris (6-2, 185, Fr.) Any remaining minutes at point guard should go to Harris, who was also recruited heavily by Ivy League schools.

A little help? Obviously beyond the five listed above, there's still a lot of playing time to be covered. The problem is that there's little indication as to who is willing to step up and fill in the holes. Dawkins brought one additional freshman to the program in **Andy Brown (6-8, 225)**, but the perimeter-oriented forward tore his ACL in October and won't see action. **Andrew Zimmerman (6-9, 215, So.)** is another newcomer to the program, but he struggled against WCC competition in his only previous season of D-I experience. With 6-10 would-be senior Will Paul on academic suspension for the season, Zimmerman is going to get minutes. After that you have guys that were on the roster last season, but saw little action.

UCLA

2009: 26-9 (13-5 Pac-10), lost to Villanova, 89-69, NCAA Second Round
In-conference offense: 1.13 points per possession (1st)
In-conference defense: 1.02 points allowed per possession (5th)

What UCLA did well: *Score (in a tempo-free way).*

The first game I watched for comprehension last season was the November 14 contest between UCLA and the Miami RedHawks. It was a hideously slow paced game. The Bruins scored 64 points in the 54 times they had the ball. Against what would end up being arguably the best defense in the MAC, it was a pretty good performance. However, the game wasn't decided until the final minute, leaving observers like myself questioning what was in store for UCLA the rest of the season.

I didn't know it then, but I didn't need to watch another Bruins' game. The game against Miami was a microcosm of their season. Their offense was a machine whose ability was often masked by a slow pace, and the Bruins were in far too many close games because of a defense that couldn't get enough stops.

What we learned in 2009: *There's nothing that could possibly happen for Ben Howland to shed the reputation of a defensive genius.*

I recognize that our way of looking at the game is not going to permeate the national consciousness overnight. I'm fairly patient, and I still hold out hope that one day every rebound will have an adjective and that in some future time, possessions will be listed as part of the box score. But I give up on advancing the notion that Ben Howland's ability to coach outstanding defense is overstated. Even a cursory analysis from last season would reveal that when UCLA failed, it was almost always on defense.

Taking their five Pac-10 losses collectively, the Bruins allowed 387 points in 325 possessions for a whopping 1.19 points per possession. And they bowed out to Villanova giving up 1.29 points per possession. There aren't too many offenses in the history of the game that can overcome a defense like that.

What's in store in 2010: Youth takes over this season and even though three seniors will find a spot in the regular rotation, it's possible none of them will be starters. Howland's challenge is to figure out how to replace the dynamic backcourt trio of Darren Collison, Jrue Holiday, and Josh Shipp. Fortunately, his roster is littered with many freshmen and sophomores who were highly-rated recruits.

Prospectus says: UCLA is the reverse image of Oregon State heading into this season. Hindered by a poor record in close games and given a tournament draw where they were forced to play a road game in the second round, the Bruins were a very good team for most of the season whose national reputation never caught up to their performance. That performance, mainly on the offensive end, was often excellent. Just not for the last 40 minutes of the season at the Wachovia Center. You can do the math—a six-seed minus four starters equals, what in 2010, flirting with a double-digit seed maybe? Not so fast.

There are certainly some questions floating over the

Bruins regarding their ability to contend for a Pac-10 title. But there's a ton of size and athleticism on this team, so perhaps the defense can improve. Given that the offense is not being run by Darren Collison any longer, there may be some more desperation to play defense because the points won't come as easily. The rest of the Pac-10 should beware: There's so much young talent on this team that some of these guys are bound to exceed expectations. The Bruins are still going to be a tough out.

Meet the Bruins

Drew Gordon (6-8, 235, So.) If Gordon can transfer the rebounding rates he posted as a reserve last season to a starting role this season, he will be widely praised as a beast of the boards. He was one of just 13 players that had an offensive rebounding rate above 15 percent and a defensive rate above 20. The only other big-conference players in that club were Jordan Hill, Jon Brockman, and DeJuan Blair. With an average usage rate, Gordon made 57 percent of shots and got to the line a respectable amount. True, all of this was accomplished in spot duty against easier competition than a starter would have seen, and his offensive arsenal was notably limited as a freshman. Even so, there is a lack of quality big men in the Pac-10 this season; with a little more polish to his game Gordon has a great opportunity to produce a pretty impressive season.

Malcolm Lee (6-5, 180, So.) Like every UCLA freshman not named Holiday last season, we didn't see enough of Lee to get a great idea of what he brings to the table. We do know that as a two-guard, he's less stationary than Michael Roll and will do more of his damage going to the basket. We'll see more of him this season.

Jerime Anderson (6-1, 165, So.) As an understudy to Collison last season, Anderson struggled with both turnovers and shooting. (Curiously, he finished second on the team in block percentage. Maybe he's playing out of position.)

Tyler Honeycutt (6-9, 180, Fr.) Honeycutt may be a year (and a few pounds) away from becoming a serious force in the Pac-10, but if he can start at one of the wings, Ben Howland is going to have a very tall front line for opponents to contend with.

Mike Moser (6-8, 195, Fr.) Moser's a lanky wing from Portland, Oregon, who backed out of a commitment to Arizona when the coaching merry-go-round began there.

Brendan Lane (6-9, 205, Fr.) "I want to have the defensive mentality they have at UCLA. The mentality that Ben Howland coaches," Lane has been quoted as saying. Argh.

Michael Roll (6-5, 200, Sr.) Roll's niche as a part-time three-point specialist should continue for his senior year. He made just over half of his 99 three-point attempts last season en route to a lofty offensive rating of 126. He's also more skilled at setting up teammates than the typical shooting guard.

J'Mison Morgan (6-10, 248, So.) Morgan saw 114 minutes of action and took 37 shots last season. That converts to about 13 shots per 40 minutes, a remarkably high figure for someone that didn't see action in 14 games due to his coach's decision. (For reference, Josh Shipp was the most frequent Bruin shooter last season at 14 attempts per 40.) While Morgan was overmatched last season, his level of activity suggests that better things are possible. Whether that means a future comparable to Brian Zoubek or Marreese Speights (two bigs who spent their freshman season providing bursts of activity in limited playing time) remains to be seen.

Nikola Dragovic (6-9, 216, Sr.) The Serbian made 21 starts as a junior and was often matched up against the opposing four on the defensive end. Offensively, he functions as a shooting forward, taking 60 percent of his shots from beyond the arc.

James Keefe (6-8, 238, Sr.) Keefe made the 14 starts that Dragovic didn't. Keefe's game is more of a traditional power forward and he provided a spark with his offensive rebounding. He will take a few three-pointers himself and isn't a bad shooter from out there.

USC

2009: 22-13 (9-9 Pac-10), lost to Michigan St., 74-69, NCAA Second Round
In-conference offense: 1.04 points per possession (6th)
In-conference defense: 1.01 points allowed per possession (4th)

What USC did well: *Get up off the mat.*

USC lost six of seven games it played in February, finishing the month at 7-9 in Pac-10 play. True, the February slate was not one that you would have expected many teams to have success with—five of the seven games were on the road and none of the games involved the Oregon schools. It wasn't just that the Trojans lost games, but most of them were lost decisively, and one—the roadie at Arizona State—featured a memorable on-court meltdown by head coach Tim Floyd.

But the Trojans weren't dead. They closed the regular season by sweeping the homestand against Oregon and Oregon State and then winning the Pac-10 tournament. They then knocked off Boston College rather easily in the first round of the NCAA tournament and lost to eventual runner-up Michigan State by only five after coming up empty on their final six possessions.

What we learned in 2009: *Coaching changes at USC are never normal.*

At least under athletic director Mike Garrett, they're not. Since being selected for that position in 1993, the hiring of a new head coach for the men's basketball team has always been an interesting process. And despite seeing four different coaches leave the program, Garrett's never experienced the typical departure. You know, where the coach leaves for a better job or gets fired, either of which happens days after the season ends.

To review: In September 1994, George Raveling decided to retire after being involved in a serious car accident. Top assistant Charlie Parker was named interim coach, only to be given the permanent title prior to the '95-'96 season. He was fired with over a month left in that season and replaced by Henry Bibby on an interim basis. Bibby was named permanent coach in the following off-season and actually brought stability to the program, but he was fired in December of 2004 just four games into the season. Jim Saia finished that season with the interim tag, whereupon Floyd was hired (after Rick Majerus accepted then rejected an offer from Garrett).

That brings us to the present off-season when Floyd abruptly resigned in June. I guess if there's a silver lining to this transition it's that for the first time under Garrett, there was no need for an interim coach to be named.

What's in store in 2010: A whole lot of change. Kevin O'Neill replaces Floyd as the head coach, and truth be told, it was a pretty impressive hire given the mid-June timing of Floyd's resignation and the possibility of NCAA investigators descending on campus. The Trojans' top three players from last season—Daniel Hackett, Taj Gibson, and DeMar DeRozan—all declared early for the NBA draft. However, even with all this turmoil the cupboard isn't completely bare. This isn't nearly the situation Tom Crean inherited when he took over for Kelvin Sampson at Indiana last season. Still, USC is notably lacking a point guard, and having Daniel Hackett getting a bunch of minutes in that spot for the past three seasons will make one notice that absence much more easily.

Prospectus says: O'Neill has a reputation as a coach that stresses defense, but there's little in the statistical record from his previous jobs at Arizona and Northwestern to suggest that he has a special formula in that area. In addition, he's coached for 12 seasons and has a career record of nine games below .500. This is not completely fair to O'Neill—he had to coach at Northwestern for three seasons—but I think it indicates that Trojan fans shouldn't be expecting miracles. He does inherit more talent than he had a right to expect given the circumstances of his hiring, but not enough to expect any bubble talk come March.

Meet the Trojans

Dwight Lewis (6-5, 215, Sr.) Lewis has a reputation as a great defender. His offense has been overshadowed by the likes of Mayo, Hackett, and DeRozan the last two seasons, but Lewis has shown an ability to create shots, cracking the 400 mark in field goal attempts last season. However, far too many of those were in the 10 to 20 foot range, resulting in a two-point shooting percentage in the low 40's.

Alex Stepheson (6-9, 235, Jr.) Stepheson walks into a great situation to put up some points. However, he was never the model of efficiency in playing a limited role for two years at North Carolina. Be advised that once Stepheson gets the ball, the possession is going to end with him somehow. He has just 10 assists in 778 career minutes.

Leonard Washington (6-7, 230, So.) Spending the season as the fifth starter or first guy off the bench, Washington showed promise on the offensive end. How that translates to a more prominent role remains to be seen. We'll have to wait until late December to find out while he gets his grades in order.

Marcus Johnson (6-6, 210, Sr.) Johnson saw very limited playing time last season. His track record going back to his days at UConn is that his value is almost entirely on defense where he's regarded as a lock down defender.

Nikola Vucevic (6-10, 220, So.) Vucevic was a very good rebounder who hit 62 percent of his shots the few times he touched the ball.

Donte Smith (5-11, 180, Jr.) Smith is expected to fill the very large point-guard shoes of Daniel Hackett this season. Smith averaged less than 10 minutes per game (and didn't even appear in 11 games) and committed a bunch of turnovers while he played. One every eight minutes to be exact. Consequently, he played a total of 10 minutes over the team's last 13 games.

Marcus Simmons (6-6, 200, Jr.) Simmons saw of surge of playing time down the stretch, even starting a few games. Much like Johnson, he's asked to defend and stay out of the way on offense. Shooting 38 percent (eFG, no less) will do that to you.

Mike Gerrity (6-1, 180, Sr.) Gerrity is the safety net for Donte Smith. He brings experience from two Division I institutions, Pepperdine and Charlotte. He'll see some minutes at point guard, that of the pass-first variety.

Kasey Cunningham (6-7, 225, Jr.) It's tough to find a player more injury prone than Cunningham. For the third straight year his season ended early with knee problems. You could easily write him off given the circumstances, but in his personal season-ender he scored 11 and rebounded six against Missouri. Working in his favor is the relative lack of big-time talent on the roster. If Cunningham's knees can somehow hold up, he should give the Trojans quality minutes off the bench.

Washington

2009: 26-9 (14-4 Pac-10), lost to Purdue, 76-74, NCAA Second Round
In-conference offense: 1.07 points per possession (5th)
In-conference defense: 0.98 points allowed per possession (1st)

What Washington did well: *Create a new identity.*

Nationally, of course, it was completely missed in the blur of possessions that the Huskies crammed into each contest, but the Dawgs were a defensive force. After languishing in the middle of the Pac-10 in defensive efficiency over the past three seasons, head coach Lorenzo Romar was able to put together a D that led a less-than-spectacular offense to a Pac-10 regular-season title.

What we learned in 2009: *Washington's pace malaise wasn't permanent.*

I have to admit I didn't see it coming. I figured Romar had been dragged down by the move by his fellow Pac-10 coaches toward a glacial pace of play. However, 2009 provided a change of course.

Re-Accelerating: Washington Adjusted Tempo, 2006-09		
	Adj. Tempo	**National Rank**
2004	75.1	3rd
2005	73.0	14th
2006	72.8	11th
2007	70.0	54th
2008	70.0	57th
2009	73.5	5th
Adj. Tempo: possessions per 40 minutes, adjusted for pace of the opponent		

The unexpected turnaround can be explained by the unexpected emergence of Isaiah Thomas. A freshman who didn't get a lot of publicity before the season, Thomas started all but one game and his ability to lead the fast break pushed the Huskies' tempo to a level that few could match.

What's in store in 2010: UW has to figure out how to replace Jon Brockman and Justin Dentmon. The loss of Dentmon may be felt less simply because the Huskies add freshman point guard Abdul Gaddy, who has the ability to do what Thomas did—start from day one. By dropping the often-lumbering Brockman and going to a three-guard lineup more often, Washington should maintain the frenetic pace.

Prospectus says: Losing Brockman might be seen as a major blow to the Huskies' front line, and his scoring ability will be missed. But his offensive rebounding may not be. The last non-Brockman team featured a smallish front line that managed to post the fourth best offensive rebounding rate in the nation. There may be a drop in offensive rebounding without Brockman, but it might not be all that noticeable.

Overall, this edition of the Huskies may not be as big or quite as talented as it was last season, but it's close enough that a significant drop in the level of play would be a surprise. Just coming close to the performance of last season will be good enough to compete for another conference title.

Meet the Huskies

Isaiah Thomas (5-8, 185, So.) The diminutive lefty was 2009's best example of a really short guy exceeding the expectations of recruiting services. As a slashing point guard, he was at the heart of the Huskies' increase in tempo. Thomas wasn't a great shooter, but if you're under six feet, shooting over 50 percent inside the arc is a tall order. Thomas came close (47.5 percent), but his inability to hit three-pointers (29.1 percent) was the obvious weak spot in his game. Since he's the early favorite to lead the team in three-point attempts this season, this could be an issue.

Quincy Pondexter (6-6, 215, Sr.) Pondexter's career at UW has been marked by solid, if not spectacular play. He's not an outstanding rebounder, but decent for his size on the offensive end. He shoots well (an effective field goal percentage of 51.5 last season),

but considering he's been the third or fourth concern of opposing defenses, you might expect better. Given that the team's offense was significantly weaker than the defense in '09, one might expect that Pondexter will need to be more productive for that to change.

Abdul Gaddy (6-3, 190, Fr.) A consensus of recruiting services has pegged Gaddy as one of the best point guards in his class. He was originally headed to Arizona until the coaching change in Tucson last summer.

Venoy Overton (5-11, 185, Jr.) Overton has spent his first two seasons battling for playing time in the backcourt and his junior year won't be any different. He has consistently had a prodigious turnover rate (and not in a good way), and therefore it makes sense that most of the backcourt minutes are going to go to Thomas and Gaddy. However, no UW player under Romar has averaged as many as 32 minutes per game, so Overton is still going to see plenty of action, either when one of those two needs a breather or as part of a three-guard lineup. He posted the third-best steal rate in the conference in each of the last two seasons which supports his reputation as a disruptive defender.

Darnell Gant (6-8, 225, So.) Gant is part of a dying breed in college hoops—the mid-range specialist. There may not have been another player in a major conference that took more of his shots from the awkward two-point jump shot distance last season. As a result, he only made 36.6 percent of his field goal attempts and hardly ever got to the free-throw line. With Brockman gone, there should be more opportunities for closer looks.

Matthew Bryan-Amaning (6-9, 240, Jr.) It helps to have an MBA in today's fast-paced job market, but what if your MBA struggles to find a role in your fast-paced offense? That has been the problem facing Washington fans the past two seasons. Bryan-Amaning managed to raise his true shooting percentage from hide-your-children numbers as a freshman to around 48 percent as a sophomore. In the battle for Brockman-vacated minutes this season, that number is going to have to rise further for the Englishman to hold down a starting spot.

Elston Turner (6-4, 205, So.) Turner did his best Ryan Appleby impression during his freshman season, although his long-range attempts were rarer than Washington's previous three-point specialist.

Justin Holiday (6-6, 180, Jr.) The lesser-known of the Pac-10's Holiday brothers, Justin had his moments last season in limited minutes. However, he was one of the most timid shooters in the conference, and despite appearing in each of the Huskies' 35 games, he never scored more than six points in any contest.

Clarence Trent (6-5, 225, Fr.) Trent arrives on campus billed as an über-athletic wing—the type that will fit nicely in Romar's frenetic system.

Tyreese Breshers (6-7, 255, Fr.) He redshirted his first year in Seattle rehabbing from what can best be described as a variety of leg injuries. That process continued through the summer, but the thinking from the program is that he'll be ready for the season opener on November 13. Breshers was hotly pursued out of high school, and with a little luck on the health front could find anywhere from a few minutes of action to a starting role on the front line.

Washington State

2009: 17-16 (8-10 Pac-10), lost to Saint Mary's, 68-57, NIT First Round
In-conference offense: 0.99 points per possession (8th)
In-conference defense: 0.98 points allowed per possession (2nd)

What Washington State did well: *Duh. Defend.*

With Tony Bennett off to ply the coaching trade in the ACC, it's worth reviewing the era of Pac-10 defensive dominance that the Bennett clan presided over in Pullman.

Locking It Down: Washington State Defensive Efficiency Since 2005		
Year	DE	Conf. Rank
2005	0.93	1st
2006	0.98	2nd
2007	0.95	1st
2008	1.01	4th
2009	0.98	2nd
Pac-10 games only		

This run occurred with the kind of talent that wasn't exactly envied around the rest of the conference. Granted, the defensive stats were partially built on an offense that didn't take many chances with respect to offensive rebounds. In addition to the pack-line principles, the Bennetts' mission was to prevent any fast break attempts and lock down the defensive boards. If anyone in the game wants a blueprint to prevent opponents from scoring, it could be found at Washington State for the past five years.

What we learned in 2009: *Forcing opponents to miss shots and rebounding all of those misses will yield good results on D.*

Yes, it really can be that simple, and that's what Washington State did last season. With the turnover-forcing ability of Kyle Weaver and Derrick Low finding a professional home in Oklahoma City and France, respectively, the Cougars' defensive turnover rate plummeted. Whatever turnovers were committed by opposing offenses pretty much happened by accident because only one team in the country (Iowa State) forced fewer steals per possession than Wazzu. However, the Cougars led the conference in two-point percentage defense and defensive rebounding, a combination that very often produces great D.

What's in store in 2010: If nothing else, Ken Bone will put a halt to the rapidly sliding pace of the average Pac-10 game. Bone's Portland State teams were slightly faster than the D-I average in terms of pace, but for a fan base that is used to Tony Bennett's version of average (last season was actually the slowest of the Bennett regime), Bone's style will seem like it was ripped from Duggar Baucom's VMI playbook.

Prospectus says: With the departure of Tony Bennett, it should be remembered that Washington State is the historic doormat of the Pac-10. (Over the past 31 seasons, Wazzu has 26 fewer wins than any other Pac-10 team.) It is not easy to build a successful basketball program in Pullman. Fortunately for Bone, there are enough parts leftover from the Bennett era for the Cougars to pick up some wins in the conference this season. However, if Bone is unable to sustain Bennett's success in coming years, it's not necessarily because Bone is incapable of running a major D-I program.

Meet the Cougars

Klay Thompson (6-6, 200, So.) If ever a positional label fit a player, it was "shooting guard" to "Klay Thompson" as a freshman. Make no mistake, Thompson could shoot—he made 41 percent of his 165 three-point attempts, a figure which rose to 48 percent in conference play. However, he was the very rare bird that took threes in bulk, made a whole lot of them, and yet wasn't a terribly efficient scorer. For one thing, Thompson wasn't married to the three-point line but also couldn't get to the bucket. Thus, a large chunk of his two-point attempts were no easier that his three-point shots, and his two-point accuracy was just 43 percent. Thompson also got to the line but rarely, averaging less than one free throw attempt per game. Among all D-I players that got starters' minutes, he was one of only five that took fewer than one free throw for every ten field goal attempts. Without Taylor Rochestie and Aron Baynes around, much of the offensive load is going to fall on Thompson's shoulders. He'll need to diversify his game in order for the Cougars' offense to have a chance at being effective.

DeAngelo Casto (6-8, 231, So.) When he was on the floor, one could make the case that Casto was the most influential freshman on the squad last season. Casto played just 16 minutes per game (compared to Thompson's 33), but his stat-line typically included a smattering of points, free throws, boards on both ends of the floor, and blocks. Casto will be a season-long starter this season, and should see his per-game numbers explode with the increase in both minutes and pace.

Nikola Koprivica (6-6, 221, Sr.) Koprivica, like Thompson, is basically going to take jump shots on the offensive end. Fortunately, he shoots about half as often—his three years in Pullman have produced a career three-point accuracy of 23.6 percent.

Brock Motum (6-9, 205, Fr.) Motum is an Australian import who has some range. The height and nationality indicate a potential for him to be an Aron Baynes clone, but Motum relies much more on a face-up game.

Marcus Capers (6-4, 180, So.) Capers struggled to make the adjustment to the collegiate level (shooting 29 percent, for example), but continued to find some minutes as the season progressed due to his value on the defensive end.

Abe Lodwick (6-7, 200, So.) Lodwick played 132 minutes last season with 51 of those coming in the first four games. Despite the size, Lodwick will be spending a lot of his time on offense outside the arc.

Mike Harthun (6-3, 181, So.) Harthun had trouble getting off the bench during his freshman season, but there are enough questions in the backcourt that there's reason to believe he'll be more than a practice player as a sophomore.

Others? At Portland State, Bone treated his squad much more like a 5th grade rec league team than Bennett did at Pullman, meaning just about everyone on the team got a chance to play. Thus the seven players listed above will see their minutes supplemented by some newcomers who, frankly, weren't given a lot of ink during the recruiting process. Nonetheless, DeAngelo Casto fell into this category a year ago, and he managed to be an important contributor as a freshman. So the hope has to be that one or more of **Anthony Brown (6-4, 206)**, **Reggie Moore (6-1, 178)**, **Xavier Thames (6-3, 186)**, and **Steven Bjornstad (6-10, 217)** can follow in Casto's footsteps.

In April of 2007 when Florida cut down the nets in Atlanta to mark their second consecutive national championship, few would have guessed that the Gators' conference was about to endure a brief but harsh winter of tournament futility. Of the 32 entrants in the 2008 and 2009 Sweet 16s, just one—Tennessee in 2008—was from the SEC.

That's likely to change this year, thanks in more or less equal measure to who's arriving and who's returning.

I trust you've heard that John Calipari and John Wall are arriving. Whether or not the NCAA officially recognizes the fact, the truth of the matter is that the erstwhile Memphis coach has now led his teams to the last four Sweet 16s, a statement that no other coach—not Roy Williams, Bill Self, Ben Howland, or anyone else—can make. He was hired at Kentucky on April 1 to extend that personal streak on behalf of the Wildcats.

Calipari would appear to have his third consecutive one-and-done scoring point guard waiting in the wings in the person of Wall. The freshman from Raleigh, North Carolina, is widely expected to be picked at or very near the top of the 2010 NBA draft. In the meantime he'll be called upon to lead a Kentucky team that many observers are rating as the favorites to win the SEC. The Wildcats will indeed have a loaded roster, one featuring not only Wall and McDonald's All-American DeMarcus Cousins but also veteran Patrick Patterson, who last year achieved amazing results where offensive efficiency by a fea-

tured player is concerned, yet still couldn't land himself a spot on the All-SEC first team. That oversight is not likely to be repeated this season.

Before Patterson and his talented mates can clear a spot in the trophy case, however, they'll have to go through Tennessee, which has won more league games the past four seasons than any other program. Coming off a year where the Volunteers went 10-6 in-conference, Bruce Pearl has returned his entire roster intact from top to bottom. Tyler Smith would represent the "top" there; he leads a veteran team that ranked second in the league in offensive efficiency last year. Nor will Devan Downey and A.J. Ogilvy allow South Carolina and Vanderbilt, respectively, to fall far behind the Wildcats and Volunteers—if indeed they fall behind at all.

And that's speaking only of the SEC East. In the West things promise to be no less interesting, with or without Mississippi State's would-be freshman Renardo Sidney. The McDonald's All-American from Jackson, Mississippi, by way of L.A. was a godsend for bored college hoops writers looking for material in the offseason. In a nutshell: The NCAA has declared that Sidney's amateur status is "not certified," due to questions that arose when his family took up residence in an L.A. home that rented for at least $4,000 a month. At this writing discussions between the NCAA and the Sidneys are still at an impasse.

Yet even without Sidney, Mississippi State returns five starters, including the nation's top shot-blocker,

SEC PROSPECTUS			
	2009 Record	Returning Minutes (%)	2010 Prediction
EAST			
Tennessee	10-6	99	12-4
Kentucky	8-8	64	12-4
South Carolina	10-6	79	10-6
Vanderbilt	8-8	91	10-6
Florida	9-7	66	8-8
Georgia	3-13	60	1-15
WEST			
Mississippi St.	9-7	94	10-6
Ole Miss	7-9	72	9-7
Alabama	7-9	58	8-8
Arkansas	2-14	83	7-9
Auburn	10-6	60	5-11
LSU	13-3	42	4-12

Jarvis Varnado. And while Arkansas likewise returns all five starters (most notably Michael Washington), it may be the Bulldogs' archrival, Ole Miss, that challenges MSU for supremacy in the West—assuming the Rebels can avoid last year's spate of injuries. Ole Miss shooting guard Terrico White could be a first-round pick as soon as next summer, point guard Chris Warren is arguably the better college player, and criminally underrated big man Murphy Holloway may be just as valuable as any of the above.

Among all the conference's returning starters, however, surely no returnee brings more experience to the court than LSU wing Tasmin Mitchell, who by my reckoning should be about 33 years old by now. He started alongside Tyrus Thomas and Glen Davis on the Tigers' 2006 Final Four team, yet somehow he is still here, the SEC's senex figure.

Experience is the key word this season not only in the West but conference-wide, where over 73 percent of last year's minutes are back for 2009-10. Conferences that return at least 70 percent of their minutes tend to do very well. In the past three seasons there have been just three major conferences that have brought back that level of experience. Two of those conferences, the ACC and Big East last year, accounted for the entirety of the 2009 Final Four. The third such conference is the SEC this year. I'm not predicting they'll sweep this season's Final Four or anything, but I do think the SEC should be able to match the last two years' combined output of Sweet 16 teams with room to spare.

A significant portion of those returning players will be overseen this season by someone new, as the SEC is welcoming three new coaches to the league this season: Calipari, Alabama's Anthony Grant, and Georgia's Mark Fox. That's noteworthy because it didn't used to be noteworthy.

Three or so new guys a year used to be the norm in the major conferences, but the current economy has changed more than a few norms, right? Not in the SEC. While the other five major conferences have to varying degrees fallen prey to a strange new frugality, one where struggling coaches are often retained rather than bought out, the SEC operates in some kind of free-spending perceptual oxygen tent where it's still 2006. They still fire coaches in this conference, for goodness sake. Then again the SEC can afford to, thanks not only to the conference's big-dollar football programs, but also to the separate deals the league recently signed with CBS and ESPN that should bring in around $3 billion over 15 years. The very rich athletic directors in the SEC are different from you and me.

If my read of the conference in the coming season is correct, those AD's may see some rather pronounced imbalances this year. The top of the East figures to be both populous and brutal, as multiple strong teams pillage the bottom third of their own division and the lower two-thirds of the West for a lot of wins. I think teams like Auburn, LSU, and Georgia will find it's hard to win games when so much of the league is very experienced, very good, or both.   *John Gasaway*

Alabama out

2009: 18-14 (7-9 SEC), lost to Tennessee 86-62, SEC Quarterfinals
In-conference offense: 1.03 points per possession (7th)
In-conference defense: 1.05 points allowed per possession (9th)

What Alabama did well: *Navigate the transition.*

Last year marked the second consecutive season where a struggling but by no means terrible SEC West team said goodbye to its coach around the time of the Super Bowl and then finished its season in a calm and even somewhat capable manner under an interim replacement. In 2008 it was LSU that said au revoir to John Brady and bonjour to interim head coach Butch Pierre, who guided the team to a 5-4 finish. After the season ended the Tigers hired Trent Johnson away from Stanford.

Then in 2009 Alabama enacted the same script. The Crimson Tide parted ways with Mark Gottfried on January 26, tapped assistant Philip Pearson to finish the year on an interim basis, and then hired Anthony Grant of VCU as the new head coach on March 27.

The Tide went 6-7 in the Pearson interregnum, a record that included a regular season-ending 70-67 win at Tennessee. Alabama can only hope the eerie parallels with LSU continue and that their team posts a 13-3 record in the SEC in 2010, as did the Tigers last year.

What we learned in 2009: *Success in college hoops isn't always a steady progression.*

Gottfried coached ten full seasons and part of an eleventh in Tuscaloosa but was just 49-35 in the last three years of his tenure. Clearly that was adjudged by his superiors as not good enough.

In retrospect his best shot at March success was arguably his first NCAA tournament team at Alabama in 2002. Featuring Erwin Dudley and Rod Grizzard, the Tide arrived at the tournament that year sporting a two-seed and a 23-6 record, but were sent home in the second round by Kent State, then coached by Stan Heath. Gottfried went on to do great things, relatively speaking, guiding Alabama to five consecutive NCAA appearances (falling just short of Wimp Sanderson's record of six). But he never again coached a team with a seed as high as that 2002 group. His best opportunity came early.

Ironically, the same might be said in spades of Heath. The former assistant to Tom Izzo at Michigan State was in his first year at Kent State when the Golden Flashes made it all the way to the 2002 Elite Eight. Heath parlayed that run into a job at Arkansas, where he was fired after the 2007 season. Now starting his third season at South Florida, Heath is 0-2 in NCAA tournament games since leaving Kent State.

What's in store for 2010: Alabama has missed the last three NCAA tournaments, but they might be able to rectify that situation as soon as this year, thanks to the return of four starters.

Prospectus says: Alabama's limiting factor last year was its defense, which wasn't terrible but wasn't very good either. In fact where the Tide improved noticeably on offense late in the season, the defense remained the same—below-average—under both the Gottfried and Pearson regimes. Grant should start with the defensive glass, where 'Bama was awful last year, worse than any SEC team other than South Carolina. Opponent possessions just kept going and going in 2009. The talent is on hand to change that in 2010. (Note for instance that, paradoxically, this was the best offensive rebounding team in the conference last year.) When Grant puts that talent to work on D, the "return" of Alabama will be at hand.

Meet the Crimson Tide

Senario Hillman (6-1, 190, Jr.). Hillman is a capable combo guard trapped in the body of a hapless perimeter shooter. He has now played two years of college ball and has made 24 percent of his threes. It may be time for Hillman to close that book for good and focus instead on slashing to the basket, assists, defense—anything.

JaMychal Green (6-9, 220, So.). Aside from being much too foul-prone, Green had a very nice freshman campaign considering he was a McDonald's All-American who nevertheless didn't have to be the Man for his team (thanks to the presence of the now-departed Alonzo Gee). Most notably, Green was an absolutely ferocious offensive rebounder, posting the SEC's best rebound percentage on that end of the floor. Assuming he can stay away from foul trouble, Green's role in the offense will likely increase this year. That will likely be a good thing for his team.

Mikhail Torrance (6-5, 210, Sr.). Speaking of players needing to make themselves more prominent in the offense, meet Mikhail Torrance. Grant's to-do list in his first season should include simply telling Torrance, "Go to it. (Inside the arc.)" Note that the season totals here are a little misleading. When Ronald Steele left the team in mid-January, Torrance's minutes shot up. Over the Tide's last 17 games he averaged 28 minutes and 13 points per contest. Burdened with a shaky perimeter shot, Torrance is most effective when he gets to the line, where he makes 88 percent of his freebies.

Justin Knox (6-9, 240, Jr.). The Tide's fourth returning starter, Knox is on the floor primarily to defend and rebound, though he does get hacked with regularity and shoots 70 percent at the line.

Anthony Brock (5-9, 165, Sr.). Brock arrived in Tuscaloosa last year as a junior college transfer and picked up 32 steals in a little over 300 minutes, enough to classify him as a clear threat to opposing ball-handlers. He also made 45 percent of his rare threes.

Ben Eblen (6-1, 180, Fr.). Praised as a "true" point guard, Eblen could compete for minutes at that spot as a freshman.

Andrew Steele (6-3, 215, So.). Steele averaged a healthy 15 minutes a game off the bench as a freshman but stylistically he is yet to declare himself, so to speak. Is he an all-pass no-shoot point guard? The lone three-point specialist on a team that never shoots them? Stay tuned.

Chris Hines (6-8, 220, Jr.). A junior college transfer from Southwestern Illinois CC, Hines has already achieved unanticipated importance for two reasons. In May 6-9 reserve Yamene Coleman graduated from the University and announced he would not return to the team for an available fifth season of eligibility. Then in late September 6-8 reserve Demetrius Jemison ruptured his Achilles tendon and is expected to miss the entire season. Hines may well see more minutes than Mark Gottfried thought he would when the young man was signed in November of 2008.

Arkansas

2009: 14-16 (2-14 SEC), lost to Florida 73-58, SEC First Round
In-conference offense: 0.98 points per possession (11th)
In-conference defense: 1.09 points allowed per possession (12th)

What Arkansas did well: *Prove conclusively that fretting about turnover margin is a football thing.*

One might assume that a really young team with a 2-14 record would commit its fair share of turnovers. Au contraire! These notably youthful Razorbacks in fact sported a very nice TO margin, coughing up the ball on just 19 percent of their trips while forcing opponents into turnovers on 21 percent of theirs. The Hogs thus had the ball-possession wind at their backs, so to speak, getting more looks at the basket than their opponents.

And look what it got them.

What we learned in 2009: *Non-conference home games mean nothing.*

Arkansas had a home stand to remember as 2008 became 2009, beating Blake Griffin and previously undefeated Oklahoma 96-88, and then taking care of Texas by the score of 67-61 seven days later. Both teams came to Fayetteville ranked in the top ten nationally and left with a loss.

The resulting headlines were understandable (John Pelphrey was touted as the odds-on favorite to win SEC Coach of the Year), but sometimes what's understandable now proves incomprehensible later on. Bud Walton Arena may have been a death trap for elite Big 12 opponents but visiting SEC teams subsequently went 6-2 there. Alabama and Georgia, two teams that fired their coaches in January, were the only opponents to share the fate of the Sooners and the Longhorns.

What's in store for 2010: Everyone's back for Arkansas, yet a lot of players left. Embrace the paradox! Reserves Jason Henry, Andre Clark, and Brandon Moore are all gone. (Henry was suspended during the season and has since left the team. Clark and Moore transferred.)

Still, even with the turnover on the bench this is a team that returns all five starters. If you're thinking that sounds familiar you're right. Just two short years ago Pelphrey was in a similar situation, putting a team on the floor that returned all the starters from the previous season. It's worth taking a glance back to see how exactly that played out for the Razorbacks:

Arkansas 2010, The 2008 Prequel: Razorback Performance When 'Everyone's Back'				
	2007	2008	2009	2010
Returning minutes (%)		96		83
Offense (PPP)	1.02	1.04	0.98	?
Defense (Opp. PPP)	0.99	0.99	1.09	?
Record	7-9	9-7	2-14	?
NCAA result	1stRd	2dRd	no bid	?
Conference games only				
PPP: points per possession. Opp. PPP: opponent points per possession				

Note that the 2008 team returned more minutes (96 percent) from a more successful group (7-9) than does this year's edition of the Razorbacks (83 percent and 2-14). Little wonder that the team two years ago was tapped as preseason favorites to win the SEC West. When they instead finished three games behind Mississippi State they were branded as underachievers, though the legacy of that team is arguably in the eye of the beholder. (The Hogs limped into the NCAA field that year as a nine-seed, where they had the tremendous good fortune to draw an Indiana team that had just parted ways with Kelvin Sampson and was thus in chaos. It can truly be said of that Arkansas team that they at least made the second round, before they were snuffed 108-77 by North Carolina.)

Suffice it to say that if 2008 is any guide Arkansas fans are justified in expecting improvement this season. They may also want to bear in mind, however, that this team has a lot of room for improvement on both sides of the ball.

Prospectus says: Pelphrey is facing a host of off-court issues with this team, not the least of which is a university investigation into three unnamed players' involvement in an alleged sexual assault on campus in August. Thus far the coach has said only that one player (as yet unidentified) will be suspended for two to three games. The turmoil surrounding this program—suspensions, arrests, roster turnover, etc.—calls to mind Mike Anderson's first two years at Missouri. In that case the coach was able to right the ship and take his team all the way to the Elite Eight. Arkansas fans hope that Pelphrey can duplicate that trajectory in Fayetteville.

Meet the Razorbacks

Courtney Fortson (5-11, 180, So.). I really need to draft a Gasaway's Law for Fortson's exact situation in 2008-09, the precociously talented freshman point guard who's given free rein over his team's offense. I swear you can bank on the ensuing statistical fuzz tone every time: Tons of assists, turnovers, and missed shots. Given that Fortson makes just 60 percent of his free throws, I expect his 31 percent three-point shooting will stay pretty much where it is. So his best bet for future development may lie in the Jonny Flynn direction, as an undersized yet surprisingly effective source of offense inside the arc. Fortson would also be well advised to model Flynn's can-do demeanor. The Arkansas floor general was suspended for one game in February by Pelphrey for what were termed attitude issues. Then in September Fortson famously sent out an ill-advised tweet referencing three teammates' involvement in an alleged sexual assault. He may face further disciplinary action as a result.

Michael Washington (6-9, 240, Sr.). Washington submitted his name for the NBA draft last April but pulled out in mid-May. He's a monster on the defensive glass who made 59 percent of his twos while playing a big role in the offense in 2008-09. Washington now appears on at least one reputable mock board as a first-rounder in 2010. I hope he fares better in his ascension to the next level than did the SEC West's last vertically challenged 20-something big man with huge stats, Alabama's Richard Hendrix.

Rotnei Clarke (6-0, 185, So.). Pretty much the personification of the term "pure shooter," Clarke hit 39 percent of his frequent threes and 93 percent of his infrequent free throws last year.

Michael Sanchez (6-8, 235, So.). As a freshman Sanchez pulled down the few defensive boards that hadn't already been swallowed up by Washington, but his minutes were limited by his fouls.

Stefan Welsh (6-3, 185, Sr.). Though he had a ghastly year shooting the rock in 2008-09, Welsh reportedly fared even worse off the court this summer, earning an "indefinite" suspension from Pelphrey in July.

Marcus Britt (6-3, 200, Jr.). Speaking of indefinite suspensions, Britt earned one of those after he was arrested under suspicion of driving while intoxicated in June.

Marshawn Powell (6-7, 220, Fr.). For what it's worth, the Arkansas coaching staff is talking up Powell something fierce. The terms "beast" and even "NBA" have been flung about.

Auburn out

2009: 24-12 (10-6 SEC), lost to Baylor 74-72, NIT Quarterfinals
In-conference offense: 1.04 points per possession (5th)
In-conference defense: 0.98 points allowed per possession (2nd)

What Auburn did well: *Transform themselves completely on defense.*

Jeff Lebo was entering his fifth season at Auburn last year with a program that had gone 4-12 in the SEC in three of the coach's first four years at the helm. He also embarked upon the year with a defense that was headed in the wrong direction, having given up 1.08 points per possession in-conference in 2007 before allowing a whopping 1.14 points per trip in 2008.

So what happened last year was more than surprising, it was stunning: The Tigers played magnificent defense in 2009. In fact no major-conference team over the past three seasons has improved its D in league play as much as Auburn did last year.

Defensive Miracles: Largest Improvements On Defense, Major-Conference Teams, 2007-09				
School	Year	Previous year	New	Diff.
Auburn	2009	1.14	0.98	-0.16
Missouri	2009	1.10	0.96	-0.14
DePaul	2007	1.09	0.98	-0.11
Notre Dame	2007	1.12	1.01	-0.11
South Carolina	2009	1.10	0.99	-0.11
Opponent points per possession Conference games only				

No, the Tigers didn't welcome some freshman shot-blocking sensation to campus last year. In both 2008 and 2009, Lebo's team was an undersized group that encouraged opponents to shoot threes. The largest single difference last year was simply that opponents' shots stopped going in, both from outside and from inside.

What we learned in 2009: *Korvotney Barber was a very important player.*

The magnitude of the transformation here was far too large to credit to just one player. Clearly Auburn stepped up their game in multiple areas at once: Perimeter D, post play, and defensive rebounding, to name a few. Still, it would appear that the presence of Korvotney Barber in the lineup in 2009 was a necessary condition for the sudden defensive clamp-down.

Though listed at a mere 6-7, Barber actually qualifies as a big man in Tiger terms. In 2007-08 he played just ten games before being sidelined for the rest of the season with a broken bone in his hand. His return to health last year was a significant benefit to this defense, one that more than offset the damage that his 47 percent shooting at the line did to the Auburn offense. Barber provided Lebo with excellent defensive rebounding, an occasional blocked shot, and perhaps most crucially the ability to play the other four Tigers at something approximating their natural defensive positions.

Last year was Barber's final season of eligibility

and despite the heroics described here he didn't make much of a perceptual mark either locally (he didn't make it onto the seven-player All-SEC first team) or nationally (he went undrafted in June). But make no mistake: His absence this year leaves a big hole for Jeff Lebo to fill.

What's in store for 2010: The Tigers will be more youthful than last year's 10-6 team, with just two starters returning. (Note for example that this team will be without the services of Indiana transfer Brandon McGee, who was dismissed from the program by Lebo on August 11. McGee thus holds the distinction of having been shown the door at two major-conference programs within 15 months. He was sent packing at IU by new coach Tom Crean in May of 2008.) If Lebo wants to see this glass as half-full, however, he could tell his charges that as accomplished as this team was last year on D, there's still room for improvement on offense. Better perimeter shooting and more offensive boards could help offset what is virtually certain to be a decline on D this season.

Prospectus says: This would figure to be a transition year at Auburn, naturally, which is notable inasmuch as this team does project to have three seniors in the starting lineup. Meaning the next two years, at a minimum, will likely see a good deal of roster turnover. That kind of change isn't always bad, of course. But for a program that hasn't been to the NCAA tournament since 2003 (however agonizingly close they came to a bid last year), "transition" is becoming a familiar label.

Meet the Tigers

DeWayne Reed (6-1, 175, Sr.). Reed recorded a commendable number of steals while functioning a little like a scoring point guard in 2008-09, dishing assists more frequently than any other Tiger at the same time that he led the team in shots from the field. Moreover he's trustworthy with the ball and that should not be underrated. Indeed, holding on to the rock was the strength of an otherwise average offense last season, as Auburn committed turnovers on just 17 percent of their trips in SEC play. Still, Reed's production inside the arc is middling (he made 45 percent of his twos as a junior) and his career 63 percent foul shooting suggests his results from the perimeter will likewise continue to be uneven.

Tay Waller (6-2, 180, Sr.). A three-point specialist who made 37 percent of his treys in 2008-09, Waller arrived last year as a junior college transfer from Okaloosa-Walton College in Florida.

Lucas Hargrove (6-6, 205, Sr.). Hargrove started 14 games as a junior and provided surprisingly accurate shooting from both sides of the three-point line, albeit in a supporting role. With the departure of Barber, the defensive boards that Hargrove hauls down will become even more important to his team.

Frankie Sullivan (6-1, 185, So.). For a player who rarely recorded assists, Sullivan brought the ball up the floor for the Tigers with surprising frequency, most notably against Florida in the SEC tournament quarterfinals. The freshman's willingness to push the pace against the Gators made a visible difference in the Tigers' 61-58 win, a victory that at the time appeared to keep Auburn's NCAA hopes alive. Sullivan bears watching, particularly if he becomes a little less foul-prone.

Kenny Gabriel (6-8, 200, So.). Gabriel was to have been a freshman at Auburn last year but did not qualify academically and played last season at Paris Junior College in Paris, Texas.

Tony Neysmith (6-5, 205, So.). A member of the same recruiting class at Oklahoma that included Blake Griffin, Neysmith actually started four games for the Sooners in the heart of the 2008 Big 12 season. Alas, those minutes represented the exception and not the rule for the Atlanta-area product: Neysmith attempted ten shots from the field all season. He therefore transferred to Auburn in search of more playing time.

Andre Malone (6-5, 200, Fr.). Malone could see minutes this season as a freshman at shooting guard.

Earnest Ross (6-4, 185, Fr.). See above: Ross and Malone are both first-year shooting guards who are arriving with roughly equal levels of hype.

Florida

2009: 25-11 (9-7 SEC), lost to Penn State 71-62, NIT Quarterfinals
In-conference offense: 1.10 points per possession (1st)
In-conference defense: 1.03 points allowed per possession (6th)

What Florida did well: *Maintain their usual excellence on offense.*

It's been feast or famine the last four years at Florida. Either the Gators win the national championship, as they did in 2006 and 2007, or they miss the NCAA tournament entirely, as they have in each of the past two seasons.

Given this Jekyll-and-Hyde record, it's fair to ask why Billy Donovan's offense has been so consistently superb over that same span.

No Change, No Change, No Change: Florida Offense, 2006-09			
Year	PPP	Year	PPP
2006	1.10	2008	1.11
2007	1.13	2009	1.10
Conference games only PPP: points per possession			

The truly amazing figure here is of course the one from 2008, a season in which the Gators had just said

goodbye to all five starters from the previous year's national champions. Few could have foreseen that having Marreese Speights as a sophomore and Nick Calathes as a freshman would result in an offense that for all intents and purposes was as good as those populated back in the day by the likes of Horford, Noah, and Brewer. Little surprise, then, that Florida was able to weather Speights' departure last year and keep right on scoring points. (Preventing opponents from scoring points, of course, was another matter.)

Now the question is whether Donovan's team can continue to score without Calathes, who in May announced his intention to play professionally in Greece.

What we learned in 2009: *Nick Calathes deserves at least a look at the next level. (Domestically.)*

Don't be fooled by the relative obscurity in which Calathes toiled (Florida was not exactly a fixture on ESPN the past two seasons) or by the fact that he barely made the All-SEC team (he finished in a three-way tie for the fifth and final spot with Mississippi State's Jarvis Varnado and LSU's Tasmin Mitchell). The truth is the erstwhile Gator has shown more than enough ability to merit the continued interest of the Dallas Mavericks, who grabbed the rights to Calathes in a deal with Minnesota after he was drafted in the second round by the Timberwolves.

To be sure, a 6-6 point guard who doesn't look terribly fleet afoot presents some undeniable problems of "fit" when it comes to the NBA. If it's hard to envision Calathes defending against the league's elite young (i.e., quickest) point guards, it's equally difficult to envision any coach happily switching defensive assignments so that his shooting guard or wing has to expend that same energy. I understand the tide Calathes is swimming against here, truly.

All I know is that for a point guard to carry far and away the largest load in his team's offense, make 55 percent of his twos, hit 39 percent of his threes, dish the lion's share of his offense's assists, take prodigiously good care of the rock, and even perform well on the defensive glass is exceptional in the literal sense of that term: I don't know of another point guard who did as many things as well. Calathes was a host unto himself last year, a multi-dimensional freak who almost single-handedly made the absence of Speights a moot (offensive) point in 2008-09.

One thing Calathes does have going for him in NBA terms is youth. He won't turn 21 until February, meaning in theory he could arrive back on these shores as a still-lively youngster, even with a couple good seasons under his belt as a member of Panathinaikos Athens. Remember his name.

What's in store for 2010: In addition to losing Calathes, the Gators have also said farewell to Walter Hodge, in effect the last remaining link to the national championship teams (notwithstanding the 70 points Dan Werner scored in 2006-07). For Florida to continue its high-scoring ways, multiple players will be required to shoulder more of the load on offense this year.

Prospectus says: Last year Florida somehow acquired a label as a team that "can't defend." With an offense this good it's true the D was their liability, but keep in mind that the defense was in fact right at the conference average in SEC play. It was, however, a visually misleading form of "average," one achieved in part because the Gators simply fouled so rarely. With some more height down low, Florida should be able to defend the paint better than they have the last two years. (Note that last year was actually an improvement over 2008 in this department.) And if Kenny Boynton is ready to score points right away, the drop-off for this team in its post-Calathes incarnation can be smaller than expected.

Meet the Gators

Alex Tyus (6-8, 220, Jr.). Immediately following the end of last season, Tyus announced his intention to transfer, only to change his mind ten days later and say he would return to Florida for his junior year after all. He was reportedly unhappy that he had been asked to play center when one of the forward spots would be more to his liking. Tyus may have been playing out of position but the young man from St. Louis actually did quite well in 2008-09, making 59 percent of his twos while performing capably on the defensive glass, albeit nowhere near the level attained by Marreese Speights the year before.

Kenny Boynton (6-2, 185, Fr.). Boynton is a McDonald's All-American from Pompano Beach, Florida, who arrives in Gainesville with a reputation as a prolific scorer.

Dan Werner (6-8, 230, Sr.). Werner is this program's chronological tweener. He was younger, obviously, than the fabled gang that won two national championships for Donovan. Then again he was also older than a new generation that's already come and gone, namely Calathes. Werner has thus settled into his Gator dotage as a supporting player on offense, one who made 36 percent of his threes last year.

Erving Walker (5-8, 170, So.). You might think a 5-8 freshman wouldn't get much playing time on a team where the point guard job was already occupied, but Walker averaged a robust 24 minutes per contest last year by hitting 42 percent of his threes.

Chandler Parsons (6-9, 215, Jr.). In each of his first two seasons Parsons has shot almost as many threes as twos. The good news is he's a career 60 percent shooter inside the arc. The bad news is he's hit just 31 percent of his shots outside it.

Vernon Macklin (6-10, 240, Jr.). A transfer from Georgetown, Macklin will likely be called upon to take a goodly portion of the minutes in the post that Tyus so plainly does not want.

Kenny Kadji (6-10, 250, So.). Whatever playing time Macklin doesn't occupy in the paint may well go to Kadji.

Erik Murphy (6-9, 215, Fr.). Murphy is a forward from Southborough, Massachusetts, who could see some playing time thanks in part to Allan Chaney's

decision to transfer after last season.

Nimrod Tishman (6-5, 180, Fr.). In October Donovan announced that Tishman will indeed be eligible to play this season. An Israeli who averaged 18 points a game at the Under-18 European championships in July, Tishman could provide immediate help for the Gators. His eligibility had previously been in doubt because he played for the club team Maccabi-Tel Aviv during high school.

Georgia *out*

2009: 12-20 (3-13 SEC), lost to Mississippi St. 79-60, SEC First Round
In-conference offense: 0.88 points per possession (12th)
In-conference defense: 1.06 points allowed per possession (10th)

What Georgia did well: *Help put 17 percent of SEC coaches on the unemployment line.*

The Bulldogs said goodbye to Dennis Felton on January 29 and finished the year under interim head coach Pete Herrmann, before luring Mark Fox away from Nevada on April 3. But the coaching dominoes didn't stop tumbling there. Don't forget UGA's pivotal role in getting Billy Gillispie fired at Kentucky.

When Herrmann and the Dawgs arrived at Rupp Arena to play the Wildcats on March 4, they were 2-12 in the SEC and had just lost a road game to last-place Arkansas by 22 points. Kentucky on the other hand was 8-6 and still fighting for an NCAA berth. The home team that night had Jodie Meeks and Patrick Patterson. The visitors did not.

Final score: Georgia 90, Kentucky 85.

No single game seals a coach's fate, of course. If Kentucky had been undefeated before losing at home to the Bulldogs, Gillispie would still be in Lexington. But the fact is the Wildcats weren't undefeated, and you'd have to search long and hard to find a single game that collided so decisively with a coach's continued employment as this game.

What we learned in 2009: *Regression to the mean is a gravitational force, but escape velocity in the wrong direction is in fact possible.*

The following statement expressly includes an Oregon State team that went 0-18 in the Pac-10 in 2008, so brace yourselves: I've never seen a major-conference offense this bad, where "bad" is defined

as said offense's relation to the conference average. Your garden variety SEC team last year scored 1.03 points per trip in conference play. Georgia's figure there was 0.88.

This team winning at Kentucky by scoring 90 points in a 75-possession game was more than an upset. It was a rupture in the hoops time-space continuum.

What's in store for 2010: The reboot starts this year. Georgia will struggle. Fox will recruit feverishly, trying to build for tomorrow. He has brought in former Alabama interim head coach Philip Pearson as an assistant to help him land the region's top prospects.

Prospectus says: Trey Thompkins provides Fox with a nice building block. Let the rebuild commence, one that will of course take longer than a single season.

Meet the Bulldogs

Trey Thompkins (6-10, 245, So.). Along with former Bulldog Mike Mercer, Thompkins would rank as the most highly-touted recruit that Felton successfully brought to Athens. (Louis Williams, now a member of the Philadelphia 76ers, possessed renown even greater than that of Thompkins or Mercer when he committed to Georgia in 2004, but he subsequently jumped directly to the NBA.) As a freshman last year Thompkins showed he can take care of the defensive glass and displayed surprising range from the perimeter, making 38 percent of his threes. And while he was jarringly ineffective inside the arc, I'm inclined to grant a onetime statistical waiver to a freshman who during his minutes took 29 percent of the shots for a hopelessly overmatched team in the midst of programmatic chaos. (For one thing he was the second-leading scorer on the USA team that won the FIBA Under-19 title in July.) Keep an eye on him.

Dustin Ware (5-11, 180, So.). Ware started 17 games at point guard last year and shot exactly 36.4 percent from both sides of the arc, meaning he was pretty good on his threes and horrific on his twos. As one might expect from a freshman point guard on a struggling team, turnovers were plentiful, but in Ware's defense this could be said of virtually the entire team. The Bulldogs gave the ball to the opponent on a whopping 26 percent of their possessions in conference play.

Albert Jackson (6-11, 265, Sr.). Jackson and his dreadlocks (which by the way Fox has said might have to go) have paid some serious dues. During his time at Georgia the Dawgs are 15-33 in SEC games. He's on the floor for his defense but foul trouble tends to limit his minutes.

Travis Leslie (6-4, 200, So.). One of the few exceptions to the Bulldog rule of committing lots of turnovers, Leslie missed Georgia's last six games to "focus on academics." Nominally a guard, Leslie never shot threes but attempted twos with such frequency during his limited minutes as to suggest that he might someday emerge as a featured player in the offense. He was also notably effective on the defensive glass.

Jeremy Price (6-8, 265, Jr.). Price's minutes declined dramatically late in the season, perhaps because his frequent misses and turnovers were paired with infrequent rebounds.

Ricky McPhee (6-1, 185, Sr.). Last year McPhee was a walk-on whose minutes increased as the year progressed.

Chris Barnes (6-8, 240, Jr.). Barnes was tasked with defense and rebounding in 2008-09 and averaged 16 minutes a game off the bench.

Vincent Williams (6-0, 160, Fr.). The first recruit signed by Fox, Williams is a point guard from Homestead, Florida.

P: Wall
W: Bledsoe, Patterson
B: Cousins

Kentucky

2009: 22-14 (8-8 SEC), lost to Notre Dame 77-67, NIT Quarterfinals
In-conference offense: 1.02 points per possession (8th)
In-conference defense: 0.98 points allowed per possession (3rd)

What Kentucky did well: *Be the most talked-about 22-14 NIT team of all time.*

On November 14, 2008, Kentucky lost its first game of the season to VMI at Rupp Arena by the score of 111-103. It marked the second year in a row that the Wildcats under Billy Gillispie had suffered a shocking early-season loss at home to a member of the Big South. (In November 2007 it was Gardner-Webb.)

Indeed from UK's first game right up until its last, an NIT loss to Notre Dame overshadowed completely by speculation on Gillispie's status, the Wildcats provided a compelling spectacle. Had they been merely a talented team that imploded, Kentucky could have been written off by January and forgotten. Instead the 'Cats were a talented team that played well, even very well, at times. Gillispie's team, after all, went 5-0 to begin SEC play, a mark which included an 18-point

win at Tennessee. Yet this same talented team insisted on continually flirting with disaster, until finally disaster said: OK, here I am.

Gillispie was let go on March 27. Five days later Kentucky announced that it had hired John Calipari away from Memphis.

What we learned in 2009: *Role players matter.*

You could make a case that with the notable exception of Ty Lawson and Tyler Hansbrough at North Carolina, no two stars in the country last year were more effective together on offense than were Jodie Meeks and Patrick Patterson. Their combined level of performance was astonishing, though in truth few people were astonished by it due to all the turmoil surrounding Gillispie. (Recall for example that Patterson didn't even make first-team All-SEC.)

Together Meeks and Patterson made 57 percent of their twos (and the duo shot almost exactly as many of the things as the rest of the team combined), while Meeks personally hit 41 percent of his threes. Also note that, notwithstanding Meeks' nine-turnover effort against Kansas State at the Las Vegas Invitational in November, both players were in fact remarkably TO-free when their season totals are adjusted for their outlandishly prominent roles in the offense. Lastly, both Meeks and Patterson made regular trips to the line, where they shot a combined 85 percent. (Kentucky was the most accurate major-conference team in the nation from the line last year.) The season that these two players had together comes pretty close to defining the upper limit of what's possible on offense. Lawson and Hansbrough did better still, yes—and, not coincidentally, their team won the national championship.

So Meeks and Patterson were unbelievable. And the twosome absorbed a huge share of the possessions and took a disproportionately large portion of the shots for Kentucky.

One then might wonder how in the world the Wildcats could have had merely the SEC's eighth-ranked offense, one that was less effective in league play than even Alabama's, to pick one ignominious example.

The Apparent Irrelevance Of Jodie Meeks And Patrick Patterson: SEC Offenses, 2009			
	PPP		PPP
Florida	1.10	Alabama	1.03
Tennessee	1.09	**Kentucky**	**1.02**
LSU	1.08	Vanderbilt	1.02
Ole Miss	1.05	South Carolina	1.02
Auburn	1.04	Arkansas	0.98
Mississippi St.	1.03	Georgia	0.88

Conference games only
PPP: points per possession

What killed Kentucky's season was simply that their two stars received no help from their teammates in the crucial area of taking care of the ball. Players not named Meeks or Patterson, almost to a man, gave the thing away like crazy: Gillispie's team as a unit coughed up the ball on almost exactly one in every four trips in SEC play. Only Georgia had a higher rate of turnovers.

Conversely when the Wildcats did *not* commit a TO and their two stars were allowed to do what they could do, this team in fact had the best offense in the league.

The Actual Importance Of Jodie Meeks And Patrick Patterson: SEC Offenses, 2009			
	PPeP		PPeP
Kentucky	**1.36**	Ole Miss	1.31
Tennessee	1.33	Mississippi St.	1.26
Florida	1.32	Auburn	1.25
Vanderbilt	1.32	South Carolina	1.24
LSU	1.31	Arkansas	1.21
Alabama	1.31	Georgia	1.18

Conference games only
PPeP: points per effective (TO-less) possession

Keep in mind UK had a very good defense last year, one that allowed SEC opponents less than a point per trip. So it's not too much to say that the turnovers committed by role players loomed larger than any other single factor in Kentucky's disappointing and tumultuous 2008-09 season.

What's in store for 2010: The good news for UK fans is that the players who committed so many turnovers last year are likely to see reduced minutes this season, thanks to an incoming class that has generated just a little attention.

Prospectus says: To me the most interesting question about this team is whether Calipari will be able to get them playing Memphis-level defense—and if so, how soon. As seen here, Kentucky was no slouch in that department last year. Even so, Coach Cal's record at his previous school suggests we'd be wrong to assume we've seen Wildcat D at its stingiest. With better defensive rebounding and fewer turnovers on offense, this team can think about fulfilling its expectations. And that's saying quite a lot.

Meet the Wildcats

John Wall (6-4, 195, Fr.). Wall is the consensus pick as both the top freshman in the nation and as the likely number one overall pick in the 2010 NBA draft. At this writing, the October flare-up concerning Wall's eligibility is said to be just that—a momentary concern that will not result in him missing much if any playing time. Anyway, let's assume that's the case.

Let's also assume for the purposes of forecasting that Wall is precisely what he's reputed to be, Calipari's third consecutive scoring point guard who: a) will be selected with one of the top four picks in the draft after his freshman season; b) is average or worse when shooting threes; and c) more than offsets any perimeter issues with assists, production inside the arc, and, not least, defense. If this is indeed Wall's future, now's a good time to take a look back at those previous two Memphis point guards, Derrick Rose and Tyreke Evans, as well as at the numbers Meeks posted at Kentucky in 2008-09 as a pure shooting guard.

Rose, Evans, And Meeks					
Player	Season	ARate	%Poss.	%Shots	3FG pct.
Rose	07-08	30.4	27.2	24.5	33.7
Evans	08-09	30.0	33.5	32.1	27.4
Meeks	08-09	11.7	28.2	34.1	40.6

Player	Season	2FG pct.	TORate	ORtng.
Rose	07-08	52.1	19.1	111.8
Evans	08-09	51.4	21.6	101.0
Meeks	08-09	52.1	15.6	117.4

The numbers for offensive rating suggest that of the three players it was the one who wore Kentucky blue who had the most positive impact on his team's offense. That doesn't mean the NBA was "wrong" not to draft Meeks until the middle of the second round. It means simply that he had one incredible year, like a good but not great golfer who comes in with a 65 in the final round.

My prediction: John Wall will commit turnovers at a higher rate and make a lower percentage of his shots than Jodie Meeks did last year (no shame in either, surely), but it won't matter because Kentucky as a team is not about to give the ball away on 25 percent of their SEC possessions two years running.

Patrick Patterson (6-9, 235, Jr.). See above on the incredible, if somewhat camouflaged, year Patterson had on offense in 2008-09. He also blocks a fair number of shots without getting into foul trouble and last year served as his team's best defensive rebounder. Patterson is projected as a borderline lottery pick in next summer's draft.

DeMarcus Cousins (6-11, 260, Fr.). A McDonald's All-American, Cousins is currently listed as a 2010 first-round pick on more than one reputable mock board.

Eric Bledsoe (6-1, 190, Fr.). In theory the second point guard in UK's freshman class, Bledsoe arrives with enough advance praise to trigger speculation that he'll play alongside Wall in the starting lineup.

Ramon Harris (6-7, 220, Sr.). During a game against Lamar on December 3, Harris collided with teammate Michael Porter and injured his neck. In effect, Harris missed an entire month and didn't return to the starting lineup for good until the beginning of conference play. When healthy, Harris served as the Wildcats' main perimeter defender.

Perry Stevenson (6-9, 210, Jr.). Stevenson started 34 games in 2008-09 and earned his minutes mainly through D. Holding playing time equal, Stevenson was the Wildcat most likely to block a shot.

Darius Miller (6-7, 225, So.). Miller was highly touted coming out of high school and he had a really nice 17-point game against Tennessee on February 21. But overall his playing time as a freshman was limited by an abundance of both turnovers and fouls.

Daniel Orton (6-10, 255, Fr.). In most years Orton would be the highest-rated member of the incoming class at Kentucky. This season, however, he has the luxury of starting his career outside the limelight. Orton is billed as an outstanding defender and shot-blocker.

Darnell Dodson (6-7, 215, So.). A junior college transfer from Miami-Dade CC, Dodson is reputed to be a good perimeter shooter, perhaps the only talent this otherwise loaded roster might be lacking.

DeAndre Liggins (6-6, 200, So.). As a freshman Liggins functioned something like a point guard in the body of a wing, and the results weren't always pretty. As much as any returning Kentucky player, Liggins struggled with turnovers last year. He also famously refused to re-enter the game against Kansas State in November. This did not endear him to the previous coaching staff.

Josh Harrellson (6-10, 265, Jr.). Harrellson saw his playing time decline dramatically as the season progressed last year and it was therefore assumed he might be something of an afterthought under Calipari. Then the new coach arrived on campus, watched individual workouts, and started talking up, of all people, Josh Harrellson. Stay tuned.

LSU ꞯout

2009: 27-8 (13-3 SEC), lost to North Carolina 84-70, NCAA Second Round
In-conference offense: 1.08 points per possession (3rd)
In-conference defense: 0.97 points allowed per possession (1st)

What LSU did well: *Surprise everyone, possibly even themselves.*

A year ago at this time the expectations for LSU were relatively modest. Coach Trent Johnson was about to start his first season in Baton Rouge and the Tigers had lost Anthony Randolph, who jumped to the NBA after his freshman year. In the SEC's preseason poll last year, Tennessee, Florida, and Kentucky were tapped as the favorites to win the conference. No team from the West received a single first-place vote.

Johnson had other plans. LSU won the West with a 13-3 record, three games ahead of Auburn, not to mention three games better than what Tennessee and South Carolina posted in the East.

The Tigers pulled their surprise thanks to simultaneous and dramatic improvement on both sides of the ball. Basically LSU did everything better last year than in 2008. When you improve markedly on both offense and on defense it results in a turnaround of prodigious magnitude.

School	Year	Previous year	New	Diff.
Missouri	2009	-0.06	0.12	+0.18
LSU	2009	-0.06	0.11	+0.17
Oregon St.	2009	-0.30	-0.13	+0.17
Northwestern	2009	-0.21	-0.04	+0.17
Washington St.	2007	-0.07	0.09	+0.16

LSU's Turnaround: Largest Improvements In Major-Conference Performance, 2007-09

Efficiency margin (points per possession – opponent PPP) Conference games only

Johnson has given himself a tough act to follow.

What we learned in 2009: *Junior college transfers can become stars.*

Speaking of modest expectations, Marcus Thornton arrived at LSU in the summer of 2007 as a little-known transfer from Kilgore College in Texas. He left in the spring of 2009 as the reigning SEC Player of the Year.

Thornton was the best weapon this team had on offense even when Randolph was in uniform in 2007-

08. Then last year as a senior, Thornton stepped up his game even further, becoming one of the finest dual-threat shooting guards in the nation. His shots from both sides of the arc simply went in, and his turnover rate was so low it looked like a typo. Thornton was the catalyst behind LSU's remarkable improvement on offense. This is one junior college transfer who will be missed.

What's in store for 2010: The Tigers this season will be one of the least experienced teams in the SEC, having lost not only Thornton but also fellow starters Garrett Temple and Chris Johnson.

Prospectus says: Last year Johnson showed what he can accomplish given a good but not necessarily great team. And bear in mind that next year the Tigers are slated to welcome well-regarded wing Matt Derenbecker, along with Ole Miss transfer (and Baton Rouge product) Malcolm White. But this year Johnson simply lacks bodies.

Meet the Tigers

Tasmin Mitchell (6-7, 235, Sr.). It's simply not possible that a player who started all 36 games on LSU's 2006 Final Four team alongside Tyrus Thomas and Glen Davis has any eligibility remaining, but somehow Tasmin Mitchell is still here. Undoubtedly the most famous three of the SEC season last year was the one Mitchell made on February 28 to beat Kentucky at Rupp Arena, a play that so enraged the Wildcat faithful that the Commonwealth's secretary of state took to Twitter to complain that his team couldn't even defend a simple pick-and-roll by Mitchell and Thornton. Actually the game-winner that day was just Mitchell's tenth made three of the year. He appeared to hand over the perimeter shooting to Thornton and Bo Spencer almost entirely last year, after making 37 percent of his 106 attempts in 2006-07. (Mitchell missed all but three games of 2007-08 with a stress fracture in his left shin.) In the wake of Thornton's departure, he may well resume his perimeter shooting this season. Mitchell's already a force to be reckoned with inside the arc, having made 52 percent of his twos while attempting a Harangody-like 410 of the things last season.

Bo Spencer (6-1, 185 Jr.). Spencer is referred to as LSU's point guard, though the way assists were spread around last year the term is as honorific as it is descriptive. He became a starter as a sophomore in 2008-09 and gave Johnson a pure shooter, one who made 84 percent of his free throws and 40 percent of his threes. Spencer is however notably less effective when shooting inside the arc.

Chris Bass (6-0, 180, So.). Bass was the first recruit to commit to Johnson at LSU. When Spencer missed a couple games last year with an ankle sprain, Bass stepped in and acquitted himself well,

dishing five assists in 26 minutes against Arkansas on February 18.

Aaron Dotson (6-4, 195, Fr.). A freshman from Seattle, Dotson is expected to see minutes immediately as a shooting guard.

Storm Warren (6-7, 220, So.). Though he scored 11 points in 22 minutes in LSU's second game last year, Warren was restricted almost entirely to spot duty as a freshman.

Eddie Ludwig (6-9, 205, Fr.). Ludwig is an in-state product (Metairie) who's billed as a good perimeter shooter.

Alex Farrer (6-5, 205, Sr.). For whatever reason, Farrer's minutes declined noticeably after 2008 became 2009.

Mississippi

2009: 16-15 (7-9 SEC), lost to Kentucky 71-58, SEC First Round
In-conference offense: 1.05 points per possession (4th)
In-conference defense: 1.07 points allowed per possession (11th)

What Ole Miss did well: *Inflict season-ending injuries on their left knees.*

Last year Ole Miss couldn't even get to the first game without a major injury. The carnage began on November 6, when sophomore guard Trevor Gaskins suffered a season-ending injury to his left knee in practice. Just 12 days later coach Andy Kennedy learned that starting guard Eniel Polynice would also be out for the year, following arthroscopic surgery on his left knee.

Then came the coup de grace. On December 18 starting point guard Chris Warren, a unanimous selection on the SEC's 2008 All-Freshman team, tore the ACL in his left knee in the closing seconds of the Rebels' 77-68 loss to Louisville. He missed the remainder of the season.

As a result the Rebels were never close to full-strength in 2008-09. And yet even in their depleted state they went 7-9, a very respectable mark under the circumstances. If Kennedy's team can stay healthy in 2010, they can win some games.

What we learned in 2009: *The job of starting big man should be Murphy Holloway's to lose, even with a hotshot freshman coming in this season.*

The Rebels received some good news nearly a year-and-a-half ago when Memphis product Reginald Buckner committed to Ole Miss before his final year in high school. A 6-8 shot-blocker who went on to win Tennessee's Mr. Basketball award as a senior, Buckner was a nice recruiting prize for Kennedy, one that he's understandably eager to get on the floor. ESPN's Andy Katz talked to the coach in September and came away with the sense that this season Ole Miss will be "a perimeter-based team with a Buckner-led presence in the middle."

But a funny thing happened after Buckner announced his decision in the summer of 2008. A much less highly-rated big man, Murphy Holloway, had an outstanding freshman season for Ole Miss in 2008-09. I'm not entirely sure Kennedy noticed said season, however, for the coach is now speaking somewhat paternally of Holloway as though the sophomore were just another work-in-progress big man. "He understands now that things aren't as new," Kennedy told the Daily Mississippian before the season, "which gives him a better grasp as to what to expect."

Is it possible, nay conceivable, that Kennedy doesn't

realize he has one of the best offensive rebounders in the country right under his nose?

Hype's Irrelevant On The Offensive Glass: Best SEC Offensive Rebounders, 2008-09		
Player	**School**	**OR%**
JaMychal Green	Alabama	15.6
Murphy Holloway	**Ole Miss**	**15.1**
Brian Williams	Tennessee	13.6
Korvotney Barber	Auburn	13.5
Jeffery Taylor	Vanderbilt	12.9
OR%: offensive rebound percentage		

Holloway didn't even make the eight-player SEC All-Freshman team, despite the fact that his offensive rating (118.1) was higher—in most instances, way higher—than that of any player so honored. Yes, he played a smaller role in his offense than did many of his fellow freshman studs. I'm not saying he should be the workhorse in this offense. The kid just does his job.

Of course offense is just half the equation, and Buckner's sure to block more shots than Holloway (who, not to put too fine a point on it, never blocks shots). But a lack of blocked or altered shots wasn't the issue with this weak defense last year. The problem was an abysmally low turnover rate for opponents, as SEC foes gave the ball away on just 15 percent of their possessions. The Ole Miss D simply drowned in opponents' shot attempts; bringing in a shot-blocker will address that problem only indirectly, if at all. A healthier and deeper backcourt will get at the root of the matter and, presumably, that's exactly what the Rebels will have with the return of Warren, Polynice, and Gaskins.

Kennedy's already said that he'll play a lot of "four out, one in" sets on offense this season (rightly, given his personnel), so Buckner and Holloway are competing for minutes in a largely zero-sum setting. Even with his iffy free throw shooting, Holloway was demonstrably the single most effective player on Kennedy's offense last year, thanks to offensive boards and 55 percent shooting on his twos. Instead of being nudged toward the bench because he's been out-hyped, Holloway should be given starts and minutes until he's been outperformed.

What's in store for 2010: Ole Miss is teed up just about perfectly to improve over last year. Their offense in 2009 was surprisingly good even with all the injuries. And their defense is almost certain to at least move in the right direction, as opponents commit a number of turnovers that is merely normal.

Prospectus says: Another element of Ole Miss's defensive struggle last year was their frequent fouling. No SEC team sent conference opponents to the line as often as did the Rebels. However this appears to have been merely the plaintive cry of an injury-ravaged roster and not something more systemic. In 2008 a healthy Ole Miss fouled at a rate equivalent to the league average. So this season I anticipate fewer fouls, better D, and more wins. Assuming this team's left knees hold up.

Meet the Rebels

Chris Warren (5-10, 165, Jr.). As noted above, Warren missed the balance of last year with a torn ACL. In 2007-08 he started 34 games at point guard and did exceptionally well for a freshman flung into that role. Specifically, he was able to record a lot of assists without committing a lot of turnovers, something of a rarity for first-year point guards who also look for their shot. Note additionally that Warren was right to look for his shot. He made 39 percent of his threes and 80 percent of his free throws that season.

Terrico White (6-5, 210, So.). White had a really nice freshman season last year as a shooting guard, making 35 percent of his threes and nearly half his twos while taking excellent care of the ball. Be advised additionally that his season totals are misleading: From February on White averaged 21 points per contest for the Rebels. Over the summer he scored seven points a game for the USA team that won the gold medal at the FIBA Under-19 championships. White's also listed as a likely first-round pick in 2010 by multiple mock draft boards. If there's a worry here it's that he shot just 63 percent from the line, suggesting that 35 percent from the outside might be his ceiling and not the floor.

Eniel Polynice (6-5, 225, Jr.). Because Polynice missed all but one game last year, we turn the clock back to 2007-08 and find that he gave Ole Miss the moral equivalent of a second point guard on the floor alongside Warren that season, recording a high number of assists while making half his twos. Unfortunately he shot just 51 percent at the line, indicating it may not be wise to have him on the floor late in close games.

Murphy Holloway (6-7, 225, So.). See above. Holloway is the SEC's lil' DeJuan Blair. (No, he's not as good as Blair. I speak merely of stylistic markers.)

Reginald Buckner (6-8, 210, Fr.). See above. Between Holloway and Buckner, Kennedy might have the ingredients for a really nice offense-defense rotation in the post, one that can be deployed as the situation requires.

Zach Graham (6-6, 225, Jr.). Graham gives Kennedy some needed length on the perimeter. He started 23 games last year and made 38 percent of his rare threes, but struggled to make shots inside the arc.

Trevor Gaskins (6-2, 205, So.). Somewhat similar to Graham in terms of end-result on offense: As a sophomore in 2007-08, Gaskins started eight games and made 39 percent of his frequent threes while faring far worse on his twos.

Terrance Henry (6-9, 190, So.), and **DeAundre Cranston (6-9, 250, Sr.).** Henry and Cranston will back up Buckner and Holloway.

Mississippi State

P: Boot
W:
B: Varnado
Augustus

2009: 23-13 (9-7 SEC), lost to Washington 71-58, NCAA First Round
In-conference offense: 1.03 points per possession (6th)
In-conference defense: 1.03 points allowed per possession (4th)

What Mississippi State did well: *Get into the NCAA tournament.*

For two years in a row now the winner of the SEC tournament has been a dark horse who won four games in four days and thus took away an NCAA bid from a bubble team. In 2008 that dark horse was Georgia (who famously won two games on the same day, after a tornado in Atlanta forced a postponement). Last year it was Mississippi State, which beat defending champ UGA in the first round and then upset higher seeds South Carolina, LSU, and Tennessee to claim the title.

The Bulldogs got their NCAA bid thanks exclusively to defense. Anyone who saw the SEC semifinal between MSU and LSU, for example, knows it was not a thing of beauty on offense for either team. (The Bulldogs and Tigers were a combined 42-of-131 from the floor that day.) For four days in Tampa, Rick Stansbury's team simply refused to let their opponents make shots, as MSU's tournament foes made just 29 percent of their threes and, more importantly, 37 percent of their twos. It wasn't pretty, but it got Mississippi State to the dance, where they were promptly defeated by Pac-10 regular season champion Washington.

What we learned in 2009: *Having the best shot-blocker in the country doesn't mean your team's interior D is automatically outstanding.*

What's interesting about Mississippi State's lockdown D in the SEC tournament is that it was preceded by a season's worth of surprisingly mediocre defense from these same Bulldogs. The mediocrity was unexpected because this team has Jarvis Varnado, the nation's premier shot-blocker. As a sophomore in 2007-08, Varnado had led a defense that shut down the interior entirely.

The question, then, is what in the world happened last year. Varnado kept right on being Varnado—ranking number one in the nation in block percentage—but his team suddenly became weirdly hospitable to opponents attempting two-point shots.

How Can This Be Happening? Mississippi State Interior D, 2008 Vs. 2009		
Year	Opp. 2FG%	SEC rank
2008	39.9	1st
2009	47.0	3rd
Conference games only *Opp. 2FG%: opponent two-point FG percentage*		

Stansbury hopes that in 2010 he sees the interior D his team played in the SEC tournament, and not the interior D they played during the regular season. If the conference tournament was indeed a sneak preview of this season, MSU will make life miserable for opposing offenses.

What's in store for 2010: Mississippi State returns all five starters, but the Bulldogs have been in the headlines more or less constantly since last spring because of the player they're trying to add to that starting five: McDonald's All-American Renardo Sidney. The 6-11 freshman is rated as one of the top big men in the country, but concerns over his amateur status led both UCLA and USC to withdraw scholarship offers, at which point MSU entered the picture.   Prior to Sidney's decision to play in Starkville, when a family spokesman was asked by the L.A. Times if Mississippi State was "the front runner" for the player's services, the reply was that the Bulldogs were "the only runner."

When MSU offered Sidney a scholarship at the end of April, they may well have thought this was a no-brainer. If Sidney is subsequently certified as eligible by the NCAA, then Mississippi State will have one of the best players in the country. If he isn't, well, then he'll never see the floor. But since the Bulldogs extended their offer, the ground may have shifted under their feet.

Four days after Mississippi State signed Sidney, the LAT published a story detailing the Sidney family's living arrangements after their 2006 move to southern California from Jackson, Mississippi. One of their homes, which they occupied until September 2008, carried a market value of $1.2 million and rented for $4,000 to $5,000 monthly, an amount that Sidney's mother, Patricia, paid by personal check. The family's attorney says Sidney's father is employed by Reebok and Patricia is his personal assistant.

Then on August 20 the NCAA ruled that Memphis had to vacate its 2007-08 Final Four season, declaring that Derrick Rose was retroactively ineligible. In the Rose case Memphis specifically argued that they couldn't be punished for what they didn't know at the time. (Rose's SAT score was invalidated by Educational Testing Service immediately following the 2008 season, when an internal investigation by ETS raised questions about whether it was indeed Rose who had taken the test.) The NCAA dismissed that line of reasoning, saying it didn't matter what Memphis knew or didn't know: Rose was never truly eligible in the first place.

This represents a significant change in the NCAA's tune. The organization famously let Duke's 1998-99 season stand, for example, even though Corey Maggette later acknowledged having received compensation from an agent as a high school player. At a press conference at the 2004 Final Four, NCAA Vice President of Enforcement David Price said the issue was "whether [Duke] knew or should have known

that Maggette was ineligible." However that line of defense, apparently, no longer obtains for a school brought before the NCAA on charges that their player was ineligible.

The implications of the Memphis ruling for Mississippi State are therefore huge. Assuming Sidney does play for the Bulldogs at some point, the NCAA's new standard expressly makes the program liable for what they don't know with regard to their freshman. At this writing the NCAA has declared Sidney "not certified" and his attorney is vowing loudly to take the NCAA to court to get his client on the court. Who knows, legal action might succeed. But the decision to actually play Sidney, and take the risk that any resulting wins will be wiped out by the NCAA at a later date, would still be Mississippi State's alone to make.

Prospectus says: Last year Mississippi State was one of the most perimeter-oriented major-conference teams in the nation, devoting 45 percent of their attempts to threes in SEC play. Whether or not the Bulldogs adjust their style on offense this season, they should have the experience and depth to win the SEC West. Anything beyond that, however, may require a return to 2008-level defense.

Meet the Bulldogs

Jarvis Varnado (6-9, 210, Sr.). Varnado is paying his own way at Mississippi State this year, opening up a 13th scholarship for Sidney. It's a marvelous gesture but, since it's unclear whether the freshman will ever get on the floor, I hope Sidney gets his money's worth in the classroom in Starkvillle. He can thank Varnado for his free education. Speaking of Varnado, he's the best shot-blocker in the country, one who, significantly, is able to record all those rejections without getting into foul trouble. The big news, though, is that last year he expanded well beyond the confines of being a shot-blocking specialist. Varnado improved on the defensive glass and increased his role in the offense dramatically while making 55 percent of his twos. The NBA may continue to be leery of him because of his age (too old) and physique (too short and slender), but he is unquestionably a dominant college player on D.

Barry Stewart (6-2, 170, Sr.). Last year Stewart came very close to what I term Greg Paulus/Darren Collison territory, meaning he almost shot a higher percentage on his threes (36.5) than he did on his twos (37.0). His struggles inside were apparently related to a slightly increased role in the offense, one he inherited following the departures of Jamont Gordon and Charles Rhodes after the 2008 season.

Dee Bost (6-2, 170, So.). Bost was the starter at point guard from the first game of his freshman year and he did pretty well, recording a fair number of assists while making one in every three treys. If there are areas for improvement they are accuracy inside the arc (coincidentally, both Stewart and Bost were 54-of-156 on their twos last year) and turnovers. Bost's TO rate for the season appears acceptable for a freshman point guard, but he did have a worrisome stretch in that department in February.

Ravern Johnson (6-7, 175, Jr.). The Bulldogs' most frequent and accurate three-point shooter, Johnson hit 40 percent of his threes in 2008-09.

Phil Turner (6-3, 170, Jr.). I know I'm sounding like a broken record here, but Turner is still another good three-point shooter. Last year Stansbury surrounded Varnado on offense with four guys who each had a green light on the perimeter. Turner is MSU's fifth returning starter.

John Riek (7-2, 240, Fr.). Riek created something of a sensation in July 2007 when he appeared, seemingly out of nowhere, at the LeBron James Skills Acade-my and started swatting away the shots of other elite prospects. The talk at the time was that the Sudanese shot-blocker would be in the NBA sooner rather than later, possibly even as the number one overall pick. One serious knee injury later Riek is a freshman at Mississippi State, where he'll sit out the first nine games. His clearance by the NCAA has triggered a lot of talk about MSU having "a great front line," even without Renardo Sidney, but I'll be interested to see how many minutes Varnado and Riek are actually on the floor together. That would be a formidable defensive combination, but it's not clear how well the two big men would work together in a high-low offensive set against a tall opponent (bearing in mind that Varnado carries out his shot-blocking heroics despite being "just" 6-9).

Kodi Augustus (6-8, 220, Jr.). A starter for the first nine games of last year, Augustus was sent to the bench in December and saw his minutes drop off drastically, going entire games without seeing the floor. Late in the year, however, he somehow made it out of that doghouse and again saw serious playing time, kicking off the Bulldogs' successful SEC tournament run, for example, with a 19-point effort against Georgia.

Elgin Bailey (6-8, 270, Jr.). Bailey is a large body on an otherwise notably svelte team, but he suffered a ghastly ankle injury against Florida on March 4 and has been rehabbing ever since. (And I do mean ghastly. Do not type "Elgin Bailey" into YouTube.)

South Carolina

2009: 21-10 (10-6 SEC), lost to Davidson 70-63, NIT First Round
In-conference offense: 1.02 points per possession (10th)
In-conference defense: 0.99 points allowed per possession (4th)

What South Carolina did well: *Pick up the pace.*

Last year was Darrin Horn's first season at the helm at South Carolina and, as coaches often will, he immediately put his stamp on his new team's style. In Horn's case this meant speeding up the tempo. While Travis Ford garnered most of the headlines last year for pushing his new Oklahoma State team to operate at a much faster pace, he clearly had nothing on Horn in this respect. The new man in Columbia added almost ten full possessions to South Carolina's conference games, giving Gamecock fans their hoops money's worth in a tight economy. (See table, next page.)

That other "Carolina" north of Columbia has trained us to think of an up-tempo style as fuel for the fire on offense. Horn doubtless hopes that comes to pass someday for his Gamecocks as well, but last year the faster pace made itself felt exclusively on the defensive end for USC. This team was already adept at forcing opponents to commit turnovers in 2008, but last year South Carolina took this to a whole new

The Master Of Faster: Largest Accelerations By Major-Conference Teams, 2007-09				
School	Year	Pace yr. before	Pace	%change
South Carolina	2009	65.0	74.8	+15.1
Duke	2008	67.4	75.3	+11.7
Virginia Tech	2008	65.2	72.2	+10.7
Oklahoma St.	2009	64.6	71.5	+10.7
Texas Tech	2008	64.5	70.4	+9.1

Conference games only
Pace: possessions per 40 minutes

level, as SEC foes gave the ball away on 26 percent of their possessions. This was easily the best mark in the league and indeed it was the distinguishing characteristic of a team with a pretty good defense and a below-average offense.

What we learned in 2009: *Darrin Horn owes Dave Odom a beer.*

Or a thank-you note. Or a hearty pat on the back. Or a gift card from Netflix. Whatever the preferred mode is in Columbia for expressing one's appreciation, Horn should indulge in that behavior toward his predecessor.

In his seventh year at the helm at USC, Odom announced in January 2008 that he would retire after that season at the age of 65. Odom had a contract that ran through 2010 but he chose to leave two years early, saying he was "on the back end" of his career.

Maybe Odom's critics accelerated his decision, or maybe he feared not making it to 2010. Odom denied such speculation vehemently. In any case, I do know this: By choosing to leave when he did, Odom gave his successor a very good situation. In 2008-09, first-year Indiana head coach Tom Crean would have killed for the kind of roster continuity that first-year South Carolina coach Darrin Horn enjoyed. The Gamecocks last season returned fully 87 percent of their minutes from the previous year. It showed, as USC improved from 5-11 to 10-6 in SEC play.

Certainly Horn deserves a good deal of the credit for that improvement. Indeed we've seen how he unquestionably made his mark on the program in just his first season. My point is simply that he was able to think of improvement and making a mark because he had the players and the experience in the first place. For that he can thank Odom, who left the cupboard relatively well-stocked.

What's in store for 2010: Speaking of having a lot of returning minutes, such is again the case in Columbia this year. The Gamecocks return four starters from last season, having lost only Zam Fredrick.

Prospectus says: South Carolina's conference opponents this season should be better prepared for 40 minutes of Horn now that they've seen it in action. Put another way, forcing the other team into a turnover 26 percent of the time for two seasons running is a long shot. Then again, this team is hardly a one-trick pony. Even when opponents didn't turn the ball over, they achieved below-average results from both sides of the three-point line. Indeed the only success those opposing offenses achieved was in getting offensive rebounds (and, truth be known, in getting fouled). No, the Gamecocks aren't going to dominate the boards, but this is still a solid and experienced team, one that plainly likes the pedal-to-the-metal style they're playing.

Meet the Gamecocks

Devan Downey (5-9, 175, Sr.). Downey presents a profile that's well-nigh irresistible to the popular imagination. Listed at just 5-9 and playing in the SEC, he nevertheless averaged nearly 20 points a game as a scoring point guard last year. Nor is the popular imagination entirely unfounded. Downey accounted for a larger share of the possessions in his offense in 2008-09 than did any other player in the SEC, more than Jodie Meeks, Courtney Fortson, or Marcus Thornton. He's no slouch on D, either. Last year he posted a simply outrageous steal percentage—one eclipsed only by Seton Hall's Paul Gause and Purdue's Chris Kramer among major-conference players—thanks in no small measure to Princeton and North Carolina Central, who unwittingly accounted for fully 14 of Downey's steals in just 56 minutes of floor time. If there are refinements we can offer to this picture, they merely round out the image we already have of Downey. Inside the arc he took the ball to the hole fearlessly the entire season and his results, if merely "good," were in fact consistently good from beginning to end. On the perimeter, conversely, the longer the year went on the lower Downey's three-point percentage dipped, until he finished the season right at the major-conference average: 35 percent. Lastly, his assist and turnover rates—both very good—have been notably stable for two consecutive seasons.

Mike Holmes (6-7, 230, Jr.). One of the few "big men" on a fast team, Holmes was Horn's best defensive rebounder last year, pulling down 19 percent of opponents' misses during his minutes. The defensive boards that Holmes provided were essential in 2008-09, because South Carolina was a wretched rebounding team on both sides of the floor, ranking 12th and 10th in the SEC on the defensive and offensive glass, respectively. A 46 percent free throw shooter, Holmes is however something of an expensive luxury for South Carolina to have on the floor late in close games.

Dominique Archie (6-7, 200, Sr.). Though he plays a supporting role in the offense, Archie is far and away the Gamecocks' most efficient source of made shots inside the arc; Horn could give him a few more looks just to see what happens. Archie also improved noticeably on the defensive glass last year, giving some needed help to Holmes.

Lakeem Jackson (6-5, 215, Fr.). Jackson arrives from Charlotte, North Carolina, as a highly touted wing esteemed for his athleticism.

Sam Muldrow (6-9, 215, Jr.). Last year Muldrow sat out the early season due to academic issues, only to injure his elbow in practice and miss an additional month of action. After working his way back into the lineup he made 15 starts and earned a reputation for himself with his shot-blocking. If he can avoid foul trouble he can help this team.

Brandis Raley-Ross (6-2, 195, Sr.). Speaking of early-season absences, Raley-Ross sprained his knee in the first game of the season last year and sat out six contests. Nominally a spot-up shooter, Raley-Ross has played a very limited role in the offense now for two years running.

Evaldas Baniulis (6-7, 210, Sr.). A pure shooter who last year sank 48 percent of his threes, Baniulis averaged 18 minutes a game off the bench.

Austin Steed (6-8, 215, Jr.). Steed sees spot duty only, in part because he's so foul-prone (he fouled out against Kentucky last year in ten minutes), but he has given indications of being very good on the offensive glass.

Tennessee

2009: 21-13 (10-6 SEC), lost to Oklahoma State 77-75, NCAA First Round
In-conference offense: 1.09 points per possession (2nd)
In-conference defense: 1.04 points allowed per possession (8th)

What Tennessee did well: *Bottom out gracefully.*

I realize that programs and coaches are traditionally praised only when they go a long way in the tournament, but I rise today to salute the 2008-09 Tennessee Volunteers, a team that was sent home in the first round by an eight-seed (Oklahoma State).

It's a tribute to how far Bruce Pearl has brought this program in just four seasons that a 10-6 conference record and a first-round NCAA exit comprise a down year. It's true the Volunteers were rebuilding last year in the wake of departures by Chris Lofton and JaJuan Smith. Still, it's surely worth noting that this particular rebuilding year achieved better results than the Vols used to see in their peak years.

Pearl's been in Knoxville long enough now to see his roster turn over completely, and yet the Vols have won no fewer than 10 conference games and made the NCAA tournament every year. When he was hired

Truly A Shirtless Wonder: Tennessee With And Without Bruce Pearl		
	Conf W-L	NCAA W-L
Four seasons with Pearl	46-18	5-4
Previous four seasons	29-35	0-0

away from Wisconsin-Milwaukee in 2005, it was thought that in time he'd build a team that would succeed by virtue of an up-tempo pressing style. From the omniscient perch of 2009, however, we can say that not only did the coach achieve the anticipated success without any initial suffering, he did so with teams that have defied narrow categorization. Last year for example the Volunteers operated at a pace that was significantly slower than the conference average—and still scored well over a point per trip.

The coach has built a strong program, one that figures to produce one of its best teams yet in 2009-10.

What we learned in 2009: *Threes matter.*

In keeping with our theme of Volunteers bottoming out gracefully, we note that last year's offense in Knoxville was a step down from what the team achieved in 2007-08, yet still these post-Lofton Vols ranked second in the league in scoring efficiency.

What's interesting about that step down is not that it still left Pearl's team at a lofty altitude, but rather that the small decline took place in the midst of so many clear improvements. Tennessee bettered their two-point accuracy significantly in conference play last year at the same time that they took slightly better care of the ball. Traditionally those are two leading indices of your offense right there.

It didn't work that way last year for the Vols, however, who in SEC play suffered through easily their worst year of perimeter shooting in the Pearl era.

Make, Make, Make, Miss: Tennessee Three-Point Shooting, 2006-09		
	SEC 3FG%	Rank
2006	39.1	2nd
2007	38.8	2nd
2008	37.7	2nd
2009	**32.3**	**11th**
Conference games only		

If opponents are looking for confidence against an NCAA tournament team that went 10-6 last year and returns five starters, here it is: Tennessee's yet to prove they can be repeatedly dangerous from outside. (OK, and their D wasn't so very scary last year, either.)

What's in store for 2010: In multiple seasons of wanton and promiscuous major-conference previewing, I have never seen the phrase "everyone's back" be more appropriate than it is with Tennessee this year. Across the broad expanse of the 2008-09 season, Ryan Childress and Tanner Wild each played eight minutes for the Volunteers. Additionally Justin Jackson logged one minute last year. Alas, those three players and their 17 total minutes are gone. The good news is the other 13 players and their 6,808 minutes return. Everyone's back.

Prospectus says: The shortest route between Tennessee and improvement is better interior D: SEC opponents made 52 percent of their twos against the Volunteers last year, making this the conference's most permissive unit inside the arc. Pearl's men don't fig-

ure to lead the league in this department, of course, but being merely average here should be plenty good enough for a deep veteran team that's above-average in so many other areas.

Meet the Volunteers

Tyler Smith (6-7, 215, Sr.). With the peripheral exception of perimeter shooting, Smith's an excellent player to build your offense around. He's quick enough to get to the rim and long enough to finish. The incessant praise of his "athleticism," while understandable, obscures the fact that he takes exceptionally good care of the ball and finds open teammates. And he gets to the line more frequently than any other Volunteer. No, Smith doesn't light it up from outside, but at least last year he had the sense to shoot almost four two-pointers for every three he tried. Interestingly he took an even more total vow of three-abstinence as a sophomore in 2007-08 and the results were encouraging, as Smith tried just one three per game and made 38 percent of his attempts. But in the two seasons where in effect he's given the perimeter a fair try—last year and as an Iowa Hawkeye in 2006-07—he shot a combined 28 percent from outside the arc. His overall efficiency on offense dipped a bit last year as he transitioned from playing alongside Chris Lofton to being pretty much the Man. But the larger point is that Smith *is* the Man for Tennessee.

Wayne Chism (6-9, 245, Sr.). Chism is an absolute monster on the defensive glass and, unless Brian Williams is giving him a breather, he is all the Volunteers have in this department. Known for his habit of opening Volunteer games with a made three, Chism makes a solid 55 percent of his twos and even blocks an occasional shot for Pearl.

Scotty Hopson (6-7, 200, So.). Don't be surprised to see Hopson take on a larger role in the Tennessee offense this year. And by "don't be surprised" I of course mean he should do so. The former McDonald's All-American is Pearl's best bet for a made three. Indeed Hopson gives every indication of developing, sooner rather than later, into a workhorse as a dual-threat wing.

J.P. Prince (6-7, 205, Sr.). Prince made an astounding 62 percent of his twos last year, albeit in a supporting role. Pity, then, that he's been strangely yet consistently foul-prone for two seasons in a row now.

Bobby Maze (6-3, 195, Sr.). He doesn't necessarily look for his shot (nor, perhaps, should he from the perimeter), but Maze posted the highest assist rate on the team last year, edging out Prince and Smith for the honor. Maze does find the open man.

Cameron Tatum (6-6, 195, So.). Among players who saw regular playing time last year, Tatum was the only one who shot more threes than twos and, it would appear, in this respect the freshman was betrayed by early success. In the season's first five games Tatum shot 53 percent on his threes, including a dazzling 5-of-6 performance from beyond the arc in the Volunteers'

90-78 win over Georgetown at the Old Spice Classic. From November 30 on, though, he made just 29 percent of his treys.

Brian Williams (6-10, 280, Jr.). As noted above, Williams gives Pearl the exact equivalent of Wayne Chism on the defensive glass, and that is no small thing. As would be expected from a big man coming off the bench, Williams has been known to commit the occasional foul.

Josh Tabb (6-4, 195, Sr.). In late September Tabb was suspended "indefinitely" by Pearl for the proverbial unspecified violation of team rules. Note that the eight players shown here constituted Pearl's rotation last year, with Smith averaging 33 minutes per contest and the other seven Vols averaging between 16 and 26.

Vanderbilt

2009: 19-12 (8-8 SEC), lost to Alabama 82-75, SEC First Round
In-conference offense: 1.02 points per possession (9th)
In-conference defense: 1.04 points allowed per possession (7th)

What Vanderbilt did well: *Follow the example of versatility set by their university's founder.*

Cornelius Vanderbilt, "the Commodore," got his start in business by ferrying passengers between his native Staten Island and Manhattan. When steam power revolutionized passenger ships, Vanderbilt adopted the technology early and expanded his network rapidly. Later, when railroads began to draw passenger traffic away from water craft, the Commodore earned fresh millions by becoming a leading figure in overland transport. Throughout his career, Vanderbilt demonstrated an uncanny ability to adapt to changing conditions.

Vanderbilt, the college basketball team, was kind of like that in 2009. What previously had been a perimeter-oriented team centered around Shan Foster became a group much more oriented toward ruling the paint. For example, the Commodores actually attempted fewer threes than the SEC average last year. That may not sound like a big deal but it represented a decided stylistic shift for Kevin Stallings' team.

The 'Dores had good reason to change their ways on offense. The constant in the equation has been A.J. Ogilvy, who's now entering his third season of patrolling the paint in Nashville. Where Ogilvy once shared the spotlight on offense with the perimeter-oriented

A Sudden Change In Priorities: Percentage Of Vanderbilt FG Attempts That Are Threes, 2006-09		
Year	3FGA/FGA(%)	SEC avg.
2006	38.3	33.7
2007	43.8	35.7
2008	41.3	35.7
2009	**33.3**	**34.1**
Conference games only		

Foster, however, he now splits the shots and possessions with the decidedly more interior-focused Jeffery Taylor. Foster had a spectacular senior year in 2008 (he made 47 percent of his threes that season), but in its own somewhat less prominent way this Ogilvy-Taylor nucleus does give Stallings a trusty source of offensive efficiency. There were just three teams that made more than half their twos in SEC play last year: Tennessee, Florida, and Vanderbilt.

What we learned in 2009: *The transitive property is totally useless in college basketball.*

Though it gets wheeled out every March when debates heat up over who should be invited to the NCAA tournament, the transitive property, that hoary old chestnut of school days gone by, was arguably gutted like a fish by the 2008-09 edition of Vanderbilt. It's all very well to say that if A is greater than B and B is greater than C, then A is greater than C. But last year Kevin Stallings and his players proved once and for all that sometimes A can beat B and lose to C despite the fact that B and all the other letters of the alphabet stomped on C by 20 points or more.

Consider these mileposts in the Vanderbilt season....

December 3, in Nashville: Illinois-Chicago 74, Vanderbilt 55. (The Flames finished the season 8-11 in the Horizon League.)

December 6, in Atlanta: Georgia Tech 63, Vanderbilt 51. (The Yellow Jackets finished the season 2-14 in the ACC.)

February 25, in Athens: Georgia 61, Vanderbilt 57. (The Bulldogs finished 3-13 in the SEC.)

March 4, in Baton Rouge: Vanderbilt 75, LSU 67. (The Tigers finished 13-3 in the SEC.)

Please, I beg of you. When March rolls around this year, strangle every use of the transitive property promptly and remorselessly. Call it the Vanderbilt refutation.

What's in store for 2010: In most years the Commodores would stand out for returning 91 percent of their minutes from last year's team. In what promises to be a rugged and experienced SEC this season, however, Vandy takes a backseat in this department to Tennessee and Mississippi State, who each return an even higher percentage of last year's playing time. Vanderbilt will be improved. Their competition will be too.

Prospectus says: Turnovers hurt Vanderbilt on both sides of the ball last year. The Commodores gave the ball away to the opponent on 23 percent of their trips in SEC play, but those same opponents rarely returned the favor, coughing up the rock on just 17 percent of their own possessions. If Stallings can redress this imbalance, his 'Dores can improve markedly. They already defend the paint, make their twos, and get to the line. Life in the SEC East won't be for the faint of heart in 2010, but Vanderbilt will pose its own challenge to the likes of Tennessee, Kentucky, and South Carolina.

Meet the Commodores

A.J. Ogilvy (6-11, 250, Jr.). At first glance Ogilvy's efficiency on offense took a small hit last year, but be not alarmed. One factor behind the hit was totally extraneous to his core mission: He somehow got it into his head to

try 27 threes. (Go figure, he made just seven.) When not floating on the perimeter, however, the sizable Aussie was the motive force behind a team that led the SEC in such varied yet unmistakably Ogilvy-related activities as trips to the line and defensive rebounding. He also blocks a shot now and then. The list of big men nationally who combine production on offense with rebounding and shot-blocking on defense as well as Ogilvy is a very short one.

Jeffery Taylor (6-7, 210, So.). Having arrived on campus as a freshman last year with a minimum of buzz from evaluators of recruits, Taylor has to qualify as a wonderful surprise for Stallings. (In defense of the evaluators, it was probably easy to lose track of a recruit who made his way to Nashville via Norrkoping, Sweden, and Hobbs, New Mexico.) The per-game numbers are a little deceiving because the coach rotates his frontcourt, including Taylor, so liberally. As a result Taylor appears to the world at large as merely a 12-point-a-game third option for an 8-8 team. (Yawn.) The world at large should look closer: Taylor's a beast on the offensive glass who makes 55 percent of his twos while playing a huge role in the offense, albeit while averaging a mere 26 minutes per game. (Stallings is an old Missouri Valley hand who doles out playing time for his frontcourt the way Dana Altman does at Creighton for the whole team. In both cases the minutes are limited not by foul trouble or by a desire to rotate in fresh legs on an up-tempo team, but simply by coach prerogative within a preset pattern.) Yes, Taylor needs to either give up the threes or start making them, but he's still pretty clearly on a trajectory to "emerge" here sooner rather than later.

Jermaine Beal (6-3, 205, Sr.). Stallings may rotate his frontcourt but Jermaine Beal, along with backcourt mate Brad Tinsley, stays on the floor. Last year in the wake of Foster's departure, Beal grabbed the lion's share of the perimeter shots that suddenly became available and made 40 percent of his threes.

Brad Tinsley (6-3, 210, So.). Like Beal, Tinsley is a combo guard who shot better than 40 percent from beyond the arc in 2008-09 while opposing defenses paid a lot of attention to Ogilvy and Taylor.

John Jenkins (6-4, 215, Fr.). Having noted that Taylor pretty much came out of nowhere, I suppose we should be leery of statements like this, but: Depending on who's doing the rating, Jenkins, a shooting guard from Gallatin, Tennessee, may rank as Vanderbilt's most highly-rated recruit since Foster.

Steve Tchiengang (6-9, 240, So.). Tchiengang started 16 games as a freshman but had real trouble staying on the floor, picking up at least four fouls in ten of the 25 games where he saw action.

Darshawn McClellan (6-7, 240, Jr.). McClellan, like Tchiengang, got a look as a defensively-oriented fifth starter last year.

Festus Ezeli (6-11, 255, So.). A Nigerian native who redshirted in 2007-08, Ezeli provided the Commodores with Ogilvy-level shot-blocking while averaging 12 minutes a game as a freshman.

Andre Walker (6-7, 220, So.). Walker injured his knee in the third game of the season last year and received a redshirt. As a freshman in 2007-08 he averaged 11 foul-filled minutes a game.

ATLANTIC 10 CONFERENCE ⑤
(in predicted order of finish)

Dayton *Fringe*

2009: 27-8 (11-5 Atlantic 10)
Lost to Kansas 60-43, NCAA Second Round
Adjusted Off. Efficiency: 102.3 (150th nationally)
Adjusted Def. Efficiency: 91.5 (27th nationally)

The Flyers are the team to beat in the Atlantic 10 as they have four starters and ten of their top 11 scorers back from a team that went to the second round of the NCAA tournament last year. The offense runs through senior forward Chris Wright, who was 91st in the nation in percentage of shots (28.2) last season while averaging 13.3 points a game. Senior guard London Warren is vastly underrated as he was tenth in the country in assist rate (39.0) and 20th in steal percentage (4.6). Dayton has combined for 50 victories the last two seasons.

Xavier *In* W: Crawford (Brey) B: Love

2009: 27-8 (12-4 Atlantic 10)
Lost to Pittsburgh 60-55, NCAA Sweet 16
Adjusted Off. Efficiency: 110.5 (50th nationally)
Adjusted Def. Efficiency: 89.0 (11th nationally)

Chris Mack was promoted from his assistant's job to replace head coach Sean Miller, who left for Arizona, and inherits just two returning starters from a team that advanced to the Sweet 16 for a second straight season. Senior forward Jason Love will be counted on to carry much of the scoring and rebounding load. He was 52nd in offensive rebounding percentage (13.4). Sophomore guard Jordan Crawford becomes eligible after sitting out a season following his transfer from Indiana and reached cult hero status over the summer for dunking over LeBron James at the NBA megastar's summer camp.

Princeton O
3-2 matchup D ### Richmond *In*
2009: 20-16 (9-7 Atlantic 10)
Lost to UTEP 81-69, CBI Semifinals
Adjusted Off. Efficiency: 105.7 (101st nationally)

lack bigs

P: Gonzalvez (w)
W: Anderson B
B:

Adjusted Def. Efficiency: 100.6 (155th nationally)

Junior center Dan Geriot, one of the top players in the Atlantic 10 two seasons ago, returns after missing last season because of knee surgery. He averaged 14.3 points a game in 2007-08. He combines with senior guard David Gonzalvez (16.0 ppg) and junior guard Kevin Anderson (16.6 ppg) to give the Spiders an outstanding trio of scorers. Anderson ranked 24th in percentage of minutes (90.9) and Gonzalvez was 66th with 88.0. Senior forward Ryan Butler is a key defender as he was 21st in steal percentage (4.6).

LaSalle

2009: 18-13 (9-7 Atlantic 10)
Lost to Saint Louis 62-60, Atlantic 10 First Round
Adjusted Off. Efficiency: 104.3 (122nd nationally)
Adjusted Def. Efficiency: 98.4 (119th nationally)

The Explorers believe this is the season they can make a run at the Atlantic 10 title as they have a legitimate star in senior guard Rodney Green. He averaged 17.6 points a game last season while ranking 83rd in percentage of minutes played (86.7). Senior forward Vernon Goodridge provides a strong inside presence as he was 68th in block percentage (7.8) and 86th in defensive rebounding percentage (21.9).

Duquesne

2009: 21-13 (9-7 Atlantic 10)
Lost to Virginia Tech 116-108 in NIT First Round
Adjusted Off. Efficiency: 114.7 (23rd nationally)
Adjusted Def. Efficiency: 104.5 (237th nationally)

The Dukes made a surprising run to the championship game of the Atlantic 10 tournament last season before losing to Temple and being denied their first trip to the NCAAs since 1977. They did make their first NIT appearance since 1994 and figure to be legitimate post-season contenders again. Junior wing

Bill Clark was 42nd in effective field goal percentage (60.8) and 57th in true shooting percentage (62.8), junior forward Damian Saunders was 54th in effective field goal percentage (60.2) and 74th in block percentage (7.4) and senior guard Jason Duty was 66th in offensive rating (120.1).

Temple

2009: 22-12 (11-5 Atlantic 10)
Lost to Arizona State 66-57, NCAA First Round
Adjusted Off. Efficiency: 108.7 (68th nationally)
Adjusted Def. Efficiency: 92.8 (40th nationally)

Dionte Christmas, winner of the last three scoring titles in the Atlantic 10, is gone along with two other starters but the Owls feel they can be competitive with the inside-outside duo of junior forward Lavoy Allen and senior guard Ryan Brooks. Allen was 18th in offensive rebounding percentage (14.6), 30th in offensive rating (123.5) and 81st in effective field goal percentage (59.2).

Charlotte

2009: 11-20 (5-11 Atlantic 10)
Lost to Saint Joseph's 72-62, Atlantic 10 First Round
Adjusted Off. Efficiency: 102.6 (146th nationally)
Adjusted Def. Efficiency: 100.6 (156th nationally)

The 49ers return six players who averaged at least 18 minutes a game last season to go with a transfer from Boston College in junior forward Shamari Spears and a top recruit in freshman forward Chris Braswell. Senior guard DiJuan Harris will lead the way after ranking 12th in assist rate (37.9) and 31st in percentage of minutes (90.6). Senior center Phil Jones was 42nd in block percentage (8.8) and senior guard Ian Andersen was 93rd in turnover rate (12.1).

Massachusetts

2009: 12-18 (7-9 Atlantic 10)
Lost to Duquesne 91-81, Atlantic 10 First Round
Adjusted Off. Efficiency: 104.2 (123rd nationally)
Adjusted Def. Efficiency: 101.2 (169th nationally)

Derek Kellogg has some rebuilding to do in his second season as coach, for the Minutemen have just two starters back. Freshman wing Terrell Vinson could wind up being the go-to guy in this offense and senior guard Ricky Harris is one of the conference's most exciting players.

Rhode Island

2009: 23-11 (11-5 Atlantic 10)
Lost to Penn State 83-72, NIT Second Round
Adjusted Off. Efficiency: 112.5 (38th nationally)

Adjusted Def. Efficiency: 99.6 (135th nationally)

The Rams have won 63 games in the last three seasons, so their senior core group of guard Keith Cothran and forwards Delroy James and Lamonte Ulmer has tasted success. Cothran will be counted on heavily to provide scoring punch after averaging 13.2 points a game last season.

St. Bonaventure

2009: 15-15 (6-10 Atlantic 10)
Lost to Richmond 65-49, Atlantic 10 First Round
Adjusted Off. Efficiency: 97.0 (238th nationally)
Adjusted Def. Efficiency: 99.4 (132nd nationally)

The Bonnies have four starters back from a team that snapped a streak of five losing seasons last winter. Sophomore forward Andrew Nicholson was 12th in block percentage (10.7) and 58th in effective field goal percentage (60.2), while winning Atlantic 10 Rookie of the Year honors. Senior guard Jonathan Hall was 74th in percentage of minutes (87.5) while averaging 12.9 points a game.

Saint Joseph's

2009: 17-15 (9-7 Atlantic 10)
Lost to Temple 79-65, Atlantic 10 Quarterfinals
Adjusted Off. Efficiency: 104.7 (116th nationally)
Adjusted Def. Efficiency: 97.8 (99th nationally)

After spending last season playing their home games at the Palestra, the Hawks move back on campus to the refurbished Michael J. Hagan '85 Arena, which used to be Alumni Memorial Fieldhouse and now seats 4,900. The Hawks will have a hard time replacing Ahmad Nivins, last season's Atlantic 10 Player of the Year, though senior guard Darrin Govens (12.5 ppg) should pick up some of the slack. Senior guard Garrett Williamson is a lockdown defender.

Saint Louis

2009: 18-14 (8-8 nationally)
Lost to Xavier 66-47, Atlantic 10 Quarterfinals
Adjusted Off. Efficiency: 100.1 (192nd nationally)
Adjusted Def. Efficiency: 98.2 (117th nationally)

The Billikens will be one of the youngest teams in the nation with no seniors and one junior as Rick Majerus continues to try to rebuild the program in his third year as coach. Sophomore guard Kwamain Mitchell (11.0 ppg) is the top returning scorer.

George Washington

2009: 10-18 (4-12 Atlantic 10)
Did not qualify for post-season play
Adjusted Off. Efficiency: 101.0 (178th nationally)

Adjusted Def. Efficiency: 102.7 (195th nationally)

Ninth-year coach Karl Hobbs, once considered a rising star in the profession, finds himself on the hot seat following last season's disaster and has a young team that includes six newcomers. The Colonials do have a reliable player in senior forward Damian Hollis, who was 91st in true shooting percentage (61.3).

Fordham

2009: 3-25 (1-15 Atlantic 10)

Did not qualify for post-season play

Adjusted Off. Efficiency: 91.5 (301st nationally)
Adjusted Def. Efficiency: 111.1 (316th nationally)

The Rams are another young team as six of their 13 players are freshmen. There are some talented young veterans, though, including sophomore guard Jio Fontan, who ranked 26th in assists rate (34.3), 37th in percentage of possessions (30.5) and 85th in percentage of minutes (86.6) while averaging 15.3 points. Junior forward Jacob Green (8.0) was 64th in block percentage and sophomore guard Alberto Estwick was 78th in turnover rate (11.7).

CONFERENCE USA
(in predicted order of finish)

Tulsa *Out?*

2009: 25-11 (12-4 Conference USA)

Lost to Auburn 74-55, NIT Second Round

Adjusted Off. Efficiency: 104.7 (117th nationally)
Adjusted Def. Efficiency: 92.2 (37th nationally)

The Golden Hurricane, coming off back-to-back 25-win seasons, seem poised to end Memphis' run of dominance in Conference USA, particularly with senior center Jerome Jordan leading the way. He was 20th in the nation in both defensive rebounding percentage (25.0) and block percentage (9.8) last season, 56th in true shooting percentage (62.9), 89th in fouls drawn per 40 minutes (6.0), 93rd in effective field goal percentage (58.6) and 94th in free throw rate (60.6). Senior guard Ben Uzoh was 54th in percentage of minutes (89.1) while averaging 14.0 points a game. Senior forward Bishop Wheatley was 67th in free throw rate (65.7).

Memphis *Out?*

2009: 33-4 (16-0 Conference USA)

Lost to Missouri 102-91, NCAA Sweet 16

Adjusted Off. Efficiency: 114.1 (25th nationally)
Adjusted Def. Efficiency: 82.5 (1st nationally)

Josh Pastner takes over a program that has had nine straight 20-win seasons, being promoted from his assistant's role to replace John Calipari, who left for Kentucky. Pastner has a major rebuilding job with only one returning starter in senior guard Doneal Mack, who was 39th in turnover rate (10.6). Junior forward Will Coleman, a junior college transfer, might only be in the program one year before moving on to the NBA.

UTEP *Frye*

2009: 23-14 (10-6 Conference USA)

Lost to Oregon State 81-73, CBI Championship Series

Adjusted Off. Efficiency: 107.6 (77th nationally)
Adjusted Def. Efficiency: 97.3 (89th nationally)

The Miners have an experienced squad with 11 juniors on their 13-man roster. Two of those juniors, Julyan Stone and Randy Culpepper, make up a potent backcourt. Stone was 35th in assist rate (32.8) and 50th in free throw rate (67.9) while Culpepper was 63rd in percentage of shots (31.3) and averaged 17.5 points a game. Sophomore forward Arnett Moultrie was 90th in offensive rebounding percentage (12.5).

Houston

2009: 21-12 (10-6 Conference USA)

Lost to Oregon State 49-45, CBI First Round

Adjusted Off. Efficiency: 107.7 (73rd nationally)
Adjusted Def. Efficiency: 95.7 (70th nationally)

Senior guard Aubrey Coleman, the Newcomer of the Year in Conference USA last season, gives the Cougars hope they can make a run for at the title. He averaged 19.4 points a game while ranking 20th in percentage of possessions (32.1), 41st in fouls drawn per 40 minutes (6.5), 48th in steal percentage (4.1) and 60th in percentage of shots (31.5). Senior guard Kelvin Lewis (18.0 ppg) was 19th in percentage of minutes (91.6) and 26th in turnover rate (10.2).

Marshall

2009: 15-17 (7-9 Conference USA)

Lost to Rice 60-59, Conference USA First Round

Adjusted Off. Efficiency: 105.1 (108th nationally)

Adjusted Def. Efficiency: 104.1 (228th nationally)

The Thundering Herd expects to make some noise with four returning starters. They get a boost from senior guard Darryl Merthie getting another year of eligibility due to academic progress.

Tulane

2009: 14-17 (7-9 Conference USA)
Lost to Memphis 51-41, Conference USA Quarterfinals
Adjusted Off. Efficiency: 97.3 (232nd nationally)
Adjusted Def. Efficiency: 96.8 (79th nationally)

The Green Wave has nine lettermen and three starters back, including senior forward Kevin Sims. He was 88th in percentage of minutes (86.5) while averaging 13.0 points a game. Junior guard Kris Richard was 50th in steal percentage (4.0).

SMU

2009: 9-21 (3-13 Conference USA)
Lost to Houston 85-76, Conference USA First Round
Adjusted Off. Efficiency: 101.1 (176th nationally)
Adjusted Def. Efficiency: 104.7 (241st nationally)

The Mustangs expect improvement after relying heavily on their freshman class last season. Senior guard Derek Williams is this team's rock, though, and he was 92nd in fouls called per 40 minutes (1.9). Ultra-quick sophomore guard Paul McCoy adds excitement.

UAB Frye

2009: 22-12 (11-5 Conference USA)
Lost to Notre Dame 70-64, NIT First Round
Adjusted Off. Efficiency: 108.1 (72nd nationally)
Adjusted Def. Efficiency: 92.2 (39th nationally)

The Blazers lost six seniors and more than 90 percent of their scoring and rebounding, leaving coach Mike Davis to put the pieces back together. Senior forward Howard Crawford will be counted on heavily after finishing 74th in turnover rate (11.7).

East Carolina

2009: 13-17 (5-11 Conference USA)
Lost to Tulane 69-59, Conference USA First Round
Adjusted Off. Efficiency: 108.8 (67th nationally)
Adjusted Def. Efficiency: 113.2 (336th nationally)

Mack McCarthy has increased the Pirates' win total in each of his first two seasons as coach and will try to make it three straight this winter. Sophomore forward Darrius Morrow led the nation in free throw rate (94.7) last season and was 41st in offensive rebounding percentage (13.7). Junior guard Brock Young was second in assist rate (45.0), junior guard Junior Abrams was 68th in effective field goal percentage (59.4) and 73rd in true shooting percentage (62.0) and junior center Chad Wynn was 96th in block percentage (6.6).

UCF

2009: 17-14 (7-9 Conference USA)
Lost to Southern Mississippi 77-53, Conference USA First Round
Adjusted Off. Efficiency: 104.9 (112th nationally)
Adjusted Def. Efficiency: 102.4 (191st nationally)

The Knights will have another young team as they have only one senior and eight freshmen. Sophomore guard A.J. Rompza was 28th in assist rate (33.7). Freshman forward Keith Clanton figures to make an immediate impact after passing up scholarship offers from Florida and South Carolina and sophomore guard Isaac Sosa is an outside shooting threat.

Southern Miss

2009: 15-17 (4-12 Conference USA)
Lost to UAB 74-73, Conference USA Quarterfinals
Adjusted Off. Efficiency: 105.0 (110th nationally)
Adjusted Def. Efficiency: 103.9 (223rd nationally)

Larry Eustachy has made slow progress in turning the Eagles around during his six seasons as coach and will likely take a step back this winter after losing three starters. Junior guard R.L. Horton will be counted on heavily as he was 72nd in percentage of minutes played (87.6) while averaging 12.7 points a game.

Rice

2009: 10-22 (4-12 Conference USA)
Lost to Tulsa 73-51, Conference USA Quarterfinals
Adjusted Off. Efficiency: 96.9 (240th nationally)
Adjusted Def. Efficiency: 103.8 (220th nationally)

The Owls have four starters and nine lettermen back to go with a good recruiting class but appear to be a season away from being a contender in the conference.

MID-AMERICAN CONFERENCE
(in predicted order of finish)

EAST DIVISION

Akron

2009: 23-13 (10-6 MAC)
Lost to Gonzaga 77-64, NCAA First Round
Adjusted Off. Efficiency: 103.0 (140th nationally)
Adjusted Def. Efficiency: 94.7 (59th nationally)

The Zips have a veteran team with four returning starters and 13 lettermen. The offense will run through Brett McKnight, who was 37th in the nation in percentage of shots (32.6) and 39th in percentage of possessions (30.4) last season while averaging 11.2 points a game. His brother, senior forward Chris McKnight, was 53rd in free throw rate (67.2). There are also high hopes for freshman center Zeke Marshall, perhaps the most-highly touted recruit landed by a MAC program in recent years.

Buffalo

2009: 21-12 (11-5 MAC)
Lost to Wichita State 84-73, CBI First Round
Adjusted Off. Efficiency: 101.1 (175th nationally)
Adjusted Off. Efficiency: 97.2 (88th nationally)

After setting a school record with 21 victories last seasons, the Bulls will again be a major factor in the MAC. Senior guard Rodney Pierce was 90th in percentage of shots (30.4) and averaged 14.3 points a game. Senior wing Calvin Betts can play any position on the floor and be an asset.

Kent State

2009: 19-15 (10-6 MAC)
Lost to Oakland 80-74, CollegeInsider.com First Round
Adjusted Off. Efficiency: 101.8 (159th nationally)
Adjusted Def. Efficiency: 97.6 (97th nationally)

The Golden Flashes will have a senior-dominated starting lineup, led by guard Chris Singletary. He was 58th in percentage of possessions (29.3) and averaged 12.1 points a game. Forward Anthony Simpson, another senior, was 66th in defensive rebounding percentage (22.5).

Miami OH

2009: 17-13 (10-6 MAC)
Lost to Akron 73-63, MAC Quarterfinals
Adjusted Off. Efficiency: 101.0 (179th nationally)

Adjusted Off. Efficiency: 94.7 (60th nationally)

The RedHawks were hit hard by graduation but they have the dean of MAC coaches in Charlie Coles and a potential impact freshman in center Drew McGhee.

Bowling Green

2009: 19-14 (11-5 MAC)
Lost to Creighton 73-71, NIT First Round
Adjusted Off. Efficiency: 101.4 (171st nationally)
Adjusted Def. Efficiency: 99.1 (127th nationally)

The defending MAC regular-season champs will have a hard time staying near the top of the standings this season. Senior center Otis Polk lends stability in the frontcourt as he was 13th in offensive rebounding percentage (15.4). Junior guard Joe Jakubowski is a good distributor.

Ohio

2009: 15-17 (7-9 MAC)
Lost to Bowling Green 74-61, MAC Quarterfinals
Adjusted Def. Efficiency: 99.7 (203rd nationally)
Adjusted Def. Efficiency: 101.0 (165th nationally)

John Groce will continue building the Bobcats' program in his second season. One player to keep an eye on is sophomore guard Steven Coleman, who was 73rd in steal percentage (3.8). Ohio also has a pure shooter in junior guard Tommy Freeman.

WEST DIVISION

Central Michigan

2009: 12-19 (7-9 MAC)
Lost to Ball State 64-61, MAC Quarterfinals
Adjusted Off. Efficiency: 97.2 (235th nationally)
Adjusted Def. Efficiency: 105.2 (250th nationally)

The Chippewas look like the favorite in what is clearly the weaker of the MAC's two divisions. Senior guard Jordan Blitzer was 57th in steal percentage (4.0).

Ball State

2009: 14-17 (7-9 MAC)
Lost to Buffalo 64-52, MAC Semifinals
Adjusted Off. Efficiency: 93.2 (286th nationally)
Adjusted Def. Efficiency: 100.7 (157th nationally)

Sophomore forward Jarrod Jones was the MAC

Freshman of the Year last season when he was 81st in defensive rebounding percentage (22.0). He will be counted on to carry a big scoring and rebounding load for the Cardinals.

Northern Illinois

2009: 10-20 (5-11 MAC)
Lost to Kent State 64-61, MAC First Round
Adjusted Off. Efficiency: 92.4(293rd nationally)
Adjusted Def. Efficiency: 105.8 (255th nationally)

The Huskies should be dangerous with their entire starting lineup and 13 lettermen returning. Junior guard Darion Anderson is their central figure as he was 44th in percentage of possessions (29.9) and 89th in percentage of shots (30.4) while averaging 16.9 points a game. Senior forward Najul Ervin was 82nd in steal percentage (3.7).

Western Michigan

2009: 10-21 (7-9 MAC)
Lost to Ohio 62-55, MAC First Round
Adjusted Off. Efficiency: 95.8 (256th nationally)
Adjusted Def. Efficiency: 104.3 (235th nationally)

Senior guard David Kool gives the Broncos a chance

Eastern Michigan

2009: 8-24 (6-10 MAC)
Lost to Central Michigan 62-49, MAC First Round
Adjusted Off. Efficiency: 88.3 (329th nationally)
Adjusted Def. Efficiency: 104.0 (225th nationally)

The Eagles have three starters back, including one of the top players in the MAC in junior forward Brandon Bowdry. He was 12th in percentage of possessions (33.1), 61st in percentage of shots (31.4) and 73rd in fouls drawn per 40 minutes while scoring 14.8 points a game.

Toledo

2009: 7-25 (5-11 MAC)
Lost to Akron 93-92, MAC First Round
Adjusted Off. Efficiency: 91.0 (307th nationally)
Adjusted Def. Efficiency: 105.6 (254th nationally)

The Rockets lost two top players from a 25-loss team in Tyrone Kent and Jonathan Amos, leaving them in a major rebuilding phase.

MISSOURI VALLEY CONFERENCE
(in predicted order of finish)

Northern Iowa

2009: 23-11 (14-4 MVC)
Lost to Purdue 61-56, NCAA First Round
Adjusted Off. Efficiency: 109.5 (64th nationally)
Adjusted Def. Efficiency: 98.7 (122nd nationally)

The Panthers are undoubtedly the cream of the crop in an improved conference as they have all five starters returning from an NCAA tournament team. Senior center Jordan Eglseder is poised for a big finish to his career after ranking eighth in the nation in defensive rebounding percentage (28.1), 39th in offensive rebounding percentage (13.8) and 50th in percentage of shots (31.7) last season while averaging 10.2 points a game. Senior forward Adam Koch was ninth in free throw rate (83.3) and 37th in fouls drawn per 40 minutes (6.6). Junior forward Lucas O'Rear finished 28th in offensive rating (123.8).

Creighton

2009: 27-8 (14-4 MVC)
Lost to Kentucky 65-63, NIT Second Round
Adjusted Off. Efficiency: 110.0 (59th nationally)
Adjusted Def. Efficiency: 98.1 (113th nationally)

The Bluejays will have one of the MVC's most athletic teams, led by junior guard P'Allen Stinnett. Senior guard Justin Carter can play four different positions and freshman point guard Andrew Bock can distribute and score. Junior center Kenny Lawson, who was 35th in block percentage (9.0), provides an intimidating presence in the middle.

Illinois State

2009: 24-10 (11-7 MVC)
Lost to Kansas State 83-79, NIT First Round
Adjusted Off. Efficiency: 107.7 (76th nationally)
Adjusted Def. Efficiency: 94.5 (56th nationally)

The Redbirds are looking to break through after losing in the championship game of the MVC tournament the past two seasons. Senior forward Dinma Odiakosa is poised for a breakout season after ranking 29th in effective field goal percentage (61.8) and 42nd in both offensive rebounding percentage (13.6) and free throw rate (69.1). Senior guard Osiris Eldridge is a potential NBA player.

Wichita State

2009: 17-17 (8-10 MVC)
Lost to Stanford 70-56, CBI Quarterfinals
Adjusted Off. Efficiency: 102.2 (151st nationally)
Adjusted Def. Efficiency: 99.2 (128th nationally)

The Shockers look to build on the momentum they gained at the end of last season by winning eight of their last 12 conference game and making it to the postseason. Slight senior guard Clevin Hannah was 25th in assist rate (34.3).

Southern Illinois

2009: 13-18 (8-10 MVC)
Lost to Bradley 67-55, MVC Quarterfinals
Adjusted Off. Efficiency: 99.9 (197th nationally)
Adjusted Def. Efficiency: 99.7 (137th nationally)

The Salukis are confident they can bounce back after having their streak of 11 straight winning seasons snapped last winter. Sophomore guard Kevin Dillard was 29th in assist rate (33.6) and is also a three-point shooting threat.

Bradley

2009: 21-15 (10-8 MVC)
Lost to Old Dominion 66-62, CollegeInsider.com Championship Game
Adjusted Off. Efficiency: 104.0 (126th nationally)
Adjusted Def. Efficiency: 100.0 (143rd nationally)

The Braves could be a sleeper after making a deep run in the inaugural CollegeInsider.com tournament last spring. They have five of their top six starters back and will welcome back junior guard Andrew Warren, who sat out last season with a stress fracture in his foot.

Indiana State

2009: 11-21 (7-11 MVC)
Lost to Northern Iowa 73-69, MVC Quarterfinals

Adjusted Off. Efficiency: 101.6 (164th nationally)
Adjusted Def. Efficiency: 103.8 (219th nationally)

Senior guard Henry Marshall was 81st in assist rate (81.5) and gives the Sycamores a chance to be dangerous this season as he leads a deep backcourt. Their frontline is the question mark.

Missouri State

2009: 11-20 (3-15 MVC)
Lost to Wichita State 59-46, MVC First Round
Adjusted Off. Efficiency: 97.5 (230th nationally)
Adjusted Def. Efficiency: 100.8 (159th nationally)

Cuonzo Martin will continue the rebuilding process in his second season as coach. Sophomore forward Kyle Weems, who was 59th in turnover rate (11.2), is one of the building blocks. The Bears are also counting on junior guard Adam Leonard, a transfer from Eastern Kentucky.

Drake

2009: 17-16 (7-11 MVC)
Lost to Idaho 69-67, CollegeInsider.com First Round
Adjusted Off. Efficiency: 100.1 (190th nationally)
Adjusted Def. Efficiency: 98.6 (120th nationally)

The Bulldogs went from winning the conference in 2008 to finishing eighth last season and will look to rebound this winter. Craig Stanley was 42nd in fouls called per 40 minutes (1.7) and 68th in assist rate (31.0) and fellow senior guard Josh Young was 79th in fouls called per 40 minutes (1.9) and 97th in fouls drawn per 40 minutes (5.9).

Evansville

2009: 17-14 (8-10 MVC)
Lost to Belmont 92-76, College Insider.com First Round
Adjusted Off. Efficiency: 101.9 (155th nationally)
Adjusted Def. Efficiency: 98.9 (126th nationally)

The Purple Aces lost four starters from last year's post-season team and coach Marty Simmons will be in rebuilding mode in 2009-10.

MOUNTAIN WEST CONFERENCE
(in predicted order of finish)

BYU

2009: 25-8 (12-4 MWC)
Lost to Texas A&M 79-66, NCAA First Round
Adjusted Off. Efficiency: 113.4 (28th nationally)

Adjusted Def. Efficiency: 91.8 (31st nationally)

Junior guard Jimmer Fredette, who had a 111.7 offensive rating last season, leads a group of four returning starters for the Cougars. He ranked 29th in the nation in fouls called per 40 minutes (1.6). Senior forward Jonathan Taverni figures to be heavily involved in the offense as he was 29th in turnover rate (10.3), 84th in percentage of shots (30.5) and 90th in defensive rebounding percentage (21.8) while averaging 15.7 points a game. Junior guard Jackson Emery was 54th in offensive rating (120.9), 72nd in true shooting percentage (62.1) and 74th in effective field goal percentage (59.3).

San Diego State

2009: 26-10 (11-5 MWC)
Lost to Baylor 76-62, NIT Semifinals
Adjusted Off. Efficiency: 109.0 (66th nationally)
Adjusted Def. Efficiency: 91.2 (24th nationally)

The Aztecs figure to be strong despite losing three starters from a team that made the NIT's final four. Leading what should be a very balanced attack is junior forward Billy White, who had a 117.5 offensive rating. Coach Steve Fisher landed an outstanding recruiting class, led by freshman forward Kawhi Leonard.

UNLV

2009: 21-11 (9-7 MWC)
Lost to Kentucky 70-60, NIT First Round
Adjusted Off. Efficiency: 105.1 (109th nationally)
Adjusted Def. Efficiency: 93.7 (48th nationally)

Junior guard Derrick Jasper, a transfer from Kentucky, will make an immediate impact for the Runnin' Rebels after they lost three starters. Junior guard Tre'Von Willis was 99th in free throw rate (60.3). Sophomore wing Chase Stanback, a transfer from UCLA, will also help.

New Mexico

2009: 22-12 (12-4 MWC)
Lost to Notre Dame 70-68, NIT Second Round
Adjusted Off. Efficiency: 112.1 (41st nationally)
Adjusted Def. Efficiency: 94.6 (58th nationally)

Junior guard Dairese Gary leads a group of three returning starters for the Lobos after ranking 34th in assist rate (33.0). Sophomore guard Nate Garth was 40th in assist rate (32.5) and senior forward Roman Martinez was 97th in effective field goal percentage (58.6).

Utah

2009: 24-10 (12-4 MWC)
Lost to Arizona 84-71, NCAA First Round
Adjusted Off. Efficiency: 109.6 (63rd nationally)

Adjusted Def. Efficiency: 91.4 (26th nationally)

The Utes will miss the inside presence of center Luke Nevill but do have three starters back, including junior forward Carlon Brown and senior guard Luke Drca. Brown is a very athletic player, who will allow Utah to run the floor more this season.

Wyoming

2009: 19-14 (7-9 MWC)
Lost to Northeastern 64-62, CBI First Round
Adjusted Off. Efficiency: 105.4 (104th nationally)
Adjusted Def. Efficiency: 102.7 (194th nationally)

The Cowboys have just two starters back but could be a dark horse thanks to the presence of sophomore wing Afam Muojeke, last season's MWC Freshman of the Year. Sophomore guard JayDee Luster is expected to provide an immediate impact after transferring from New Mexico State.

TCU

2009: 14-17 (5-11 MWC)
Lost to Utah 61-58, MWC Quarterfinals
Adjusted Off. Efficiency: 101.4 (168th nationally)
Adjusted Def. Efficiency: 98.0 (108th nationally)

Senior forward/center Zvanko Buljan will lead the way after winning MWC Newcomer of the Year honors last season. He was fourth in the nation in defensive rebounding percentage (28.9). Senior guard Edvinas Ruzgas was 13th in turnover rate (9.6).

Colorado State

2009: 9-22, (4-12 MWC)
Lost to Air Force 71-67, MWC First Round
Adjusted Off. Efficiency: 105.5 (102nd nationally)
Adjusted Def. Efficiency: 107.2 (272nd nationally)

Despite having three starters back, this season figures to be another struggle for the Rams. Junior forward Travis Franklin was a bright spot last season as he was 54th in fouls drawn per 40 minutes (6.3).

Air Force

2009: 10-21 (0-16 MWC)
Lost to BYU 80-69, MWC Quarterfinals
Adjusted Off. Efficiency: 96.9 (239th nationally)
Adjusted Def. Efficiency: 102.7 (196th nationally)

The Falcons have only one starter back but that might not be a bad thing considering they did not win a conference game in the regular season last winter. The lone returnee is junior guard Evan Washington.

WEST COAST CONFERENCE
(in predicted order of finish)

In Gonzaga

2009: 28-6 (14-0 WCC)
Lost to North Carolina 98-77, NCAA Sweet Sixteen
Adjusted Off. Efficiency: 118.4 (fifth nationally)
Adjusted Def. Efficiency: 90.5 (18th nationally)

The Bulldogs are heavy favorites to win a tenth consecutive WCC title and make their 12th straight appearance in the NCAA tournament despite losing three starters from a Sweet 16 team. Junior guard Steven Gray was 60th in offensive rating (120.3) and 68th in turnover rate (11.3) last season. Senior guard Matt Bouldin was 74th in offensive rating (119.3). The Bulldogs also have a lockdown perimeter defender in sophomore guard Demetri Goodson and a potential star in freshman forward Mangisto Arop.

bg slow Guards,

Portland

2009: 19-13 (9-5 WCC)
Lost to Pacific 82-76, CollegeInsider.com First Round
Adjusted Off. Efficiency: 105.9 (97th nationally)
Adjusted Def. Efficiency: 100.0 (141st nationally)

The Pilots have all five starters back and 12 lettermen, giving them hope of ending Gonzaga's long run of WCC dominance. Junior guard Jared Stohl is one of the most unappreciated players in the country as he was second in fouls called per 40 minutes (1.2), sixth in true shooting percentage (68.0), seventh in offensive rating (128.0) and ninth in effective field goal percentage (66.2). Senior guard T.J. Campbell was seventh in true shooting percentage (67.1), 13th in effective field goal percentage (65.4) and 75th in assist rate (30.7). Junior forward Luke Sikma was 25th in defensive rebounding percentage (24.6) and senior guard Nik Raivio was 97th in percentage of shots (30.2) while averaging 16.0 points.

Saint Mary's *Fringe*

2009: 28-7 (10-4 WCC)
Lost to San Diego State 70-66, NIT Quarterfinals
Adjusted Off. Efficiency: 110.4 (53rd nationally)
Adjusted Defensive Efficiency (95.6 (69th nationally))

The Gaels have just one starter back from a team that set a school record for victories but Randy Bennett has built a program that has reached the status of perennial contender. Senior center Omar Samhan is a strong inside presence and was 19th in offense rebounding percentage (14.4) and 88th in offensive rating (118.7).

San Diego

2009: 16-16 (6-8 WCC)
Lost to Santa Clara 80-69, WCC Semifinals
Adjusted Off. Efficiency: 96.4 (246th nationally)
Adjusted Def. Efficiency: 97.4 (92nd nationally)

The Torreros got good news when the NCAA granted a fifth year of eligibility to guard Brandon Johnson, who ruptured his Achilles tendon eight games into last season. He is one of two returning starters and eight lettermen.

Santa Clara

2009: 16-17 (7-7 WCC)
Lost to Gonzaga 94-59, WCC Semifinals
Adjusted Off. Efficiency: 100.0 (195th nationally)
Adjusted Def. Efficiency: 98.0 (109th nationally)

The Broncos will miss center John Bryant, who was a real force underneath, and have just two starters back from a sub.-500 team. One of them is sophomore guard Kevin Foster, the WCC co-Newcomer of the Year last season. He was 49th in percentage of shots (31.8) and averaged 14.9 points a game.

Pepperdine

2009: 9-23 (5-9 WCC)
Lost to Portland 69-45, WCC Semifinals
Adjusted Off. Efficiency: 90.0 (313th nationally)
Adjusted Def. Efficiency: 104.3 (232nd nationally)

The Waves have 12 lettermen back who accounted for 82 percent of last season's scoring. Sophomore guard Keion Bell figures to be the focal point of the offense as he was 18th in percentage of possessions (32.3) and 87th in percentage of shots (30.4) while averaging 12.9 points a game. Sophomore center Corbin Moore was 70th in offensive rebounding percentage (13.0).

San Francisco

2009: 11-19 (3-11 WCC)
Lost to Pepperdine 93-85, WCC Quarterfinals
Adjusted Off. Efficiency: 102.3 (149th nationally)
Adjusted Def. Efficiency: 110.2 (349th nationally)

Senior forward Dior Lowhorn, the two-time defending WCC scoring champion, is one of four returning starters for the Dons. He averaged 20.1 points while ranking fifth in percentage of shots (37.4), ninth in turnover rate (9.3) and 42nd in percentage of possessions (30.1).

Loyola Marymount

2009: 3-28 (2-12 WCC)
Lost to San Diego 62-56, WCC Quarterfinals
Adjusted Off. Efficiency: 87.5 (330th nationally)
Adjusted Def. Efficiency: 106.7 (267th nationally)

The Lions look for stability after head coach Billy Bayno resigned early last season and was replaced by assistant coach Max Good, who now has the job on a permanent basis. Sophomore guard Jarred DuBois is a player to build around as he was 90th in percentage of minutes played (86.4) and averaged 13.5 points a game.

WESTERN ATHLETIC CONFERENCE
(in predicted order of finish)

Utah State

2009: 30-15 (14-2 WAC)
Lost to Marquette 58-57, NCAA First Round
Adjusted Off. Efficiency: 116.0 (17th nationally)
Adjusted Def. Efficiency: 100.7 (158th nationally)

Stew Morrill, one of the top mid-major coaches in the nation, has the Aggies poised to win a third straight WAC title with four returning starters. Junior guard Tyler Newbold was sixth in the nation in offensive rating (128.1) last season, 38th in fouls called per 40 minutes (1.7) and 47th in turnover rate (10.9). Junior forward Tai Wesley was 70th in effective field goal percentage (59.4) and 71st in true shooting percentage (62.1) and senior guard Jared Quayle was 55th in offensive rating (120.8).

Nevada

2009: 21-13 (11-5 WAC)
Lost to UTEP 79-77, CBI First Round
Adjusted Off. Efficiency: 104.7 (115th nationally)
Adjusted Def. Efficiency: 97.9 (105th nationally)

Sophomore forward Luke Babbitt, last season's WAC Freshman of the Year, leads a group of three returning starters and eight lettermen for new head coach Mark Carter, promoted from his assistant's job to replace Mark Fox, who left for Georgia. Babbitt had a 111.8 offensive rating. Junior guard Armon Johnson was 20th in fouls called per 40 minutes (1.5) and 71st in assist rate (30.8). Sophomore forward Dario Hunt was 14th in block percentage (10.5).

New Mexico State

2009: 17-15 (9-7 WAC)
Lost to Utah State 71-70, WAC Semifinals
Adjusted Off. Efficiency: 107.7 (75th nationally)
Adjusted Def. Efficiency: 104.2 (230th nationally)

The Aggies will again try to take advantage of their offensive prowess by playing at a quick pace. The strong work on the glass by junior forward Wendell McKines, who was 57th in offensive rebounding percentage (13.4) and 64th in defense rebounding percentage (22.5), helps gets get the fast break going. Sophomore center Hamidu Rahman was 90th in block percentage (6.7) and junior guard Gordo Castillo was 94th in offensive rating (118.4).

Idaho

2009: 17-16 (9-7 WAC)
Lost to Pacific 69-59, CollegeInsider.com Quarterfinals
Adjusted Off. Efficiency: 103.1 (137th nationally)
Adjusted Def. Efficiency: 102.8 (198th nationally)

The Vandals are looking to continue building on the momentum of their first post-season appearance since 1990 and first winning season since joining the WAC in 2005. Senior guard Mac Hopson was seventh in assist rate (40.8) and 52nd in percentage of possessions (29.6) while averaging 16.4 points a game. Senior center Marvin Jefferson was 28th in block percentage (9.4) and senior guard Kahif Watson was 63rd in free throw rate (66.1). Senior guard Steffon Johnson, a transfer from Pacific, is good enough to crack a veteran lineup.

Louisiana Tech

2009: 15-18 (6-10 WAC)
Lost to Nevada 77-68, WAC Semifinals
Adjusted Off. Efficiency: 100.4 (188th nationally)
Adjusted Def. Efficiency: 98.8 (124th nationally)

The Bulldogs have an experienced team with nine lettermen, four of whom are seniors. One of those seniors, guard Kyle Gibson, is the leader as he was 92nd in percentage of minutes (86.3) and averaged 16.1 points a game. Senior forward/center Magnum Rolle was 75th in block percentage (7.4).

San Jose State

2009: 13-17 (6-10 WAC)
Lost to Nevada 78-69, WAC Quarterfinals
Adjusted Off. Efficiency: 101.4 (167th nationally)
Adjusted Def. Efficiency: 104.0 (226th nationally)

The Spartans have hopes of finishing above .500 for the first time since 2001, as they have four returning starters. The offense runs through junior guard Adrian Oliver, who was 33rd in percentage of possessions (30.7) and 51st in percentage of shots (31.7) while averaging 17.1 points a game. Senior center Chris Oakes is a force inside as he was 44th in offensive rebounding percentage (13.6) and 62nd in defensive rebounding percentage (22.7).

Boise State

2009: 19-13 (9-7 WAC)
Lost to Stanford 96-76, CBI First Round
Adjusted Off. Efficiency: 101.4 (169th nationally)
Adjusted Def. Efficiency: 100.6 (154th nationally)

The Broncos don't have a blue floor at Taco Bell Arena but they are 47-9 at home the last three seasons. They also have four starters returning, including senior forward Ike Okoye, who was 30th in both defensive rebounding percentage (24.2) and block percentage (9.2).

Fresno State

2009: 13-21 (3-13 WAC)
Lost to Utah State 85-68, WAC Quarterfinals
Adjusted Off. Efficiency: 98.3 (222nd nationally)
Adjusted Def. Efficiency: 102.2 (186th nationally)

The Bulldogs have three starters back but are still a very young team with only one senior. Sophomore forward Paul George had a 107.1 offensive rating. Senior forward Sylvester Seay has the potential to sneak into the lower part of the first round of the NBA draft with a big season. Freshman center Greg Smith, a Fresno native, should help right away.

Hawaii

2009: Lost to Fresno State 62-58, WAC First Round
Adjusted Off. Efficiency: 95.1 (265th nationally)
Adjusted Def. Efficiency: 98.8 (125th nationally)

The Rainbow Warriors have players from six different states and five different countries, including four who started last season, but diversity won't be enough to keep them from the basement. Senior forward Petras Balocka was 33rd in fouls drawn per 40 minutes (6.6) and 98th in percentage of possessions (28.1) while averaging 8.7 points a game. Senior forward Roderick Flemings was 46th in percentage of minutes (89.5) and averaged 16.6 points.   *John Perrotto*

Best Of The Rest

A look at the top teams in each of the conferences that historically receive one NCAA tournament bid

Boston University

2009: 17-13 (11-5 America East Conference)
Lost to Maryland-Baltimore County 79-75, America East Quarterfinals
Adjusted Off. Efficiency: 102.8 (144th nationally)
Adjusted Def. Efficiency: 103.0 (200th nationally)

The Terriers were expected to win the America East the last two seasons but came up short. Now they hope new coach Pat Chambers, who was a Villanova assistant, can get them over the hump. Sophomore forward Jake O'Brien was 80th in turnover rate (11.8) last season. Junior wing John Holland might have an NBA future. Defending champion Binghamton figured to challenge for the title until six players were dismissed from the team in September.

27th place
Injuries

Vearley [W + Hayward, Howard]

Butler B

2009: 26-6 (15-3 Horizon League)
Lost to Louisiana State 75-71, NCAA First Round
Adjusted Off. Efficiency: 110.0 (61st nationally)
Adjusted Def. Efficiency: 93.8 (50th nationally)

Howard foul trouble

The Bulldogs have the best chance of any team from a non-power conference to make a Final Four run, with junior forward Matt Howard, the Horizon League Player of the Year last season, leading the way. Howard was fifth in free throw rate (85.1), seventh in fouls drawn per 40 minutes (7.6), 50th in offensive rating (121.3) and 55th in true shooting percentage (62.9). Sophomore forward Gordon Hayward was 17th in true shooting percentage (65.7), 33rd in offensive rating (123.4) and 36th in effective field goal percentage (61.1).

College of Charleston

2009: 27-9 (15-5 Southern Conference)
Lost to Richmond 74-72, CBI Quarterfinals
Adjusted Off. Efficiency: 107.3 (85th nationally)
Adjusted Def. Efficiency: 106.9 (270th nationally)

The Cougars took down Davidson and Stephen Curry twice last season but came up short of the NCAA tournament when they lost to Chattanooga in the championship game of the SoCon tournament. Junior guard Andrew Goudelock was 28th in fouls called per 40 minutes (1.6) and will take Curry's place as the best shooter in the conference. The Citadel figures to challenge Charleston in the South Division while Appalachian State and Western Carolina should battle for first place in the North Division.

Cornell

2009: 21-10 (11-3 Ivy League)
Lost to Missouri 78-59, NCAA First Round
Adjusted Off. Efficiency: 107.4 (81st nationally)
Adjusted Def. Efficiency: 100.5 (152nd nationally)

The Big Red is the clear favorite to win a third consecutive conference title, as they have last year's Ivy League Player of the Year in senior guard Louis Dale and Rookie of the Year in sophomore guard Chris Wroblewski. Senior center Jeff Foote was 73rd in block percentage (7.5) but the best player of all is senior forward Ryan Wittman, who has an NBA future.

Holy Cross

2009: 18-14 (11-3 Patriot League)
Lost to American 73-57, Patriot League Championship Game
Adjusted Off. Efficiency: 97.8 (227th nationally)
Adjusted Def. Efficiency: 98.3 (118th nationally)

Coach Ralph Willard left after last season to become Rick Pitino's top assistant at Louisville but the Crusaders found a capable replacement in long-time Notre Dame assistant Sean Kearney. He inherits a talented roster that includes junior guard R.J. Evans, who was 77th in percentage of shots (30.8) while averaging 13.4 points a game. Also back are junior forward Andrew Keister, who was 98th in offensive rebounding percentage (12.5), and sharp-shooting junior guard Andrew Beinert. Lehigh looms as the Crusaders' biggest threat in the conference race.

Jackson State

2009: 18-15 (15-3 Southwestern Athletic Conference
Lost to Alabama State 65-58 in SWAC Champ. Game

Adjusted Off. Efficiency: 96.1 (250th nationally)
Adjusted Def. Efficiency: 104.8 (244th nationally)

The Tigers are a veteran group with three returning starters and ten lettermen. The top returnee is senior forward Grant Maxey, who was 92nd in percentage of shots (30.3) and averaged 16.4 points a game.

Jacksonville

2009: 18-15 (15-5, Atlantic Sun Conference)
Lost to Florida 84-62, NIT First Round
Adjusted Off. Efficiency: 106.7 (91st nationally)
Adjusted Def. Efficiency: 103.2 (204th nationally)

Senior guard Ben Smith, an adept playmaker, leads a group of four returning starters. He was 44th in percentage of minutes played (89.6) and 82nd in fouls called per 40 minutes (1.9) while scoring 16.9 points a game. Senior forward Ayron Hardy was 16th in effective field goal percentage (64.2), 20th in true field goal percentage (65.4) and 21st in offensive rating (125.3).

Long Beach State

2009: 15-15 (10-6 Big West Conference)
Lost to Pacific 65-60, Big West Quarterfinals
Adjusted Off. Efficiency: 103.1 (138th nationally)
Adjusted Def. Efficiency: 104.0 (224th nationally)

Two years removed from a six-win season, the 49ers enter 2009-10 as the Big West favorites despite starting four sophomores. Sophomore forward T.J. Robinson was 73rd in defensive rebounding percentage (22.3) and he is joined by sophomore wing Larry Anderson, who is a lockdown defender, and senior guard Stephan Gilling, a long-range shooting threat. UC Santa Barbara should also be a contender for the conference crown.

Morehead State

2009: 20-16 (12-6 Ohio Valley Conference)
Lost to Louisville 74-54, NCAA First Round
Adjusted Off. Efficiency: 100.4 (187th nationally)
Adjusted Def. Efficiency: 99.4 (133rd nationally)

Junior forward/center Kenneth Faried was one of the nation's best-kept secrets last season as he was second in defensive rebounding percentage (33.8), eighth in offensive rebounding percentage (16.4), 77th in block percentage (7.2) and 79th in steal percentage (3.7). He is a major reason why the Eagles are the favorites in the OVC. Senior guard Maze Stallworth was 56th in offensive rating (120.8) and 61st in turnover rate (11.3). The Eagles should get a challenge from Murray State.

Morgan State

2009: 23-12 (13-3 Mid-Eastern Athletic Conference)
Lost to Oklahoma 82-54, NCAA First Round
Adjusted Off. Efficiency: 98.7 (217th nationally)
Adjusted Def. Efficiency: 97.5 (93rd nationally)

Todd Bozeman has resurrected his once-tarnished coaching career by winning back-to-back regular-season titles in the MEAC. This year the Bears are poised to make it three in a row. Senior guard Reggie Holmes was 22nd in turnover rate (10.1) and sophomore forward Kevin Thompson was 86th in offensive rebounding percentage (12.6).

Mount St. Mary's

2009: 19-14 (12-6 Northeast Conference)
Lost to James Madison 69-58, CollegeInsider.com First Round
Adjusted Off. Efficiency: 100.2 (189th nationally)
Adjusted Def. Efficiency: 97.9 (107th nationally)

The Mountaineers lost in the NEC championship game to Robert Morris last season after winning the season before and are poised to return to the top of the conference this year. Senior guard Jeremy Goode was 91st in fouls called per 40 minutes (1.9) and was among the nation's top 500 in nine different Pomeroy categories. Meanwhile, junior guard Jean Cajou is an excellent defender and could give the Mountaineers an edge in what figures to be a tight NEC race, one in which Quinnipiac and Robert Morris should also contend.

Northeastern #23 big good shooter

Oakland

2009: 23-13 (13-5 Summit League)
Lost to Bradley 76-75, CollegeInsider.com Quarterfinals
Adjusted Off. Efficiency: 113.4 (32nd nationally)
Adjusted Def. Efficiency: 106.0 (259th nationally)

The Grizzlies' 23 victories last season were their most since moving to Division I and they should be even better this season with four starters returning. Junior center Keith Benson had a spectacular under-the-radar season in 2008-09 as he was 14th in offensive rating (126.3), 26th in both effective field goal percentage (62.2) and block percentage (9.5), 27th in turnover rate (10.2), 34th in true shooting percentage (64.1), 68th in free throw rate (65.5) and 75th in defensive rebounding percentage (22.2). Senior guard Johnathon Jones was ninth in assist rate (39.7) and 11th in percentage of minutes played (93.2) while scoring 13.3 points a game. Junior forward Will Hudson's 120.1 offensive rating ranked 65th.

Old Dominion

2009: 25-10 (12-6 Colonial Athletic Association)
Defeated Bradley 66-62 in CollegeInsider.com
Championship Game
Adjusted Off. Efficiency: 104.6 (120th nationally)
Adjusted Def. Efficiency: 95.9 (72nd nationally)

The Monarchs will be strong again as they return all five starters from a 25-win team that captured the inaugural CollegeInsider.com tournament last spring. Junior forward Frank Hassell was 23rd in offensive rebounding percentage (14.2) and MVP of the CIT. Junior wing Junior wing Ben Finney was 78th in steal percentage (3.7) and sophomore wing Kent Bazemore was 90th in the same category (3.6). Junior guard Darius James is a top-notch playmaker. VCU figures to give Old Dominion strong competition for the CAA title. *Very small team*

Radford

2009: 21-12 (15-3 Big South Conference)
Lost to North Carolina 101-58, NCAA First Round
Adjusted Off. Efficiency: 99.1 (213th nationally)
Adjusted Def. Efficiency: 101.0 (164th nationally)

The Highlanders jumped from seventh place in 2008 to first last season and are poised to repeat as Big South champions. Senior center Art Parakhouski was 20th in offensive rebounding percentage (14.3) and 52nd in defensive rebounding percentage (23.1), and provides a strong inside presence. Senior point guard Amir Johnson runs the show with a steady hand.

1-2-2 halfcourt press
3S pace
NY Albany

Siena

p: Moore pure
w: B: Rossiter

2009: 27-8 (16-2 Metro Atlantic Athletic Conference)
Lost to Louisville 79-72, NCAA Second Round
Adjusted Off. Efficiency: 110.3 (57th nationally)
Adjusted Def. Efficiency: 96.7 (78th nationally)

The Saints will no longer sneak up on anyone after going a combined 85-44 in Fran McCaffrey's four seasons as coach and making NCAA tournament appearances the last two seasons, including a win over Ohio State in the first round last March. MAAC Player of the Year Kenny Hasbrouck graduated but there is still plenty of talent on hand, including junior forward Ryan Rossiter, who was eighth in true shooting percentage (67.0), 11th in offensive rating (126.9), 23rd in effective field goal percentage (62.4) and 97th in free throw rate (60.4). Senior guard Ronald Moore was 53rd in assist rate (31.9) and 97th in fouls called per 40 minutes (1.9) while senior forward

Edwin Ubiles was 27th in fouls called per 40 minutes (1.6) and senior forward Alex Franklin was 33rd in free throw rate (71.7).

Sam Houston State

2009: 18-12 (12-4 Southland Conference)
Lost to Texas-San Antonio 83-74, Southland Quarterfinals
Adjusted Off. Efficiency: 106.1 (96th nationally)
Adjusted Def. Efficiency: 102.4 (190th nationally)

A veteran backcourt led by senior guard Ashton Mitchell makes the Bearkats the favorites in what should be a competitive Southland. Mitchell was fourth in assist rate (44.0), 55th in free throw rate (66.9) and 86th in fouls drawn per 40 minutes (6.0). Texas A&M-Corpus Christi figures to challenge Sam Houston State in the West Division. The East Division is wide open with Nicholls State, Southeastern Louisiana and Stephen F. Austin all having title hopes.

Weber State

2009: 21-10 (15-1 Big Sky Conference)
Lost to San Diego State 65-49, NIT First Round
Adjusted Off. Efficiency: 102.1 (152nd nationally)
Adjusted Def. Efficiency: 97.5 (94th nationally)

The Wildcats easily won the Big Sky regular-season championship last season but wound up in the NIT after suffering a crushing loss to Montana State in the semifinals of the conference tournament. However, do-everything sophomore guard Damian Lillard should give Weber State the edge in a hotly contested race against Montana State and Portland State this season.

Western Kentucky

2009: 25-9 (15-3 Sun Belt Conference)
Lost to Gonzaga 83-81, NCAA Second Round
Adjusted Off. Efficiency: 110.4 (56th nationally)
Adjusted Def. Efficiency: 100.9 (163rd nationally)

The Hilltoppers are the clear favorites in the East Division and the Sun Belt's top team as they return four starters after winning a combined three games in the last two NCAA tournaments. Senior forward Jeremy Evans appears poised for a breakout season as he was 18th in effective field goal percentage (63.4), 20th in offensive rating (125.3), 22nd in true shooting percentage (65.3) and 54th in block percentage (8.4). Junior wing Sergio Kerusch was 32nd in defensive rebounding percentage (24.2). The Hilltoppers also have another star in senior guard A.J. Slaughter. North Texas is the top team in the West Division.

John Perrotto

Author Bios

Will Carroll writes about injuries and topics in sports medicine. Called the "industry standard" by Peter Gammons and a "must read" by Peter King, Will has been published at Baseball Prospectus, Football Outsiders, Basketball Prospectus, ESPN, the New York Times, Puck Prospectus, and Popular Science, among others. He's written two books and has contributed to nine others. Will also believes that Crash Davis should add "single-class basketball in Indiana" to his famous rant.

Bradford Doolittle has written on sports ranging from major league baseball to arena football, and just about everything in between. He was an editor and baseball columnist for the Kansas City Star and its companion website for six years. His work has also appeared at ESPN, Slate, Deadspin, The Hardball Times, Heater, and Sports Illustrated. He's written for Basketball Prospectus since 2007 and is the creator of the NBAPET basketball analysis system. He attended the University of Missouri and is now a freelance writer based in Chicago, where he lives on the North Side with his wife Amy.

John Gasaway bores his wife Nicole with stories about the time during his sophomore year at Springfield High School when he scored an unprecedented eight points against Urbana in a game where he functioned as an efficient low possession-usage role player behind featured scorers Mike Lee and Steve Jeffers. Drawing on this rich fund of first-hand experience he has spent the last five years holding forth on how to play college basketball. John's "deft writing" was praised in the last issue of Play Magazine ever published by the New York Times, a fact he views as correlation and not causation.

Dan Hanner has been writing about college basketball at Yet Another Basketball Blog since 2007. In addition to the Big East preview in this volume, Dan's analysis of this year's Kansas team can be found in the Jayhawk Tipoff 2009-10, published by Maple Street Press. Dan loves tempo-free stats but his real passion is Division I's underrated tournaments, like the Old Spice Classic and the Missouri Valley's Arch Madness.

Kevin Pelton has analyzed the NBA (and occasionally college hoops) for Basketball Prospectus since the site's inception in 2007. Previously his NBA commentary appeared at Hoopsworld, 82Games, Sports Illustrated, and CourtsideTimes. Having covered the WNBA's Seattle Storm for the team's official site since 2003, Kevin additionally spent four seasons as the beat writer for supersonics.com. He will always remember 2008-09 as the year that his alma mater, the University of Washington, won the Pac-10 regular season title for the first time since he was three years old.

John Perrotto has covered college basketball for a quarter-century and has been with Basketball Prospectus since the beginning in 2007. A graduate of Geneva College (birthplace of college basketball), he lives with his wife Brenda in Beaver Falls, Pennsylvania (birthplace of Joe Willie Namath).

Ken Pomeroy has been a lifelong fan of both college basketball and math, experimenting in quantitative analysis since 2002 and publishing advanced stats at kenpom.com since 2004. The popularity of the site has grown each season and the stats have been used in the scouting process by Final Four teams. Ken's work has been cited by numerous media outlets, including ESPN, Sports Illustrated, the New York Times, and the Wall Street Journal. His formative years were spent in ACC country, but Ken has spent most of his adult life in the Mountain time zone. While he never played the game at the collegiate level, Ken claims proudly to have officiated exactly one college basketball game in his life.

2-20-10

Colonial Winner: ODU? (180)

Horizon Winner: Butler (178)?

MAAC: Siena (180)

<u>Look At</u>

Baylor

New Mexico

BYU

Big Sky   Weber St/N. Colorado

Illinois

Northeastern (Colonial), ODU, G. Mason, William & Mary, VCU

Vandy

Arkansas

Florida

Wichita St

Wm & Mary

Made in the USA
Lexington, KY
23 November 2009